QUALITATIVE DATA ANALYSIS WITH NVIVO

Sara Miller McCune founded SAGE Publishing in 1965 to support the dissemination of usable knowledge and educate a global community. SAGE publishes more than 1000 journals and over 800 new books each year, spanning a wide range of subject areas. Our growing selection of library products includes archives, data, case studies and video. SAGE remains majority owned by our founder and after her lifetime will become owned by a charitable trust that secures the company's continued independence.

Los Angeles | London | New Delhi | Singapore | Washington DC | Melbourne

WINDOWS & MAC

3rd EDITION

QUALITATIVE DATA ANALYSIS WITH NVIVO

KRISTI JACKSON & PAT BAZELEY

Los Angeles | London | New Delhi
Singapore | Washington DC | Melbourne

Los Angeles | London | New Delhi
Singapore | Washington DC | Melbourne

SAGE Publications Ltd
1 Oliver's Yard
55 City Road
London EC1Y 1SP

SAGE Publications Inc.
2455 Teller Road
Thousand Oaks, California 91320

SAGE Publications India Pvt Ltd
B 1/I 1 Mohan Cooperative Industrial Area
Mathura Road
New Delhi 110 044

SAGE Publications Asia-Pacific Pte Ltd
3 Church Street
#10-04 Samsung Hub
Singapore 049483

Editor: Jai Seaman
Editorial assistant: Charlotte Bush
Production editor: Ian Antcliff
Marketing manager: Susheel Gokarakonda
Cover design: Shaun Mercier
Typeset by: C&M Digitals (P) Ltd, Chennai, India
Printed in the UK

Library of Congress Control Number: 2018960485

British Library Cataloguing in Publication data

A catalogue record for this book is available from
the British Library

ISBN 978-1-5264-4993-1
ISBN 978-1-5264-4994-8 (pbk)

CONTENTS

Figures   viii
Tables   xiii
About the authors   xiv
Preface to the third edition   xvi

    What makes this book innovative?   xvi
    How to use this book   xvii
    Organization of the book   xvii
    Organization of each chapter   xviii
    Online resources   xix

Online resources   xx
Acknowledgements   xxi

1 Where to begin?   **1**

    1.1 Introduction to qualitative research with NVivo   2
    1.2 Conceptual grounding in qualitative research purposes and NVivo   6
    1.3 Using NVivo to get started on your research   9
    1.4 Chapter 1 Takeaways   34

2 Designing an NVivo Project   **39**

    2.1 Introduction to designing an NVivo Project   40
    2.2 Conceptual grounding in the Project structure   41

2.3 Using NVivo to store and manage data   53
2.4 Chapter 2 Takeaways   58

3 Coding foundations   **63**

3.1 Introduction to coding foundations   64
3.2 Conceptual grounding in Coding   65
3.3 Coding in NVivo   77
3.4 Chapter 3 Takeaways   97

4 Advanced coding   **101**

4.1 Introduction to advanced coding   102
4.2 Conceptual grounding in advanced coding   103
4.3 Advanced coding with NVivo   113
4.4 Chapter 4 Takeaways   130

5 Cases, Classifications, and comparisons   **135**

5.1 Introduction to Cases, Classifications, and comparisons   136
5.2 Conceptual grounding in Cases and Classifications   137
5.3 Cases and Classifications in NVivo   145
5.4 Chapter 5 Takeaways   161

6 Surveys and mixed methods   **165**

6.1 Introduction to surveys and mixed methods   166
6.2 Conceptual grounding in surveys and mixed methods   167
6.3 Surveys and mixed methods in NVivo   175
6.4 Chapter 6 Takeaways   194

7 Querying data   **199**

7.1 Introduction to Queries   200
7.2 Conceptual grounding in Queries   201
7.3 Working with Queries in NVivo   217
7.4 Chapter 7 Takeaways   232

8 Literature reviews and pdf Files   **235**

8.1 Introduction to literature reviews and pdf Files   236
8.2 Getting grounded in literature reviews and pdf Files   237
8.3 Literature reviews and pdf Files in NVivo   246
8.4 Chapter 8 Takeaways   253

9 Working with multimedia Files   **257**

9.1 Introduction to pictures, audio, and video   258
9.2 Conceptual grounding in pictures, audio, and video   259

9.3 Pictures, audio, and video in NVivo   263
9.4 Chapter 9 Takeaways   281

10 Twitter, Facebook, YouTube, and web pages   **285**

10.1 Introduction to Twitter, Facebook, YouTube, and web pages   286
10.2 Conceptual grounding in Twitter, Facebook, YouTube, and web pages   287
10.3 Twitter, Facebook, YouTube, and web pages in NVivo   292
10.4 Chapter 10 Takeaways   303

11 Teamwork   **307**

11.1 Introduction to teamwork   308
11.2 Conceptual grounding in teamwork   309
11.3 Teamwork in NVivo   317
11.4 Chapter 11 Takeaways   335

12 Moving on – further resources   **339**

References   341
Index   346

FIGURES

1.1   NVivo for Windows main interface: *Ribbon,*
      Navigation View, List View, Detail View   13
1.2   NVivo for Mac main interface: *Ribbon, Navigation View,*
      List View, Detail View   13
1.3   *Navigation View* in Windows (left) and Mac (right)   14
1.4   Showing and hiding subfolders in the *Navigation View*   15
1.5   Opening *Barbara* in the *Detail View*   16
1.6   Opening *Community change* in the *Detail View*   16
1.7   Open items in the *Detail View* with individual tabs (Windows)   17
1.8   The 'Open Items' list in the *Navigation View* and the *Menu bar*
      above the *Ribbon* (Mac)   17
1.9   Creating a Project in Windows (left) and Mac (right)   19
1.10 Creating a Memo to use as a journal   21
1.11 Mind Map to launch the *Researchers* Project   24
1.12 Becoming a researcher: preliminary Concept Map   26
1.13 Creating an Annotation (Windows)   28
1.14 Pasting a See Also Link (Windows only) to a specific location
      (in a File) from a specific location (in a Memo)   31

2.1   Tagging a paper copy of a document   44
2.2   Different types of Cases in the *Environmental Change* Project   46
2.3   Sample transcription format for focus groups and interviews   50

2.4	Microsoft Word table format displays entire row when a portion of a cell is coded.	51
2.5	Customizable Folder structure for NVivo Files	55
2.6	Customizable Set structure for NVivo Files	56
2.7	Customizable Case structure for NVivo Files	57
3.1	*Frank's* document showing application of multiple codes to each passage of text, and Annotations (see Chapter 1 for Annotations)	71
3.2	NVivo mimicking the conventional strategy of coding: making copies and placing them in categories/concepts	78
3.3	NVivo actually tagging the text with the Node	78
3.4	The Node Properties window	80
3.5	Coding to an existing Node via drag-and-drop	81
3.6	Creating a Node and coding at the same time	81
3.7	Coding for *Family* displayed by the Node	82
3.8	Uncoding from the File with a right-click	82
3.9	Viewing Coding Stripes in a File	83
3.10	Viewing narrow coding context in a Node	85
3.11	Viewing Coding Stripes in a Node	85
3.12	Jumping from a Reference in a Node to the File	86
3.13	Shortcut keys to Copy in Windows (left) and Mac (right)	87
3.14	Coding and uncoding alternatives: *Ribbon*, right-click, Quick Coding bar (Windows)	87
3.15	Coding and uncoding alternatives: *Ribbon*, right-click, Coding Panel (Mac)	88
3.16	Merging Nodes	89
3.17	Window to Customize Current View in the *List View*	90
3.18	Customized Node *List View*	90
3.19	Node Chart of Files coded to *Balance* based on the percentage coverage	94
3.20	Comparison diagram showing which farmers adopted one or other or both innovative practices	95
3.21	Coding Query in the *Environmental Change* Project on the Nodes *Community change* and *Economy*	96
4.1	The online catalogue hierarchy	104
4.2	A viral coding structure	108
4.3	A vista coding structure	109
4.4	A Matrix Coding Query of *Strategies* by *Valence*	109
4.5	A Hyperlink to the File from the *Detail View* of the Node	115
4.6	Sorting Nodes into hierarchies using a Concept Map	117
4.7	Node hierarchy with parent Nodes and child Nodes	118
4.8	Creating a subnode (or child) Node	119
4.9	Fixing a viral coding structure	122
4.10	Visualizing coding structure with a Project Map	123
4.11	Using a Set for a metaconcept	125

4.12	Word Frequency Query with stemmed words	127
4.13	Text Search Query using the alternator, OR, with stemmed words	129
5.1	Individual participant transcripts imported as Files and converted into Cases	138
5.2	Cases, Attributes, and Values	139
5.3	The structure of Classifications, Attributes, and Values	141
5.4	An NVivo Project with two Case Types (*Employees* and *Organizations*) and two Case Classifications (*Employee* and *Organization*)	142
5.5	Using a Crosstab Query to view data sorted by Attribute Values	143
5.6	Coding multiple Files to a New Case (Windows)	147
5.7	Selecting a method for Auto Coding (Windows)	148
5.8	Entering speaker names in Step 2 of the Auto Code Wizard (Windows)	149
5.9	Identifying the Case Type (Classification) and location for the new Cases in Step 3 of the Auto Code Wizard (Windows)	149
5.10	The Auto Code by Speaker panel (Mac)	150
5.11	Adding an Attribute and Values in Windows (left) and Mac (right)	151
5.12	Classification Sheet with Attribute Values for interview participants (Windows)	152
5.13	Crosstab Query interface (Windows)	156
5.14	Crosstab Query interface (Mac)	156
5.15	Crosstab Query Results Display, showing cell content options selected from the *Ribbon* (Windows)	158
5.16	Crosstab Query Results display, showing options selected from the Results tab (Mac)	158
5.17	Grouped column chart displaying results from the Crosstab Query shown in Figure 5.15 (Windows)	159
5.18	Selecting Attribute Values in a Group Query (Windows only)	161
6.1	Examples of Folder structures for projects with multiple File types	175
6.2	Survey data, prepared using an Excel spreadsheet	176
6.3	The *Survey Import Wizard*	178
6.4	Choosing question type in Step 4 of the *Survey Import Wizard*	179
6.5	Nodes and Matrix display of results from Auto Coding themes related to wellbeing (NVivo Plus)	179
6.6	Choosing question type in Step 3 of the Import Dataset Assistant (Mac)	180
6.7	Using a Framework Matrix to construct a Joint Display	183
6.8	Crosstab combining qualitative text with quantitative scaled data	184
6.9	Crosstab specifications used for transformation of coding to variable data (Windows)	185
6.10	Crosstab specifications used for transformation of coding to variable data (Mac)	185
6.11	Using a Matrix Coding Query with Sets (Windows)	187
6.12	Matrix data based on qualitative coding for export from NVivo for use in statistical analyses	188

6.13 Selecting the operator for combining rows and columns 189
6.14 Dendrogram and associated statistics based on clustering Nodes
by word similarity (Windows) 190
6.15 Three-dimensional cluster diagrams, based on clustering
Nodes by word similarity (Windows) 191

7.1 Word Frequency Query with visualization 205
7.2 Text Search Query with visualization 206
7.3 Crosstab Query with visualization 207
7.4 Matrix Coding Query with visualization 208
7.5 Coding Query with visualization 209
7.6 Compound Query (Windows only) with visualization 211
7.7 Group Query (Windows only) with visualization 212
7.8 Coding Comparison Query with visualization 213
7.9 Framework Matrix cell content using the Auto Summarize feature 216
7.10 Word Frequency Query interface in Windows (top) and Mac (bottom) 218
7.11 Text Search Query interface in Windows (top) and Mac (bottom) 220
7.12 Crosstab Query interface in Windows (top) and Mac (bottom) 221
7.13 Matrix Coding Query interface in Windows (top) and Mac (bottom) 222
7.14 Coding Query interface in Windows (top) and Mac (bottom) 223
7.15 Compound Query interface (Windows only) 224
7.16 Group Query interface (Windows only) 226
7.17 Coding Comparison Query interface in Windows (top) and Mac (bottom) 227
7.18 Filter options in a Case Classification Summary Report (number
of Cases with each Attribute Value) (Windows only) 231

8.1 Selection and retrieval of text in a pdf File 247
8.2 Selection and retrieval of text in a line-numbered pdf File 248
8.3 Selection and coding of a region in a pdf File 249
8.4 Selecting options in the import dialogue for reference
material from EndNote (Windows) 251
8.5 Compound Query Results (Windows only) in the
Environmental Change Project 253

9.1 Thumbnail display of Files (Windows only) 266
9.2 A picture Region with an associated log and Coding Stripe 266
9.3 Picture with a newly inserted log entry 267
9.4 The picture content of a Node open in *Detail View* 269
9.5 The Playback group in the *Video Ribbon* (Windows) and
the Player controls (Mac) 271
9.6 The playhead moving across the timeline of an audio or video
File in Windows (top) and Mac (bottom) 272
9.7 Entering a new transcript row (Windows) 273
9.8 Entering a new transcript row (Mac) 274
9.9 Coding Stripes and Shadow Coding Stripes on a media file (Windows) 278

9.10   Turning the results of a Group Query (Windows only) into a Set   279
9.11   A Connection Map of the Files coded to *Natural environment* and
         Real estate development   280

10.1   NCapture icon showing in the Chrome menu (top) and Internet
         Explorer Command bar (bottom)   293
10.2   Capturing a Twitter hashtag (left) and Twitter home page (right)
         with NCapture   294
10.3   Selecting an NCapture file to import   295
10.4   Auto Code Wizard   296
10.5   *Detail View* with a Map of a social media Dataset   297
10.6   Collecting a YouTube video with NCapture   298
10.7   Collecting a web page with NCapture via Internet Explorer   300
10.8   Selecting an NCapture file for importing as a web page   301
10.9   A web page converted into a pdf and opened in NVivo   301
10.10 Web page captured and imported into NVivo   302

11.1   *List View* of Memos with *Detail View* closed or on the bottom   325
11.2   Setting the Application Options to 'Prompt for user on launch'
         in Windows (left) and Mac (right)   325
11.3   The initial window showing an original Project and
         copies with Title and Path   327
11.4   Changing the Project Title to match the Project Path
         (or File Name) (Windows)   328
11.5   Coding Stripes showing the work of three coders on a File (Windows only)   333
11.6   Statistical output from a Coding Comparison Query in
         Windows (top) and Mac (bottom)   333

TABLES

2.1   Formatting strategies to facilitate case construction from
different types of sources   52

2.2   Differences between Folders, Sets, and Cases for managing Files   58

3.1   Simulation of Matrix Coding Query output   92

4.1   Three differences between Merging and Aggregating Nodes   121

6.1   Complementary analysis strategies   170

6.2   Comparative analysis strategies   171

6.3   Transformative analysis strategies   173

6.4   Comparison of Crosstab Query and Matrix Coding Query   189

11.1   Choosing a Project storage and management strategy   319

ABOUT THE AUTHORS

Kristi Jackson is a Qualitative Senior Scientist at Optum (www.Optum.com), where she supports a broad range of qualitative studies in Patient Reported Outcomes (PRO). PRO studies are designed to better understand patients' experiences related to conditions, their treatments, and the healthcare system. She has a background in evaluation research and in 2002 she founded Queri (www.Queri.com) to provide resources and coaching to NVivo users worldwide. With over 25 years of experience in qualitative research design, data collection, analysis, reporting, and stakeholder relations, she is an expert in a diverse array of qualitative methodologies. Her theoretical frames tend to be sociological, and her research interests include conceptualizations of qualitative research transparency and the constantly changing spaces where qualitative researchers and technologies meet.

Pat Bazeley is Director of Research Support P/L and Adjunct Professor in the Translational Research and Social Innovation group at Western Sydney University. Since graduating in psychology, she has worked in community development, project consulting and in academic research development. For almost 30 years, Pat has been providing research training and serving as project consultant to academics, graduate students, and practitioners representing a wide range of disciplines across Australia and internationally. Her particular expertise is in helping researchers to make sense of qualitative, survey, and mixed methods data, and to use computer programs for management and analysis of data. Pat's research has focused on qualitative and mixed methods data analysis, the development and performance of researchers, and the wellbeing of older women. She has published books, chapters, articles, and reports on these topics. She serves on the Editorial Boards of the *Journal of Mixed Methods Research* and *Qualitative Health Research*, and was 2015–2016 President of the Mixed Methods International Research Association.

PREFACE TO THE THIRD EDITION

WHAT MAKES THIS BOOK INNOVATIVE?

Along with the materials from the second edition that researchers found most helpful, we incorporated a wealth of new information and approaches in this third edition:

- Easy-to-use instructions and screen shots that explicitly assist both Windows and Mac users.
- Rich, methodological discussions in the first half of each chapter to help prepare you to think qualitatively in relation to the technology in the second half of the chapter.
- Discussions that complement the NVivo Help so you understand why and when you might use various tools instead of just how to use them.
- Explanations regarding the most sophisticated options and creative combinations of tools.
- A multipronged approach to help all users understand the Queries in NVivo:
  - Specific examples in the context of each chapter.
  - A chapter on Queries that provides a brief textual and visual orientation to each one.
  - Screen shots that map the Query interface options in both Windows and Mac.
- A new concluding section of each chapter with Takeaways to help you reflect on the material in the chapter and to assist instructors who use the book in methods courses.

- A new chapter on Twitter, Facebook, YouTube, and web pages, based on the burgeoning analysis of data generated in online communities.
- Pointers to relevant materials in other Chapters, including page numbers when relevant.
- An expanded set of online resources (https://study.sagepub.com/jackson3e), including videos, sample projects and a range of supplementary materials that exceed the size limitations of the book.

This third edition of *Qualitative Analysis with NVivo* is designed for qualitative researchers who work on their own and are looking for support. It is also ideal for qualitative researchers working in teams, instructors incorporating NVivo into their qualitative methods courses, and users transitioning from earlier versions of the software. We carefully crafted the chapters to accommodate a range of learning styles via conceptual discussions, specific clicks, visualizations, research ideas, examples from other researchers, and sample project data. In addition to our 40+ years of combined experience working with a range of NVivo users, in this third edition we also drew from the expertise and feedback of many QSR Platinum NVivo Trainers to help clarify our narrative and expand on our examples (see the Acknowledgements page for names and contact details).

HOW TO USE THIS BOOK

The average user of any software program typically accesses only a small portion of its capabilities; this is no doubt true for users of NVivo also. If you are using NVivo for a small descriptive project, you can work without having to learn complex procedures, but if you are undertaking complex analytical tasks, you can find the additional tools you need. Choices about what tools to use and how to use them is entirely up to you. Although the chapters of this book can be fluidly followed in chronological order, you might find yourself jumping around among them based on your needs. The table below shows the structure to guide your customized journey.

ORGANIZATION OF THE BOOK

Start here if you are …	Chapter
… serious about using the book strategically and need to know how to install the software, create a project, and develop Maps, Memos, Annotations, Memo Links, See Also Links, and Hyperlinks.	1. Where to begin?
… interested in getting a better handle on how all of the pieces of the NVivo Project fit together and the implications this has on the way you format Files. This will also help you eliminate tools that you do not need.	2. Designing an NVivo Project
… ready to learn all the basics of coding in NVivo and also want tips and tricks for thinking about how to develop your codes.	3. Coding foundations

(Continued)

(Continued)

Start here if you are ...	Chapter
... confident with the basic skills of creating and managing Nodes but want to learn about all the bells and whistles, including (but not limited to) management of Node hierarchies, automation, and text mining.	4. Advanced coding
... comfortable with the tactics you will use in the database to code and want to dive into the ways NVivo matches any quantitative or demographic data with the qualitative data.	5. Cases, Classifications, and comparisons
... taking a mixed methods approach and already understand the way NVivo handles qualitative data (primarily through coding), Cases, Classifications, Attributes, and Values, but want to apply and extend this knowledge (including surveys combining qualitative and quantitative data).	6. Surveys and mixed methods
... unclear about the way NVivo helps find patterns in your data (usually based on the prior work you do to read, write about, and code your data).	7. Querying data
... diving into NVivo with the intent of conducting a literature review or want to see the unique issues in handling pdf Files.	8. Literature reviews and pdf Files
... focusing on the most common, non-text data types.	9. Working with multimedia Files
... interested in strategies for examining user-generated content in online communities.	10. Twitter, Facebook, YouTube, and web pages
... planning for the structure and process of a team project and want to begin with some tips before learning the technical details of managing a database.	11. Teamwork

ORGANIZATION OF EACH CHAPTER

Conceptual introduction followed by clicks

As we argue in the opening section of the first chapter, we ardently support an understanding of methods-with software as mutually constituting activities. This position is in alignment with current understandings about the social shaping of technology and encourages researchers to move beyond simple binaries such as researcher/technology, method/software, and manual/digital (Jackson, 2017). Despite this position, we purposefully (and somewhat warily) separate most of the methodological/theoretical discussions in each chapter from the descriptions of NVivo tools. This structure is based on two factors that swayed our approach in this third edition of the book:

- The commitment to help both Windows and Mac users in a single publication while making it easy for users of each platform to ignore irrelevant material without constantly flipping back and forth through pages.
- Feedback from qualitative methods instructors who use this book in their courses and want to more easily direct students to the appropriate section of the chapter, depending on whether they need methodological help and guidance or assistance with specific software tools.

Four sections

The following guide to the four subsections within each chapter will help you find relevant material if you have a specific question or issue to investigate about a topic (e.g., coding).

- **Section 1** introduces the purpose of the chapter and sets the stage for the subsequent conceptual and methodological detail. We end this introductory section with a brief explanation of related material in other chapters to help redirect your attention, in the event that another chapter is more closely related to your immediate needs.
- **Section 2** explores conceptual and methodological grounding through a range of traditions in qualitative research practice. Much of this material is designed to prompt ideas about handling data whether you use Qualitative Data Analysis Software (QDAS) or not. This section is not intended to be exhaustive but provides enough diversity and variation in methodologies and strategies to help avoid cookie-cutter approaches to handling qualitative data. We sometimes address methodological debates and we also occasionally articulate our stances on professional practice. The online resources (https://study.sagepub.com/jackson3e) will help you dig more deeply into the literature.
- **Section 3** details the NVivo tools that can facilitate your analysis and provides instructions on clicking through the most frequently used options. Instructions common to Windows and Mac users are in purple font and where they diverge you will follow grey font if you are using Windows and black font if you are using Mac. Furthermore, we provide and update these instructions in the online resources. Both Mac and Windows users can download a Click Guide to all of the instructions pertaining to the material we cover in the book (https://study.sagepub.com/jackson3e).
- **Section 4** wraps things up with Takeaways including:
  - Key points from the chapter.
  - Tips, challenges, and warnings relating to tools covered in the chapter.
  - Pointers to applicable videos.
  - Practice questions that help reinforce the methodological and technical material while exploring the terrain where researchers and technologies meet.

ONLINE RESOURCES

The website provides a wealth of additional material that will be updated as the NVivo interface changes. You will find a complete compendium of clicking instructions, videos, sample projects, and other supplementary materials (https://study.sagepub.com/jackson3e).

ONLINE RESOURCES

This book is supported by a wealth of carefully curated online resources that support your learning and research, available at **https://study.sagepub.com/jackson3e**

Watch screencast video tutorials on how to navigate NVivo, with top tips from co-author Kristi Jackson about how to use the main tools the software offers.

Learn how to master NVivo with clear, up to date, click by click instructions that show you how to use the software in Mac and Windows.

Explore NVivo at your own pace with sample project files from authors.

Gain insight from watching videos of co-author Pat Bazeley discussing tips and hints for using NVivo.

Connect with a network of experts from the NVivo community who can help you tackle your project head on.

Read handy guidelines on how to use NVivo that offer practical support and information about coding qualitative data.

ACKNOWLEDGEMENTS

PUBLISHER

The authors welcome the opportunity Sage provided to create a new and improved third edition of this book and appreciate the work of our editor, Jai Seaman, to guide us through the process.

MAC INSTRUCTIONS

The commitment to develop a book that specifically assists both Windows and Mac users came to fruition in large part thanks to our colleague and friend, Clare Tagg. The Mac instructions in the book and the logical order of the material were influenced by her keen eye for detail and her balanced view of user experience. Clare's contact information is provided below if you would like to reach her.

REVIEWERS

We are thankful for the assistance of some of the QSR Certified Platinum NVivo trainers who work with individuals and organizations around the world as instructors, coaches, and mentors. They carefully reviewed the chapters, pointed out gaps in our explanations, improved the language, and added examples from their research to bring the instructions to life. Together, Kristi, Pat, and these additional trainers/consultants represent many decades of experience working with or teaching others how to use NVivo. This book benefited from our combined expertise and our evolving collaboration. We provide basic contact information for all those involved in the development of this edition, in the event you would like to reach out for additional training or consultation. Contributors in alphabetical order by first name:

- Amma Buckley   a.buckley@curtin.edu.au
- Anuja Cabraal   anuja.cabraal@gmail.com (http://anujacabraal.wordpress.com/)
- Ben Meehan   benm@qdatraining.eu (www.qdatraining.com)
- Christina Silver   christina.silver@qdaservices.co.uk (www.fivelevelqda.com)
- Clare Tagg   clare@taggoram.co.uk (www.taggoram.co.uk)
- Claude Julie Bourque bourque.cj@gmail.com (http://ca.linkedin.com/in/cjbourque)
- Elif Kuş Saillard   elif@namqda.com (www.namqda.com)
- Fiona Wiltshier   fiona@concorsco.com (www.concorsco.com)
- Hideki Nakazato   nakazato@konan-u.ac.jp (researchers.adm.konan-u.ac.jp/ html/208_en.html)
- Jenine Beekhuyzen   jenine@adroitresearch.com.au (www.adroitresearch.com.au)
- Jennifer Patashnick   jennifer.patashnick@qdaservices.com
- Kristi Jackson   kjackson@queri.com (www.queri.com)
- Laura Lagendyk   laura@quoteswork.ca (www.quoteswork.ca)
- Linda Sweet   (www.flinders.edu.au/people/linda.sweet)
- Lyn Lavery   lyn@academic-consulting.co.nz (www.academic-consulting. co.nz)
- Marie-Hélène Paré   info@mariehelenepare.com (www.mariehelenepare.com)
- Pat Bazeley   (www.researchsupport.com.au)
- Patsy Clarke   patsy@qualitania.com (www.qualitania.com)
- Stuart Robertson   info@robertsoneducational.com (www.robertsoneducational. com)

In addition to these independent trainers, the staff at QSR International (developers of NVivo) have been responsive and helpful as we crafted this independently written and published book. We would especially like to thank Silvana di Gregorio for her thoughtful review and excellent suggestions throughout. Nearly two decades of collegial interactions with Silvana have proven again and again that her professionalism and her camaraderie are top notch. We offer our sincere gratitude for her attention to the book.

ADDITIONAL THANKS

Kristi Jackson: I took more than one 'dissercation' while working on my PhD; journeys under the guise of a vacation that provided opportunities to write intensively without distractions. This book followed suit with some 'bookations'. Thanks to these playful, supportive, and low-maintenance friends/colleagues, I was able to survive the long hours. I adore and appreciate all of you:

- My satellite office at Shift Workspaces (Bannock) in Denver, Colorado – Maggie Smith, Crystal Harris, Sabrina Read (you're so wonderful, it sometimes feels like a vacation!)
- The equine, canine, and feline refuge in Berthoud, Colorado – Samantha, Jeff, Chase, Athena, and the whole menagerie (Dante, Hansel, Savvy, Pretty, Gracie, Terra, Rosie, Zoe … and Beans).
- HGVC Tuscany in Orlando, Florida – Mason Mouisset, Jason de Knegt, Ana Castillo, Mario Atesiano.
- The Grand Mayan, Acapulco – Gretchen Mann.
- The Timber Run sanctuary in Winter Park, Colorado – Andrew Nixon.

Pat Bazeley: Pat is just grateful she could hand over the 'lion's share' of the task of updating this book to Kristi!

1

Section 1.1: Introduction to qualitative research with NVivo 2

Section 1.2: Conceptual grounding in qualitative research purposes
and NVivo 6

Section 1.3: Using NVivo to get started on your research 9

Section 1.4: Chapter 1 Takeaways 34

WHERE TO BEGIN?

Maintaining a craft-like approach to research can help to open up critically imaginative ways of working with computers (as techniques of representation) and avoiding the tendency for these programmes to become black-boxes or demonised gadgets. (Hinchliffe, Crang, Reimer, & Hudson, 1997: 1123)

SECTION 1.1: INTRODUCTION TO QUALITATIVE RESEARCH WITH NVIVO

Before diving into NVivo, it is important to understand the contexts in which this software evolved and the various arguments researchers have made about the role of software in qualitative research. You are likely to hear a range of perceptions about the utility of the software (or problems with using it). Having a background in this debate will help you decide where you stand and will provide some ideas as you start shaping your claims about the use of NVivo in your research. After this introduction, we encourage you to play with your ideas and your data (this could be supplementary data, like literature). You do not need an exceptionally clear idea about where you are going yet. This chapter is simply designed to get you started and get you thinking.

In this chapter you will

- Learn the basic arguments exchanged between camps regarding the utility of software like NVivo (summarized via the metaphors of snake oil, silver bullet, and cart/horse).
- Find out why we advocate a methods-with mantra (Jackson, 2017) rather than a methods-first mantra.
- Consider strategies for getting started and thinking about your data.
- Discover how to install the software.
- Understand how to get familiar with the software by exploring the Sample Project.
- See how to create a Project of your own.
- Learn tactics for reflecting on your ideas with Maps, Memos, See Also Links, and Hyperlinks.

Qualitative research

Qualitative methods are a powerful choice when you want to understand details of a process or experience, need more information to determine the boundaries or characteristics of the issue being investigated, or assess – for a variety of reasons – that the best information available is non-numeric (e.g., text or visual). The questions that could benefit from a qualitative approach emerge from many fields such as criminal justice, education, finance, health care, marketing, organizational development, public policy, sports, and user experience. For example:

- After participating in an alternative drug treatment programme, what do incarcerated young adults think about their opportunities after release?
- How does a customized, after-school biology programme for girls influence their interest in a career in science?
- How do company reports explain 'negative news' (e.g., losses, legal challenges, declining share values) to shareholders?
- What are physician perceptions of barriers to diagnosing and treating diabetes among immigrants?
- Why does a specific marketing strategy for fire alarm/smoke detectors work well in urban areas but not in rural areas?
- When organizational leaders incorporate meditation practices into their businesses, how do relationships between employees change?
- What processes need to be in place for health impacts to be considered when infrastructure development is being planned?
- What factors are taken into account before a professional gymnast considers moving away from home for intensive coaching?
- How do NVivo users perceive the relevance of a new software tool?

The diversity of fields and multitude of questions are part of the thrill of qualitative research and you will find questions that invite qualitative data and analysis around every corner as you continue building your expertise.

This 'big tent' also brings unique challenges, primarily regarding the many choices that need to be made about how to handle the data. Choices will vary depending on whether the research involves, for example, exploration, description, comparison, pattern analysis, theory testing, theory building, or evaluation. Another important choice is the methodology or combination of methodologies used, and these are constantly evolving and sometimes overlapping. They include action research, conversation analysis, ethnography, life history, grounded theory, and phenomenology. Methodologists routinely urge researchers to assess the fit between purpose and method, with the choice to use a qualitative approach being determined by the research question and purpose, rather than by prior preference of the researcher (Maxwell, 2013; Richards & Morse, 2012). The same is true regarding the use of NVivo, where tools used should be informed by the goals of the research rather than just ease of use, visual appeal or familiarity.

Origin and evolution of NVivo

Most researchers engaged in qualitative data analysis have heard of Qualitative Data Analysis Software (QDAS) or Computer Assisted Qualitative Data AnalysiS (CAQDAS) and know that NVivo is one of the options for storing, managing, and analysing qualitative data. However, few qualitative researchers are aware of how long the software has been around or know the ways in which it has been discussed alongside (or in comparison with) 'manual' methods. While you need not be an expert in the history of the various camps that debate the dangers and opportunities of using QDAS, it is wise to understand the general lay of the land and the traditions that inform the diverse uses of NVivo. In this chapter we discuss some of this background to help you begin situating yourself amidst the diversity and we provide suggestions to help you clarify your qualitative approach and get excited about your unique research. We end by walking you through some basic steps to write about and map your research plans to help you sort through and frame your early thoughts with your research questions and your data.

The current version of NVivo is based on the work of Lyn and Tom Richards, who began developing the software in 1981. They founded Qualitative Solutions and Research (later becoming QSR International) in 1995 and since that time NVivo has retained the core features of handling text data via coding, writing, linking, adding demographics, searching for patterns, and reporting or exporting data. Since the construction of these early tools, the subsequent software developers incorporated additional capabilities to analyse a wide range of data types (pdf files, audio, video, images, surveys, reference managers, web pages, social media, etc.) with increasingly complex searches and modes of output (textual, numeric, and visual – via graphs, charts, and maps).

Three metaphors

Depending on the people you know who use NVivo, the kinds of research they do and whether you are a novice or have considerable experience with qualitative research, your impressions of the software will vary. Your use and discussion of the software will be influenced by your theoretical frameworks and research questions, the colleagues with whom you work, the types of data you handle, the modes you intend to use for communicating your results, and the stakeholders who are interested in the implications of your research. When you read accounts of QDAS – including arguments about the potential dangers and opportunities of using it – you will become aware of three metaphors in the literature. As with most metaphors, these carry a grain of truth. However, the oversimplification and subsequent strategic use of these metaphors by many authors to justify their own positions have nearly robbed them of their merits and have often turned them into clichés.

The silver bullet

The enthusiasm of the early adopters regarding the potential of QDAS was articulated by Miles and Huberman (1994), who argued that the flexible, recursive, and iterative capabilities of software provided unprecedented opportunities to challenge researcher conceptualizations. The Richards (1994) agreed and stated that as they began developing NUD*IST (subsequently becoming NVivo) their analysis 'became far surer, with provision for constant interrogation of themes. The processes of building and interrogating themes gave an impression of constant working at theory built up and peeled back in onion skin layers' (p. 164). Despite the cautions, warnings and limitations that were articulated by these same scholars, their claims have been problematically oversimplified and reiterated too narrowly. When you receive marketing materials or review research articles that describe the use of QDAS, beware of statements that argue or infer that QDAS inevitably leads to more transparent, rigorous, credible, or accurate research. Follow the trail of such citations and you will find they are not based in trustworthy research, a comprehensive theory, or a conceptual framework.

The snake oil salesman seeks profit, not remedy

The *snake oil* metaphor was perhaps an inevitable (and sometimes warranted) push-back on the use of computers to assist with qualitative research. Early in the evolution of QDAS, Seidel (1991) warned about the 'dark side' of such software because it might prompt researchers to overemphasize volume of data or distance researchers from data. Agar (1991) said he 'kept having nightmares about two studies – a lousy computer analysis and a beautiful analysis done by hand – where the community of researchers would immediately gather around the [computer] printout and celebrate its form rather than its content' (p. 185). However, both Seidel and Agar raised these possibilities as part of the overall picture, not as an inevitability of using QDAS. Agar argued that QDAS has 'powerful and positive consequences for what we do' (p. 182) and Seidel was one of the first qualitative researchers to begin building QDAS, writing extensively on the benefits of such software. As with the overstated benefits of QDAS in the literature, use caution when reading claims that QDAS inevitably leads to more sloppy, corrupted, quantified, or mechanized research. (For a detailed example of the appropriation of these early claims, their modification and subsequent misuse, see Jackson, Paulus, & Woolf, 2018.)

Don't put the cart before the horse

Many qualitative researchers make a reasonable claim that the software can be used appropriately only insofar as it follows (rather than leads) the research methodology. The Five-Level QDA® method (Woolf & Silver, 2017) is perhaps the most detailed example of a resource that helps researchers articulate methodological strategies and walks them through the appropriate tactics in the software in order to satisfy the ultimate goals of those strategies. In many respects, this approach is in sync with the early developers of QDAS who were crafting tools that satisfied the research practices already used via 'manual' methods. The logic of this approach appeals to qualitative researchers who do not use software, those who do, and a wide array of experts in methodology. However, a (sometimes unintended) consequence of the cart/horse metaphor is that qualitative researchers who eschew the use of software for a wide range of reasons are able to justify their avoidance by putting QDAS in a permanent back seat. This methods-first mantra is slowly becoming less viable.

Our stance: *methods-with* software

The early tools developed in QDAS were an immediate and direct result of attempts to translate manual methods (using paper, pencil, highlighters, and Post-it notes) into digital tools that provide similar tactics to mark, tag, and sort. Part of the reason the methods-first metaphor continues to thrive is because of this evolution. In our research and in our consultation with other qualitative researchers who use NVivo, we almost always begin by asking about the design and logic of the study (including the methodology) before determining which software tools to use and how we will use them (as many tools are multi-purpose). However, to assume that there is a one-directional and linear relationship between human thought and tool production (or use) is outmoded and no longer an accepted view within the sociology of technology. Researchers in a wide array of disciplines are looking more closely at the ways society and culture influence the construction of technologies and how these technologies also influence society and culture. To accept this view means accepting that our qualitative work is sometimes influenced by NVivo.

Therefore, as an alternative to the methods-first mantra, we advocate a *methods-with* mantra (Jackson, 2017). This view acknowledges the potential for mutual influence between researcher and software and urges us to let go of the fear that the software is hijacking the process. We still need to learn more about the contexts in which software influences us and with what results. Unfortunately, few studies have explicitly sought to carefully explore the spaces where qualitative researchers and technologies meet (for exceptions see Gilbert, 2002; Jackson, 2014; Saillard, 2011). Some of our reflective questions in the Takeaways section of each chapter are designed to help you think more reflexively about the role of NVivo in your work.

SECTION 1.2: CONCEPTUAL GROUNDING IN QUALITATIVE RESEARCH PURPOSES AND NVIVO

Getting ready for qualitative analysis

If you feel comfortable and familiar with qualitative research, you will see many places where NVivo mimics the handling of qualitative data through highlighting, writing notes, and connecting ideas. If you are new to qualitative research, you will learn a lot about handling qualitative data as you experiment with different software tools. While we will provide you with tips and tricks and pragmatic issues to address, much of what you learn will come through patience and experimentation.

Understand your methods

If you are coming to NVivo without first meeting qualitative methodology or methods, then you are strongly advised to read some general texts or introductory texts from within your own discipline. Then use the recommended reading lists in those texts to further explore the methodological choices available to you. Qualitative methods are a rich, diverse, and complex sphere of knowledge and practice.

Develop questions

Qualitative research often begins with a vaguely defined question or goal. It may well begin 'with a bit of interesting "data"' (Seale, Gobo, Gubrium, & Silverman, 2004: 9). Record your early reflections as you set out. In NVivo, you can create a Memo (a research journal) to record them. They will help you maintain focus as you work, and then later to evaluate the direction you are taking. Keep notes about thoughts you have around those questions as you read, discuss, observe, or simply reflect on issues as they arise, and date these. Keeping a record will allow you to keep track of your ideas and to trace the path those ideas have taken from initial, hesitant conceptualizations to final, confident realizations.

Visualization techniques (Mind Maps and Concept Maps in NVivo) and thought experiments can also help to clarify what might be useful questions (Bazeley, 2013; Maxwell, 2013). They can facilitate your examination and framing of various camps in your areas of research or how particular theories might overlap. As you work, your initial Maps might help refine your questions (or generate new ones), so more deliberate (purposive) data gathering can occur. These visual explorations become part of your data and can be explored, managed, and tracked within NVivo. Later in this chapter we help you explore journaling and mapping tools for thinking about your project before getting to the nuts and bolts of setting up a project.

Identify assumptions

Previous knowledge is a prerequisite to gaining understanding. Qualitative researchers who investigate a different form of social life always bring with them their own lenses and conceptual networks. They cannot drop them, for in this case they would not be able to perceive, observe and describe meaningful events any longer – confronted with chaotic, meaningless and fragmented phenomena they would have to give up their scientific endeavour. (Kelle, 1997: paragraph 4.2)

Previous knowledge brings with it assumptions about what you might find. Rather than deny their existence, you should recognize them, record them, and become aware of how they might be influencing the way you are thinking about your data – only then can you effectively control (or at least, assess) that impact. Maxwell (2013) recommends creating a 'researcher identity memo' to explore personal goals, recognize assumptions, and draw on experiential knowledge. You could add such a Memo to your research notes or create a conceptual map that captures what you are expecting to see.

Explore existing data

Data relevant to your project often exist before you make new data. Try starting with one or more of the suggestions listed here.

- *Observations of yourself and of others.* Field notes or diary records could play a significant early role. Adapt the instructions for creating a Project journal to create documents in which to record your observations.
- *Data already in the public sphere.* Examples include newspapers, novels, radio, internet, or archived data. These can provide valuable learning experiences as you master both software and analysis strategies.

- *Expository or research literature.* The belief that an inductive approach to inquiry requires researchers to come to their data without having been influenced by prior reading of the literature in their field and without bringing any theoretical concepts to the research is generally no longer seen as feasible, nor is it broadly supported. Strauss and Corbin (1998: 47) declared: 'Insights do not happen haphazardly; rather they happen to prepared minds during interplay with the data.' In many fields, qualitative researchers are expected to gain a firm grasp of the relevant literature, and for university-based research, prior understanding of the literature on the topic is an essential element of a funding application or doctoral research proposal.

How NVivo will support your analysis

NVivo provides you with a set of tools that will *assist* you in undertaking an analysis of qualitative data. The use of a computer is not intended to supplant time-honoured ways of learning from data or to diminish the role of the qualitative researcher in exploring and interpreting rich data. NVivo was created by researchers who used precisely these kinds of manual methods. The many benefits of this technology include the ability to:

- mimic manual strategies for handling qualitative data;
- develop an efficiently searchable warehouse of data that records the choices made during analysis and can be examined and re-examined with relative ease;
- increase the efficiency of the more mundane and administrative tasks in organizing data;
- extend the longevity and reusability of data because it is not stuck in a shoebox under someone's bed, with prior insights long forgotten;
- push the boundaries of what qualitative researchers are able to do manually by providing a few tools that open new opportunities;
- improve the efficiency and effectiveness of teamwork through consistent processes that capture and combine individual work in one comprehensive Project.

NVivo continues to be developed with extensive, qualitative researcher feedback to support researchers in the diverse ways they work with data.

The average user of any software program typically accesses only a small portion of its capabilities; this is no doubt true for users of NVivo also. If you are using NVivo for a small descriptive project, you can work without having to learn complex procedures, but if you are undertaking complex analytical tasks, you can find the additional tools you need. Choices about what tools to use and how to use them are entirely up to you. There are, nevertheless, some common principles regarding the most effective use for many of the tools, regardless of methodological choices. For example, the labels used for coding categories will vary depending on the project and the methods chosen, but the principles employed in structuring those categories into a branching coding system are common to many methods where coding takes place. These common principles allow us to describe in general how you might use the various tools. It is then your task to decide how you might apply them to your project.

Using NVivo during the analysis of qualitative data will help you:

- Manage data – to organize and keep track of the many messy records that go into making a qualitative project. These might include not just raw data files from interviews, questionnaires, focus groups or field observations, but also published research, images, diagrams, audio, video, web pages, other documentary sources, rough notes and ideas jotted into memos, information about data sources, and conceptual maps of what is going on in the data.
- Manage ideas – to organize and provide rapid access to conceptual and theoretical knowledge generated in the course of the study, as well as the data that support it, while at the same time retaining ready access to the context from which those data have come.
- Query data – to ask simple or complex questions of the data, and have the program retrieve from your project all information relevant to determining an answer to those questions. Results of queries are saved to allow further interrogation, and so querying or searching becomes part of an ongoing enquiry process.
- Visualize data – to show the content and/or structure of cases, ideas, concepts, sampling strategies, timelines, etc., at various stages of the interpretive process, and to visually represent the relationships among these items in a range of (often interactive) displays.
- Report from the data – using contents of the qualitative project, including information about and in the original data sources, the ideas and knowledge developed from them, and the process by which these outcomes were reached.

Although specific tools such as Nodes, Memos, and Cluster Analyses were sometimes designed with one strategy in mind, you will discover that these and other software tools can be adapted for multiple strategies. The tools are not so isolated or independent in practice and the strategies they support work best when they are carried out as integrated activities.

SECTION 1.3: USING NVIVO TO GET STARTED ON YOUR RESEARCH

We start by providing basic installation information, to ensure you are able to access the software, and we introduce you to two sample Projects to which we will be referring throughout the book. Then, in the remainder of this chapter, we help familiarize you with the software via the Sample Project and our introductory videos and then walk you through the creation of your own Project. In the process, we help you develop good practices for thinking and writing by:

- creating a Project journal;
- visualizing ideas in a Mind Map and assumptions in a Concept Map;
- importing and thinking about a pdf (or Word) file;

- writing an Annotation;
- developing a Memo;
- connecting a Memo to a File with a Memo Link;
- creating a web of connections between your evidence and your ideas with See Also Links;
- connecting your data or ideas to items outside of the project with a Hyperlink.

We also detail the steps for saving and creating backup Projects and if you do not work through this chapter in one sitting, you might skip to the final instructions about backups when you are ready to take a break.

NVivo terms used in this section

Annotation

Concept Map

Memo

Memo Link

Mind Map

NVivo Project

Hyperlink

See Also Link

Install the software and become acquainted with NVivo

Upgrading from an earlier version on the same computer

If you have an earlier version or the trial version of NVivo on your computer, you do not need to remove it before installing your new licence of NVivo. All you will need to do is enter and activate a new licence key to extend your existing licence. If, however, you have more than one version of NVivo on your system, your computer will default to open the most recent software, even if you launch from a project created in an earlier version. NVivo will then walk you through the steps to convert your older project so it can be used in the new version.

- As a result, you will have two copies of the same project in two different versions of the software. NVivo adds the name of the version to the end of the name of your Project so you can distinguish them easily, or you can rename the Project (see Chapter 11 for details about Project names, pp. 327–328).
- If you convert a Project to the new version of NVivo, you cannot reopen or resave that new copy of the Project in an earlier version of the software.

How to follow our instructions

- For NVivo clicking instructions we use purple font to indicate steps you will take in the software.
- When click instructions diverge, we use grey font for Windows users and black font for Mac users.
- When the screen shots from Windows and Mac are similar, we will use one or the other as a visual. When they are different we will label the Figure to indicate Windows or Mac.
- When a tool is available in only the Windows or Mac version of NVivo, we indicate this in the section heading with parentheses. We will also occasionally do so in the body of the text.
- To help acquaint you with these instructions, we provide two, brief videos in the online resources (https://study.sagepub.com/jackson3e) that serve as a 'Primer for following the click instructions.'

Download, install, launch, and activate

If you have not yet done so, use these instructions to download, install, launch, and activate the software (which requires an internet connection). If you were using the trial, you do not need to uninstall and reinstall the software. All you will need to do is to enter and activate a new licence key to extend your existing version.

1.a.

⇒ **www.qsrinternational.com** > **NVivo** > **Learn More** > **Select Free Trial** or **Buy Now**.
⇒ Follow the instructions to > **Download** > **Install** > **Launch** > **Activate**.

If this is the first time you launch the software, you will be asked for your name and initials to help track the work you do in the software.

- This prompt for the current user occurs once only, unless you change the default to ask for the user each time.
- More about the potential need to change this default and instructions for doing so are in Chapter 11 on Teamwork (pp. 325–326).

1.b.

⇒ After launching the software > **Sample Project** / **Create a Copy of Sample Project** > provide a new name > **Save**.
⇒ **Quick Start Steps tab** (right hand side of the screen) > **Let's Get Started with NVivo for Windows** > watch the video.

Sample data

Two sample projects are provided throughout the book to help bring the conceptual and methodological issues to life. One project is referred to as the 'Sample Project' or the 'Environmental Change Project' and is included in NVivo; the other is an example from Pat's research and is referred to as the 'Researchers Project'. Before you begin playing with these projects, the following information will help you understand them.

Environmental Change Project

The *Environmental Change Down East* Project explores the attitudes of individuals in 13 communities in an area of North Carolina known as 'Down East'. The goal of the data collection and analysis was to foster dialogue among stakeholders (residents, land developers, legislators, business owners, etc.) regarding community planning, land use, and sustainable development. This Project accompanies every licence as an embedded sample.

Researchers Project

The *Researchers* Project comprises focus groups, extracts from interviews, and some other sources designed to help answer the questions of what brings people to engage in research, and what it is about their experience that keeps them researching. This Project is available in the online resources (https://study.sagepub.com/jackson3e)

In addition to these two Projects, we pull from a broad array of other studies from our own experiences, research from the literature, and research stories and examples from our colleagues. In a few instances, we also provide a vignette to help illustrate a point. When available, we provide references, but these examples tend to come from our memories of collegial conversations rather than materials that can be perused in greater detail in another publication.

NVivo's basic interface

In our subsequent instructions on clicking through the software, we almost always begin with one of the screen locations shown in Figures 1.1 and 1.2. Knowing these terms will be helpful because they also serve as the foundation on which most Project items are built.

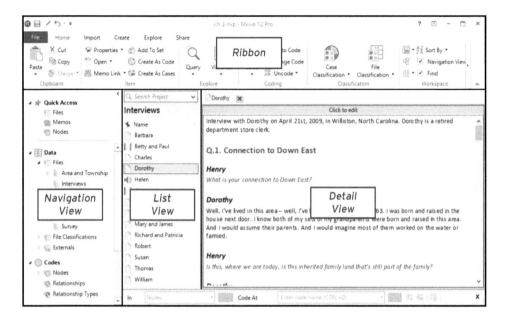

Figure 1.1 NVivo for Windows main interface: *Ribbon, Navigation View, List View, Detail View*

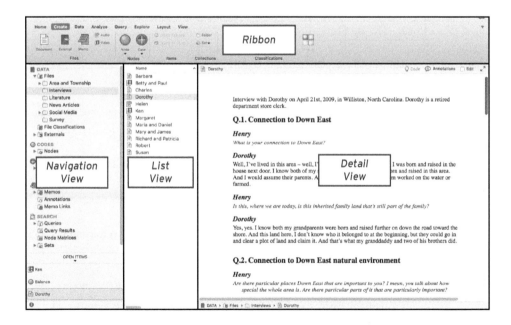

Figure 1.2 NVivo for Mac main interface: *Ribbon, Navigation View, List View, Detail View*

In the *Navigation View* on the left side of the screen (Figure 1.3) there are standard buttons and subfolders (Windows users also have a customizable Quick Access area).

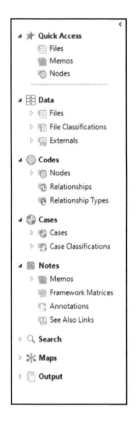
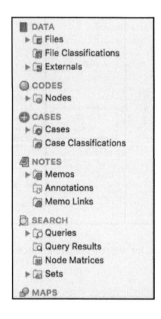

Figure 1.3   *Navigation View* in Windows (left) and Mac (right)

- **Data** are neatly organized in Files (e.g., transcripts, audio, video, surveys, social media).
- **Codes** are organized to help you examine conceptual or thematic Nodes that run across your Files (e.g., *Communication, Time, Trust, Vaccination*).
- **Cases** contain qualitative data as well as demographic and/or quantitative data for your units of analysis (e.g., *Barbara, Dorothy, Susan*).
- **Notes** help store your ideas and are sometimes linked to Files or Nodes (e.g., your Memo for *Initial Interpretations*).
- **Search** allows you to ask about connections among items in the project, usually through Queries or Sets.
- **Maps** provide an area to explore and express ideas visually.
- **Output** offers pre-established formats for getting data out of the software (Windows only).
  - Items can usually be easily exported from Windows and Mac with a right-click. You will do that later in this chapter.
  - Mac users who do not currently right-click should see the Tips, Challenges, and Warnings subsection at the end of the chapter for guidance.

In addition to this orientation to the screen, visit the online resources (https://study.sage pub.com/jackson3e). Here you can watch a two-minute video, 'Orientation to the NVivo interface.' We provide a video for Windows users and a video for Mac users. At the same time, you can take stock of the supplementary materials on the companion website that you can access any time.

Now we will help you look more deeply into the project and familiarize yourself with the *Navigation View, List View* and *Detail View* (use Figures 1.1 or 1.2 if needed).

1.c.

Exploring the Sample Project

⇒ *Navigation View*: **Data** > **Files** > **Interviews**.

Throughout these instructions, keep in mind that items in the *Navigation View* sometimes require an extra step in order to see the subfolders (Figure 1.4).

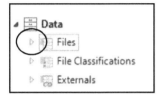

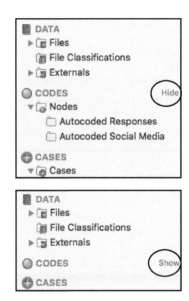

| Windows and Mac users: On the left side of a Folder, click on the right-facing triangle to see subfolders. When displaying subfolders, the triangle points down. Click on this downward triangle to hide the subfolders. | Mac users: In addition to the triangle on the left side of the folder, you will see a 'Hide' and 'Show' option if you move your pointer to the right of the main options (e.g., 'Data', 'Codes', 'Cases:'). |

Figure 1.4   Showing and hiding subfolders in the *Navigation View*

⇒ *List View*: **Double-click** on **Barbara** (Figure 1.5).

(Continued)

(Continued)

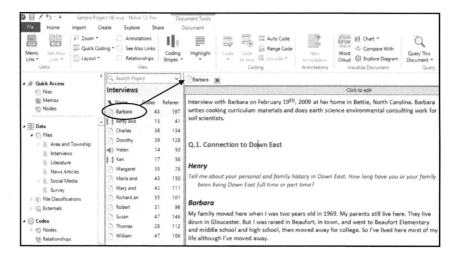

Figure 1.5 Opening *Barbara* in the *Detail View*

⇒ *Detail View*: This File inside NVivo looks similar to the file in Microsoft Word, but NVivo has made a copy of the original file.
⇒ *Navigation View*: **Codes** > **Nodes**.

  o Nodes are your concept containers and we will discuss them in detail in Chapter 3.

⇒ *List View*: **Double-click** on the Node, **Community change** (Figure 1.6).

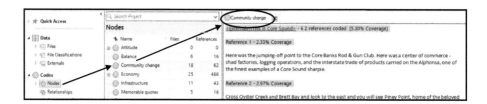

Figure 1.6 Opening *Community change* in the *Detail View*

⇒ *Detail View*: This Node points to passages in various Files that have been coded to the Node (and calls each coded passage a Reference).
⇒ *File*: **Open Project Event Log** (this tracks every action taken in the Project and can help you problem-solve; we will show you how to turn this on when you create your own Project).

Windows users

As you open items in the Project, they will continue to stack in tabs in the *Detail View* (Figure 1.7). You can leave many items open and access them via their tabs. You can also close any item by clicking on the X in any tab.

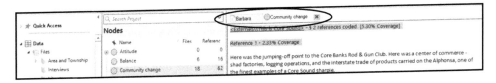

Figure 1.7 Open items in the *Detail View* with individual tabs (Windows)

Mac users

As you open items in the Project, they will continue to stack at the bottom of the *Navigation View* in the Open Items list (Figure 1.8). You can leave many items open and access them with a single click. You can also close any item by clicking on the X to the right of the item name. Mac users should also be aware that the *Menu bar* at the top of the screen provides additional options (e.g., File … Window, Help). We will occasionally send you to the *Menu bar* to access software features.

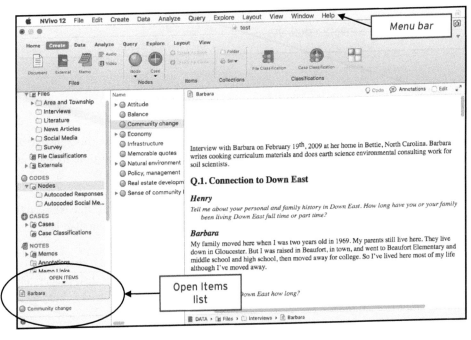

Figure 1.8 The 'Open Items' list in the *Navigation View* and the *Menu bar* above the *Ribbon* (Mac)

Continue exploring the *Environmental Change* Project

Continue clicking around in items in the *Navigation View* to get a sense of the tools and their locations – although the rest of the book will click you through these tools with specifically focused chapters. In addition, you can watch our video on 'The main tools in NVivo' in the online resources (https://study.sagepub.com/jackson3e) for an extended tour of these tools and a guide to the chapters where you will find additional information about these tools. After opening a few items (some of which will make sense and others which might look strange), you will have a general sense of a fully populated Project. You will continue in the remainder of this chapter by creating your own Project from scratch (even if you have not yet finalized your research questions or collected the data to answer your research questions). When you are ready, exit the Sample Project.

═══════ **1.d.** ═══════

Exit the Sample Project

⇒ *File:* **Close.**
⇒ *Menu bar:* File > **Close.**

This will close the project without closing the software. If you want to quit working in NVivo until another time you can close the Project and the software simultaneously:

⇒ **Select** the X on the upper right.
⇒ *Menu bar:* **NVivo12 > Quit NVivo.**

Create your own Project

Your Project begins from the time you start asking questions – from the thought that X, Y, or Z might be something interesting to investigate. This is also a good time to start using software!

- Early use of software ensures you do not lose precious early thoughts. Indeed, sketching ideas and writing even rough notes will help to clarify thinking as you plan your project.
- Starting early will give you a gentle introduction to the software and a chance to gradually develop your skills as your Project builds up. This is better than desperately trying to cope with learning technical skills in a rush as you become overwhelmed with data and the deadline for completion is looming.
- Starting with software early acts as a reminder that data collection and data analysis are not separate processes in qualitative approaches to research.

So, let's start now! We will help you create a new Project and record your preliminary ideas in a Project journal, Mind Map, and Concept Map. You will then import a pdf or Microsoft Word document, and create Annotations, a Memo, and a See Also Link to start writing about ideas prompted by the document.

1.e.

Creating a Project

It is *very important* that you only work with NVivo Projects on your hard drive unless you have purchased **NVivo for Teams**. There are instances of projects getting corrupted if you work off an external drive, server, or jump drive (unless you are using NVivo for Teams, Chapter 11, pp. 318–319). Don't panic: you can save backups to an external drive or a server and we show you how to do this at the end of this chapter. However, as you work through the instructions below to create a Project, we recommend that you save it in your Documents folder.

⇒ **Launch NVivo** › **Blank Project** / **Create new project** (Figure 1.9).
⇒ Provide a name in the **Title** / **Save As window**.
⇒ Add a **Description** for the Project (these can be changed later).
⇒ NVivo assigns a matching **File name** (or **Path**) for the Project file.
⇒ Check the box to **Write user actions to project event log** (you can turn this on and off later).
⇒ Identify the location of your Project (default is usually the **Documents** folder unless you recently used another location to save an NVivo Project).
⇒ **OK** / **Create.**

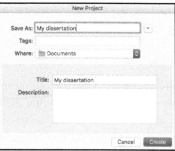

Figure 1.9   Creating a Project in Windows (left) and Mac (right)

⇒ Profiles and passwords: If you want to customize User profiles or establish Password protection, see Chapter 11 on Teamwork (pp. 324–326).
⇒ Save your project regularly, but if you have not taken an action in the Project since your last save, the option to 'Save' will be greyed out.
   ○ *File:* **Save.**
   ○ *Menu bar:* **File › Save.**

Windows users will discover that every 15 minutes NVivo will ask if you want to save your changes in case of power failure or crash. When you are working on your own Project, it is strongly recommended that you save each time you are asked, unless you are simply experimenting, do not want to save your changes, or you are in the middle of an Undo operation.

One or many Projects?

Your research may have a number of components:

- data generated from different sources (rural and urban; companies A, B, and C);
- data from different phases of the project (pilot phase and main data collection; wave 1, 2, and 3 of interviews);
- data of different types (literature, observations, interview transcripts, a dataset, pictures or video, web pages).

NVivo provides data management tools that allow you to compare or isolate different components within your Project. What this means in practice is that it is best to incorporate all those components into a single NVivo Project, rather than make separate Projects for each component. Having everything together in one NVivo Project will allow you to gather together all you know on any topic, regardless of the source, and to make instant comparisons across different Files, phases, types of data, or Cases. If you wish, you will still be able to interrogate just one component of the data by placing relevant Files within a specific subfolder, or by identifying that component as belonging to a defined Set or having a specific Attribute Value. (Chapters 2 and 5 will show you how to create and use Folders, Sets, and Attribute Values to manage your data.)

Journaling

In an NVivo Memo, you can journal any insights gained as you shape your research questions and your approaches to analysing the data. These reflections can alert you to include certain kinds of people in your sample, to collect information in alternative ways, or to explore a broader (or narrower) context. Begin by recording the questions, assumptions, or other ideas you are bringing to the Project. The following prompts might help:

- Why are you doing this research?
- What do you think it's about?
- What are the questions you're asking, and where did they come from?
- What do you expect to find and why?
- What have you observed so far?

Qualitative researchers typically keep a journal to document how they have moved from initial forays in their research to arrival at their conclusions; hence some refer to the journal as an audit trail for the study. Lyn Richards (2015) compares the journaling process to keeping a ship's log with its careful account of a journey, and provides detailed suggestions about what might be recorded there:

- How insights were triggered and ideas were developed.
- Fleeting ideas that are captured before additional data and ideas march into your consciousness.

- Lists of things you want to do at another time.
- The core concepts amidst the sometimes overwhelming options you could (but perhaps shouldn't) pursue in the data to answer your research questions.
- How you pulled together the evidence to support your conclusions.

Unlike the ship's log, however, the journal can be a private document and you might also record your frustrations and your joys as you work through your research. Perhaps the best advice of all, as you focus on ideas and your responses to them (rather than dry description), is to enjoy the journaling task. Write freely without worrying about formality of style or 'correctness' of thoughts. Writing 'often provides sharp, sunlit moments of clarity or insight – little conceptual epiphanies' (Miles & Huberman, 1994: 74).

In NVivo a journal is a Memo, and it will always be available for modification as you are working in the Project. You will be able to establish links (Memo Links and See Also Links) from your written ideas to entire Files or to the specific passages which prompted those thoughts. Additionally, you will be able to code the journal as you write it, making it easy

1.f.

Creating a journal

⇒ *Ribbon:* **Create** > **Memo** (Figure 1.10).

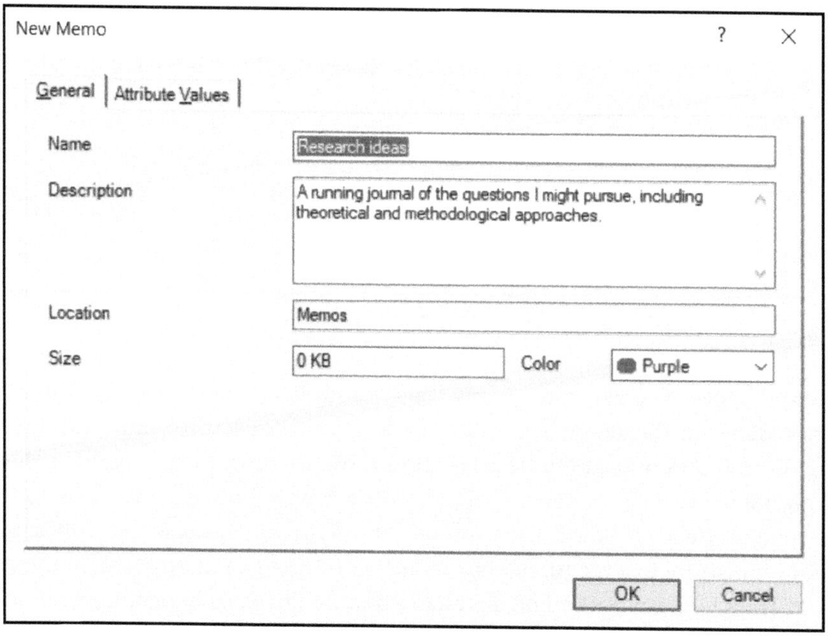

Figure 1.10   Creating a Memo to use as a journal

(Continued)

(Continued)

- ⇒ **Name** (provide a concise title)
- ⇒ **Description** (an optional, additional, brief overview of the Memo)
- ⇒ **Colour** (use as an optional strategy for grouping items, such as Memos about methodology)
  - o **OK / Done**.

If you have a journal already started in a document outside of NVivo you can import it into the Project:

- ⇒ *Ribbon*: **Import / Data** > **Memos** > Select the File > **Open** > **Import**.

If you are importing only one Memo, you will encounter the Memo Properties window where you can rename, add a colour, etc. (this can also be done later through the Memo Properties window) > **OK / Done.**

Journal writing, saving, closing, reopening and editing

- ⇒ *Ribbon*: **Edit / Home** > **Insert** > **Insert Date/Time** to keep track of the evolution of your ideas (note the alternative shortcut keys: **Ctrl / Cmd + Shift + T**).
- ⇒ *Ribbon*: **Edit / Home** to adjust **Format** (colour), **Style**, etc.
- ⇒ *Detail View*: Write some ideas about your expectations for the Project or a list of things to do next as you move forward with your design and analysis.
- ⇒ *File / Menu bar*: **File** > **Save** (although you do not need to save it before you close the Memo, only before you close the Project).
- ⇒ *Detail View*: **Select** the **X** in your Memo tab (just above your date/time stamp) to close the Memo.
- ⇒ *Navigation View*: in the Open Items list, **Select** the **X** to the right of the Memo to close the Memo (see Figure 1.8).
- ⇒ To reopen the Memo:
  - o *Navigation View*: **Notes** > **Memos**.
  - o *List View*: **Double-click** on the **Memo** to re-open.
  - o *Detail View*: **Click to edit** with the blue bar just below the name of your Memo / check box on the far right above your Memo > add more thoughts.

---

to retrieve the ideas you generate on any topic – and this is something you can do with any other Memo or document you create within your Project. No more coloured tags hanging off the sides of pages to help you find those insightful ideas. Perhaps the most important advice is that it does not matter if the typing or the grammar is rough, as long as you get the ideas down. Later, if you can discuss the ideas with a colleague, the conversation is likely to strengthen your reflective thinking about the text and its interpretation. Then you can clarify and augment your Memo. Consider coding your Memos as well as coding your other data, to help sort your thoughts thematically and to keep them at the forefront when you read coded data later. We will show you the basics of coding in Chapter 3.

Create a Map

We will show the various Maps, Graphs, and Charts available in NVivo as they become relevant in each chapter. Sketching your ideas about your Project at this stage is a particular form of journaling what you think it is you are asking or doing – great for those who prefer to think and work visually, and beneficial even for those who sometimes struggle to work visually. Maxwell (2013) argues strongly for creating an early concept map to help clarify the conceptual framework or theoretical underpinning of a study. In NVivo, two different types of Maps can be created to pursue this clarity:

- use a Concept Map when you want to visualize concepts or categories in your research questions or theoretical framework and explore the possible links between them;
- use a Mind Map when you want to explore a main idea and visualize a hierarchy or web of topics associated with that idea.

Maps can be used throughout your Project. In this chapter, we will use the Mind Map and the Concept Map as you begin shaping your research. This is a way of reflecting on the assumptions you bring to the Project as well as the concepts, relationships, or patterns you expect to find. This helps clarify your research questions and plan your data collection. If you have already collected data, the Maps can help you start tracking the ideas that are already emerging.

If you find it a struggle to develop a Map, then try some of Maxwell's (2013: 62) suggestions:

- Think about the key words you use in talking about your topic, or in things you've already written about your research.
- Take something you've already written (your research proposal, or a preliminary literature review perhaps) and map the implicit theory within it.
- Ask someone to interview you about your topic, then listen to the tape and note the terms used.

━━━━━━━━━━ **1.g.** ━━━━━━━━━━

Create a Mind Map (Figure 1.11)

⇒ *Ribbon*: **Explore** > **Mind Map** > Provide a **Name** for your Mind Map > OK / **Done.**
⇒ *Detail View*: Name your Main Idea for this Project.

Connect an Idea

⇒ Select the Idea you created (Main Idea) and add a Sibling or Child Idea to it.
    ○ Use the icons in the *Ribbon* > **Mind Map.**
    ○ Use the icons at the top of the *Detail View.*

Alternatively

⇒ With the main idea selected > **Right-click** > **Insert Child Ideas** > **Name** the idea.

(Continued)

(Continued)

⇒ Create a Sibling idea: **Right-click** on an idea > **Insert Sibling Idea** > **Name** the idea.

To move an item from one branch to another:

⇒ **Right-click** > **Cut** > **Right-click** on the destination item > **Paste.**

Create a floating idea

⇒ *Detail View:* In the white space **Right-click** > **Insert Floating Idea** > Label the idea. Floating ideas are used when there is not (yet) an obvious connection to the other ideas.

Create Nodes from a Mind Map

⇒ *Detail View:* **Click** anywhere on white space to ensure the *Detail View* is active.
⇒ *Ribbon:* **Mind Map** > **Create As Nodes or Cases** > Select Location > **Nodes** > **OK.**
⇒ *Detail View:* At the top > Create as **Nodes** > Nodes > **Select.**

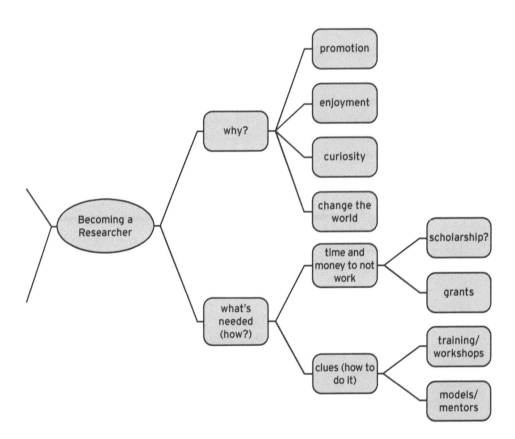

Figure 1.11 Mind Map to launch the *Researchers* Project

Create a Concept Map (Figure 1.12)

⇒ *Ribbon*: **Explore** > **Concept Map**.
⇒ Provide a **Name** for your Concept Map > **OK** / **Done**.

The *Detail View* will open with a collection of Shapes and an empty workspace in which to use them.

⇒ *Detail View*: **Select** a **Shape** and drag it to the workspace area to represent one of your concepts or categories.

The *Detail View* will open with an empty workspace. At the top of the empty Map you will find options to add Shape, Connector, and Project Item.

⇒ Click on **Shape** (sometimes this a is very small icon with no label just above the empty space of the Map) to add one to the workspace area.
⇒ **Double-click** on the Shape to label it. You might want to use different Shapes to represent different categories or theoretical concepts.
⇒ Add another Shape to the workspace, and label it. Add as many as you need to capture all of your concepts.

Managing shapes and connections

To illustrate real or potential connections between concepts or categories, you can add connecting lines between items.

⇒ *Ribbon*: **Concept Map Tools** > switch from Pointer to **Connector** / **Select** a Connector from the menu above the *Detail View*.
⇒ *Detail View*: **Select** one item, then while **holding** the left mouse button, **drag** to another item, to make a connection.

To change the type of Connector:

⇒ **Select** the Connector you want to change.
⇒ *Ribbon*: **Change Connector** /*Detail View*: **Format** pane: **Connector** > **Select** from the drop-down options.

To rearrange items

⇒ *Ribbon*: Switch back to **Pointer** to rearrange items in your Concept Map.
⇒ **Select** any item and hold the left mouse button to drag the item.

Other options

Select any item or items in your Map, to change their colour and border.

⇒ *Ribbon*: **Concept Map Tools** > Format Shape / *Detail View*: **Format Tab** > **Select** **Fill**, **Border Colour**, and **Border Width** to modify the appearance of the item.

If your mapping has prompted fresh thoughts about your Project, record those in your Project journal. Maps can be copied and pasted into the Project journal, as well.

(Continued)

(Continued)

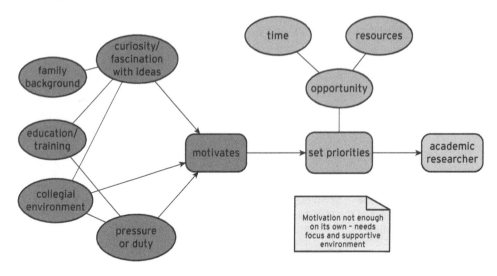

Figure 1.12   Becoming a researcher: preliminary Concept Map

Import and reflect on a data item

Now you are ready to import and explore a document. Consider using any of the following:

- an article or report;
- notes from your reading;
- the text of a preliminary interview;
- field notes from a site visit;
- the transcript of (or notes from) a conversation about your research with a colleague or your dissertation advisor or supervisor; or
- text from a web page.

We provide the types of Files that can be imported in the context of specific chapters, but a complete list of the various formats for qualitative data that can be incorporated into an NVivo Project can be found in the online resources (https://study.sagepub.com/jackson3e). With the exception of YouTube videos (Chapter 10) and non-embedded audio and video (Chapter 9), NVivo makes a copy of the Files when you import them. Changes you make to the File in NVivo will not be reflected in the original, and changes in the original will not update into the NVivo copy.

Text File types that can be imported include *.doc and *.docx (Word files), *.txt (text files), *.rtf (rich text files), and *.pdf (portable data format files). If you use a pdf file at this stage, make sure it is one that allows you to copy specific text onto your clipboard. Identify a file or two that you are interested in importing, thinking through and writing about, and make sure they are closed but accessible through your computer.

━━━━━━━━━━━━━ **1.h.** ━━━━━━━━━━━━━

Importing and viewing a text-based document

⇒ *Navigation View*: **Data** > **Files** (to establish the location where the Files will import).
⇒ *Ribbon*: **Import** > **Files** / **Data** > **Documents** > **Select** the File(s) > **Open** > **Import** > **OK** / **Done**.
⇒ *List View*: **Double-click** on the File to open in the *Detail View*.

Your first reading of a document should be rapid but purposeful, directed but not bound by your research questions. The idea is to get a sense of the whole, so as you begin to identify specific points or issues in the data, you will see them in the context of the whole (see Bazeley, 2013: chapter 4). Reading right through before you start coding is especially important if it is some time since you gathered this particular item of data, or if your recent work on it was piecemeal. Many people prefer to scribble on hard copy at this stage, on scrap paper, or in a notebook, but there is a real advantage in making notes on the computer – they do not get lost, and you have tools to help connect them with other Project items if you wish.

Mark text with Annotations

As you read (or later, as you code) in NVivo, you might Annotate words or phrases in the text. Annotations in NVivo are similar to a comments field or a footnote in Microsoft Word. Whereas Memos are more useful for storing (often extensive) reflective thoughts and ideas from the text, Annotations are useful for adding (usually brief) comments or reminders about a particular segment of text. You might use them to:

• clarify an acronym;
• note the intonation of the voice at a point in the conversation;
• identify a translation or transcription problem;
• comment on some aspect of the discourse.

━━━━━━━━━━ **An Annotation in the** ━━━━━━━━━━
Environmental Change Project

In the *Environmental Change* study, Susan refers to herself as an 'Islandberger' in her response to the first question in the interview. The researcher notes, with an Annotation, that Susan has strong ties to both Harkers Island and Marshalberg, and that locals have developed hybridized names to express these ties. Fellow researchers will therefore know that they will not find 'Islandberg' in a list of nearby cities.

━━━━━━━━━━ **1.i.** ━━━━━━━━━━

Annotating text

⇒ *Detail View*: **Select** a word or a few words in the passage to be Annotated (usually short) > **Right-click** (on the highlighted text) > **New Annotation**.

⇒ A space for typing will open at the base of the *Detail View* (Figure 1.13).

⇒ A box will open in the *Detail View*.

⇒ Type your Annotation.

⇒ *Detail View*: Passages with an Annotation will be indicated with a blue highlight (click anywhere in the *Detail View* to release your selection to see this).

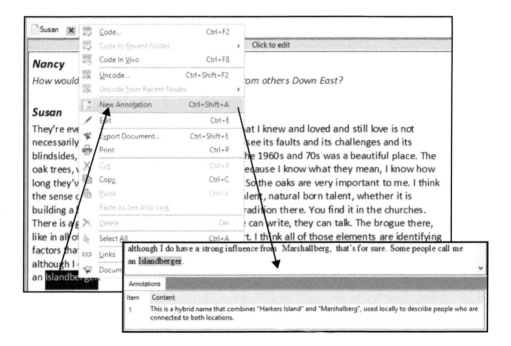

Figure 1.13   Creating an Annotation (Windows)

To turn Annotations off or on

⇒ *Ribbon*: **Document** > check or uncheck **Annotations**.

   o *Detail View*: **Click** anywhere in the blue highlighted text to see the matching comment at the bottom of the screen; or

   o **Select** the number next to a comment to see the associated blue highlight in the text (which will turn a darker blue).

⇒ *Detail View*: At the top, **select Annotations.**

   o *Detail View*: **Click** anywhere in the blue highlighted text to see the matching comment; or

   o **Select** a comment to see the associated blue highlight in the text (which will turn a darker blue).

Reflect on a specific File using a Memo Link

You can use a Memo to reflect on the data you imported, but, depending on the nature of your data, you might also create a Memo that is linked to a particular File. This allows a quick pathway between the File and the Memo (although, as an alternative, you could also develop a naming scheme that simply allows you to find the Memo that is associated with a particular File efficiently in the *Navigation View*). There are two key restrictions to note when using a Memo Link:

- A Memo Link does not allow you to jump from a specific place in a Memo to a specific place in a File.
- Each File in NVivo can be assigned only one Memo. A File and a Memo are monogamous when it comes to a Memo Link.

These restrictions do not apply to a See Also Link (covered later).

Because a Memo Link will focus on a particular File, rather than on overarching concepts or a list of things to do at another time, they have a different use, including:

- field notes generated during data collection about the participant whose File is linked, such as unrecorded comments, observations, and debrief discussions with a co-interviewer;
- a summary of the main points in the File, or notes about your overall impressions from the File;
- thoughts about the meaning or significance of statements in this File such as inconsistencies or unique metaphors.

Whether you decide to create a Memo for particular Files in your Project or simply use a general journal will be a matter of methodological choice and/or pragmatic decision-making and will vary from Project to Project. A link between a File and a Memo is not necessarily useful for all Projects. For example, for data where responses are brief, it may be more useful to record a summary of key issues for each File (or Case) in a single combined 'issues' journal, and to use a separate journal for reflecting on what you are learning from various Cases and for noting common themes to explore. For any Project dealing intensively with rich data for a small sample, however, the Memo for each File becomes a valuable resource holding a reminder of key points learned, interpretive thoughts, and ideas to follow up in later analyses.

1.j.

Creating a Memo Link to a File

⇒ *Navigation View*: **Data** > **Files** > **Select** a File > **Right-click** > **Memo Link** > **Link to New Memo.**

⇒ **Name** the Memo > **OK / Done**.

(Continued)

(Continued)

⇒ Date and time stamp your entry > **Ctrl / Cmd + Shift + T**.

⇒ Record your ideas about that **File** in the **Memo** and come back to it any time to review and revisit your interpretations.

    o *List View*: **Select** the **File > Right-click > Memo Link > Open Linked Memo** (or **Ctrl / Cmd + Shift + M**).

    o At the top of the *Detail View*: **Click to Edit / Tick Edit** if you want to edit/ augment your existing thoughts.

Link ideas with evidence, using a See Also Link (Windows only)

Although the Memo Link provides quick access to your Memo, it does not link specific ideas to specific passages. This extra specificity is available in one of our favourite tools, the See Also Link. You can use this to jump to a specific place in a File from a location in another File or Node (not available in the Mac). An additional bonus is that the File containing the links can be exported to an MS Word document and the associated See Also Links also export as endnotes in the document. This provides a far better solution than copying and pasting text directly from a File into a Memo. Pasting text rather than linking is problematic, because

- the segment has become disconnected from its identifying File and context;
- any coding on that text will be pasted as well, generating double retrievals when you review the coding. (You can fairly easily Uncode all the coding from a Memo if this occurs.)

1.k.

Create, view, and export a See Also Link (Windows only)

Create a See Also Link

⇒ Read an interesting passage in a File that gives you an idea and **Copy** it (remember it is now on your Clipboard as you do a few additional things).

⇒ *Navigation View*: **Notes** > **Memos**.

⇒ *List View*: **Double-click** on an existing **Memo**, such as your Project journal, to open it > **Select Click to edit** at the top of the *Detail View*.

⇒ *Detail View*: Write your interpretation or idea in the Memo (Figure 1.14) > **highlight** what you wrote (or a key phrase in your writing) > **Right-click** on this material > **Paste As See Also Link**.

Viewing the See Also Link

⇒ After following the above instructions, click inside your Memo to release the black highlight. The text associated with the See Also Link will now be highlighted in pink. If you do not see the See Also Link at the bottom of your screen:

    o *Ribbon*: **Document** > check the box next to **See Also Links**.

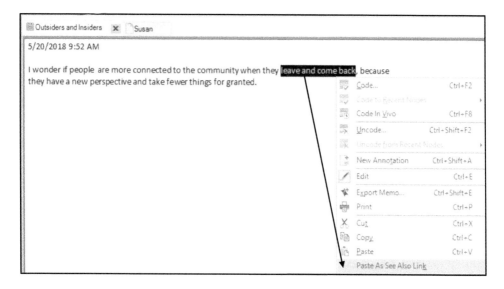

Figure 1.14   Pasting a See Also Link (Windows only) to a specific location (in a File) from a specific location (in a Memo)

⇒ When you do see the See Also Link at the bottom of the screen:
  o *Detail View*: **Double-click** on the **See Also Link** at the bottom of your screen to jump to the original location.

Exporting the Memo with its associated See Also Links

⇒ *Detail View* (or *List View*): **Right-click** in the **Memo** > (**Export** >) **Export Memo** > select a location and rename it if you wish.
  o under **Related Content > Tick** See Also Links.
  o Tick **Open on Export > OK.**

A See Also Link identifies the File, provides context, and can be viewed or printed along with the ideas you added in your Memo. This helps you pull together the argument you are developing for your article, report, or thesis, along with quotes from the Files. Examples of how you might apply the See Also Link include:

- Link interpretation of text to the passage that gave rise to the interpretation. In the *Environmental Change* Project, this is evident when interpretations of what it means to be local (in the Local identity and knowledge Memo) are linked to what was said in interviews.
- Identify questions or issues that you want to return to later. In the *Environmental Change* Project this is evident in the *EDR Research Journal* (a Memo written by Effie). If you open this Memo, you will find a See Also Link connected to a portion of the interview with *Thomas*, where community newcomers are referred to as 'dingbatters'.

Effie wants to return to this later to examine whether the designation should become a node or not.

- Use the capacity to create a See Also Link from one passage to another in the same document to point up contradictions in a narrative, or where one passage provides an explanation for or expansion of the other.
- Create a See Also Link where the transcript illustrates something you read in the literature. Link from that transcript to the relevant material in a reference document, such as a passage in a pdf article you imported.
- Communicate with and respond to other team members. In the *Environmental Change* Project you will find an entry in the *WWS Research Journal* on 6/4/2010 where Wanda is responding to an observation Henry made in his *HGP Research Journal*.
- Eliminate the need to repeatedly articulate processes or protocols by adding See Also Links to point to where they have been described and/or used. In the *Environmental Change* Project, the *Project protocol memo* contains such a link dated 5/15/2010 to the location where Wanda explains the process she used for assigning pseudonyms.
- Link across documents to build a sequentially ordered picture of an event or a life history through the eyes of one or more tellers, or to trace an evolving idea or saga. When a See Also Link is accessed, the linked item is opened with the selected passage highlighted. That passage might contain another link, allowing a further link in the web of ideas you created.

Connecting across your Project – more on See Also Links

There are two types of See Also Links, and each does something slightly different. The first and most commonly used way of creating a See Also Link is to select a passage of text or part of a media file, copy it, then paste it elsewhere as a See Also Link – as described above. Use this method when you are linking a specific portion of one File to a specific portion of another File. The second way of creating a See Also Link (which is also only available in Windows) is to link a whole Project item to an anchor at a specific location within a File or a Memo. We do not see this used as often, but it could be useful to you.

Create links in your Memos to whole Files, Nodes, or Project Maps to illustrate or provide evidence for what you are reflecting on in the Memo. For example, when you have explored an association within your data using a Query, write about what you discovered in a Memo with a link to the Node that contains the stored Query Results.

━━━━━━━━━ **1.I.** ━━━━━━━━━

Creating a See Also Link to a whole Project item (Windows only)

⇒ *Detail View:* **Select** text to act as an anchor for the See Also Link > **Right-click** > **Links** > **See Also Link** > **New See Also Link**.

  ○ **From** > shows the File name for the content you just selected.
  ○ **To** > provides options of existing items > **Select** > **OK** > **OK**.

⇒ The anchoring text will be highlighted in pink to indicate the presence of a linked item, and a tab in the *Detail View*, below the text of your File, will indicate the name and location of the linked item.

⇒ View See Also Links as described earlier. If you export a copy of the File, it will provide the name and location of the linked item for this type of See Also Link, but not the content (because it is linked to an entire item).

Connecting beyond your Project – Hyperlinks

Perhaps your interviewee referred to a report that is online, or to an ongoing blog; the group discussion was based around a book or video; or there is a cross-reference from an article you have imported to one that is on file but which you are not importing into your Project. For such situations, Hyperlinks allow you to make direct connections from a specific location within a File to items that are not in the Project (online data or any digitally stored material on your computer), such as books or reports, pictures, web pages, video or audio files. You can also use Hyperlinks to link from your journal to records of meetings with advisors, emails from colleagues, and other sources of influence on your developing thinking as well, as part of an audit trail for the Project.

▬▬▬ 1.m. ▬▬▬

Create and view a Hyperlink

⇒ *Detail View*: **Click to edit / Tick Edit** > **Select** the text that will be an anchor for the link > **Right-click** > **Links** > **Hyperlink** > **New Hyperlink** and select one of the following options:

    o   Enter a URL in the window; or

    o   **Browse** your filing system for the object to be linked.

⇒ **OK.**

⇒ To open the Hyperlink, use one of the following options on the **underlined blue text** that marks the anchor for the link:

    o   **Ctrl / Cmd** + **click**; or

    o   **Right-click** > **Links** > **Hyperlink** > **Open Hyperlink**.

Saving and backing up your Project

Save your Project periodically as you work. Of course, you should always save as you exit the Project as well. For safety, you should create backup copies as you work. Our recommendation is to make a backup on your working computer at the end of each day's work, and to copy that to another medium (a disk, memory stick, server, or cloud that is independent of that computer) on a regular basis. You might also want to retain copies from important transition points, for example, before and after a major restructure, before and after combining the work of team members, or when you've developed key Maps or understandings of the Project. These copies will help you write up the methods section of your final product. They can also help you communicate about how your ideas developed and thus help convince a reader about the legitimacy of your findings.

1.n.

Backing up after you close your Project

⇒ Go into Windows Explorer or your File Manager / Go to Finder > **Copy** the Project > **Paste** into a backup folder and rename or add a date to the backup.
⇒ Windows users might want to match the Title with File (or Path) name (Chapter 11, pp. 327–328).

Backing up your Project while you are working in NVivo (Windows only)

⇒ **File: Save.**
⇒ **File: Copy Project.**
⇒ The **Copy** window identifies the Project you are in and that is about to be copied.
⇒ The **Copy to** window allows you to select a version for your copy.
⇒ The **Location** window allows you to rename the copy

   o We use an international date format (year-month-day) added to the name, so they sort in date order (from oldest to newest).
   o Identify a location place for the copy, and we recommend an external drive. Remember, however, you should never open and work on a Project on an external drive unless you are using NVivo for Teams.
   o Windows users might want to match the Title with File (or Path) name (Chapter 11, pp. 327–328).

Be aware that in the process of copying your Project, NVivo will copy your Project but then return you to the original. In contrast to *Save As* (in Microsoft Word and many other programs), you do not end up in the copy at the end of the procedure.

SECTION 1.4: CHAPTER 1 TAKEAWAYS

Key points from this chapter

o It is important to think about ways NVivo can follow your methodological choices rather than lead them.
o We believe that society and culture influence the construction of technologies and that these technologies also influence society and culture. To accept this view means accepting that our qualitative work is sometimes influenced by NVivo.

o Start using the tools in NVivo that are designed to help you think before you start coding:

- Maps

- Memos
- Links

o Establish a consistent process for saving your Project and creating clearly named backups.

Tips, challenges, and warnings

- Do not work on an external drive unless you have NVivo Server.
- Save and create backups regularly.
- If you rush through the process of writing and thinking you will end up with a messy journal that is likely to be hard for you to understand.
- Start using NVivo early in your research so you can learn the tools gradually and without as much pressure.
- If you are a visual thinker, use Maps to sort through your ideas.
- Whenever you are not sure what to do or where to look for an action when you are working in NVivo, a context-sensitive menu can be accessed by right-clicking in the *Navigation View, List View,* and *Detail View.*
- Mac users are encouraged to use one of the following options to enable a right-click:
  o Purchase an external mouse with a right-click option.
  o In your System Preferences, configure your 'Secondary click' to engage as a right-click with one of three options: Click or tap with two fingers, Click on bottom right corner, or Click on bottom left corner.
  o Press **Control (Ctrl) + click** to access right-click options. This works for a 1-button mouse, MacBook trackpad, or with the built-in button on the standalone Apple Trackpad.
- See Chapter 11, pp. 324–326 if you want to set up User profile and Password protection.

Videos and online resources (https://study.sagepub.com/jackson3e)

Videos

- 'Primer for following the click instructions' (Mac, Windows)
- 'Orientation to the NVivo interface' (Mac, Windows)
- 'The main tools in NVivo' (Mac, Windows)

Help files

- *File*: Help.
- *Menu bar*: **Help > NVivo Help.**

Search for any of the following:

- Concept maps
- Create a new project
- Explore the sample project
- Links
- Memos
- Mind maps
- Save and copy projects
- Using NVivo

Practice questions

1   How do you think the software might lead you? Articulate the circumstances in which this might be a good/bad thing.
2   Think about the theoretical framework(s) that underpin your research. Try creating a Concept Map to visualize them.
3   What kinds of Memos (or topics within Memos) are likely to help you with your research?
4   What topics, themes, and patterns do you anticipate finding in your work? Create a Mind Map to diagram them, then turn the ideas into Nodes. Or, create a Memo and write about them, linking to available material (e.g., literature) when available.

2

Section 2.1: Introduction to designing an NVivo Project   40

Section 2.2: Conceptual grounding in the Project structure   41

Section 2.3: Using NVivo to store and manage data   53

Section 2.4: Chapter 2 Takeaways   58

DESIGNING AN
NVIVO PROJECT

Using software is a creative process since qualitative software packages – in essence and in design – are inherently flexible. There might well be an efficient way of proceeding, but there are multiple pathways to reaching a particular end-point and multiple purposes for doing so. (Silver & Lewins, 2014: 3)

SECTION 2.1: INTRODUCTION TO DESIGNING AN NVIVO PROJECT

In this chapter we provide practical guidance on structuring your NVivo Project. However, you will need to triage some of the information because you can customize your use of NVivo so it fits into the theoretical and methodological traditions that are relevant to you. Furthermore, your values, world-views, research questions, and the stakeholders interested in your work, will inform what tools you will use and how you will use them. The combination of these factors can result in a different Project design each time you use NVivo. Fortunately, there are some elements of the software that can be adopted by a broad range of researchers and NVivo offers a high degree of flexibility regarding the use of specific tools. A cogent plan for structuring your NVivo Project has definite benefits, but if elements of your qualitative research change over time as you come to new understandings, you will be able to rewrite, recode, reorder, reconfigure, redefine, revamp, and reframe as necessary. There are, of course, limits to this flexibility, so this chapter identifies the aspects of your Project that warrant your attention early on.

In this chapter you will

- Identify what a case is in your research.
- Think through how you might utilize Folders, Sets, and Cases to organize your Files and compare subgroups in NVivo.
- Learn how to prepare your text Files.

Other chapters with related materials

While you might find all the material related to your current needs in this chapter, you should also consider these other chapters that contain closely related information:

Chapter 5: Cases, Classifications, and comparisons

Chapter 5 helps you think conceptually about what a case is in your research with details about types of NVivo Cases. This area of the software is especially helpful if your research requires the comparison of subgroups, particularly if there are additional design complexities such as the examination of change over time.

Chapter 7: Querying data

The structure of your NVivo Project is likely to influence and be influenced by the use of Queries. Therefore, having a general sense of the different Queries and what they can do might help you think through the structure of your Project.

Chapter 8: Literature reviews and pdf Files

NVivo's tools can be easily applied to reference materials like articles. Because of a few unique issues around managing pdf files and reference manager programs (EndNote, Mendeley, RefWorks, Zotero), we focus on this data in Chapter 8.

Chapter 9: Working with multimedia Files; Chapter 10: Twitter, Facebook, YouTube, and web pages

If you want to handle non-text data such as pictures, audio, video (Chapter 9) or capture data from the web (Chapter 10), you will also benefit from exploring how these items are stored and handled in an NVivo Project.

SECTION 2.2: CONCEPTUAL GROUNDING IN THE PROJECT STRUCTURE

By recording and selecting materials for your research, you make them into data. The challenge with qualitative data is not in generating them, which as Richards (2009) noted is 'ridiculously easy', but in making useful and manageable data records (transcripts, notes, etc.) that can be used for analysis. Qualitative data records are often large. An hour of interviewing, for example, can generate 25 pages or so of single-spaced text. Qualitative data records are also messy and complex. Participants say unexpected things, you need to relate your records to a larger context, and it takes repeated review of the data to identify meaning or patterns. Mentoring, practice, and good judgement will help you determine what data to emphasize.

Given the many different types of qualitative data now supported in NVivo, it is worth noting Coffey and Atkinson's (1996: 11) warning against making data 'in a spirit of careless rapture … with little thought for research problems and research design'. Such enthusiasm tends to lead to the predicament of having too much data and not knowing what to do with it. In a similar vein to Maxwell (2013), Coffey and Atkinson (1996) emphasized the necessity of an overall methodological approach that links research questions, design, data, and analytic approaches. However, each of these is potentially subject to modification throughout the life of the research. Because of the importance of combining a thorough, logical and clear qualitative research design with a degree of flexibility, we offer the following suggestions:

- Be careful about adopting the first approach you encounter (e.g., ethnography, or phenomenology) as the only approach.

- Do not assume that because you are working inductively from data that you are doing grounded theory.
- Learn about the relevant methodological debates within a tradition that appeals to you, so you understand the various camps. Think critically about how these camps argue for particular approaches to data collection, management, and interpretation.
- Find specific research publications that are closely related to your design, noting the things you like and do not like.
- Remember that information is everywhere; it becomes data when you attend to it and collect it.

Qualitative researchers often think about working with transcribed records of interviews or focus group discussions, but not all interviews can be recorded, and not all data require full transcription. Consider also using:

- open-ended comments at the end of quantitative questionnaires;
- notes from observations;
- existing material such as media releases, participant-generated notes, web material, administrative records, films, and novels;
- secondary files obtained from qualitative data archives.

NVivo can be used for the analysis of any form of qualitative data. Although it is often used – and particularly well suited for – the analysis of free-flowing texts, you need not be limited to that form of data. We focus on text-based data in this chapter to simplify our discussion about the basics of preparing to work in an NVivo Project. However, many of the methods and strategies we describe will apply to data from other media as well. See our pointers to other chapters at the beginning of this section.

Making transcriptions

Interviews and other files for sociolinguistic, phenomenological, or psychological analysis generally should be fully transcribed to capture as much of the exchange as possible. What appears at first sight as a purely mechanical task is, in fact, plagued with interpretive difficulties. Transcribing involves translating auditory or visual information, and transcripts are not copies or representations of some original reality. They are interpretative constructions that are useful tools for given purposes (Kvale, 1996: 165). When transcribing, the value of using a high-quality recorder becomes apparent. This is particularly the case when recording focus group discussions or other encounters where several participants are involved, so you can accurately distinguish between participants' contributions. This will be facilitated if you can use two audio recorders. It is also valuable to do your own transcribing, if at all possible. Doing so supports familiarity with your data. At the very least, if another person or automated service produced the transcripts, it is absolutely essential for the person who did the interview to review and edit the transcript while listening carefully to the recording. A typist who unintentionally reorders or omits words can reverse the intended meaning in some sentences.

The flat form of the written words can lose the emotional overtones and nuances of the spoken text, so it is beneficial for the interviewer to format or annotate the text to assist in communicating these overtones and nuances, with a view to the kinds of information that will facilitate analysis. 'Transcription from tape to text involves a series of technical and interpretational issues for which, again, there are few standard rules but rather a series of choices to be made' (Kvale, 1996: 169). The goal in transcribing is to be as true to the conversation as possible, yet pragmatic in dealing with the data. Kvale (1996) and Mishler (1991) provide useful discussions and examples of issues involved in transcription, and Bazeley (2013) lists general guidelines to follow when transcribing. Whatever procedural decisions are made, they should be recorded as clear decisions and formatting guidelines. This promotes consistency from transcriptionists and in your own Project journal. You will notice the benefits of following these guidelines when you are writing up your findings. If you are a doctoral or masters student, the construction of a methods section or chapter will also benefit from your documentation of these decisions.

Text in a document will be imported into NVivo with most of the familiar richness of appearance that word processors provide, such as changes in font type, size and style, colour, spacing, justification, indents, and tabs. So, when you are making notes or transcribing your interview, focus group, or field observations, make use of this to help shape your data, express emphasis, convey the subtleties of what is happening, clarify how your respondents were expressing themselves, or draw attention to critical statements.

Working without verbatim transcripts

When nuances of expression are not needed for the analytic purpose of the research, verbatim transcriptions might not be needed; summary notes can be adequate for the task. As with transcripts, however, keep the comments in their spoken order and context rather than rearranging them into topic areas.

▬▬▬▬▬▬ Deciding what to transcribe ▬▬▬▬▬▬

Pat had assistants interviewing researchers about the impact of receiving a small financial grant on their development as researchers. Although the conversations were recorded, much of the discussion was not directly relevant to the topic of her research (researchers have an irrepressible urge always to tell what their research is about). The interviewers made notes from the recordings, supplemented by occasional verbatim quotes, and this data was used for the analysis.

Then there are always times when you discover the audio recorder was not working or times when your participant opens up just as you have your hand on the door to leave; there are many reasons why you might have data in the form of notes rather than verbatim transcripts.

Two ways of tagging qualitative data

Tagging part of a text document

Imagine you are reading a paper copy of an interview or a journal article (Figure 2.1). Working on paper, you might use a highlighter pen to emphasize an interesting segment of data and create a bracket in the margin that surrounds that paragraph. Then you can tag the ideas you have about what is interesting and meaningful in the paragraph using a few labels: *School, Family, Gratitude.* These labels might end up becoming codes later in your analysis. We will look at coding in much more detail in Chapters 3 and 4, but for our present purpose this very simple example will suffice.

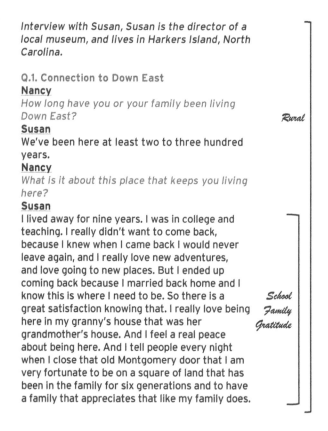

Figure 2.1 Tagging a paper copy of a document

Tagging the entire document

While reading this interview or article you also become aware that the entire document might warrant additional tags. For instance, if you are reading a rural resident's interview, you might want to tag the entire document as *Rural.* Or, reading an article from 2019, you might want to tag the entire document as one published in that year. Borrowing from our first image about creating a bracket around a paragraph, you would draw a line down every page in the margin, and label it with *Rural* or *2019* (Figure 2.1). Eventually you could look at all the documents you bracketed with *Rural* and all the documents you bracketed with *Urban*, and sort them into two stacks. Then you could look through the *Urban* interviews, hunting for your bracket for *Gratitude*, and then repeat this with the other stack, to compare with what the *Rural* residents said about *Gratitude*. Through the years, researchers developed cumbersome document management systems to facilitate sorting and comparing data in this way, always with limitations on what and how much was within reason to group and sort. NVivo breaks through some of these barriers by allowing you to more efficiently store and sort by a large number of characteristics over a wide array of document types (e.g., transcripts, pictures, videos).

Tagging with Attributes and Values

Our use of the tags *Urban* and *Rural* to sort data in this example are demographic categories, but in other situations we might tag entire documents with other variables like a response to a Likert scale question or whether someone is taking *Medication A* or *Medication B*. NVivo refers to variables (e.g., *Location of residence* and *Medication type*) as Attributes and to the specific values (e.g., *Urban, Rural; Medication A, Medication B*) as Values. In Chapter 5, you will learn more about other reasons you might tag the entire entity (in this instance, the entity is a person's transcript). For now, let's stay with our example of the demographic labels, *Urban* and *Rural*. At present, the important distinction is that some tags are specific to a portion of the data (e.g., *Gratitude*), and some tags pertain to the entire document (e.g., *Rural*), as in Figure 2.1. This could be true also of video, audio, picture, and other kinds of data besides text, but for now we are using an example of a paper copy of a transcript.

Understanding these two kinds of tags and how to handle them in a database such as NVivo presents new opportunities that impact both efficiency and complexity. Instead of taking a pen and drawing down each page of *Susan's* interview to label her as *Rural*, you can instruct NVivo to identify her not only as *Rural*, but also as someone *Employed full-time*, in her *40s*, and any other relevant factors. In most databases, this process of adding tags such as *Urban* and *Rural* to the entire document happens in a different location and with a different technical process than the more discrete coding of pieces of a document to *School, Family,* and *Gratitude*. Nonetheless, the purpose and the outcome of adding tags for *Urban* or *Rural* is the same as if you were working on paper: creating subgroups in order to make comparisons.

Cases

Thinking about Cases

When you put *Urban* residents into one pile and *Rural* residents into another pile, you are sorting Cases. In NVivo, the use of the term Case is not intended to imply that you are undertaking case study research. Rather, Cases are employed in NVivo as a unit of analysis in a research study, and there might be more than one type of Case in a single Project. For instance, you might have Cases that represent *People*, who will be associated with Values such as *Doctor, Nurse,* or *Patient*. You could also have Cases that represent *Communities* that will be associated with Values such as *Coastal, Island,* or *Landlocked*. In the sociological and anthropological literature, a case is typically regarded as a specific and bounded (in time and place) instance of a phenomenon selected for study. Cases are generally characterized on the one hand by their concreteness and circumstantial specificity and on the other by their theoretical interest or generalizability (Schwandt, 1997: 12). With this claim in mind, you should strive to define the boundaries of your Cases in your research and then use them as a foundation for building theories and making claims.

In the *Environmental Change* study, *Barbara, Charles,* and *Dorothy* are Cases, as are the communities of *Atlantic, Cedar Island,* and *Marshallberg* (Figure 2.2). In Chapter 5 we will show you how to manage Cases and ensure that all the data for *Barbara*, for example, is contained in her Case. This includes all qualitative data and all Attribute Values.

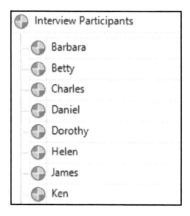 

Figure 2.2   Different types of Cases in the *Environmental Change* Project

Alternatively, you may be working in a Project where policies, schools, or less visible entities like mathematical theories are Cases. This all depends on your research question(s), and it could also change as you analyse your data and realize that the kind of Case you started with is not the one you are currently interested in examining. For instance, you may initially be looking at individual people, thinking you will compare *Urban* and *Rural* residents and later decide that instead you want to focus on friendship clusters and compare *Insular* and *Open* clusters.

Even if you are doing a single case study (a methodology), you still might end up with multiple Cases (a tool in NVivo). For instance, if you are following a single Olympic athlete's journey to the summer games, you might be investigating this one person's experience through the letters he writes, with each letter being treated as a Case in NVivo. By doing so, you can easily sort the letters written to *Parents, Siblings,* or *Friends* (Attribute Values for the recipient of each letter), so you can focus on a more detailed interpretation of the content of the letters and compare across these subgroups. Your Cases in NVivo should follow your research design, and therefore it is important to think about this aspect of your Project early in your use of NVivo.

Identifying your Cases

Much has been written about selection of cases in qualitative work. Patton (2002) and Flick (2007) each give a thorough overview of the range of sampling and selection possibilities. Case structures are often simple, but they can also be quite complicated. The main case unit(s) sometimes have illustrative cases embedded within them, for example, when a corporation is the case and one or more specific departments or products are illustrative cases within the study of that corporation (Yin, 2003). Alternatively, they might be layered, for example where schools, classes, and the students in them are each treated as cases at different levels.

Yin (2003) warns to 'beware' of cases which are not easily defined in terms of their boundaries – their beginning and end points. 'As a general guide, your tentative definition of the unit of analysis (and therefore of the case) is related to the way you have defined your initial research questions,' and 'selection of the appropriate unit of analysis will occur when you accurately specify your primary research questions' (Yin, 2003: 23, 24). If your questions and conceptual framework are clear, it should take only minutes to define the type of case (e.g., *Company*) and the specific Cases (e.g., *Earthbound Organics, Applegate Organics, Nature's Path*) (Miles & Huberman, 1994). Even if you do not intend to compare subgroups, you will probably benefit from understanding cases and how they help your work in NVivo.

Cases in NVivo

As you can see, a Case is often a core structural element in NVivo. Each Case unites all the different components of qualitative and quantitative data you have about that entity (e.g., *Barbara*) in one place. Cases are incredibly flexible in three ways, all of which are important for you to understand at the outset.

1   After you import a document with qualitative data into NVivo, it is referred to as a File. You will be able to include just a single File, multiple Files, and/or portions of Files in a Case. For example:

   - If you interview 30 people and as a result have 30 transcripts, generally these will be turned into 30 Cases.
   - If you are doing a longitudinal study with several Files for a single person, a Case can include all waves of data collected from that person (multiple Files).
   - If you have focus group discussions, with several participants within each transcript, you might turn portions of a single File into Cases, to capture all the contributions each individual speaker makes in the discussion.
   - If you have collected data from the same people using different data collection strategies (for instance you have observed their behaviour, and interviewed them), you can place both forms of data at each Case.

2   Each Case might include only one File format, such as text in participant transcripts; or it could bring together information from multiple formats, such as photographs taken by the participant and videos of family celebrations.

3   You can connect demographic and numeric (Attribute Value) data with the text (or other qualitative data) to each Case. For example, an Attribute Value such as *Urban* or *Rural* is applied to all data for the person who is that Case. This is true regardless of type of data, volume, or how many Files pertain to a single Case.

Cases in an ethnographic study

For an ethnographic study reviewing issues of research production and performance for academics in the arts, humanities, and social sciences disciplines of a university, Pat created a Case for each member of academic staff, with Attributes for academic unit, discipline, and level of seniority. Data for the study comprised administrative records of research funding received by each staff member and details of research publications produced by them (originally in two Excel spreadsheets), individually completed surveys, web profiles, media releases, field observations, interview notes, other official records, and incidental documentary Files. The Cases brought together data from all or part of the various documents, so Pat could instantly access everything she knew about a particular academic. Additionally, once all the data were coded for issues raised, and for the scholars' research areas (interpersonal violence, pedagogy of mathematics, or religious experience, for example), she could easily discover which academics were interested in which issues, whether there was sufficient interest in any particular topic to create a research group, and who might want to be part of such a group, including details of what their contribution might be.

In NVivo, each Case acts as the 'container' that holds all data (e.g., qualitative, demographic, and quantitative).

Why does it matter now?

Creating Cases can be one of the first things or one of the last things you do in NVivo, with no negative effects on the analysis. Given this reality, why are we asking you to consider the issue of Cases carefully before you begin? Because formatting the Files can help you efficiently create and manage your Cases. Five considerations are relevant at this stage:

1   separating data into different Files;
2   naming Files;
3   formatting, with an awareness of the information that will be retained and ignored;
4   identification of speakers (usually in order to create Cases or to separate interviewer and respondent speech);
5   planning for Attribute Values (to efficiently associate them with your Cases later).

Separating text data into different Files

If you are generating text data via interviews, focus groups, field notes, video, audio, etc., you will find the following guidance useful. One of the first decisions you will encounter is whether or not to separate data into different documents, called Files in NVivo. This decision can have implications regarding the ease of creating Cases. Our first recommendation is to keep every episode of data collection, such as an interview, in its own File. Thus, you will create two Files in each of the following examples:

- You interview someone at Time 1 and again at Time 2.
- In a household, you first interview a parent and then you interview (or observe) a child.
- You observe two classrooms in a school.

We advise separating data into two documents for each of these examples, because later it will be easy in NVivo to use other tools to group Files together in a flexible way, either as Cases, or as all interviews done at Time 1 or Time 2. Therefore, in the above examples, you will still be able to examine or sort data according to a single person (or time point), a single household, or a single school, respectively.

However, in each of the following examples, you will create one File because you want to analyse the exchanges among participants:

- You interview a parent and a child at the same time in a household.
- You conduct a focus group.

If you format these Files in a way that identifies individual speakers, it will be possible, later, to separate individuals out into separate Cases, to help you compare subgroups.

Naming Files

NVivo will sort Files alphabetically by Folder and File name and prioritize numbers in a list if you have both numeric and text names. We recommend preparing Files outside of NVivo and then importing them, instead of creating a new empty File inside of NVivo. Having an external copy is an additional backup precaution. It is best to keep the File name reasonably brief and straightforward as the names will look truncated in various locations of the Project, making them difficult to discern if they have names such as 'Transcript of interview with ....' Dates or demographic details or even details of the context of the interview are more appropriately recorded in other locations, including:

- the first paragraph of the text as a document description;
- a spreadsheet if they are demographics you want to import later (Chapter 5, p. 153);
- a Memo linked to the File (Chapter 1, pp. 20–22).

Files prepared for importing into NVivo can be stored anywhere, although you will find it useful to have them all together in a clearly identified folder.

Standard formatting issues to consider

We recommend keeping transcripts simple when it comes to the issue of being able to isolate or compare the data from different speakers in the same text File. If you are looking for guidance on formatting data to differentiate speakers in other types of Files, you should take a look at other chapters with additional detail (Chapter 9 for audio and video; Chapter 6 for surveys; Chapter 10 for social media). In conventional text transcripts, we recommend the format in Figure 2.3, because NVivo can Auto Code by speaker (Chapter 5, pp. 148–150) to place each speaker's contributions into a Case or to separate out the interviewer from the respondent. You can use the same tool in NVivo to separate data by questions if you have a structured interview guide, so add the question number to the transcript, if relevant.

Example 1: Focus Group	Example 2: Interview
Q.01	Q.01
Facilitator: What is the first thing you tell people about your family?	Interviewer: Tell me about the things you considered before accepting this job offer.
Dagmar: My family has a strong sense of supporting each other...	Respondent: Well, location was probably most important. But, we also considered the health benefits...
Daniella: My family is scattered across the continent, because...	Interviewer: What were you thinking during your relocation?
Ricardo: My family is in a lot of transition right now with three...	Respondent: How exhausting it is to ...
Q.02	Q.02
Facilitator: How would your closest family members react to this description?	Interviewer: What did your children think about moving?
Ricardo: They would all agree because ...	

Figure 2.3 Sample transcription format for focus groups and interviews

The ability to Auto Code by speaker in the interview transcript could be useful if, for instance, you will run a Text Search Query (Chapters 4 and 7) on the word *"Sustainability,"* but want NVivo to look only in the Respondent speech.

Most of the other formatting features researchers tend to include in a File will be retained when they are imported, although a few kinds of formatting will be ignored. These are the most common considerations we encounter when working with researchers regarding other formatting issues in their Files.

Microsoft Word File features that will be retained in NVivo:

- Formatting that helps enrich or clarify the presentation of text, including heading levels, bold, italics, different font types, and coloured fonts.

- Text in different languages (and alphabets), even within the same document.
- Embedded items such as images, text boxes, and illustrations, although if they are included as part of a text document, you can only code the entire embedded image, text box, or illustration, not portions of these items. In contrast, when you import pictures as jpeg or another supported format (Chapter 9), you can code portions of the image.
- Tables, but the text coded into a Node from a cell will appear in the context of its entire row when you open a Node. We discourage the use of tables in a text File (Figure 2.4).

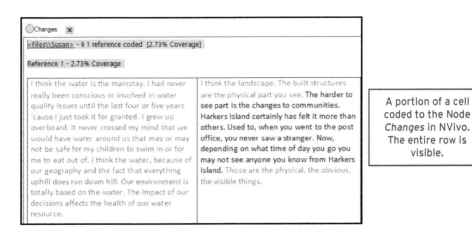

Figure 2.4 Microsoft Word table format displays entire row when a portion of a cell is coded.

Microsoft Word File features that will be ignored by NVivo (although the documents will still import):

- Headers, footers, page numbers
- Line numbering
- Shapes
- Highlight
- Comments

Planning for Attribute Values

While you are preparing your data, we offer the following suggestions:

- Record Attribute Value data (e.g., demographic details) as you gather your qualitative data. Try to think of all the kinds of comparisons you are likely to want to make, and record these details during data collection. For example, if you want to compare what is said by people from different locations, then you should collect information about where each person lives.
- It is much more helpful to have Attribute Values recorded in data collection forms or, even better, in a spreadsheet, than to extract them from within the text of interview documents (where it is also a waste of transcription time).

Preparing data records is one of those areas where 'fools rush in', so use careful editing and thoughtful structuring or you will waste valuable time later. As an analyst, you are dependent on the representation of reality that is contained within those records. If you have any unusual formatting features, experiment by running a pilot; import and check how the coded text and other items look in a Node before you spend time preparing all the others.

Table 2.1 provides the most common possibilities with formatting suggestions that maximize your ability to efficiently create Cases later.

Table 2.1 Formatting strategies to facilitate case construction from different types of sources

Structure of Files prior to import	The qualitative data that will be included in each Case (in addition to demographic and/or numeric data)	Formatting to facilitate efficient handling of Cases (other methods applied later will be much slower)
Each File contains all the data for only one Case (e.g., text of an interview, a video, a picture).	One File only.	No special formatting required. However, if there is a need to differentiate speakers (e.g., the interviewer and the interviewee), it is useful to precede each person's speech with a consistent identifier to enable Auto Coding by speaker later (e.g., interviewer and interviewee as in Figure 2.2).
Multiple Files for each Case, where each File is related to one Case only (e.g., the same person has been interviewed several times; your information comes from different people associated with a single Case; or you have different types of data, such as an interview and a picture for each Case).	Multiple, whole Files.	No special formatting required within each File. However, we suggest that each File for a particular Case has a common root name followed by a unique identifier, e.g., Beatrice 1, Beatrice 2, Beatrice 3.

Structure of Files prior to import	The qualitative data that will be included in each Case (in addition to demographic and/or numeric data)	Formatting to facilitate efficient handling of Cases (other methods applied later will be much slower)
Files with individually identified speakers in a focus group or Files with more than one interviewee or any other File that includes data relating to multiple Cases, e.g., field notes.	Portions of one or more Files.	Speakers names or IDs need to be uniquely identified, preceding the speech on the same line, separated with a colon. Alternatively, record the ID above the speech on a separate line as in Figure 2.1.
Dataset Files (see Chapter 6) with responses to a survey or questionnaire.	One or more codable fields in a Dataset, one row per Case.	Standard row and column identifiers for a Dataset.
Combinations of any of the above (e.g., where you have survey responses, focus groups, and individual interviews from the same person).	Portions of Files in addition to whole Files.	Format individual Files as above. If possible, use the same identifiers for the Case across the File types to make it easier to aggregate them later (they can be aggregated without a consistent identifier, but it will take more time).

Planning for Cases and the demographic or numeric data you will include in each Case has implications also for how you organize your coding system. Your Attribute Values for *Urban* and *Rural*, for example, can be rapidly applied to all relevant Cases (Chapter 5) yet they are kept away from your coding system. This makes the Project more efficient and effective to use.

It is helpful to be aware of these issues even if your Case structure is very simple, and we strongly suggest doing a small pilot with a small subset of your data once you have a plan for formatting Files (import, code, etc.) to ensure that your plan will yield what you need as you proceed through your analysis. Conducting a pilot with a subset of your data is perhaps one of the most important pieces of advice in this chapter. Basic instructions for importing Files for this pilot were provided in Chapter 1 (*Ribbon*: **Import** > **Files** / **Data** > **Documents** > **Select** the File(s) > **Open** > **Import**).

SECTION 2.3: USING NVIVO TO STORE AND MANAGE DATA

NVivo terms used in this section

Case

File

Folders

Node

Query

Set

Value

Storing qualitative Data in NVivo

The Data folder in the *Navigation View* has two subfolders for your qualitative data (see Figure 1.3).

- Files are your primary qualitative items in your project. These might include text documents, pictures, audio, video, surveys, or web-based material such as social media.
- Externals are proxy documents for items that cannot be imported. You might choose to use Externals when:
    - documents are not available electronically (e.g., handwritten diaries or early research journals);
    - files are too large (e.g., a 1,000 page report);
    - digital formats are not currently supported in NVivo (e.g., an entire GPS database);
    - access to the entire File for analytic purposes within NVivo is not needed (e.g., an employee handbook or detailed regulations).

For these kinds of materials, creating an External will create a record (much like a document) within the program that indicates the existence of the nonimportable file, along with a hyperlink that provides quick access to this file (if the file is available electronically). In addition, you can code any summaries or Notes you add to the NVivo External after it is created.

Managing Files in NVivo

It was the realization that computers could assist with managing data, rather than a belief that they were useful for analysis, that prompted early work in qualitative computing (Kelle, 2004). Since their early development, computer programs for assisting with qualitative data have become sophisticated toolboxes providing multiple ways to approach the management of data. Your use of NVivo's data management tools will vary throughout your project, with some being appropriate from the start, and others coming into play more as the project develops. Available tools for managing data include Folders, Sets, and Cases. Any coding you apply is preserved and links you create are updated automatically if you rearrange your Files into Folders or Sets or subsequently code them to Cases.

Managing Files in Folders

Just as you group books on your bookshelf or put nails in a different set of tins than screws, if you have Files which differ in some way you have the option to store them in different Folders to reflect these differences. In the *Environmental Change* Project, the researchers have created additional folders for separate storage of different types of data (e.g., *Interviews, Literature, News Articles*).

- You should place each File in only one Folder (i.e., Folders contain mutually exclusive items).
- We recommend considering a Folder structure that matches your organization of your data on your computer to help ease your way into NVivo, as you already know this is a meaningful way to group your data. (You can change this later, just as you can rearrange files on your computer.)
- Be mindful that you will have to click your way through Folders every time you want to select a File, so try not to create too many nested Folders. The use of many layers could be a sign that you are using folders for things better handled with Sets or Attribute Values (which we will discuss shortly).

Creating Folders (as in Figure 2.5) is fairly easy (*Navigation View*: **Data > Files > Right-click > New Folder > Name** it > OK **/ Done**). Later you can drag Files from the *List View* into the appropriate Folder (or import Files directly into that Folder). To import Files, see Chapter 1, pp. 26–27.

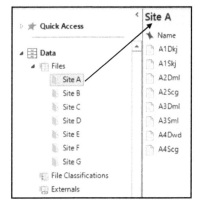

Figure 2.5   Customizable Folder structure for NVivo Files

Customizable Folders in the Violence Prevention Initiative

In the *Violence Prevention Initiative*, each community had a separate violence prevention programme with its own objectives and activities. Data were collected at multiple time points in each site from program directors as well as their staff. Figure 2.5 shows the customized Folders for the project, where researchers created a Folder for each

(Continued)

(Continued)

site and used a naming scheme to further facilitate accurate sorting of the data; each transcript in *Site A* begins with the letter 'A'. This organization facilitated separate analysis to be undertaken on all the data collected from each site, because Queries can be scoped/filtered to only the Files stored within a particular Folder (see Chapter 7). For example, with the Folder structure in Figure 2.5, the researchers could easily conduct a Word Frequency only in *Site A*.

Managing Files in Sets

In Chapter 5, you will learn how to create Sets in order to provide an additional way of organizing your Files. A Set (Figure 2.6) simply contains shortcuts to other items in the Project so you can group them together and treat them as a collective. Identifying a File as part of a Set does not alter that File or the structure of your data Files. Unlike Folders, items in Sets do not need to be mutually exclusive so your interview for *Susan* can be in a Set for *Time 1* as well as your Set for *Pilot Interviews* (for example). In other words, it is an alternative Folder structure and you can arrange (or rearrange) your Files in Sets at any time during your project. All of the Queries, such as a Word Frequency Query, can be scoped to a particular Set.

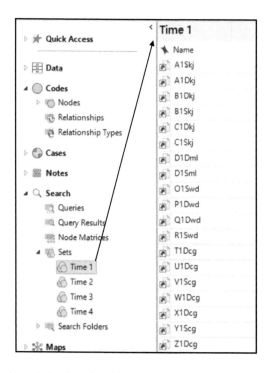

Figure 2.6 Customizable Set structure for NVivo Files

Sets in the Violence Prevention Initiative

In the *Violence Prevention Initiative*, after creating Sets of Files according to the time point in which they were collected, the researchers could run any Query to look only at a particular Time, or to compare Nodes (or other items) across Time.

Managing Files with Cases and Values

In Chapter 5 you will learn how to create Cases, Classifications, Attributes, and Values. To simplify this complexity, we discuss the utility of Cases and Values for comparing and counting subgroups in your data. A Case (Figure 2.7) is a location that combines all data (qualitative, quantitative, and demographic data) for a person.

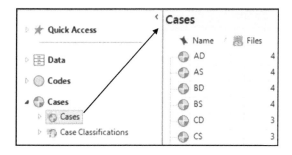

Figure 2.7 Customizable Case structure for NVivo Files

Cases in the Violence Prevention Initiative

In the *Violence Prevention* Initiative, the researchers created a Case that combined all interviews over the four time points for each person. Note that the Case for AD (the Director in community A) contains four Files in Figure 2.7. By creating this entity in the Project and assigning Values of *Rural* or *Urban* to each Case, NVivo can efficiently count the number of Rural and Urban people that discussed particular topics.

Differences among Folders, Sets, and Cases

Folders are a good place to start creating meaningful groups in NVivo and they can be used to efficiently direct NVivo to look in some of your Files when running a Query, instead of the default to look in all of them. However, you may want to use alternative groupings of Files, and some of these groups might not have mutually exclusive items – as Folders should have.

Sets are a great place to create these alternative groups because they are simply shortcuts to the Files in your Folders. While they are useful, each Set usually only pertains to one dimension (e.g., *Time 1*) and are not as effective as Cases for counting things when the project becomes larger and more complex. Cases and Values provide the most sophisticated way to organize your data into subgroups because Cases can point to entire Files, portions of Files, or both. Unlike Sets, they can easily be associated with multiple Values (e.g., a single Case could be someone who lives in a *Rural* area, is *Over 40, Employed full-time,* and ranked on *Likert question A as 3*). In a single NVivo Project, you might not use Folders, Sets, or Cases. However, we see some NVivo Projects that use all three of these, as shown in our video in the online resources (https://study.sagepub.com/jackson3e), 'A Project with Folders, Sets, and Cases.' (For more details on Sets, see Chapter 5, pp. 145–146, and for more details on Cases, see Chapters 2 and 5). Table 2.2 will help you think through your options and strategies as you prepare to structure your NVivo Project.

Table 2.2 Differences between Folders, Sets, and Cases for managing Files

	Folders	**Sets**	**Cases**
Where do I find these in the *Navigation View?*	Data > Files > Folders	Search > Sets	Cases > Cases
Can a single File be placed in more than one Folder, or added to more than one Set or coded to more than one Case?	No. The File should exist in only one Folder.	Yes. Items in Sets are not mutually exclusive (i.e., they can be added to more than one Set).	Not usually, although you might have an interview that is coded to the Case for the person (e.g., *Susan*) as well as a Case for the school (e.g., *Mapleton*).
What is the primary purpose of this tool for managing Files?	Visual organization. Sorting and management of Files.	To allow any combination of Files regardless of their Folder location.	Combining all of the qualitative, demographic, and quantitative data for a unit of analysis (e.g., *Susan*).
What is an example of using this in a Query?	To efficiently include only some of the Files in a Word Frequency Query (Chapter 7, p. 219).	To collect multiple Files into a single column or row (e.g., when comparing Sets) in a Matrix Coding Query (Chapter 7, p. 223).	Conducting an analysis of what *Urban* people who are *Over 40* say about *Changes in the community* with a Coding Query. (Chapter 7, p. 224)
			Comparing what *Urban* and *Rural* people say in a Crosstab Query (Chapter 7, pp. 221–222).

SECTION 2.4: CHAPTER 2 TAKEAWAYS

━━━━ Key points from this chapter ━━━━

o Understanding what a Case is in your study is a key element of setting boundaries or parameters around your inquiry.

o A Case in NVivo is different from a case study.

o The initial steps of preparing your Files to maximize the tools in NVivo depends on a basic understanding of Cases. A Case typically gathers all of the data for a unit of analysis in your project. For example, *Susan's* Case will gather:

- All of her qualitative data (which could be from multiple Files or parts of Files)
- All demographic or quantitative data (e.g., her age).

Tips, challenges, and warnings

- On a small subset of your data, pilot the formatting of your Files. If you intend to use Cases, jump to Chapter 5 and use the guidance there to create a small pilot of these as well.
- Develop a plan for collecting relevant Attribute Values for your study (e.g., in a spreadsheet) so that when you develop your list of Nodes these do not need to be part of your coding structure. They will go in another part of your NVivo Project.
- While it is important to have a plan for your Cases to maximize the use of some tools in NVivo, the creation of these aspects of your Project can occur at any time. They tend to be most useful when you conduct Queries.
- Folders and Files can be renamed and rearranged easily, without losing any work. Start with Folders that match your organization of the data on your computer (e.g., by *wave*, by *data type*, by *site*) and later you can adjust the structure if it facilitates the way you want to handle the data.
- Creating a lot of nested Folders will make clicking through some of the tools more cumbersome, so be prepared to adjust the structure later if you have an extensive hierarchy.
- Cases offer a very powerful and exciting aspect of handling your data in NVivo, but in a complex design, they can be difficult to master in relation to other tools in your Project. Be prepared to experiment, give it time, and ask for assistance when you hit barriers.

Videos and online resources (https://study.sagepub.com/jackson3e)

Videos

- 'A Project with Folders, Sets, and Cases'

Help files

- *File*: Help.
- *Menu bar*: **Help > NVivo Help**.

Search for any of the following:

- Bring in your files and get organized
- Cases
- Files
- Queries
- Sets and search folders

Practice questions

1   What is a Case in your research and how does/did this influence the way you collect data?

2   How might your research question(s) change to point you toward a different kind of Case in your study? Does this thought experiment change the way you are thinking about your research? If so, how?

3   What kinds of demographic or quantitative data might you want to associate with your Cases? After developing a comprehensive list, think about the analysis that waits ahead of you and what kinds of groups in your data (e.g., people who are *Motivated, Getting by,* or *In a slump*) might only be discovered through the qualitative coding you will be doing. How does this thought experiment inform the way you think about the relationship between qualitative and quantitative data?

4   What are the visual cues you like to use when handling text such as colours, bold, highlighting, indents, etc.? Experiment with these in a text file and import it into NVivo. Are there elements that will not work and require an alternative strategy? If so, how do you plan on handling them?

3

Section 3.1: Introduction to coding foundations   64

Section 3.2: Conceptual grounding in Coding   65

Section 3.3: Coding in NVivo   77

Section 3.4: Chapter 3 Takeaways   97

CODING FOUNDATIONS

The excellence of the research rests in large part on the excellence of coding. (Strauss, 1987: 27)

SECTION 3.1: INTRODUCTION TO CODING FOUNDATIONS

This chapter provides practical strategies that will help you identify meaningful labels for your codes and to begin coding your data. Coding can be labour-intensive but should not be approached as a hurdle you have to get through to eventually arrive at your analysis; it is part of an interpretive process that might shift over time and requires periodic use of other strategies. At first, your progress in working with the data might be slow. However, your project will gradually grow into a web of data, themes, and thinking, illuminating (and sometimes refining) your research question(s). As your ideas develop, coding the data is likely to become more efficient than it was when you started.

In this chapter you will

- Learn how coding can support your analysis.
- Discover the specific strategies you can use to identify and name concepts and themes in your data.
- Learn some practical strategies for managing your coding process.
- Find out where and how NVivo stores your Nodes.
- Learn how to approach the basics of coding in NVivo and viewing what you coded (e.g., coding, uncoding, Node Descriptions, using Coding Stripes and Highlighting).
- Learn how to manage your Nodes (e.g., deleting, merging, customizing your Node list, exporting a list of Nodes).
- Learn how Memos and See Also Links can help you think about your coding process and initial interpretations.

Other chapters with related materials

While you might find all the material related to your current needs in this chapter, you should also consider these other chapters that contain closely related information:

Chapter 1: Where to begin?

In many ways, Memos and Links are companion tools to coding. Instead of pulling similar themes or concepts together through coding, Memos and Links help keep track of ongoing ideas and threads of connections in your data and this is often where a good portion of your analytical work can be developed and tracked. Be sure to use Memos and Links in conjunction with coding.

Chapter 4: Advanced coding

After you master the basics of coding, you will move on to more advanced skills such as creating hierarchies, aggregating, and Auto Coding. You will also want to explore relationships among Nodes with visual Maps. You will likely want to create Node hierarchies while being mindful to use 'vista' Node structures and avoid 'viral' ones. Get acquainted with using Queries to aid coding by running a Word Frequency Query and a Text Search Query and consider turning these Query Results into Nodes.

SECTION 3.2: CONCEPTUAL GROUNDING IN CODING

In this section of the chapter, we identify ways of thinking about your coding regardless of whether or not you use software. If you want to jump to the instructions on clicking, go to Section 3.3 (Coding in NVivo). The codes, themselves, are often referred to by qualitative researchers (regardless of whether they use software or not) as issues, themes, topics, etc., and although these labels carry nuances across different methodologies, we use them here as synonyms to help orient you to the process. Another term that resonates with most newcomers to this adventure is the verb, 'tagging'. While tagging or coding the data is often an important strategy for researchers, qualitative analysis is about working intensively with rich and often unstructured data with additional strategies that are related to – but often identified as distinct from – coding. These include annotating, associating, discussing, exploring, linking, memoing, organizing, reading, reflecting, suggesting, transforming, and visualizing.

Goals for early work with data

As you begin coding, it is important to observe what is going on in the data while also paying attention to how you are reacting to the process of coding. By engaging in this self-observation you will become better at coding and you might notice that you encounter the following:

- *Excitement:* As you code data, even though you may have collected the information and transcribed it yourself, new codes and a new awareness of the relationship among your codes might emerge unexpectedly. As this happens, you will become more aware of what you can contribute to the field. Notice when this happens and write about it! (See memoing and linking in Chapter 1.)
- *Changing your mind:* Coding evolves as you handle the data over time. You might encounter compelling arguments or perspectives in the literature or among your colleagues that result in an alternative framework or definition of a concept. Notice when this happens and write about it!
- *Frustration:* You might change your mind once, and then change it back again; your timeline could get thrown by unforeseen circumstances; a brilliantly complicated coding structure that took time to develop might need to be simplified to better answer

your research questions. There are many things that can trigger frustration around the lack of predictable, fluid movement through the coding process. Notice when this happens and write about it!

- *Adjusting your gaze:* You might dive into nuances in the data to get close to the perspectives of your participants, but then occasionally see a need to step back and look at the bigger picture and how the data relates to a larger context. Moving back and forth between closeness and distance is an important part of making sense of the data and understanding your codes, although there are few prescriptions of when or how to do so. Notice when this happens and write about it!
- *Building ideas:* Strive, even from this early stage, to go beyond descriptive labelling and to think about codes beyond their relationship to a single File. Why is this information important? Where will these ideas take me? This will be reflected in the way you name codes. Notice when this happens and write about it!
- *Jumping to conclusions:* Early work with text and concepts is about laying the foundation and identifying key themes in the data. But, beware of making judgements or decisions too early. Constantly challenge your first ideas by looking for contrasts as well as comparisons, by purposively sampling diverse cases, or by reviewing what the various camps in the literature say on the topic. Notice when this happens and write about it!
- *Observing constellations of codes:* Right from the start, it is helpful to observe when you are applying multiple codes to the same content (e.g., the same portion of a transcript). Early in the coding process you should not assume these co-occurrences are correlations or indicate causation, but they could help you map constellations of concepts that facilitate your construction of theories later. Notice when this happens and write about it!

If you lay a sound foundation with your first File(s), then you will confidently move on to adopt further strategies for advancing your thinking about data, as outlined in the following chapters. For now, however, we will help guide you through the basic steps as you prepare to code.

Selecting Files (we recommend starting with text documents)

If you are just beginning to gather data, selecting a text document to work on first is probably easy because you will have only one or two to choose from. If, however, you have already completed a number of interviews or have a variety of data items, then you might identify two Files:

- Choose one which you remember as being typical in some way, or which was contributed by someone who was representative in some way of a group or subgroup in the sample.
- Choose one which seemed to be particularly interesting or rich in its detail.

These first two Files can have a significant influence on the early stages of coding. When choosing a second one, therefore, you will benefit from focusing on one that contrasts in some important way with the first in order to maximize the potential for variety in concepts (or in their forms of expression).

Two, contrasting documents to code

In the *Researchers* Project, Pat chose *Frank* and *Elizabeth* as the first two documents to work through in detail, because, as academic researchers, they provided a strong contrast in terms of career development. *Elizabeth's* path into a research career was characterized by digressions and serendipitous events, while *Frank's* path was direct and purposeful.

When Pat first worked through *Elizabeth's* document, the impact of her changing image of research was striking, and so she coded that and further documents for the way in which the speaker viewed research – only to find in later analyses that it had no particular significance for anyone else. It became more useful to see (and code) *Elizabeth's* re-visioning of research as a turning point, rather than focusing on her image of research. The codes that dealt with images of research could then be retired.

Exactly how and what you code will most certainly depend on your choice of methodology, so it is important that you familiarize yourself with the literature surrounding your methodology, including the various camps and debates therein. Coding is also influenced by your community of practice (Lave & Wenger, 1991), your discipline, your participants, your personality, and any prior experience you have in handling qualitative data. We will not cover all of these nuances although we want you to be aware of them as we provide guidance in these early stages of coding. Furthermore, we advise you to consider writing about these influences on your analytical processes.

Codes and coding

'A code is an abstract representation of an object or phenomenon' (Corbin & Strauss, 2008: 66) and it 'is most often a word or a short phrase that symbolically assigns a summative, salient, essence-capturing and/or evocative attribute for a portion of language-based or visual data' (Saldaña, 2013: 3; 2016: 4). More prosaically, Bernard and Ryan (2010) describe coding as a way of identifying themes in a text. Codes range from being purely descriptive (this event occurred in the *playground*) to more conceptual topics or themes (this is about *violence between children*) to more interpretive or analytical concepts (this is a reflection of *cultural stereotyping*) (Richards, 2009). Furthermore, all of these might be applied to the same text.

Field notes and verbatim transcripts reflect 'the undigested complexity of reality' (Patton, 2002: 463), needing coding to make sense of them, and to bring order out of chaos. Coding in qualitative research, in its simplest sense, is a way of indexing the data in order to facilitate later retrieval as singular concepts (e.g., *cultural stereotyping*) or constellations of concepts (e.g., *cultural stereotyping, employee guidelines*, and *retention*). Naming a concept or topic aids organization of data and so assists analytic thinking. As data are seen afresh through the code rather than the original document, coding allows you to 'recontextualize' your data (Tesch, 1990), assisting you to move from individual document analysis to theorizing, all the while retaining access to the original material.

Because the codes we create are inextricably connected to our world-views, 'implicitly or explicitly, they embody the assumptions underlying the analysis' (MacQueen, McLellan-Lemal, Bartholow, & Milstein, 2008: 119). In other words, codes do not magically 'emerge' from the data, but are always generated by the researcher through a range of strategies, such as the constant comparative method (Glaser & Strauss, 1967). Some methodologies (e.g., autoethnography) push researchers to engage with and understand their personal roles in producing and making sense of data, while others (e.g., hypothesis testing) de-emphasize such an examination. Regardless, there can never be a complete separation between codes and researchers, as they are engaged in an iterative process of mutual construction.

Approaches to coding

Coding is not a mechanical task. It requires continual assessment and rethinking and is part of analysis. It is a mistake to tenaciously push through coding in the hope that something interesting will tumble out of the Project when you are done. One way of understanding basic approaches to coding is to observe that there are 'splitters' – those who maximize differences between text passages, looking for fine-grained themes – and 'lumpers' – those who minimize them, looking for overarching themes (Bernard & Ryan, 2010), although most of us do some of each. A common approach is to start with general themes, then code in more detail (e.g., Coffey & Atkinson, 1996). However, those who employ grounded theory, phenomenology, or discourse analysis start more often with detailed analysis and work up to broader concepts.

━━━━━━━━━━━━━━ **Sorting the laundry and sorting codes** ━━━━━━━━━━━━━━

Lynn Kemp, Director of the Translational Research and Social Innovation Group at Western Sydney University, tells students that choices about coding are like choices in sorting the laundry. Some hang the clothes just as they come out of the basket, and, when dry, throw them into piles for each person in the family, ready for further sorting and putting away - preferably by their owner! Others hang the clothes in clusters according to their owner, so they are already person-sorted as they come off the line, although pants and shirts might be mixed up and socks still need pairing. And yet others hang socks in pairs and place other similar things together, so they can be folded in batches as they come off the line. Ultimately, the wash is sorted, people get their clothes and (hopefully) all the socks have pairs. Similarly, whether you start big and then attend to detail, or start small and then combine or group, your coding will eventually reach the level required.

Broad-brush or 'bucket' coding

This one is for lumpers! There is no need to treat coding as unchangeable and you will be able to code from broader themes to more refined subthemes. If you begin with the broad-brush approach, your initial coding task is to 'chunk' the text into more general topic areas, as a first step to seeing what is there, or to identify just those passages that will be relevant to your investigation. Beginning by coding to these broad themes does not mean they should be vague. Some researchers strategically begin here because they want to take one pass through the data without getting bogged down with a large volume of codes and they know in advance that they will be taking a second pass through each code to consider the work already done. During the second pass, researchers often take stock of the diversity of opinions in each code, the volume of data and the relative importance participants assign to them while simultaneously coding to more discrete subcodes. If you use this approach, notice that you are beginning with a deductive stance, because you hope that the answers to your research questions can be developed out of some fairly broad themes that you are applying to the data. In Chapter 11 we elaborate on the efficacy of the broad-brush approach for teams.

Selecting from broad themes for greater focus

Lynn Kemp's doctoral study of the community service needs of people with spinal injuries employed broad-brush coding as an initial sorting strategy. In response to her question, 'You came home from hospital and ...?' her interviewees talked extensively across all areas of their lives. In order to manage this large pool of data, Lynn coded her interviews first into very broad themes (e.g., *community services, employment, education, recreation*). She then coded on from the community services text (which was her immediate focus), capturing the detail of what people with spinal injury were seeking from life, what services were being offered, and how these supported or impeded their clients' capacity to fulfil their 'plan of life'. After recovering from the doctoral process, Lynn (or indeed, her students) could then focus attention on topics that were set aside, to engage in further analysis and reporting.

Coding detail

And this one is for the splitters! For some methods, most notably grounded theory (Glaser & Strauss, 1967), your initial analysis will involve detailed, slow, reflective exploration of early texts – doing line-by-line coding, reading between the lines, identifying concepts, and thinking about the possible meanings as a way of breaking open the text. You record what you learn via your work with your codes, supplemented by the notes you write along the way. At the beginning of the analytical process, you will explore each word or phrase for meaning, perhaps considering theoretically the difference it might have made if an alternative word had been used or a contrasting situation described (Strauss, 1987). You will not continue to code at this level of intensity beyond the first few files, however, unless you come upon new ideas to explore or contradictions to resolve. In practical terms, capturing the detail of the text does not mean you should segment it into tiny, meaningless chunks. Rather, the goal is to capture the finer nuances of meaning lying within the text, coding a long enough passage in each instance to provide sufficient context without clouding the integrity of the coded passage by inclusion of text with a different meaning (unless, of course, the whole passage contains contradictory messages).

Implications and nuances within the interview

In the *Researchers* Project, *Frank* begins his response to an open question about his research journey as follows:

> My PhD was both a theoretical and empirical piece of work; I was using techniques which were novel at the time. (Interruption by secretary.) I was using novel mathematical dynamic techniques and theory and also I was testing these models out econometrically on cross-country data. I think it was a strong PhD, I had a strong supervisor, he was regarded as – it is fair to say he would have been in the top 5 in his area, say, in the world.

In the first place, *Frank* begins his response by focusing on his PhD experience. In broad terms, one could simply code this passage descriptively as being about the PhD or learning phase of becoming a researcher, and indeed, that is relevant as contextual (or structural) coding even if one is looking to capture detail in the text. But this passage is also saying considerably more than just that *Frank's* research career included a PhD student phase. He implies that the PhD provided a strong foundation for his later career. Linked with that strong foundation are the kinds of work he did in his PhD and the role of his supervisor.

This text tells us also a great deal about *Frank* and his approach to research. His PhD was both theoretical and empirical (characteristics which are repeated in the next sentence). Not only does he have credibility in both these aspects of his discipline, but his work was novel. Here, he is both validating and emphasizing the strength of his foundational work. In describing his work as using novel mathematical techniques, he is also suggesting that he is making a mark on the development of the discipline – presaging a later, critical theme.

That his PhD was a 'piece of work' also suggests wholeness or completeness. So, research work can have the dimension of being partial, incomplete and ongoing, or of being finished and completed with loose ends tidied up. This, along with the dimension of research discoveries as occurring at a point in time versus occurring in incremental developments, could be interesting in relation to the nature of research activity (and being a researcher), but they are not necessarily relevant to the current question of how one becomes a researcher – and so they are noted but not coded.

Frank's emphasis on the strength of his PhD (noting repeat use of 'strong') and the strength of his supervisor supports an idea also evident in the first sentence that the status of his work matters; It is important to him that his supervisor was at the top, and Frank was moving up there too, with leading-edge work. This theme of ambition (incorporating status) is also evident in several other passages, for example:

> I then teamed up quite soon with another 'young turk' … we hit it off and both of us were interested in making some sort of an impact, so basically we were young

and single and just really went for it. ... our two names became synonymous with this certain approach, and we went around Britain and into Europe giving research papers and getting ourselves published. ... it was us carving out a niche for ourselves in the research part of the profession and that was our key to success so we kept at it.

How important is this level of ambition, both from the point of view of the research question, and for detailed coding? At this early stage, the safe move is to create a Node for *ambition*: if no one else talks in these terms, then later it can be combined within a broader category of, say, *drive* or *commitment*.

Coding for the opening passages might therefore look as shown in Figure 3.1. Other ideas and reflections prompted by the passages were recorded in annotations and in the memo attached to *Frank's* document.

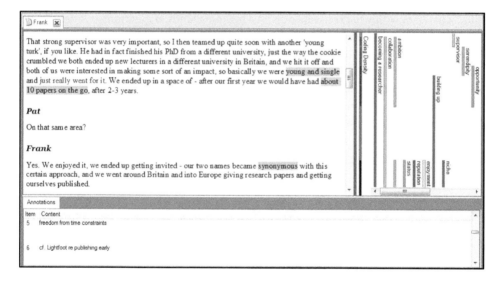

Figure 3.1 *Frank's* document showing application of multiple codes to each passage of text, and Annotations (see Chapter 1 for Annotations)

Strategies for identifying and naming codes

The idea of coding a portion of text (or audio, video, images, etc.) to index its content sounds simple enough, and observing someone else's coding can make the task look deceptively easy. When you meet your own data, however, you find many things are going on at once: something is happening in a particular setting or at a particular time, particular people or groups are involved, perhaps their responses are based on their belief systems or cultural background, and there are consequences to be considered. Perhaps there is a twist to the way this experience, belief, or feeling is being reported that makes it just a bit different from other reports or makes it difficult to pin down. Narrative is inherently complex: a group can argue about the content and meaning of just one paragraph for a very long time. In your NVivo Project, it tends to help when you code each passage to multiple codes that are all relevant (e.g., *Trust, Friends, Advice*), rather than create an overly nuanced code that attempts to capture all of them at once (e.g., *Trusted friends are sought for advice*). By using the former approach, you can later check whether this combination of codes forms a pattern, or how *Advice* AND *Trust* AND *Friends* occur in different (or similar) ways than *Advice* AND *Trust* AND *Family*.

What follows is a collection of ways in which codes might be identified and named, particularly those requiring more than a simple descriptive label. Further suggestions and extended examples of coding strategies can be found later in this chapter.

- *Look for repetitions and regularities:* People repeat ideas that are of significance for them (see the use of 'strong' by *Frank* in the example above), sometimes across a range of experiences. Identifying these repetitions can be the first step in understanding the contexts in which they are used.
- *Use questions of the text to generate codes:* Who, what, when, why, how, how much, what for, what if, or with what consequences? Asking these kinds of questions will help to ensure thoroughness of coding and to develop relational statements (do the actions or strategies change under different conditions and, if so, what are the implications?) and so will hugely benefit development of a theoretical model.
- *Compare and contrast passages of text:* Think about the ways in which they are both similar and different. This will help you go beyond simply deciding which chunks might go together: it will help you discern the dimensions within concepts, or perhaps to discern previously unobserved variables running through the text.

Gender differences and the role of parents in relationship choices

In a study of parental and peer attachment among Malaysian adolescents, Noriah Mohd Ishak, in the Faculty of Education at the University of Kebangsaan, Malaysia, found boys and girls spoke in contrasting ways about their parents' role in their relationship choices, for example:

Boy: I trust my parents with their choice; I might have a girlfriend here in America, but the girl I finally marry will depend on my parents' choice. I think theirs is always the right choice.

Girl: I choose whom I will marry. My parents might have their own choice, but how can I trust their choice, because they live in a different generation than I do!

In relation to young people's acceptance of parental leadership, then, trust is a significant dimension. Other possibly relevant concepts arising from these comparative passages are parental adaptability, parental authority, cultural expectations, and cultural change. Also of interest in the boy's comment about having an American girlfriend is what it says about attitudes toward women and commitment in relationships.

- *Compare the data with hypothetical or extreme examples:* This helps to identify dimensions within concepts.

▬▬▬ Obsession with research ▬▬▬

As his career was unfolding, Frank's total focus was on research:

> When you go out in the pub you are talking research, when you go to bed at night you are thinking it.

Seeing this as a form of addiction prompted Pat to talk with a colleague who was studying youth gambling behaviour. Researchers and gamblers can both follow a passion, often (but not necessarily) to the detriment of their health and/or family relationships; both can engage in activities that benefit from careful strategic planning but which are also subject to luck or whim; both can be characterized by emotional highs and lows; both can experience problems with self-regulation. There were differences of opinion over whether addiction was necessarily 'bad'. As the project developed further, Pat saw addiction as one expression of a larger category of obsession, which she came to define as 'driven passion' to capture the dimensions of emotional engagement and the potentially blind (unregulated) commitment of the obsessed researcher.

- *A priori, or theoretically derived, codes:* These come from your prior reading and theoretical understanding to give you a start list of concepts to work with. Use, also, the categories embedded in your research questions. Don't let your a priori codes confine your thinking, however. Strauss (1987) and Patton (2002) each referred to these as sensitizing concepts, rather than as fixed ones.
- *In vivo, or indigenous codes:* These are different from a priori codes because they are derived directly from the data (Strauss, 1987). They capture an actual expression of an interviewee or label used by participants as the title for a code, but they can sometimes have the unfortunate problem of not being useful in exactly that form for expressing what is learned from other participants. Change the term to a more general construct as the project develops but keep a record (in the description or a note) about how the code arose in the first place.

▬▬▬ The 'hard labour' of going through change ▬▬▬

When a member of a corporation that underwent a radical change programme talked about the hard labour of working through that change process, this expression was appreciated for its valuable imagery - of what goes on in a birthing process, of the punishing work of someone held in a prison - and hence became an in vivo code available for use in coding other text.

- *Explore discourse that reflects a particular construction of the topic, or of society:* In the *Researchers* data, you will find discourses of performance (being successful, competing, building a reputation), of play (following curious leads, puzzling, playing with new ways of doing things), and of romance (passion, sensuality, orgasmic) in the way participants talk about their research worlds. Coding these varying constructions provides insight into participants' motivations and approaches to navigating their research context. The field of discourse analysis encompasses a wide range of specialties and perspectives, each with implications for choice of codes. For example:

  o Critical discourse analysis: A focus on the reproduction of social power through language use (Fairclough, 2014) might result in the creation of codes for *formal or mature titles* (e.g., 'sir' or 'men') versus *informal or immature titles* (e.g., 'gals' or 'girls').

  o Rhetoric: Paying attention to the mechanisms and processes of persuasion (Anzaldúa, 2015) could entail codes that track the use of discursive strategies like 'definitively', 'certainly', 'obviously' versus 'perhaps', 'potentially', 'maybe'.

- *Narrative structure and mechanisms take account of how things were said as well as what was said:* You might note, for example:

  o transitions and turning points in the narrative, signifying a change of theme or a subject to be avoided (Duchinsky, 2013);

  o inconsistencies, endings, omissions, repetitions and silences (Poirier & Ayres, 1997);

  o repairs, hedging language, chronology (or lack thereof) (Fox, Hayashi, & Jasperson, 1996);

  o the use of metaphors and analogies (Lakoff & Johnson, 2003);

  o the sequenced, structural elements of a narrative (Elliott, 2005; Riessman, 2008); and use of articles or pronouns pointing to particularized or generalized referents, for example, 'the staff', 'my staff', or 'our staff'; indicating level and type of ownership or involvement (Morse, 1999).

'We' and 'ours' versus 'they' and 'them'

In an evaluation research project on a Violence Prevention Initiative, Kristi worked on a team where the final rounds of data collection and coding turned to a focus on how pronouns were used by community collaboration partners in 26 communities over the course of the Initiative. Prior rounds of analysis facilitated the development of codes that were descriptive (e.g., *special events* and *definition of violence*), thematic (e.g., *learning* and *conflict*), and interpretive (e.g., *critical events* and *cultural barriers*). However, the final round focused on an examination of the use of pronouns that were inclusive (e.g., *we* and *ours*) versus pronouns that indicated separations (e.g., *they* and *them*). The careful examination of pronouns in the context of the prior coding helped explore how well and in what ways the partners shifted to collaboration over time.

Generating conceptual codes

If sensing a pattern or 'occurrence' can be called seeing, then the encoding of it can be called see-ing as. That is, you first make the observation that something important or notable is occurring, and then you classify or describe it. ... [T]he seeing as provides us with a link between a new or emergent pattern and any and all patterns that we have observed and considered previously. It also provides a link to any and all patterns that others have observed and considered previously through reading. (Boyatzis, 1998: 4)

At first, you are not quite sure what is relevant, or how it will be relevant. When coding, it is very easy to be beguiled by fascinating things your participants have said and so to become sidetracked. To start, try the following three steps Lyn Richards (2009) developed for under-graduate teaching. They will help you move from 'seeing' to 'seeing as':

- *Identify:* What's interesting? Highlight the passage.
- *Ask:* Why is it interesting? This can generate a useful descriptive code or perhaps an interpretive code. It could also warrant a note to help remind you of the significance later.
- *Explain:* Why am I interested in that? This will 'lift you off the page' to generate a more abstract and generally applicable concept, which, if relevant to your project, will be very worthy of a code (and perhaps a memo).

That critical third question is giving you a way of generating concepts that will be useful across documents rather than for only one or two passages in a single document. These more general or abstract concepts are essential for moving from description to analysis and link the data to the broader field of knowledge. In a strategic sense, that third question also helps keep you on target, to keep the focus on issues relevant to your research questions.

▬▬▬▬▬ **Developing more abstract categories** ▬▬▬▬▬

In a doctoral project on the role of support groups in assisting young people with a mental health problem, a participant reported moving from sheltered to independent accommo-dation. The student deemed this to be of interest and created the Node 'accommodation' to code it. Just one participant, however, had anything to say about accommodation, and accommodation was not an issue of concern for this project. (Had the project been about issues faced by young people with mental health problems, then of course accommodation could well have been a relevant code to make.) When the student was challenged about why the text was interesting, she said it was the evidence of improvement in mental health status indicated by the young person's change in accommodation. With the code name changed to reflect this more pertinent (and more interpretive) concept, she could use this code across other documents to code other indicators spoken of in the same way, such as gaining employment or repairing a relationship. If she wished to examine the nature of the evidence given to indicate improvement in mental health status, she could simply review the text coded at the Node.

You might expect to engage in periodic rereading of earlier material, when the salience of particular texts becomes more obvious. In any case, it remains likely that you will create codes which you later drop if you heed the advice of MacQueen et al. who say, 'Don't clutter the codebook with deadwood' (2008: 133). In addition, you will occasionally miss relevant passages, but that should not be a major concern. Firstly, important ideas will be repeated throughout the data; secondly, it is likely you will pick up on missed instances of something as you review other codes, or later as you are querying your data. Above all else, keep in mind that you can change your mind about relevant concepts and even about your research questions (depending on your methodology). Fortunately, NVivo accommodates such changes.

Time and timing

How long will it take?

People often ask, but it is very difficult to say how much time is needed for coding. Our best estimate is that, once you have an established coding system, you should allow at least 3 hours per hour of transcript – the actual amount will very much depend, however, on your research questions, methodological approach and the quality of the collected data. Experienced researchers (including Miles & Huberman, 1994) routinely recommend allowing a working period for analysis of data that is two to five times as long as the period taken to make arrangements and gather the data.

When do I stop?

There are two ways you should consider walking away from the coding. The first pertains to a temporary but purposeful break that gives you time to rethink, regroup, and come back more focused. Kristi sometimes warns researchers that if they are becoming obsessed with the movement of the Scroll Bar down the right side of the screen and calculating the minutes left to code the File, it is likely time to stop. Lyn Richards commented in an online forum that: 'If you've been coding for more than two hours without stopping to write a memo, you've lost the plot.' She recommended regularly stepping out of coding, not only to write memos, but also to monitor and review the coding. Freely make new codes (rather than sweat over each one as you create it), but also periodically do a check to ensure the categories you are making are relevant. Occasionally review one or two codes in depth for a useful change of perspective on your data.

The second way to reconsider or step back from coding might be more permanent or final. If your project is one in which it is essential to code all materials in order to thoroughly test hunches/hypotheses or because counting the frequency of occurrence of codes (e.g., issues raised for a stratified sample) is part of the research strategy, you might need to persist until the task is completed. However, if you have worked sufficiently and thoroughly with enough texts to be able to generate convincing answers to your questions (or to develop your explanatory theory), it may be time to stop. Consider this if coding is becoming routine and fails to generate new themes or ideas. If you have additional data, consider reviewing these materials, just to check if any include comments or images which extend or contradict the model or theory or explanation you have generated thus far. Alternatively, if you have additional data transcribed, then import them into a separate folder for *non-coded documents* and use Word Frequency or Text Search Queries to identify text that contains especially relevant terms from within those files (see Automatic coding in Chapter 4).

SECTION 3.3: CODING IN NVIVO

NVivo has two predefined types of Codes: Nodes and Relationships (and a third, Sentiment, in NVivo Plus). In the *Navigation View* under the **Code** button you will also see Relationship Types. This is a classifying tool rather than a kind of Code and we discuss classifying tools in Chapters 5 and 6. The vast majority of NVivo users spend their time working in the Nodes area, and this will be our focus in the remainder of this chapter. Despite NVivo's flexibility in helping you apply the strategies from our earlier ideas about coding, knowing how to code in theory and making it work effectively and efficiently for your research can be two quite different things. In this section we turn to practical issues about how to apply the ideas above to the mechanics of the software, and we introduce a few tactical and practical issues that are related to coding in your NVivo Project.

NVivo terms used in this section

Codes

Codebook

Coding Reference (or Reference)

Coding Stripes

Highlight

Node

Node Description

Storing coding in Nodes

In many respects, coding in NVivo is much like the way some qualitative researchers use Post-it notes and whiteboards to develop ideas (although a digital Project is much more versatile than Post-it notes and highlighters). Because you will be doing this work in a digital Project, Files will not lose their coding when you move, split, or merge Nodes, nor will Files lose their coding if the text is modified (unless you delete all of the text instead of modifying part of it). The bottom line with coding in NVivo is that the software enables you to build on work already done and will allow you to change your mind about everything related to coding (the name of a Node, its Description, colour, location in the coding hierarchy, data coded [or uncoded], etc.).

In NVivo, you make a Node for each topic or concept to be stored, much like designating a hanging file for the cut-up photocopies in a manual system. As you code, the system interface will mimic the manual method (as if you were using paper and making copies to put them in a folder). Note the direction of the arrow in Figure 3.2.

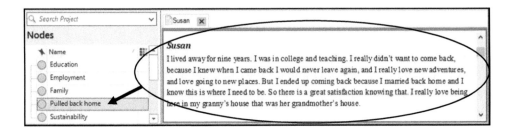

Figure 3.2 NVivo mimicking the conventional strategy of coding: making copies and placing them in categories/concepts

What NVivo keeps in a Node, however, are not actual segments of data, but pointers (references) to the exact location of the text (or audio, video, etc.) you coded in the File. Note the more accurate depiction of the direction of the arrow in Figure 3.3.

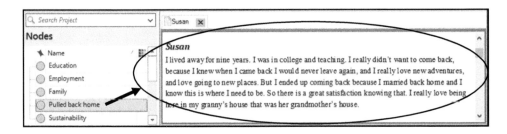

Figure 3.3 NVivo actually tagging the text with the Node

Coded passages are never copied, cut, or physically moved into the Nodes. Think of a Node as though the only thing it contains is a command that says, 'go get it!'; when you open a Node you are looking at the original text in the File. These coded passages can be short or long, according to your assessment of a meaningful range. Regardless of their size, in NVivo these passages are called References (also sometimes Coding References). A Node can point to as many References across your documents as you would like, and more than one Node can point to the same Reference, since some passages will convey multiple meanings. Because the Node is a pointer to the Reference:

- the File always remains intact;
- information about the File and location of a quote is always preserved;
- it is always possible to view the Coding Reference in its original context (because the Node is pointing to the File);

- changes to the File, such as edits, are immediately reflected in the Nodes (because the Nodes are just pointing to the File); and
- text (audio, video, pictures, etc.) can be coded at multiple Nodes (which will become especially important later when we show you how the Queries in NVivo can help you find intersections [and other patterns] among Nodes).

At first, you will probably use Nodes that do not presume any relationships or connections to each other. They serve simply as tags for data about ideas you want to track. At this stage we recommend you focus on creating Nodes without trying to sort them into different levels – it is easy to reorganize them later when you have a better understanding of the data. In the meantime, they will be listed alphabetically by default (and we will show you how to custom sort your list of Nodes later).

Creating and describing Nodes

If you do not yet have any Files in your Project (or have not even created a Project yet), see Chapter 1 (pp. 18–19) for instructions. You can create some Nodes in advance if you are using an existing framework or theory or if you are so familiar with your data that you already know some of the Nodes you want to create. (You can use many of these strategies for creating a Node while you read the data as well.) Remember each Node should only refer to one theme or concept. If you need to capture two or more elements of what is happening, use two or more Nodes to do so, applied to the same text (and NVivo will help you find the intersections later).

To follow the subsequent instructions, remember the four main areas on your screen (*Ribbon*, *Navigation View*, *List View*, *Detail View*) from Chapter 1 (Windows: Figure 1.1; Mac: Figure 1.2), as each instruction begins with one of these four locations.

Guided tour of Nodes and coding

One of the challenges in learning NVivo is there is more than one way of achieving most tasks like creating a Node or adding coding, and it takes experience to know which most suits your purpose at a particular time. We will begin with a guided tour with some activities within a File as you code and then we will walk you through some activities from inside a Node. After you are familiarized with these most common pathways through the Project, we provide alternative ways to create Nodes, code data and uncode data. After this tour, you might jump to Chapters 4 and 7 if you are interested in the ways NVivo can use Queries and Auto Coding to create Nodes, but if you intend to use these tools, you will first need to understand the basic skills we will teach you in this chapter.

Node Names and Descriptions

The two main Properties of a Node are the Name and the Node Description. Node Descriptions serve as accessible reminders about the basic meaning of the Node and they are very useful when:

- there are multiple people working on the same project;
- other responsibilities have taken you away from this project for a time;
- you need to investigate if you have multiple Nodes with similar meanings (in which case you can combine the Nodes later).

These Descriptions essentially serve as your Codebook, can be modified as your data informs your Description, and can be exported later as a reference or appendix.

━━━━━━━━━━ **3.a.** ━━━━━━━━━━

Getting ready to code

⇒ *Navigation View:* **Data** > **Files**.
⇒ *List View:* **Double-click** on the **File** so it opens.
⇒ *Navigation View:* **Codes** > **Nodes**.

Creating a Node from the *Ribbon*

⇒ *Ribbon:* **Create** > **Node** > (Figure 3.4) provide a **Name** and **Description**.
⇒ We recommend skipping the Nickname and you can always add it later.
⇒ We discuss Aggregate in Chapter 4 (pp. 120–122).
⇒ If you wish, you can assign a colour to the Node in order to sort Nodes or view these colours in the Coding Stripes (both of which we discuss later).
⇒ **OK** / **Done.**

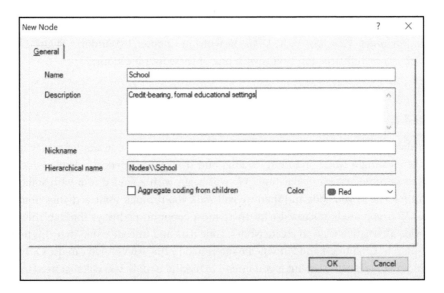

Figure 3.4 The Node Properties window

Creating a Node with a Right-click

Mac users will find that this option only works until the *List View* fills with Nodes. At that point you should use another tactic.

⇒ *List View*: In the white space (below the Node you just created) **Right-click** > **New Node** / **New top level Node** > provide a **Name** and a **Description**.

Fill in additional information as described in 'Creating a Node from the Ribbon.'

Coding to your existing Nodes

⇒ *Detail View*: Select the text to be coded > Drag selected text to a **Node** (Figure 3.5).
⇒ A brief pop-up message in the *Navigation View* (next to Nodes) confirms your action.

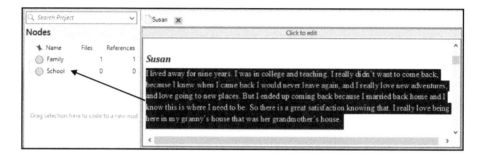

Figure 3.5 Coding to an existing Node via drag-and-drop

Creating a Node and simultaneously coding (Windows only)

⇒ *Detail View*: Highlight the text you want to code > Drag the text to the empty space in the *List View* that says, 'Drag selection here to code to a new node' (Figure 3.6) > **Name** the Node, provide a **Description** > **OK**.

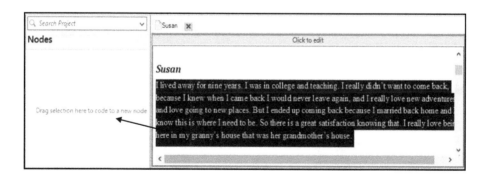

Figure 3.6 Creating a Node and coding at the same time

Seeing what you coded

⇒ *List View*: **Double-click** on the **Node** and the **Reference** will be displayed in *Detail View*.
⇒ *Detail View*: Each time you code, additional References (across Files) will stack in this window (alphabetically by Folder name and then File name).

(Continued)

(Continued)

⇒ Select the **X** on the tab you just opened to close it (Figure 3.7) but leave the File open.
⇒ *Navigation View:* Open Items list (Chapter 1, Figure 1.8) > Select the **X** next to the Node to close it.

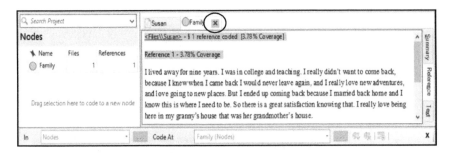

Figure 3.7 Coding for *Family* displayed by the Node

Changing a Node Description (or name, colour, etc.)

⇒ *List View*: **Right-click** on the **Node** > **Node Properties / Get Info** > change the Description (or colour, etc.) > **OK / Done**.

Uncoding from the File

⇒ *Detail View*: Select text in the **File** to be uncoded > **Right-click** and select one of the following two options:
  o **Uncode / Uncode Selection** > **At Existing Nodes or Cases** > tick the desired boxes > **OK / Select;** or
  o **Uncode from Recent Nodes** > select the desired **Node** (Figure 3.8).

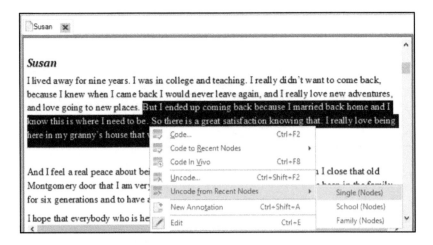

Figure 3.8 Uncoding from the File with a right-click

Re-examining your coding

As you proceed with your coding, you might want to reconsider the data you coded or to look at it in a slightly different way for a variety of reasons:

- You are still getting used to the software and want some reassurance your coding is really happening.
- You have been interrupted in your work and want to check where you stopped.
- You want to check if you picked up all important aspects for this passage.
- You want to visually show your coding on a passage to a colleague, teammate, or instructor.

You can achieve these various goals in several ways while you are working with your Files.

3.b.

Opening and managing the Coding Stripes on a File

⇒ *Detail View*: Click anywhere in the **File** so NVivo knows you are active in the *Detail View*.

⇒ *Ribbon*: **Document** / **View** > **Coding Stripes** > **Recent Coding** / **Nodes Recently Coding**.

⇒ As you scroll up or down with the **Scroll Bar** (between the text and the stripes), you see the stripes are anchored adjacent to the text you coded (Figure 3.9).

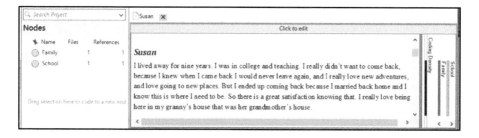

Figure 3.9 Viewing Coding Stripes in a File

Turning on the colours you assigned to the Nodes (if you did!)

⇒ *Ribbon*: **Document** / **View** > **Coding Stripes** > **Item Colours** / **Use Item Colours**.

Coding Density

⇒ With your cursor/pointer, hover over the vertical black/grey/white **Coding Density** stripe to the right of your text to see the associated Nodes (Figure 3.9).

  ○ The darker the stripe the more Nodes you have applied.

(Continued)

(Continued)

⇒ **To modify the default of seeing only seven Coding Stripes**
    o   *Ribbon*: **Document** / **View** > **Coding Stripes** > **Number of stripes** (up to 200) > **OK**.

Viewing coding with the Highlight tool

⇒ **Single-click** (not twice) on any stripe to turn on Highlighting for that Node in the File.
⇒ To turn the Highlight off go to the *Ribbon*: **Document** / **View** > **Highlight** > **None**.

Uncoding with a stripe

⇒ **Right-click** on a stripe to **Uncode** (and see additional options).

You have completed your basic, guided tour of coding from inside of the File and examining the work you have done. As you continue to work with data, however, you will occasionally want to open a Node instead of a File, in order to see things from a different perspective while asking yourself some of the following questions:

- What was said before or after this Reference?
- What if I want to code this same Reference somewhere else?
- Is this Node too general or too specific?
- Has my understanding of this concept shifted?
- Did I code too much or too little context?
- How do I uncode some or all of a Reference while I review a Node?
- To what other Nodes is this data coded?

Some of the tools we will now explore are similar to the ones you used in the File and some of them are new.

━━━━━━━ **3.c.** ━━━━━━━

Expanding Coding Context

⇒ *List View*: **Double-click** on one of your **Nodes** so it opens > **Highlight** a portion of a Reference (or multiple references) **Right-click** > **Coding Context** > **Narrow** (to get 5 words on either side as in Figure 3.10).
    o   **Broad** provides the context of the entire paragraph.
    o   **Custom** allows you to choose a number of words on either side.
⇒ On your keyboard select **Ctrl** / **Cmd** + **A** to select all of the References and then expand the Coding Context of all simultaneously by following the steps above.
⇒ Mac users might need to go to the bottom of the *Detail View* and drag up to select everything.

⇒ If seeing it as temporary context is insufficient and you want to retain some or all of the context around the coded portion, then select and code text in your usual way (e.g., drag-and-drop the additional context into the Node). It will show as coded text in the Node next time you open it.

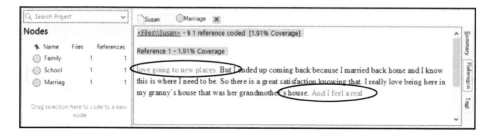

Figure 3.10   Viewing narrow coding context in a Node

Coding from a Node to another Node

⇒ *Detail View*: Select the text in a **Node** > Drag it to the *List View* to another **Node**.

  o   This does not uncode the data, it simply adds more coding to the File in the Project.

Coding Stripes in a Node

⇒ *Detail View*: Click on one of the **References** (so NVivo knows you are in this window).

⇒ *Ribbon*: **Node** / **View** > **Coding Stripes** > **Most Coding** / **Nodes Most Coding** (Figure 3.11).

Figure 3.11   Viewing Coding Stripes in a Node

Highlight in a Node

⇒ **Single-click** (not twice) on any Coding Stripe to turn on Highlighting for that other Node.

⇒ To turn the Highlight off go to the *Ribbon*: **Node** / **View** > **Highlight** > **None**.

(Continued)

(Continued)

Uncoding from the Node

⇒ *Detail View*: Select text in the **Node** to be uncoded (code the text where it belongs before you uncode it, because it is about to disappear from the screen) > **Right-click > Uncode from This Node > OK / Uncode Selection > At This Node**.

⇒ As an alternative use **Uncode / Uncode Selection > At Existing Nodes or Cases >** tick the desired boxes > **OK / Select**.

View the context in the File

⇒ To see the data in its full, original context, **Right-click** on a **Reference > Open Referenced File** (Figure 3.12).

⇒ Turn Highlight off in the *Ribbon*: **File / View > Highlight > None**.

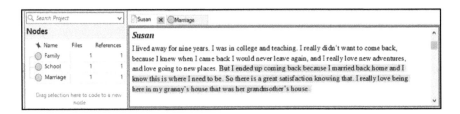

Figure 3.12 Jumping from a Reference in a Node to the File

We began this basic, guided tour in one of your Files, where we showed you how to create Nodes, code, and visualize your coding with Coding Stripes and Highlight. Then we turned to one of your Nodes to play with similar tools for coding, uncoding, and visualizing your work. We just ended back where we started, in one of the Files. You can now repeat the steps until you feel familiar with the basic tactics, explore some of the alternative ways to accomplish the same outcomes that we describe next or skip to the subsequent section on Miscellaneous Node management.

Alternative tactics for creating Nodes, Coding, and Uncoding

As with most software, many keyboard shortcuts are provided as alternatives to working with the *Ribbon* or a Right-click. You will find these while you work by noticing the additional symbols next to the names of the actions. For instance, instead of going to the *Ribbon:* **Home > Copy** / *Menu bar:* **Edit > Copy**, you can use **Ctrl / Cmd + C** (Figure 3.13).

A comprehensive list of keyboard shortcuts can be found in the NVivo Help files.

NVivo also provides other options in addition to keyboard shortcuts that you might prefer because they seem easier to you or because they are especially helpful in particular circumstances. Examples include:

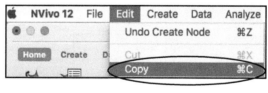

Figure 3.13   Shortcut keys to Copy in Windows (left) and Mac (right)

- The creation and naming of Nodes directly from participant speech (in vivo coding).
- Rapid review of a File to code additional text to a single Node that you recently added to your list of Nodes.
- Uncoding from multiple Nodes simultaneously.

These moves can be achieved by using the *Ribbon,* a **right-click** on selected text, or the Windows Quick Coding bar (Figure 3.14) or the Mac Coding Panel (Figure 3.15).

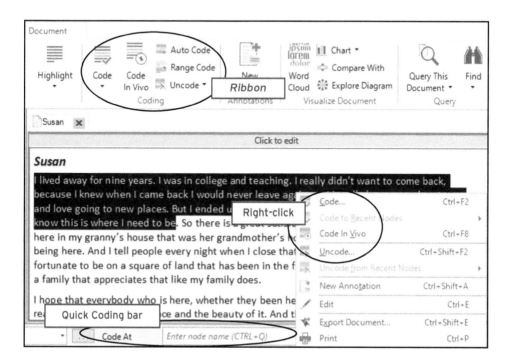

Figure 3.14   Coding and uncoding alternatives: *Ribbon,* right-click, Quick Coding bar (Windows)

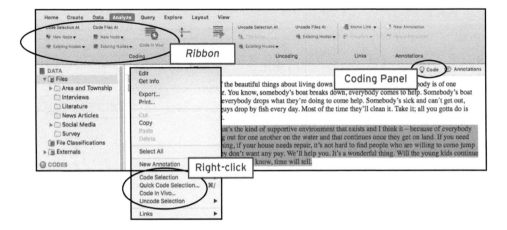

Figure 3.15 Coding and uncoding alternatives: *Ribbon*, right-click, Coding Panel (Mac)

Figure 3.14 and 3.15 might be sufficient for you to explore the options, but if you would like additional details about using these alternative tactics for coding and uncoding, see the online resources (https://study.sagepub.com/jackson3e) to view the 'Coding and uncoding alternatives' for Windows and Mac.

Miscellaneous Node management

The bottom line about your Nodes and coding is that you are never stuck with a prior decision; this includes the ability to rename, uncode, recode, change the Node Description, adjust the Node colour, etc. In addition, there are a few additional tactics for managing your Nodes that you will want to understand before we describe some of the more complex aspects of managing your Node structure in Chapter 4. These tactics are deleting Nodes, merging two or more Nodes together, and customizing your Node list.

3.d.

Moving, Deleting, and Merging Nodes

Moving Nodes

⇒ *List View*: Select the Node to move > Drag it to the destination (e.g., under another Node, creating 'parent' and 'child' Nodes. See Chapter 4, pp. 118–121).

   o To move the Node to the top level of Nodes: **Drag** the Node to the *Navigation View*: **Nodes**.

Deleting Nodes

⇒ *Navigation View*: **Codes** > **Nodes**.

⇒ *List View*: Select the **Node** to remove from your Project > **Right-click** > **Delete** (or click **Delete** on your keyboard) > **Yes / Delete**. (This also deletes all coding for that Node.)

Merging Nodes

⇒ *Navigation View*: **Codes** > **Nodes**.
⇒ *List View*: Select a **Node** > **Right-click** > **Cut / Copy** > select the other **Node** > **Right-click** > **Merge into Selected Node** > **OK / Merge** (Figure 3.16).
⇒ *List View*: **Right-click** *on original Node* > **Delete** > **Delete**.

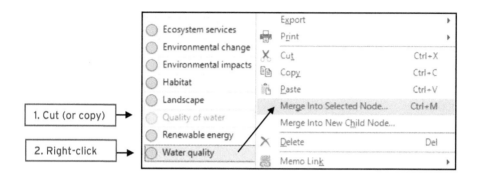

Figure 3.16 Merging Nodes

Customizing your display and listing Nodes

You can customize the display in the *List View* to show or hide information such as the Description and how many Sources or References are coded to the Node. This list can be customized independently in each of two contexts: (1) when the *Detail View* is closed (resulting a much wider *List View*, which makes it more practical to see additional information); and (2) when the *Detail View* is open (resulting in a narrower *List View*). Furthermore, once you set this customization, you can export the displayed information into a text, Excel or pdf file for your own reference, to bring to a data meeting, or to use in a report/publication.

3.e.

Customize your display (Windows only)

⇒ If you have anything open in the *Detail View*, close all items by clicking the **X** in each tab (or on any tab **Right-click** > **Close All**).
⇒ *List View*: **Single-click** on any **Node** (not twice, or it will open). This ensures your cursor is active in the *List View*.
⇒ *Ribbon*: **Home** > **List View icon** (in the **Workspace group** on the right side of the Ribbon) > **Customize**.
⇒ Use the arrows to move items left or right between **Available columns** and **Selected columns** to suit your preferences (Figure 3.17).

  o We recommend that you begin with **Description**, **Files**, and **References** in the **Selected Columns** window.

(Continued)

(Continued)

⇒ Use the **arrows** on the right to rearrange the order of these items.

⇒ **OK.**

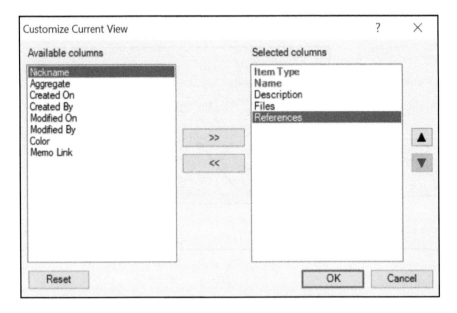

Figure 3.17 Window to Customize Current View in the *List View*

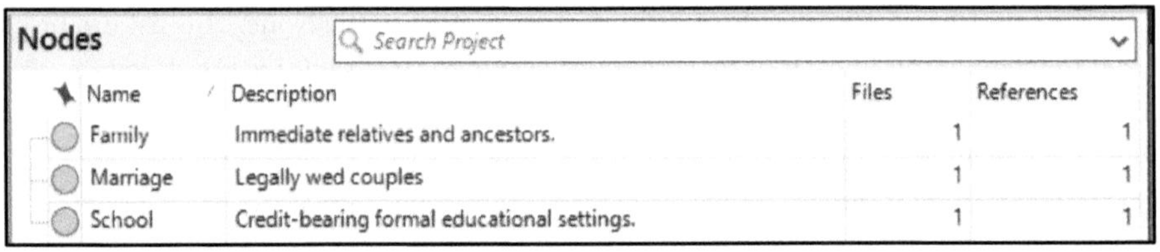

Figure 3.18 Customized Node *List View*

To customize the narrower list that appears in *List View* when items are open in the *Detail View*, simply click on any Node in the *List View* and follow the same steps to customize the view. Here we recommend not having any additional data showing.

How many Nodes should I create?

There is no set standard on 'too many' or 'too few' Nodes. The Nodes should help you generate, organize, and reconsider the concepts in your data. Having too many or too few can prevent this and you should use your judgement (and guidance from experienced qualitative researchers) to help you land on the sweet spot about the number of Nodes in your system, given your research design.

Is it Node worthy?

New Nodes proliferate early in the project, but as you work through further documents, you are more likely to add coding to existing Nodes. If you keep making a new Node for each passage, then it might be time to rethink. Very specific categories tend to be of little value for analysis. Check after a few documents to identify those Nodes that code only one passage.

3.f.

⇒   *Navigation View:* **Codes** > **Nodes**.
⇒   *Ribbon:* **View** > *Detail View* > **At Bottom.**

Then challenge each of these with Lyn Richards' question 'Why am I interested in that?' to identify a broader concept or purpose for this Node. The discipline of writing a Description for each Node in the Node Properties dialogue can also help sort out what they are about, and which you should keep, delete, or modify (*List View:* **Right-click** on a Node > **Node Properties** / **Get Info**).

Do I code the question?

When a conversation is being held about a particular topic, there is often an exchange between the participant and the interviewer while on the same topic area, such that you will want to code more than one paragraph or speaking turn. When you do so, include the interviewer's intervening text as well as the participant's text, for methodological and practical reasons:

- It is helpful to know how the interviewer was prompting or responding to what the participant was saying.
- Every time the coded passage is broken by a non-coded interviewer's turn, then the parts will be displayed as separate References and will consequently break up the text when the node is being reviewed.

Where the passage you are coding is not interrupted by the interviewer you might not need to include the question – unless it is needed to understand the participant's response (e.g., when interviewing someone who can't say more than 'yeah' or 'nah').

How much surrounding context should I select?

Coding can be applied to a word, phrase, sentence, paragraph, long passage, or a whole document. The length of the passage to be coded (which turns it into a Reference) is dependent on context and analytic purpose. You need to include a sufficient length of passage for the coded segment to make sense when you retrieve it, but at the same time, avoid coding long, drawn-out, vaguely relevant passages that are going to clutter your reading when you review the text at the Node. This is about balancing specificity and context. It helps, too, to have a basic understanding of how the reporting and Query functions of the software work (see Chapter 7 for an overview of these). As a general guideline, we advise that you tend to over-code for context rather than under-code for context. Coding very short segments could:

- make the retrievals hard to interpret, because they are too disconnected from the original context;
- increase the time it takes to code because so many more passages are chosen during the process;
- limit the utility of Queries, particularly those that are looking for intersecting content in a File.
- If you want to find whether concepts such as *Financial resources*, *Material resources*, or *Emotional resources* (for instance) are used to manage challenges like *Language barriers*, *Transportation access*, and *Peer group upheaval* (for instance) then be sure to code the passage at the resource AND at the challenge. This will allow you to use a Matrix Coding Query (Chapter 6, pp. 186–189; Chapter 7, pp. 208–209) to discover patterns of association between resources and challenges (Table 3.1). In addition to counting the intersecting data, you can also access the qualitative material by double-clicking on the cell.

Table 3.1 Simulation of Matrix Coding Query output

	Financial resources	Material resources	Emotional resources
Language barriers	45	18	22
Transportation access	55	33	12
Peer group upheaval	52	12	67

Printing and exporting Node lists and Codebooks

Periodically, you will want to move data or other information about the Project into another file, such as a report or a dissertation. At this juncture, your list of Nodes, their Descriptions and the number of Files and References would be helpful to print, export, or generate as an NVivo formatted Codebook. These three options provide a slightly different output, so experiment with them (and with the *Detail View* open as well as closed). Remember that if you want to create a list of your Nodes with descriptions (Figure 3.18), customize your *List View* to include Descriptions (Windows only).

━━━━ **3.g.** ━━━━

Print, Export as a list, or Export as a Codebook

Print

⇒ *List View*: Select a **Node**.

 o *Ribbon:* **Share** > **Print List.**
 o *Menu bar:* **File** > **Print List**.

Export

⇒ *List View*: Select a **Node**.

 o *Ribbon:* **Share** > **Export.**
 o *Ribbon:* **Data** > **Export List.**

⇒ Choose a location, provide a Name, and file type for your export > **Save / OK**.

Codebook

⇒ *Ribbon*: **Share** > **Export Codebook** / **Data** > **Codebook** > **Select**
⇒ Choose a location, provide a Name, and File type / format for your export > **Save / OK**.

Moving on

After working your way through a few Files, you will have built up quite a list of Nodes. In the next chapter, we start by thinking about how these might be organized to better reflect the structure of your data, and to make your coding system and the coding process more manageable. In the meantime, you might consider visualizing the coding you have applied to a Node or a File. There are several ways to accomplish this, but we provide one of each for you. You might also consider running a Coding Query to examine File contents where two Nodes intersect.

Visualizing your coding with a Node Chart

━━━━ **3.h.** ━━━━

Generating a Node Chart

You can instantly produce a chart that represents the Files coded to a Node (see example in Figure 3.19).

⇒ *Navigation View*: **Codes** > **Nodes**.
⇒ *List View*: **Select** any Node that is coded by multiple Files.

(Continued)

(Continued)

    ⇒ **Right-click** > **Visualize** > **Chart Node Coding** / **Chart Selected Node**.
    ⇒ *Ribbon* / **Data Tab and Format tab**
       o See additional options to change axes, values, labels, etc.

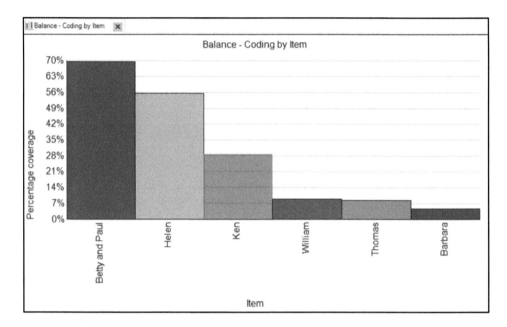

Figure 3.19 Node Chart of Files coded to *Balance* based on the percentage coverage

Visualizing your coding with a Comparison Diagram

Comparison Diagrams help you examine the way two items in the Project have shared and/ or unique connections with other items in the Project.

Farmers who adopted two strategies or only one

Philip Thomas, in a study for the Cooperative Research Centre for Sheep Industry Innovation at the University of New England in regional New South Wales, wanted to know if the farmers who adopted one kind of innovative animal husbandry practice also adopted another. Of the 48 farmers in the sample, 29 adopted the practice of scanning their ewes each season to detect those which were not pregnant, pregnant, or pregnant with multiples, so they could cull or regulate nutrition accordingly. Additionally, 22 were employing measures to reduce resistance to drenches used for worm control. Figure 3.20 shows the kind of display that can be generated from his data, to assist in answering his question about adoption of innovation.

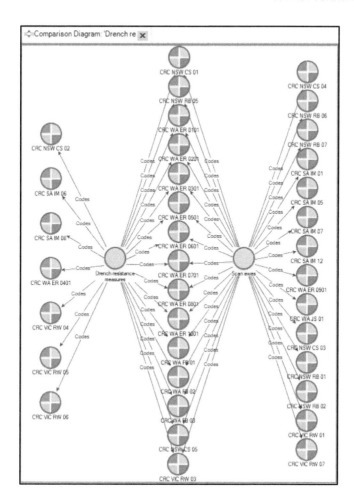

Figure 3.20 Comparison diagram showing which farmers adopted one or other or both innovative practices

3.i.

Generating a Comparison Diagram

You can generate a Comparison Diagram on the Files coded to one or more of your Nodes.

Create a Comparison Diagram

⇒ *Navigation View*: **Codes** > **Nodes**.
⇒ *List View*: **Control-click / Cmd-click** to select the two Nodes to be compared **Right-click** > **Visualize** > **Compare / Compare Selected Items.**
⇒ OR: Select one Node > **Right-click** > **Visualize** > **Compare With ...**
⇒ *Ribbon*: **Comparison Diagram / Display Tab >** Use checkboxes to modify what is included in the diagram, e.g., you are unlikely to want both Files and Cases showing.
⇒ *Detail View*: **Right-click** > **Properties / Get Info** on any item in the diagram to see its Properties.

If you have not already, you might also find it helpful to write a brief case vignette or a summary of what you learned from the File about the main issues of interest in your study in the linked Memo, potentially also using See Also Links (Chapter 1, pp. 30–33). You can also right-click anywhere in the Chart or Comparison Diagram, copy, and then paste it into your linked Memo.

Coding Query

You will learn more about the Coding Query in Chapter 7 (pp. 209–210) but for now you should experiment with a simple example of the intersection of two Nodes. Before running this Query, you might check that you know you have at least one intersecting Reference in the two Nodes.

▬▬▬ 3.j. ▬▬▬

Using the Highlight to check for intersecting content

⇒ *Navigation View*: **Codes** > **Nodes**.
⇒ *List View*: **Double-click** on the first Node to open it.
⇒ *Ribbon*: **Node / View** > **Highlight** > **Coding for Selected Items** > **tick the box** next to the second Node > **OK / Select**.

Yellow highlight indicates content coded at both Nodes. When you run the Coding Query, you will see the same content.

Figure 3.21 Coding Query in the *Environmental Change* Project on the Nodes *Community change* and *Economy*

Running a Coding Query

⇒ *Ribbon*: **Explore** / **Query** > **Coding**.
⇒ Select the '...' next to **All Selected Nodes or Cases** (Figure 3.21) / Select the arrow next to **all of these nodes** > use the left side of the window to click once on the word **Nodes** (not the tick box) > use the right side of the window to **tick the box** next to each of the two Nodes > **OK** / **Select**.
⇒ **Run Query** > the bottom half of the window displays the intersecting content.

For additional information about the options in this Query, see Chapter 7 (pp. 209–210).

SECTION 3.4: CHAPTER 3 TAKEAWAYS

■■■■■ Key points from this chapter ■■■■■

o Coding is an inherently flexible process and highly dependent on the context, research questions, methodologies, and types of data engaged in the process.

o You can change every decision you make about your coding in NVivo (Node names, descriptions, locations in the hierarchy, coded references, colours, etc.)

o A Node is simply a pointer or a link to the File. The only thing in a Node is a command that says, 'go get it!' When you code you establish these pointers and when you delete you dissolve these pointers.

o You will likely need to move beyond simple, descriptive coding to generate interesting interpretations from the data. Play around with the many strategies for constructing meaning through coding. Remember to challenge your initial interpretations of the data and take alternative views before drawing conclusions.

o Write, write, write. Use your Memos and See Also Links.

Tips, challenges, and warnings

Nodes and Coding

• If this is your first time coding, you will benefit from reading more detailed literature about the process from various perspectives and/or getting guidance from an expert.

• When you are struggling with conceptualization (and if you aren't part of a team project), connect with a group of other researchers undertaking qualitative work – the discipline area is irrelevant – and meet with them on an occasional basis. Each takes a turn to bring a short sample of data (maximum one page, de-identified) as the basis for discussion in that session.

- Spending too much time calculating how long it will take you to code or watching the scroll bar while you code to see how much is left might mean you are focusing more on time and mechanics than data.
- Chaos may reign periodically. You might occasionally need to force yourself to stop and rethink things and this can be done inside or outside of the software.
- If you are new to coding, you will feel a strong need to create the 'right' Nodes. There is no one, right approach and you might struggle to find the internal logic that makes the most sense to you as a researcher in this context (look to your theory and methods for guidance; seek advice from an experienced qualitative researcher).
- Keep Files in 'read only' mode while coding, or you might accidentally rearrange the text.
- By default, NVivo codes the entire word, so you do not need to precisely grab the first and last character of a Reference (you can change this default in the application options).
- Triple-click to quickly select an entire paragraph for coding.
- If you find you want to add further coding on either side of the passage you just coded, select overlapping text to ensure the passages connect and are combined as one passage. Text coded more than once with the same Node will show up only once, because the Node is simply pointing to the text (and that text is unique in the transcript).

Visualizing with Coding Stripes and Highlighting

- If you tend to jump around in the document while you code, turn on Highlighting for all of your conceptual/thematic Nodes to easily see what you have already coded.
- Quickly find where you left off the last time you were coding by turning on Coding Stripes for Nodes Recently Coding.
- Turn on Coding Stripes within a Node to see what else is going on to help you think.

Tracking and writing

- The description field of your Nodes is one place to write. While the goal is to end up with concise descriptions, you can add brief quotes or examples to the descriptions as long as you keep within the limit of 512 characters, including spaces.
- If you want to track the way your Nodes and Node Descriptions change over time, do so in a Memo. You can also create backup copies at key junctures to see Node structures and descriptions from prior phases.
- Use Annotations to track ideas as you code a document and then decide what to write up more formally in a Memo when you are done coding that document.
- If you are flooded with ideas while you code and fear you will have hundreds of Nodes, start by using Memos and See Also Links. Wait until you know which concepts are 'node worthy' (Richards, 2009).

Videos and online resources (https://study.sagepub.com/jackson3e)

Videos

- 'Coding and uncoding alternatives' (Windows, Mac)

Help files

- *File*: Help.
- *Menu bar*: **Help > NVivo Help.**

Search for any of the following:

- Charts
- Code files and manage codes
- Coding
- Comparison diagrams
- Export nodes
- Reorder and organize nodes
- Use coding stripes to explore coding

Practice questions

1   Select a 3–5 page section of one of your transcripts and then choose four of the eight strategies we suggest for identifying and naming nodes (p. 72). Code the pages from beginning to end using strategy 1; then again for strategy 2, etc. Write a Memo in your Project about how these strategies help you see different (or similar) things in the data and how they help you identify/create different (or similar) Nodes. Which of them might be most appropriate and fruitful as you continue coding?

2   Do you think you are more of a 'splitter' or a 'lumper' when it comes to coding? Why? How do you think this will be reflected in your use of Nodes?

3   Write a reflexive journal/Memo in NVivo about how it felt to do your first round of coding in NVivo (whether you have experience analysing qualitative data or not). What did you like? What was annoying? In what ways might NVivo facilitate your analysis? In what ways might it get in the way?

4

Section 4.1: Introduction to advanced coding   102

Section 4.2: Conceptual grounding in advanced coding   103

Section 4.3: Advanced coding with NVivo   113

Section 4.4: Chapter 4 Takeaways   130

ADVANCED CODING

It is impossible to conduct any kind of research without using some form of categorizing. Just the act of selecting a topic, recruiting participants, and deciding on relevant concepts involves categorizing. (Freeman, 2017: 25)

SECTION 4.1: INTRODUCTION TO ADVANCED CODING

After familiarizing yourself with the basics of coding and perhaps working through a few Files, three additional features in NVivo might become relevant for you. The first is the management of Node hierarchies into branches, because a long list of Nodes can be unruly without this structure. You will sometimes find that conceptually related Nodes are scattered in your list or that Nodes which initially seemed distinct need to be combined into one. Several choices are available to handle these moves with some implications for using Queries later. A second advanced move, of a different kind, pertains to use of the Auto Code tool which can do part of the work to help you organize data and look for patterns. This tool sometimes relies on the format of your Files (which we introduced in Chapter 2 and will expand on in this chapter). Finally, you might be interested in the Queries that help you look for words or phrases, which offer far more options than the simple "Find" feature you know from word processing programs.

In this chapter you will

- Learn strategies for managing your Node structure.
- Discover the merits of some of the common hierarchical structures.
- Experiment with tactics you can use to revisit and revise your coding structure as things progress.
- Understand the difference between Merging and Aggregating Nodes.
- Learn about the problems associated with 'viral' coding structures and how to avoid them with 'vista' structures. You will also see how vista structures can facilitate the use of the Matrix Coding Query.
- Consider the merits and limitations of the Auto Coder.
- Play with the Word Frequency Query and the Text Search Query as a way of examining your data.

Other chapters with related materials

Chapter 3: Coding foundations

In this chapter you learn the basic skills of creating Nodes, coding, uncoding, and starting to look at visualizations such as Coding Stripes, Highlight, Charts, and Comparison Diagrams.

You will also find information here on customizing your Node list and exporting or printing your Node list and your Codebook.

Chapter 8: Literature reviews and pdf Files

Importing and coding pdf Files is similar to coding Word documents such as transcripts and focus groups. In addition, the Region Selection tool allows you to select and code portions of images in the pdf Files, such as charts, graphs, and figures.

Chapter 9: Working with multimedia Files

Pictures, audio, and video can add a rich aspect to your research, although there are also potential disadvantages you should consider. In addition to the ability to transcribe or write notes about this media, you can code and then export it as an html File. Most of the things you learn about managing Nodes in Chapters 3 and 4 hold true for these media, with a few new tactics to practise and consider.

Chapter 10: Twitter, Facebook, YouTube, and web pages

Social media data presents interesting, new opportunities, and you will use the memoing, linking, and coding tactics you learned in Chapters 3 and 4.

SECTION 4.2: CONCEPTUAL GROUNDING IN ADVANCED CODING

Revisiting your Nodes

You see your data differently through Nodes; as noted in Chapter 3, data in Nodes are recontextualized in terms of the concept rather than the case (Richards, 2009). As you move more deeply into your data, do not be surprised if you find yourself spending as much time in your Nodes and thinking about Nodes as you spend in Files. Indeed, one of the signs of a maturing Project is that the ideas being generated from your Files become more important than the Files themselves. In viewing your data through Nodes, you will become aware of repeated ideas that are central to the experiences, events, and stories people tell (Coffey & Atkinson, 1996). You will see data linked by concepts and associations – and you will note discrepancies and misfits. You will find you want to reshape your Node Descriptions, explore alternative Nodes where References might be more appropriately coded and to consider grouping Nodes in hierarchies.

Some Nodes are easy to see as part of a larger taxonomy (the *Amusement park*, the *School*, and the *Swimming pool* are several possible locations), and others are instances of a more general concept (*Conflict, Trust,* and *Dependence* are types of interpersonal issues). It is natural to categorize and organize objects so that the category at the top of a hierarchy describes, in general terms, the items below. In NVivo, Nodes can be structured in a branching hierarchical system with categories, subcategories, and sub-subcategories. So, just as folders and subfolders in your computer filing system help you to organize your Files, Nodes in hierarchies will allow you to organize conceptual groups and subgroups.

Think about how a department store organizes its online catalogue. There will be major sections dealing with clothing, kitchen, linen, entertainment, and so on. But you can also look for items based on colour or size. Furthermore, you will find some unique items and some items in common when you browse by colour or size. A coding system that reflects this arrangement might look as shown in Figure 4.1. The shopper, after scanning the various sections, could then put together a coordinated outfit that comprises shirt, pants, jacket, and shoes in matching colours. Putting together the outfit is more like making theoretical connections between the Nodes: these things go together to build a larger concept, they occur together, or they impact on each other in some way. These kinds of connections will be shown in another way (usually through your Memos and Query Results).

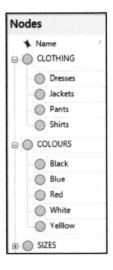

Figure 4.1   The online catalogue hierarchy

Hierarchical, branching systems are often the subject of debate and open to revision, but the principles on which you build your system should be consistent, just like your filing system on your computer. Researchers coming to the same data from different perspectives or with different questions will almost certainly create differently labelled and organized coding systems. Furthermore, the structure for your Nodes will evolve over time, particularly when you engage in a period of review to check the consistency and salience of each one and revisit your research questions. Nevertheless, most Nodes will find a place with other concepts of that type; there will be a logical fit.

Why bother sorting Nodes into hierarchies?

Using hierarchies to create a structured organizing system for concepts brings a number of benefits:

- *Organization:* The hierarchies help create order out of randomness or chaos. The logic of the system means you can find existing Nodes and you can determine where to put new Nodes.
- *Conceptual clarity:* Organizing Nodes helps to give meaning to them; sorting them into hierarchies prompts you to clarify your ideas, to identify common properties, see missing categories, and sort out categories that overlap. And you clearly see what kinds of things your project is dealing with – the structure of your data. The coding system, when established, will 'tell' your project (Richards, 2009). Indeed, when someone approaches Pat for assistance with a project, there are just two things she asks them to send ahead: their research question(s) and a list of Nodes.
- *Prompt to code richly:* Well-organized hierarchies provide a useful tool for ensuring the thoroughness of your coding as you progress. You stop to code a passage because an interesting issue is raised in the data. Capture that, but before you leave the passage, run an eye over your coding structure as a quick visual prompt to see if there are other Nodes that are relevant. Should you also code for the context, who the key players are, or how people felt or otherwise responded? Do you need reminding to always code the outcome? Coding at Nodes across all relevant hierarchies will allow for more effective and more complete answers to Queries later.
- *Identifying patterns:* Identifying patterns of association between groups of Nodes can make a significant contribution to an emergent analysis. If all *Emotions* (e.g., *Joy, Sorrow, Gratitude, Anticipation*) are organized together and all *Events* (e.g., *Recitals, Birthday parties, Weddings, Vacations*) are in another hierarchy, it becomes a simple matter to set up a Query to identify the overall pattern of the *Emotions* that are associated with types of *Events*.

Building your coding structure

To create some conceptual order in your coding system we have some tips about thinking through your Nodes (we later provide instructions about how to implement them in the Project; for now, you can think through all of these without using NVivo).

- Start with a thinking-sorting process, to decide how the Nodes might be arranged. When you ask yourself why you are interested in a particular category or concept (abstracting), ask yourself also what sort of thing this concept is about – what group it belongs to. Work through each of your Nodes in this way, making organized lists of things (if you are struggling to do this, look for ideas in the later subsection on *Kinds of hierarchies*); alternatively, revisit our suggestions in Chapter 3.
- Create a Map which holds each of your Nodes, so that you can push them around to help sort them into groups of similar things.

- Describe your project to someone. Both the telling and the discussion will help you work out the salient issues and potential branches.
- Focus on what might be top-level Nodes. You may already have some which represent broad categories (e.g., *Emotions, Events, Environmental issues*) that will remain as top-level Nodes. Others will need to be created especially for the purpose of providing a structure, rather like coat hangers for others to hang from – the way *Clothing, Colours,* and *Sizes* are in Figure 4.1.
- As you find yourself honing in on a structure, check that it serves the main ideas you set out with, and the research questions you want to answer. If part of the structure does not fit, ask whether you need to modify the structure, or your original purpose and questions.

Experience teaches that projects typically do not have more than about ten hierarchies, and that hierarchical structures usually do not go more than two or three layers deep; it is difficult to subcategorize much more than that without starting to confuse what class of thing you are dealing with. There may be a large variation in the number of Nodes within a hierarchy, although if you get too many (say, 30+) at a single level in a hierarchy, it could be time to group them into further levels or to see if some of them could be combined. Regard your coding structure as a work in progress and keep in mind that some approaches to the entire study (e.g., evaluation research) are likely to direct you to a hierarchical structure (or parts of it) much earlier in the process than others (e.g., phenomenology).

Kinds of hierarchies

It is sometimes surprising to new researchers that it is possible, ahead of time, to predict some of the hierarchies you will use in your study. For research projects that deal with the lives and interactions of people, this is broadly possible because the kinds of labels that most appropriately become top-level Nodes are typically quite general. It is extremely unlikely that all of our suggestions are going to turn up in one project. We offer them to help nudge your thinking and to remind you that by coding a passage to multiple Nodes, you can cross reference them later. Keep in mind that if any of these apply to entire Cases in your study, they could be used, instead, as Attribute Values for the Case, rather than Nodes (see Chapters 2 and 5).

- Actions – things that are done at a point in time (e.g., *Argue, Cheer, Laugh, Listen*).
- Activities – ongoing actions (e.g., *Aging, Learning, Raising children, Supervising*).
- Beliefs, ideological positions, frameworks – intellectual positions (or discourses) which are evident in thinking and action (e.g., *Honesty, Independence, Reason, Spirituality*).
- Context – the settings in which actions, events, etc. occur (e.g., *Adolescence, Downtown, School, Work*).
- Culture – social behaviours and norms that are likely to have multiple sub-branches, depending on the type of culture (e.g., *Art, Careers, Kinship, Technology*).
- Emotions – feelings (e.g., *Anticipation, Gratitude, Joy, Sorrow*).

- Events – highly structured actions or rituals (e.g., *Birthday parties, Recitals, Weddings, Vacations*).
- Issues – matters raised about which there might be some debate (e.g., *Control, Ownership, Privacy, Transparency*).
- Narrative – such as the narrative features discussed in Chapter 3 (e.g., *Contradictions, Omissions, Pronouns, Repairs*).
- People (or actors or entities) that are referred to or talked about – the locus or target of a comment, either specifically (e.g., *Dr. Almos* or *My boss*) or generally (e.g., *Employees, Managers, Nurses, The industry*).
- Valences (also sometimes called sentiments or attitudes) – the participant's implicit or explicit response to a topic (e.g., a participant says or implies they are *Conflicted, Negative, Positive,* or *Uncertain* about an event or action; or identify it as a *Barrier* or *Facilitator* to success).
- Strategies – a purposeful activity to achieve a goal or deal with an issue (e.g., *Making amends, Negotiating, Planning, Raising money*).

As well as the types of Nodes suggested above, there are several other areas worth considering that pertain more to the tactics of managing the process:

- Good quotes – an area to store References that are especially compelling, poignant, or typical. These can be cross-referenced with your other Nodes with a Coding Query (see Chapter 3) to find the quotes that pertain to a particular concept or theme to assist you in writing up your findings (but be careful about cherry picking your findings just because of these quotes).
- Suggestions – to capture the recommendations provided by participants about how things could or should be done or changed.
- Retired Nodes – to store any defunct concepts or themes in case you are not fully convinced you want to delete them.

What all this points to is that you should experiment with and revise the coding system to suit your own purposes. Be creative. We have seen Nodes called *I don't believe this, Come back to this later,* and *Outliers.* Some researchers use the NVivo Maps to help think through the hierarchies. In Chapter 1, we showed you how to use a Mind Map to help you think about your Nodes. Later in this chapter we provide assistance in using the Concept Map to help you sort your Nodes into a hierarchy and a Project Map to view the hierarchies you created.

Healthy and unhealthy hierarchies

'Viral' coding systems

New researchers are often tempted to create duplicate sets of Nodes under multiple branches of the coding structure. An example would be the placement of *Valence* Nodes for *Positive, Negative, Neutral,* and *Conflicted* under each of the strategy Nodes for *Negotiation, Raising money, Planning* (Figure 4.2).

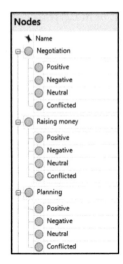

Figure 4.2 A viral coding structure

Many of us refer to such a structure as a 'viral' system because Nodes keep reproducing themselves like a virus. This is a metaphor intended to convey that such a structure can interfere with the health of your project. While the above example is fairly simple, you can see how a coding structure of 30 Nodes could instantly turn into a structure of 120, if each of them reproduced the *Valence* Nodes as subnodes. A viral structure such as this creates four main problems:

- Large structures are hard to navigate (to code, to identify items for Queries, and to review output).
- Locating all of the data coded as *Conflicted,* for instance, is no longer a simple matter of opening a single Node to review the material because it is scattered throughout the system.
- The use of some Queries will be more cumbersome because text is already divided in one particular way and could therefore require Merging groups of Nodes before some Queries can be performed.
- Once a viral structure starts, it can continue exponentially. Consider the possibility that after the *Valence* Nodes are created in the viral structure in Figure 4.2, the researcher might add, for example *Patients, Doctors,* and *Nurses* under each one, depending on the actor who is being discussed. Coding structure chaos will quickly ensue.

The solution to the viral structure is presented in Figure 4.3.

We refer to this solution as a 'vista' structure, using a metaphor that pulls from the experience of standing on the rim of a canyon. As visitors to the Grand Canyon in the United States discover, there are several viewing platforms with different vistas of the canyon. Think of your project as mounds of data that fill the canyon. When you conduct vista coding, you agree to take a stance at particular angles on multiple platforms and to look at the data from these angles and code accordingly. In the above example, the two main vistas are *Valence* and

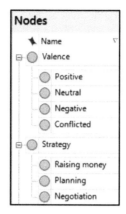

Figure 4.3 A vista coding structure

Strategy. Of course, your project could have more than two vistas, not every Node will neatly fit into a vista, and you must use caution when settling on vistas. But, as you begin solidifying your hierarchical structure, these vistas will begin doing considerable work for you. If someone discusses a *Positive* experience they had with *Planning*, the data would be coded at both Nodes.

In our discussion of the online catalogue (Figure 4.1), we also provided an example of a 'vista' structure. Later, NVivo's Queries (such as a Matrix Coding Query) can help you examine the intersections of these Nodes. For example, the following Matrix Coding Query (Figure 4.4) presents the intersections of all *Valence* Nodes by all *Strategy* Nodes. In addition to the counts in each cell, the researcher can double-click on a cell to access the text that expressed, for instance, *Positive* things about *Planning*. For detailed instructions on how to create a Matrix Coding Query, see Chapter 6, pp. 186–189 and Chapter 7, pp. 208–209.

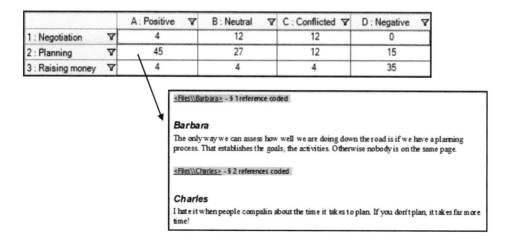

Figure 4.4 A Matrix Coding Query of *Strategies* by *Valence*

To elaborate, the use of vista coding resolves all four of the problems presented by a viral structure, because vista coding:

- tends toward parsimonious coding structures that are easy to navigate (to code, to identify items for Queries and to review output);
- enables the efficient access of data coded as *Negotiation,* for instance, because it is in one place;
- maximizes the utility of Queries that can expeditiously provide you with evidence of particular constellations of Nodes (e.g., there might be more *Positive* comments intersecting *Planning* than *Raising money*);
- Thwarts the development of viral structures (e.g., once the two vistas of *Valence* and *Strategy* are created, the researcher is likely to add separate hierarchies according to other vistas, such as the *Role* of the person being discussed or the *Culture* in which something occurs; the researcher might also become more aware of the possibility of other strategies being used and add child Nodes to that hierarchy).

There are two rules that help keep you from creating a viral coding system:

1 Each category or concept or theme (i.e., each Node) should appear in only one place in the coding system.
2 Keep Attribute data that apply to whole Cases (such as *Age* or *Ethnicity*) separate from the coding system (see Chapters 2 and 5).

You will find some sample coding systems (from real projects) in a resource file in the online resources (https://study.sagepub.com/jackson3e). These might provide you with further clarification or ideas. Additionally, if you already have a coding system which is in a tangle because of a repeating (viral) Node system, you will find suggestions about how to think through the mess. Later in this chapter we will also provide instructions on how to turn a viral structure into a vista structure.

Balancing act

As you continue working on your Node structure, you will discover that you are often trying to strike a balance between apparently opposing goals, as outlined below. However, these tensions can actually help support your successful journey through the analytical process; managing the balance between them is the key.

Flexibility and stability

It is very easy to become beguiled by a thread of thinking late in the process and wish you had developed it sooner. At the same time, to set the parameters early in the project regarding what is relevant (and limit change thereafter) is deadening. Therefore, one endeavour is to balance flexibility in coding with purposefulness and consistency. We have three main tips for handling this balance. The first two will help you modify the concept over time while keeping you focused on your current understanding:

- Use the description field in the Node properties dialogue to record what a Node is about, including perhaps a record of how the concept was developed.
- If the history or evolution of your thinking on a hierarchical structure is significant, record its development in a linked Memo (see Chapter 1, pp. 29–30).
- Discuss your coding system with others who are interested in the topic to test or brainstorm your options.

Comprehensiveness and simplicity

Coding also involves balancing between completeness (which, when it runs awry, becomes clutter) and parsimony (which can result in barely enough coded data to facilitate analysis). This balance can occur either at the Node structure level (having too many or too few Nodes) or at the Reference level (coding too much or coding too little context). Navigating this balance will become more comfortable as the project progresses and coding becomes more strategic. Two main tips will assist you in pursuing this balance:

- Ask yourself if your individual Nodes have clear Descriptions. A few Nodes that seem imprecise is not a problem and they might turn into interesting concepts later. But, this should be the exception rather than the rule. Consider combining some Nodes to simplify the overall structure and splitting others apart to add clarity to a large volume of data in a single Node.
- When in doubt, code too much context rather than too little. You can always uncode superfluous information later but if you fail to include important information you might omit it from your analysis. Ongoing review of already coded material will facilitate the right balance.

Closeness and distance with coded data

Sometimes, to understand circumstances, you need to move in close. Friends describe how hard and wonderful it is to be a new parent, how beneficial it is to meditate, or how horrible the latest influenza virus feels. You nod and smile, getting a general picture, but your knowledge pales in comparison to your deep understanding when you have children, begin meditating, or catch this year's virus. On the other hand, there are times when we simply cannot fully reflect on a situation until we have distance. When observing the activities of others, it can be easier to see their bad relationship decisions than to see our own. Or, we might have a colleague who brings amazing skills to a work setting that we can see as a distanced observer, while this colleague continues to ignore the merits of her own abilities. Sometimes we understand things better by getting a close view, and sometimes we benefit from stepping back. Knowing when to move from one to the other is one of the key skills in life and you will need to apply this to your coding, too.

One way of thinking about closeness with your data in NVivo is to carefully examine the stories of one of your participants to make sure you are focusing on his or her perceptions and experiences; you could code and recode this data and write reflective Memos. One way of thinking about distance is to alternate this close inspection with a broader view that considers the combined data from multiple participants or even the general volume of data in a Node rather than the experiences of one participant. In this regard, navigating your analysis means moving back and forth between closeness and distance to obtain different angles on the data. Such movement takes experimentation and practice; a common mistake to avoid is to simply plod through a single activity, such as coding, just to be done with it. We have three suggestions to keep you from getting stuck in a position that is too close or too distant:

- Open the two transcripts you feel least familiar with and read them (while listening to the audio recording, if available). Take detailed notes in a Memo about the experiences that are described.
- Conduct two sorting activities of your data by volume to get a different look (e.g., the transcripts that have been coded to the most Nodes versus those that have been coded to the least; the Nodes with the most coding in them versus those that have the least).
- Open a Node with Coding Stripes turned on for Most Coding (Chapter 3, p. 85). This allows you to see where this Node connects or appears independently. Should those independent References be coded elsewhere as well? Write a Memo about what you have learned about this Node.

Automatic Coding

Although NVivo was designed with an emphasis on the researcher's desire to carefully examine all of the data, a significant amount of what any researcher does is routine work on tasks which are occasionally boring but also essential to the overall project. Fortunately for researchers and for the progress of research, technology has come to our aid and machines have taken over some of the drudgery. This gives more time to concentrate on less mechanical, more interpretive work. In NVivo, we recommend you consider two advanced tools designed to assist with these administrative tasks:

- Auto Code (by speaker, question, or other structural feature in the Files).
- Text-mining Queries (Word Frequency and Text Search).

NVivo Plus users might also want to experiment with three Auto Code features that will automatically code for you more conceptually, although we advise a very high degree of caution in the use of these tools and only mention them briefly, here:

- Identify Sentiment (with predefined Nodes for *Very positive, Moderately positive, Moderately negative, Very negative*).
- Identify Theme (a text analytics algorithm that uses noun phrases such as *Family celebrations* to generate and group Nodes).

- Use Existing Coding Patterns (an experimental feature that uses your existing coding to speed up the coding process for large volumes of additional text material).

The NVivo Help states that researchers should review the material coded via these three Auto Code options and we recommend you approach all of them as experimental. They can be helpful to get started with coding a large volume. Alternatively, they can be used after you have coded to check whether you have missed anything. To date, we have found them only moderately useful in unique circumstances (primarily in large projects with short responses). An example of a testimonial of successful use of Auto Coding by sentiment and theme is a project conducted by Steve Wright: https://www.qsrinternational.com/nvivo/enabling-research/research-powered-by-nvivo/analysing-large-survey-data-using-automated-insigh

SECTION 4.3: ADVANCED CODING WITH NVIVO

Having played with some ideas about organizing your Nodes into a hierarchical structure, it is now time to start moving Nodes around. Nodes can be moved, appended, combined and split as needed. As with most other tools in NVivo, the use of hierarchies is flexible. Your ongoing review of Nodes will assist you in determining whether you need to adjust your sampling strategies, the questions you are asking of your participants, other data you are generating, or perhaps your coding strategies or Node hierarchies.

NVivo terms used in this section

Aggregate

child Node

Merge

Node hierarchy

parent Node

Strategies for reviewing Nodes

Seeing the whole (Nodes in overview)

As your Node list develops, pause to consider the following:

- Does the range of Nodes you created so far reflect the focus and range of questions your project is designed to answer?
- Are the categories and concepts embedded in your questions represented by Nodes?

- Which Nodes are being used more or less extensively for coding?
- Are there Nodes that can be Merged or coded to more discrete subcategories to facilitate analysis?
- Is there any indication you need to modify your research questions or any other portion of your methodology that is independent of NVivo?

━━━━━━━━━━ **4.a.** ━━━━━━━━━━

Exporting an overview of your Nodes

Consider customizing your list of Nodes (Windows only) to include relevant information, such as the Descriptions (see the subsection in Chapter 3 on Customizing your display and listing Nodes). The next two options will generate output that matches your customization.

Exporting a list of Nodes

⇒ *List View:* **Select** a **Node.**
⇒ *Ribbon:* **Share / Data > Export List.**

Printing a list of Nodes

⇒ *List View:* **Select** a **Node.**
⇒ *Ribbon:* **Share /** *Menu bar:* **File > Print List.**

Exporting a Codebook

⇒ *List View:* **Select** a **Node.**
⇒ *Ribbon:* **Share / Data > Export Codebook.**

Code Summary Report (Windows only)

You can also list your Nodes with a summary of the volume of data for each type of File in your project.

⇒ *Navigation View:* **Output > Reports.**
⇒ *List View:* **Double-click** on **Code Summary Report** > to the left of **Field** tick the **box > Select >** tick **Nodes > OK > OK.**

Node lists provide a historical archive of the development of your Project. When you make a list of Nodes, therefore, store the output (with the date) for review when you are writing about your methodology. Even if you do not use some of these in writing up your methodology, you are likely to find them invaluable as a reminder about the development of your ideas as you worked toward your conclusions. If you wish, they can be exported as a Word or pdf document and imported into your project as a Memo for easy access and Annotating while you analyse the data.

Seeing the parts (Nodes in detail)

Viewing all the text stored at a Node changes your perspective on the data. It is an exciting process to see your concepts come alive! Sometimes you simply want to check what is there to ensure coding consistency, but it is really beneficial to take time out occasionally from coding to reflect on the implications of Node Names, Descriptions, and contents. You may find yourself surprised by what you find. This also lays a necessary foundation for using Queries later to answer some of your research questions. We caution against printing out (or saving a copy of) all the coded material at your Nodes for this task, because you might want to recode or reorganize during your review. Handling this material on paper (or as a digitally exported document) means you will be marking up the changes on paper, so you will then need to return to NVivo to make the changes on the screen. Usually you can review and adjust simultaneously, which is far more efficient, so try to stay in NVivo as you look through the detail of your Nodes.

- Open and read the data stored at particular Nodes, so you see the data in the context of the category, rather than the original File.
    - Of course, wherever necessary, you can gain immediate access to the original File, via the blue underlined Hyperlink associated with the name of the File (Figure 4.5). This allows you to see all the data coded to the Node in its original context, perhaps to explore if you coded too much or too little.

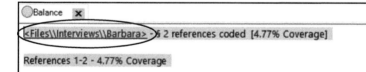

Figure 4.5 A Hyperlink to the File from the *Detail View* of the Node

- Refine the content of a Node. Think about whether you need more or less content or if this data should also be coded elsewhere.
    - Recode into other, relevant Nodes directly from the screen because you do not have to be in the File; you can code from one Node to another.
    - Uncode what is irrelevant.

--- **Adding additional categories when reviewing a Node** ---

In a study of children's self-management of asthma for her PhD at the University of New South Wales, Jacqueline Tudball had a Node for physical activity. In reviewing this Node, she found that children might use physical activity in order to stay fit and healthy and so prevent asthma attacks, or they might reduce *physical activity* as a way of managing asthma attacks when they occurred. This led her to develop two new Nodes (under *Focus*, labelled *Prevention* and *Management*). In addition to coding data to *Physical activity* (or other Nodes), she also coded whether the passage referred to *Prevention* or *Management*.

- Examine the other Nodes that are applied to the Node you are reviewing (use the Coding Stripes to do so, as detailed in Chapter 3, pp. 83–85) – and record the potential implications in the Node Memo or Project journal.
- When you complete your review, record or add to your Description for the Node (**Right-click > Node Properties / Get Info**). Note the boundaries – what is included, what is excluded – as well as typical examples.
  - o This can help you see repetitions and commonalities among Nodes.
  - o Seek to justify each Node, as a way of targeting Nodes for Merging, deleting or 'putting into storage'.

Memo Links to track your ideas about a Node

Whereas a Memo that is linked to a File (Chapter 1, pp. 21–22) stores background information and the ideas and thoughts generated by the particular document or Case, a Memo linked to a Node is likely to contain a record of more conceptual thinking. The Node Memo holds the 'story' of the category and will become invaluable in the analysis and writing-up phases of your project (Richards, 2009). For less important Nodes, you might just record those thoughts in the Project journal.

--- **4.b.** ---

Creating a Memo Link to a Node

⇒ *Navigation View*: Codes **> Nodes.**
⇒ *List View*: **Right-click** on a Node > **Memo Link > Link to New Memo.**
⇒ **Name** the Memo > **OK / Done.**
⇒ Date and time stamp your entry > **Ctrl / Cmd + Shift + T.**
⇒ Record your ideas about that Node in the Memo and come back to it any time to review and revisit your interpretations.

  - o *List View*: **Right-click** on the Node > **Memo Link > Open Linked Memo** (or **Ctrl / Cmd + Shift + M**).
  - o **Click to Edit** if you want to edit or augment your existing thoughts.

Using Maps to think about your coding structure

If you made your initial Nodes freely and without thinking too much about structure, then using a Concept Map to sort those Nodes into groups can assist the process of structuring. The visual display, the kinaesthetic activity of rearranging Nodes in the display as you explore alternatives, and the software feature that allows you to have only one copy of any Node in a Map all work together to help you see those that might belong in the same hierarchy, while avoiding duplication of Nodes in a viral structure. Figure 4.6 shows an in-progress arrangement of Nodes relating to people's descriptions of their experience when they felt they were part of a community.

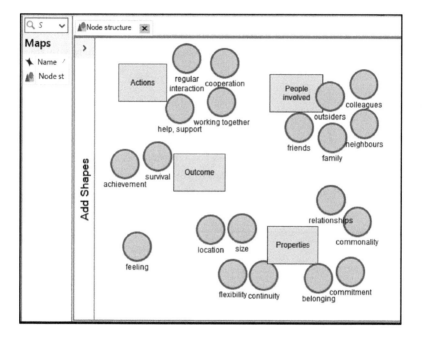

Figure 4.6 Sorting Nodes into hierarchies using a Concept Map

This arrangement, when reasonably complete, can be used as the basis for designing a hierarchical coding system. Unlike when working with a Mind Map, however, you cannot create a structure directly from the Concept Map, so to transfer what you learned through this exercise back to your coding system, you will benefit from printing a copy of the Map for reference.

━━━━━━━━━━ **4.c.** ━━━━━━━━━━

Using a Concept map to sort Nodes into groups (Figure 4.6)

⇒ Ribbon: **Explore > Concept Map >** provide a name > **OK / Done.**
⇒ Ribbon: **Add Project Items / + Project Item**, selecting all your thematic Nodes. Existing connections between them will be ignored > **OK / Select.**

(Continued)

(Continued)

⇒ **Select** a Node or Nodes to move them around the screen, forming groups based on their being 'the same kind of thing'.

⇒ **Right-click** on a Node to **Open Item / Open** if you need to check what is coded there.

⇒ Label each group of Nodes:

    o   **Add Shapes / + Shape > Select** a Shape and drag to the Map.

    o   **Double-click** on a Shape to **Name** it.

If you did start from a Mind Map when creating initial Nodes (as suggested in Chapter 1), this might be a good time to review that Map and your current Node structure to see if you want to revise that Mind Map and update it to reflect and extend where you are now with your Nodes.

Organizing and coding with Node hierarchies

As you consider these ways of conceptually grouping your Nodes, you will likely want to put them into a hierarchy. The Node at the top level of a hierarchy is a parent Node and the Node below it is a child Node. If you have three levels in your hierarchy, the mid-level Node is both a parent and a child (Figure 4.7).

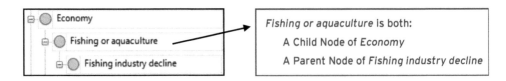

Figure 4.7 Node hierarchy with parent Nodes and child Nodes

In theory, you can build as many levels in a hierarchy as you wish, but we recommend starting with just two, and no more than three levels, for practical reasons.

━━━━━━━━ **4.d.** ━━━━━━━━

Rearranging and creating Nodes in hierarchies

Before making drastic changes to your project, make a backup copy.

Option 1 (the preferred method):

⇒ **Select** the **X** on the top right of the Project.

⇒ **Open** your Windows Explorer and copy/paste as you would any other file.

⇒ **Select** the red symbol on the top left of the Project.

⇒ **Open** your Finder and Duplicate as you would any other file.

Option 2

⇒ **File: Manage > Copy Project.**

Moving Nodes into hierarchies

Nodes can be dragged from one parent to another:

⇒ *List View:* Click once on a Node to select it > click and drag to the parent Node, or
⇒ *List View:* **Right-click** on a **Node > Cut / Copy > select** the desired parent Node >
Right-click > Paste.
⇒ **Delete** the original Node.

To place an existing Node at the top level:

⇒ *List View:* **Select** a Node > release your click and return to drag it to the *Navigation View:* **Codes: Nodes**, or
⇒ *List View:* **Right-click** on a Node > **Cut / Copy.**

o *Navigation View:* **Codes > Nodes > Right-click > Paste.**
o **Delete** the original Node.

Creating Nodes in hierarchies

⇒ *List View:* **Right-click** on the Node under which you want to create a child Node >
New Node > add a **Name** and **Description > OK / Done** (Figure 4.8).

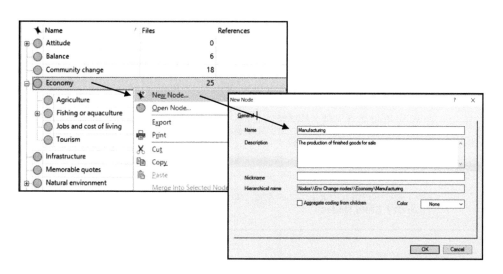

Figure 4.8   Creating a subnode (or child) Node

Code text at the parent Node also?

When you code at a child Node, the References are stored at that Node only; the data are not automatically coded at the parent Node (larger category) – nor, in general, would you want them to be unless you have a specific reason for doing so.

Node hierarchies in a motor vehicle injury study

In a project analysing injury types related to motor vehicle accidents, the team needed to consider injuries at several levels of detail; thus, *Orthopaedic* was parent to various types of *Fractures* and *Dislocations*; *Psychological* was parent to *Anxiety* and *Depression*, and so on. Most analyses in the injury study were conducted at the physical and psychological injury level, but the detail remained available if needed and helped during the development of the write-up.

If you do want the text of the child Nodes at a parent Node also, you could choose to Copy and Merge them with the parent (as described earlier), but this action occurs at a single point in time and has to be repeated if you add more data. As an alternative, you can Aggregate the parent Node, so that all coding at the child Nodes is temporarily included in the parent. Unlike Merge, an Aggregated parent Node will constantly update as you add or remove coding from the child Nodes. For the example above, you might want to leave Aggregate turned on for the parent; in most other situations, you are likely to turn it on for a specific purpose, and then turn it off again.

4.e.

Aggregate child Nodes

To automatically Aggregate child Node(s) into the parent Node as you continue coding

- ⇒ *Navigation View*: **Codes > Nodes.**
- ⇒ *List View*: **Right-click** on a (preferably empty) **parent Node > Aggregate Coding from Children / Child Nodes.**

To undo Aggregation

- ⇒ *List View*: **Right-click** on the Aggregated Node **> Aggregate Coding from Children / Child Nodes.**

As you continue to add coding to the child Nodes, they will automatically be updated into the Aggregated parent, or if you move a child Node to another location in the hierarchy, the coding will be removed from the parent. Selecting Aggregate again (to untick the option) will disaggregate the Nodes, that is, will remove the coding from the parent but not the child(ren). Aggregate only works one level at a time, so you must Aggregate at each level if you want data from the bottom level in a four-tiered hierarchy, for example, to be included in the Node at the top level.

We have two main cautions/warnings about Aggregate:

- At present, if you attempt to uncode Aggregated data from a parent Node, the action will uncode all of the data from any of the child Nodes to which it was also coded. We therefore recommend customizing your display in the *List View* (see Chapter 3, pp. 89–90, Windows only) to include the icon that informs you whether or not the Node is Aggregated. We also discourage you from uncoding at any parent Node until you confirm that it is not Aggregated.
- We discourage coding to top-level Nodes for undecided or miscellaneous material once your structure seems fairly stable, because the practice of keeping the parent Node empty will allow you to Aggregate without inadvertently mixing known things (the child Nodes) with unknown things (the miscellaneous content at the parent Node). However, it can be a mistake to create a separate child Node for every possible option under a parent Node. Instead, consider these two solutions:
  - o Create a child Node named *Transportation miscellaneous* if someone discusses a specific form of transportation that sounds unfamiliar to you and you are not sure where to code the data (you can return to it later).
  - o Create a child Node for *Transportation in general* if people talk about transportation in general terms.

Because of this recommendation to move toward a structure where the parent Nodes are empty, you might want to go back to your parent Nodes, recode the data to child Nodes and then uncode the data from the parent, so it can be appropriately Aggregated if and when it would be helpful to do so.

Merge or Aggregate?

Merging and Aggregating can sometimes free you from coding data in multiple Nodes. However, knowing when to Merge and when to Aggregate can be confusing until you understand the differences between these tools. See the video (https://study.sagepub.com/jackson3e) on 'The difference between Merging and Aggregating Nodes in Windows and Mac.' Although they both take coding from one or more Nodes and apply this coding to another Node, there are three main differences (Table 4.1).

Table 4.1 Three differences between Merging and Aggregating Nodes

	Merging	Aggregating
Does this tool allow me to cut and copy?	Yes. In fact, you must do one of these with a Node as a first step to be able to Merge data into another Node.	No. Aggregating does not depend on cutting, copying, or pasting. It is a type of command in a Node that simply points to all coded data one level down in the hierarchy.

(Continued)

Table 4.1 (Continued)

	Merging	Aggregating
Is this tool hierarchically dependent?	No. You can Merge Nodes from any part of the coding structure to any other Node. Their relationship to one another before the Merge is irrelevant.	Yes. Aggregating only adds coded data if the Node has child Nodes and will include the data from all of these immediate child Nodes.
Is this tool static or dynamic?	Static. Once you Merge, NVivo does not repeat the action, regardless of your subsequent actions in the Project. Think of it as a solitary event that occured at a particular point in time.	Dynamic. An Aggregated Node is actively pointing to all the data one level below. It is constantly working and will automatically adjust as you add to or remove coding from child Nodes.

How to fix a viral structure

The great news is that viral structures can almost always be turned into vista structures without starting over. As with all major adjustments in your Project, we recommend creating a copy of the Project (perhaps dating the copy and ending the title with 'before fixing viral structure'). After creating a copy:

1   Create two, new (temporary) Nodes at the top level of your hierarchy called *Old Nodes* and *New Nodes*.
2   Move all of your Nodes under *Old Nodes*. (See instructions on how to move Nodes earlier in this chapter.)
3   Create the new vista structure (with empty Nodes) under *New Nodes* (Figure 4.9).

Figure 4.9   Fixing a viral coding structure

4   Copy and Merge the Nodes from the Old Node structure into the New Node structure (Chapter 3, pp. 88–89). This means that in the old structure, the Node for *Positive* that was under *Negotiation* should be Merged into both *Positive* and *Negotiation* in the new structure.

5   Remember to copy and paste Nodes that are relevant to your Project but were not repeated as viral child Nodes in your initial system.

6   When you are done, save the Project and create a backup (perhaps dating the copy and ending the title with 'after converting to a vista structure').

7   Pilot the coding with this new structure. If you don't like it, you can delete the *New Nodes* and try again.

8   When it feels like the restructuring was a good move, make a copy of the Project (Chapter 1, pp. 33–34), delete *Old Nodes* (which deletes all the Nodes in this area. If you do not delete them, you are likely to find that they create noise in Coding Stripes, Queries, Reference counts, etc.).

The backup Projects will help you retrace your steps if you encounter issues later or want to pull some examples as part of your description of how you handled the data.

A Project Map (Windows only) of your refined coding hierarchy

The branching display of Nodes in the *List View* of the software is a visual display. But, if you prefer to see the structure of your coding system in diagrammatic form, you can choose to show part or all of it in a Project Map (Figure 4.10).

━━━━━━━━ **4.f.** ━━━━━━━━

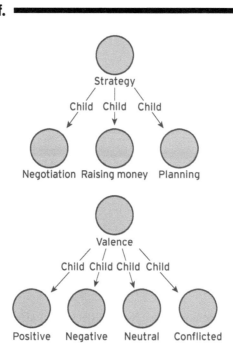

Figure 4.10 Visualizing coding structure with a Project Map

(Continued)

(Continued)

Project Map of your coding structure (Windows only)

⇒ *Ribbon*: **Explore > Project Map > Name > OK**.
⇒ *List View*: **Left-click** to select one or more parent Nodes, and drag to the *Detail View*.
⇒ *Detail View*: Expand **Add Associated Items >** select **Children** and drag to the Map.
⇒ *Ribbon*: **Project Map Tools > Layout**. Use the drop-down menu to choose the option that works best for you (e.g., Hierarchical).

Using a Set to create a metaconcept or to cluster Nodes theoretically

You will sometimes see associations or connections between Nodes that belong in different hierarchies. Sets are a great way of showing these Nodes 'hang together' because they focus around a larger concept, or because they have a theoretical (e.g., causal) association. A Set is simple to create or modify by right-clicking on a Node or groups of Nodes and then **Create As** or **Add to Set**. Putting Nodes into a Set will not change the member Nodes; Nodes can be in more than one Set; and when you add further coding to any Nodes in a Set, the Set will be updated as well. The practical advantages are: (a) an ability to choose a Set (or more than one) in a Matrix Coding Query (Windows only); (b) you can add a Set (with or without its members) to a Project Map; and (c) you can add a Set to a Concept Map without its members. The principal advantage, however, is conceptual – the Set acts as a reminder of the linkage between these Nodes.

A Set of Nodes about purposeful commitment

In the *Researchers* Project, Pat used a Set to draw together selected Nodes from the *Personal qualities* hierarchy and the *Strategies* hierarchy, to create a metaconcept of *Purposeful commitment* (Figure 4.11). The Set holds aliases for (or shortcuts to) the Nodes, rather than the Nodes themselves.

Auto Code by structural features in the File

The most useful Auto Code option simply identifies the structural features of the File. It could be used quite effectively, for example, to:

- Delineate the contributions of each speaker in an interview or focus group.

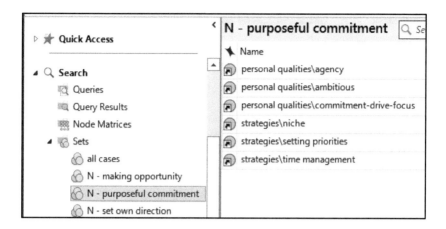

Figure 4.11 Using a Set for a metaconcept

    ○   To separate interviewer speech from respondent speech (primarily useful when going on to apply text-mining tools to examine only the text of the respondents).

    ○   To separate multiple respondents in a File in order to code each person's text to a Case (see Chapters 2 and 5 for additional detail on Cases and Classification Systems).

• Code responses for topic or the question asked, when these are standardized throughout Files and identified by a label or question number.

• Delineate the components of highly structured documents, such as meeting minutes or annual reports.

The resulting Nodes will give immediate access to, for example, all the answers to *Question 3*, everything that *Jim* said in the focus group, or all of the *Next steps* from meeting minutes. While these structural features in the File can be very useful, do not force the issue by attempting to force structure onto your data. It will be more efficient and effective to code the text interactively unless your data is highly structured.

As we detailed in Chapter 2 (Figure 2.3, p. 50), we recommend formatting your files very simply, left aligned, with a colon after the name of each speaker (or ID) followed by their speech. If you have a highly structured question format, simply enter it as a unique alphanumeric string on a line above the exchanges. With this format, you can use the Auto Code tool in NVivo to create a Node for each speaker and put it in a Case. You are unlikely to use the Facilitator as a Case, but it could be handy to include or exclude facilitator speech from various Queries, so putting it in the Case area, moving it elsewhere or deleting it later are all viable options as a way of handling the facilitator or interviewer speech. You can similarly create a Node for each question. Note that if you have headings in a Heading Style – usually applied when in Microsoft Word – you can also Auto Code by Heading Levels; consult the NVivo Help for additional assistance on the use of Heading Levels to code.

━━━━━━━━━ **4.g.** ━━━━━━━━━

Auto Coding a File by speaker name

⇒ *Navigation View*: **Data: File.**
⇒ *List View*: **Select** the **File(s) > Right-click > Auto Code > Speaker name / By Speaker > Next.**

  o Enter **Speaker names** (or question numbers) in the lines provided (see the highlight below the names for visual feedback. But, wait until all names are entered to see the distinction between all speakers) > **Next.**
  o **Create new classification >** provide a name (e.g., **Person**) > **Finish / Auto Code.**

If your question Nodes ended up as Cases, simply create a new folder in your Nodes (e.g., Interview responses by question), and cut/paste them into this new folder.

If the File you want to Auto Code is a Dataset (a spreadsheet with at least one qualitative field), such as a survey, see Chapter 6 for alternative information.

Word or phrase Queries

NVivo provides two text-mining Queries:

- Word Frequency Query, which finds up to 1000 common words in the data (or a portion of the data).
- Text Search Query, which allows you to determine words or phrases of interest as a single result (even if they are not the most common).

Word or phrase Queries might be an appropriate strategy for generating ideas for follow up with other tools in the software (or other interpretive moves by the researcher). In some forms of conversation or discourse analysis, these Queries are used to identify passages suitable for detailed coding and analysis from within the larger body of text. However, many researchers spend considerable time in these tools only to realize they should have read all the text and coded the data 'manually'. Play with the capabilities and options to hunt for words and phrases before setting in on long hours of managing the process. Even when it works well, as Lyn Richards (2009) noted, searching for words in the text is a mechanical process, so why should one expect it to help in interpretive research?

The conundrum to keep in mind with text mining is that such searches (e.g., a Query that locates the word *Feed*) almost inevitably result in a false find (a mother says, 'The children get all worked-up because they feed off of each other's energy') and false omission (a father might say, 'I just can't get her to take anything,' when describing his infant's reluctance to eat, yet never uses the word 'feed'). Like most other Queries in NVivo, both the Word Frequency Query and the Text Search Query allow you to save the Query for future use. They also provide a host of additional options (e.g., using NVivo's ability to search for synonyms, stemmed words, etc.; see Chapter 7, pp. 204–206).

Word Frequency Query

The Word Frequency Query will search selected text and identify the most frequently used words (and you can choose to limit this to selected Files, Sets, or even to selected Nodes). NVivo displays finds as a summary list or word cloud. You can review the list of words found, then follow up by reviewing particular keywords in their immediate context or save them as a Node.

4.h.

Running a Word Frequency Query

⇒ *Ribbon*: **Explore / Query** > **Word Frequency** (Figure 4.12).
⇒ **Search in** > leave as **Files and Externals** to search in everything (or go to **Selected Items** to scope the search to a narrower focus).
⇒ **Display words** > leave at **1000** most frequent or set to a lower number.
⇒ **With minimum length** > leave at **3** (increase to only find longer words; decrease to include shorter words).
⇒ Combine different forms of the same word into the same "Find" as shown in Figure 4.12).

    o   **Grouping > With stemmed words.**
    o   **Finding matches > Include stemmed words.**

⇒ **Run Query.**

NVivo will display the found words in order of frequency (Figure 4.12); you can change the sort order by selecting any of the header rows such as *Word* or *Length*.

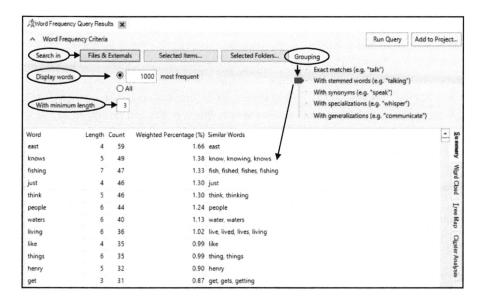

Figure 4.12   Word Frequency Query with stemmed words

If you anticipate running this Query again, perhaps in a different set of Files, select **Add to Project / Save Query** on the top right and name it. Run it again any time (*Navigation View*: **Search > Queries > Double-click** on the Query in the *List View*). Alternatively, you may modify a saved Query (*List View*: **Right-click** on the Query > **Query Properties** / *List View*: **Double-click** on the Query).

You have a number of options for viewing and working with the results from the Word Frequency Query:

- **Double-click** on a word of interest > Click on **Reference** and view it in context.

    o NVivo will provide 5 words either side as a default.
    o To see paragraphs, select one or more finds, **Right-click > Coding Context > Broad**.

- Code relevant content to a Node in your coding system as desired (not every find will be relevant). Or, save all the finds as a Node:
- Go back to the **Summary** list of results: **Right-click** on one of the words > **Create As Code > OK** > provide a **Name** and **Description > OK**.
- Stay in your Reference view > Save Results (top right) > provide a Name and Description > Save Results.

    o Save the Node in a different folder or incorporate something in the name or the description for the Node to indicate it was created as a result of an automated search, rather than through interactive coding – at least until you have reviewed the finds.

- From the list of results, choose from the tabs to the right / **buttons above** to view the finds as a Word Cloud, (or, in Windows only, as a Tree Map, or Cluster Analysis).

Stop Words

Stop Words are excluded from the search when you run either a Word Frequency Query or Text Search Query. These include such English words as *any, the*, and *yours* – words that most researchers wish to omit from their results. You might, however, be interested in seeing what follows words like "because", or "if" – and these also are listed as default Stop Words (so they don't work in either Word Frequency or Text Search Queries). You can change this in Project Properties.

━━━━━━━━━━ **4.i.** ━━━━━━━━━━

Viewing and adjusting Stop Words

Select the text search language and view the default list of Stop Words

⇒ *File:* / *Menu bar*: **File: Project Properties** (Stop Words are Project-specific) **> General.**

   o **Text content language.**
   o **Stop Words.**

Modify the Stop Words

⇒ Change words directly from the Stop Words List (in Project Properties), or
⇒ **Right-click** on any Word in the results > **Add to Stop Words List**.

Text Search Query

The Text Search Query contains options very similar to the Word Frequency Query, although it provides different visualizations because it is not comparing words and is instead retrieving all the words (and/or phrases) that satisfy the criteria you provide.

════════ **4.j.** ════════

Running a Text Search Query

⇒ *Ribbon*: **Explore / Query > Text Search**.
⇒ **Search in** > leave as **Files and Externals** to search in all Files (or go to **Selected Items** to scope the search to a narrower focus, such as one of your Sets).
⇒ **Search For** > enter the word(s) of interest (as in Figure 4.13, use the **Special** button to add your own synonyms with **OR** as an alternator between words; use quotations marks for phrases). See the NVivo Help for additional explanations.

o As an alternative, use **Find > With stemmed words / Finding matches > Include stemmed words** or any of the other options.

⇒ **Spread to** allows you to expand the result beyond the simple word or phrases you searched for (although we prefer to look at the coding context after the results are provided, as this makes it easier to identify the bolded words in the output, as in Figure 4.13).
⇒ **Run Query.**

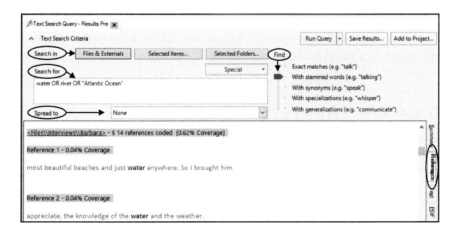

Figure 4.13 Text Search Query using the alternator, OR, with stemmed words

- The results initially show you a Summary of Files with finds. Go to the right / top of the list and change **Summary** tab to **References** in order to see the text (as in Figure 4.13).
- See Chapter 7, p. 206 for an example of a Word Tree visualization with this Query.
- If you anticipate running this Query again, save the instructions in the Query, as detailed for the Word Frequency Query.
- If you choose to Save Results, the default location is the Query Results folder which is a subfolder in *Navigation View*: **Search**.

What else can you do with Word Frequency Queries and Text Search Queries?

The word and phrase Queries in NVivo are quite versatile and you might consider adapting them to the following inquiries:

- You have a Node for *Community* and you want to know what concerns people have in this area. You can do a Word Frequency Query in the Node (instead of on the original Files), by using the **Selected Items** button to scope this Query to the Node and perhaps do additional coding based on the results.
- Use the counts from the Word Frequency Query to compare the major concerns in published articles, or changes of emphasis in annual reports.
- If you become aware of a new issue or topic or your thinking about the project takes a new direction, use Text Search Query to quickly explore across your data to see if this is a viable area for deeper investigation.
- In the course of working through a File, you might come upon a new concept or category that is 'node worthy' and then wonder whether it was there before, but you just overlooked it. Use a Text Search Query to rapidly check whether such things were indeed mentioned earlier (such a Query might be scoped to just the already coded Files).
- For routine or repetitive coding where there are clear pointers to what needs to be coded (such as known keywords in the text, like *Respirator* or *Bangladesh*), a Text Search Query can provide a viable method of locating relevant passages.
- There is too much data or too little time to read and code all of the material, so you use this strategically to hunt for words or phrases that were identified through initial coding.

SECTION 4.4: CHAPTER 4 TAKEAWAYS

═══════════ **Key points from this chapter** ═══════════

o Node structures are likely to change over time. If it is not happening naturally, force yourself to stop coding and revisit your Node structure.

o Viral coding structures can create chaotic, inefficient, and inconsistent coding practices. As viral structures emerge, learn how to recognize and adjust them into vista structures.

o Automated strategies for coding can be leveraged to handle more administrative tasks efficiently.

Tips, challenges, and warnings

- It is important to make backups and copies as the Project evolves but most people do not do it enough.
- Do not uncode data from a Node that has been Aggregated, as the action will also uncode data from coded child Nodes.
- NVivo does not track the ways you created your Nodes and the difference between open coding versus using a text-mining Query can be significant. Consider naming schemes and/or new Node folders to separate these different ways Nodes are created.
- In many instances there are two kinds of error with text-mining strategies:

  o False finds (passages that were found that do not fit what you were really looking for).
  o False omissions (passages that fit your goal but do not satisfy the automated criteria and so were omitted from the finds).

- Do not print everything. If you think you want to, just do it for one Node first, to see whether or not it is helpful.
- To expand your list of Nodes: *List View*: **Right-click > Expand/Collapse > Expand All Nodes**.
- Consider exporting a List of your Nodes, with the following columns, particularly if you are working in a team and need to train people as they join the project:

  o Node Name
  o Node Description
  o Examples (quotes that fit well)
  o Counter-examples (quotes that initially seem to fit, but belong in a closely related Node instead)

- If you want to use the Auto Code tool to separate speakers (for instance), do a small pilot on a few pages of text from a few Files. Make sure it works for you before you spend time formatting all of your data.
- Text-mining coding strategies initially look like they will be helpful but, in practice, you might have to do so much cleaning that you will wish you had read and open-coded the text. Another good reason to do a pilot.

Videos and online resources (https://study.sagepub.com/jackson3e)

Videos

- 'The difference between Merging and Aggregating Nodes'

Help files

- *File*: Help.
- *Menu bar*: **Help > NVivo Help.**

Search for any of the following:

- Automatic coding techniques
- Concept map
- Reorder and organize Nodes
- Text content language and stop words
- Text Search query
- Word frequency query

Practice questions

1   After deciding on an initial Node hierarchy, use these three strategies to push your thinking about alternative structures and then move forward with the most helpful structure:

- Copy your Project and then take an important child Node (or a few of them) and move them to the top level. What existing or new Nodes might go under this?
- Create a Concept Map of your Nodes (unconnected) and rearrange them into different groups.
- Print out a list of your Nodes with descriptions and then cut them into individual pieces of paper (one Node per piece) and ask a few of your colleagues to sort them into piles while listening to their discussion.

2   Write a Memo that reflects on your coding structure and your attempts to balance either flexibility and stability or comprehensiveness and simplicity.

3   Using the start of your coding structure, come up with two examples. One should explain why you would use the Merge feature to combine Nodes and the other should explain why you would use Aggregate.

- What is the important warning about Aggregating and uncoding?

4   Review the default Stop Words List in NVivo. Write a Memo in your Project about whether or not this list makes sense for your Project, with an accompanying rationale.

5

Section 5.1: Introduction to Cases, Classifications, and comparisons   136

Section 5.2: Conceptual grounding in Cases and Classifications   137

Section 5.3: Cases and Classifications in NVivo   145

Section 5.4: Chapter 5 Takeaways   161

CASES, CLASSIFICATIONS, AND COMPARISONS

As we know from Foucault, how we choose to name other people and groups - how we categorize them - often tells us more about us, about our stance on how things are, than it does about any truth of who they are. (Rinehart, 1998: 201)

SECTION 5.1: INTRODUCTION TO CASES, CLASSIFICATIONS, AND COMPARISONS

Whether we like it or not, our position in society and our membership in groups can influence the way we think and act, and the kinds of experiences we have. An interviewer's or interviewee's gender, class, nationality, and religion might singly, or in combination, sway what he or she says. Within an organization, it could matter what role or position one has, and perhaps how much education or training, or how many years of experience. And at a personal level, attitudes, behaviours, or experiences may relate to one's work history, education, family responsibilities, or health. To record these kinds of demographic or quantitative variables in a project becomes important, therefore, so they can be assessed. We begin this chapter by covering the various ways you can create Cases from your qualitative data in NVivo, before going on to show how you can connect, store, and use the different kinds of quantitative and demographic information you associate with your Cases.

In this chapter you will

- See the many different ways you can create Cases and add qualitative data to them.
- Discover what other kinds of information you can store with Cases, and different ways of entering this into your Project.
- Find out how to use demographic information to compare qualitative responses for different subgroups.
- Consider the use of Sets and Search Folders as an alternative way of grouping items.

Other chapters with related materials

Chapter 2: Designing an NVivo Project

Efficiently turning speakers into Cases (e.g., from a focus group) depends on the set-up of your Files. Details about formatting and labelling are provided in Chapter 2.

Chapter 6: Surveys and mixed methods

Extend what you learn about Cases and Classifications to survey and mixed method data. Chapter 6 provides additional examples of a Crosstab Query and introduces a Matrix Coding Query. Also explore multivariate and multidimensional displays.

Chapter 7: Querying data

The structure of your NVivo Project is likely to influence and be influenced by the use of Queries. Therefore, having a general sense of the different Queries and what they can do with your Cases and Classifications might help you plan this part of your Project.

SECTION 5.2: CONCEPTUAL GROUNDING IN CASES AND CLASSIFICATIONS

Understanding Cases, Case Types, Attributes, and Values

Cases

Cases serve in NVivo as units of analysis. We provided a range of examples of what Cases might look like in Chapter 2, with the goal of helping you think through who or what will be Cases in your study. If you are still unsure about what a Case is in your NVivo Project, it would be a good idea to review that part of Chapter 2 (pp. 45–48), where we also provide examples of the ways you can prepare data to make it easier to create Cases in NVivo when you are ready to do so (Table 2.1). In Chapter 4 (pp. 124–126), we provided the steps for using the Auto Coder to create Cases from speakers in a File and simultaneously add the qualitative data to these Cases. We did not explain, as we will here, how demographic or other quantitative data also can be assigned to those Cases.

However, before moving to the assignment of demographic and quantitative information to Cases, we will discuss the similarities and differences among Nodes, Cases, and Case Types. Nodes and Cases share a primary characteristic: they are containers for qualitative data. Therefore, like Nodes, there is a lot of flexibility in the kinds of data that can be associated with each Case; they can reference (i.e., code) an entire File (e.g., transcript, audio, video, photograph), multiple Files, parts of Files, or combinations of these (see Table 2.1). Data can be coded (assigned) to them, or uncoded (removed) from them at any time during the research. Although they share these characteristics, a Case is distinct from a Node because:

- a Case holds together everything you know about a particular unit of analysis, such as *Susan*, regardless of whether the data are qualitative, demographic, or quantitative; and
- a Case usually pertains to a definable unit of analysis (e.g., a *Person*, a *Place*, a *Policy*), rather than a concept (such as the Nodes for *Access*, *Anxiety*, and *Honour*).

For additional assistance in understanding Cases, see the video on 'Conceptual overview of Cases and Classification Systems' that can be found in the online resources (https://study.sagepub.com/jackson3e).

Case Types

A File such as a transcript or photograph will usually be assigned or coded to only one Case. For example, in the *Environmental Change* Project, *Barbara*, *Charles*, and *Dorothy* are all Files and you will also see that they are Cases, as in Figure 5.1.

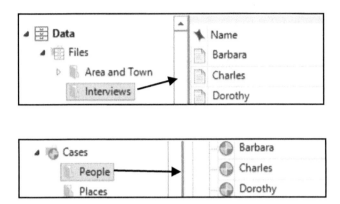

Figure 5.1 Individual participant transcripts imported as Files and converted into Cases

These Cases are nested under the folder for *People*. We refer to *People* as a Case Type. It is possible to have more than one Case Type in the same NVivo Project. Figure 5.1 shows both *People* and *Places* as Case Types in the *Environmental Change* Project. This occurs because sometimes you want to answer questions about different kinds of *People* in the study (e.g., *Younger* versus *Older*) and also want to answer questions about different kinds of *Places* in the study (e.g., *Coastal* versus *Inland*). In a study with multiple Case Types, such as *People* and *Places*, a File in your NVivo Project such as *Susan's* transcript might belong to the Case for *Susan* and also to the Case for *Harkers Island*. However, this is not usually true, and the Files in the different Case Types are likely to be mutually exclusive. For example, you might have field notes and interviews that pertain only to *Susan*, whereas aerial photographs and City Council minutes pertain only to *Harkers Island*. Regardless of how many Files are in a Case, or to how many Cases a File is assigned, within a given Case Type the qualitative data in the Cases should be mutually exclusive. In other words, *Susan's* interview transcript should only be assigned to the Case for *Susan*, and not to any other Case within the same Case Type, *People*. We will show you how to create Cases and structure them as different Case Types later in the chapter.

Attributes and Values

In NVivo, demographic or quantitative variables such as *Occupation* are referred to as Attributes (i.e., an Attribute is the same thing as a variable). Just as the variable for *Occupation* in a quantitative study might have values of *Nurse, Educator, Commercial fishing*), the Attributes in NVivo might have the same Values. These Values are then applied to specific Cases (Figure 5.2). For example, a participant might be an *Educator* in her *40s*, and a *Long-time resident*.

While we would encourage you to think about Cases, Attributes, and Values early on (because it has implications for Project design and data preparation), you can create them at any stage of the analysis. Some researchers prefer to create Cases and their system for recording Attributes as part of the preliminary construction of the Project; others prefer to

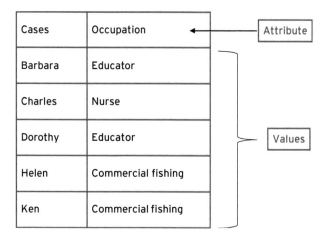

Figure 5.2 Cases, Attributes, and Values

wait until they better understand what they are doing or they are ready to start carrying out comparisons of subgroups in the NVivo Project. Depending on the research design, we sometimes recommend one over the other, but your personal preference or style is probably a good guide.

Identifying the relevant Attribute Values

Attribute Values record stable information known about a Case, whether or not it is specifically mentioned in the course of conversation; collected purposefully with a checklist or through a survey; or perhaps contained within archival records. Usually you will know all the Attributes and the Values you need ahead of time, but some of them might become evident to you only after you start to code the data.

While Attributes are routinely used to record demographic data, you can also use them to record any of a range of other kinds of data; we have listed some examples below. Use of these other kinds of Attributes will be considered in more detail in Chapter 6 on Surveys and mixed methods.

- Categorized responses to fixed-alternative questions such as those found in surveys – for example, *often*, *sometimes*, or *never*, checked in response to a structured question about experience of harassment.
- Categorical data (with broad relevance across your data) that you might generate in the course of analysing your data – for example, whether the interviewee who is caring for her mother did or did not mention getting help from other family.
- Scaled responses on instruments designed to measure attitudes or experience – for example, a visual analogue scale measuring level of pain experienced, level of attachment to community, or a score from a standardized inventory.

- Characteristics of a site or organization – for example, *Size*, where sites or organizations (rather than people) are Cases.

If you record these kinds of Attributes with the Cases, then comparisons become a straight-forward task of using NVivo's query processes or visualization tools.

Creating Cases and adding Attribute Values to the Cases has several consequences:

- Attribute Values apply to all of the data in a Case – they cannot be added to part of a Case.[1]
- Any further data added to the Case (e.g., a second interview for the same person) will automatically acquire the Attribute Values of the Case.
- Any coding you apply to passages within a File (e.g., *Trust, Love, Honour*) intersects with the Case information for that File, and thereby with the Attribute Values (e.g., *Nurse, Educator*) of that Case. This is what allows you to later run a Query to compare, for example, what *Nurses* and *Educators* said about *Trust* (or *Love* or *Honour*).

For now, the point is that once you create Cases, you will be able to add Attribute Values to these Cases with the long-term goal of using them to sort the Cases. In the discussion above, we were using the example of *People* as Cases (and comparing Attribute Values such as *Nurse* and *Educator*), but keep in mind that your Cases might be policies, groups, sites, or critical incidents; the types of Cases you study and the kinds of Attribute Values you associate with them are entirely up to you and only needed if relevant to your research questions.

Additional considerations regarding Attributes and Values

When you are planning what Attributes and Values to create, keep in mind that a primary purpose for creating Attributes is to group Cases for comparison, so if everyone, or nearly everyone, has a different Value on a particular Attribute, then that Attribute is not going to be useful for analysis and there is not much point in recording it in that way. This is often an issue, for example, with Attributes like *Age* (recorded as months or years), or with *Years of service*. You will need to categorize these into a few groups to make them useful. Make these decisions on the basis of what is likely to be most relevant to your research questions and based on what you know about developmental (or other) stages in your topic area. If you have the original data, you can always change these ranges or add another Attribute later with different ranges or groupings. Similarly, there is little point in recording an Attribute for which almost everyone has the same Value – again, it will not be useful as a basis for comparison and you will probably be well aware of the one or two Cases that are different in this regard should they also turn out to differ in some more qualitative way as well.

---

[1]This means if you want to add Values to only one of three Files within a Case – such as whether it was the first, second, or third interview – you will need to create a Set of all the Files with that characteristic, as explained in Chapter 2. Another alternative is to add Attributes directly to the Files instead of the Cases in your system, but this option is less flexible when it comes to using the information to set up Queries.

The other major planning consideration is that you can record only one Value per Attribute for each Case. If a Case has two Values (e.g., *Fred* works in two different occupations), then you have three options:

- Record the most relevant or important Attribute Value for that person and ignore the secondary one.
- Create all possible combinations of Attribute Values (e.g., *Counsellor, Coach, Educator, Counsellor/Coach, Educator/Coach, Counsellor/Educator,* and *Counsellor/Coach/Educator*). However, you should only do this if you are likely to have more than one Case with these combinations, because your goal is to compare subgroups.
- Abandon your Attribute for *Occupation* (with Values of *Counsellor, Coach, Educator,* etc.) and turn the Values into three Attributes with *Yes* and *No* as the new Values under each of them. Of course, this creates many more Attributes, and can become cumbersome if you have more than a few options.

Understanding Classifications

Although most projects have only one Case Type, we suggested earlier that it is possible to have more than one within a Project (e.g., *People* and *Places*). Each Case Type will be represented in NVivo by a Classification, and each Classification will have different Attributes and Attribute Values associated with it. *Person, Organization,* and *Policy* are examples of Classifications that you might have in NVivo (possibly all within one Project). A *Person* might have Attributes of *Occupation* and *Age; Organization* might have an Attribute of *Funding source* (or *Size* or *Length of operation*) and *Policy* might have an Attribute of *Ratification date. Occupation* will never apply to *Organization* or *Policy,* nor will *Ratification date* apply to the *Person.*

Values are associated with Attributes. Attributes, in turn, are associated with Classifications. So, to be able to create a location in the Project where you can indicate that a person has the Value of *Educator,* you create a Classification such as *Person,* and then an Attribute such as *Occupation,* and then Values such as *Educator* and *Nurse* (Figure 5.3). This is the backbone or core

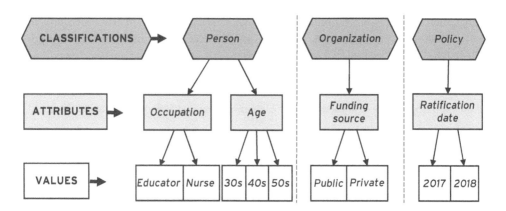

Figure 5.3   The structure of Classifications, Attributes, and Values

architecture of the possible Values of a particular Classification (e.g., *Person*) that can be applied to each associated Case (e.g., *Barbara, Charles, Dorothy*). If you have more than one Case Type in your project, you might find it helpful to plan out what your Classification system might look like by creating a diagram, like the one in Figure 5.3, on paper or in an NVivo Mind Map. For each of the three Classifications, you will have a matched Case Type (and Cases).

Even if one group of Cases can be seen as being embedded within another, such as *Employees* within *Organizations*, they are different Case Types and have different Attributes and Values. List each employee's Case in a folder for that Case Type, and list each organization in a folder for that Case Type (the left side of Figure 5.4). As stated above, a Classification system is then created for each Case Type, to store the relevant Attributes and Values (the right side of Figure 5.4).

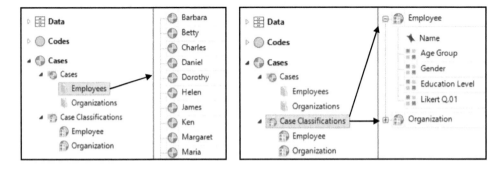

Figure 5.4 An NVivo Project with two Case Types (*Employees* and *Organizations*) and two Case Classifications (*Employee* and *Organization*)

The Cases for *Employees* might have an Attribute Value indicating the organization they were employed by, to compare individual employees on that basis. Additionally, although employees' qualitative data could also be coded to the Cases for their *Organizations*, this would not usually be necessary or appropriate. The Cases for *Organizations* are more appropriately used to reference data relating to the organization as a whole, such as annual reports or programmes or newsletters. If you have a nested sample in a research design (often in large studies in hierarchical settings, such as military institutions or school systems), start with your smallest unit of analysis, such as the *Person*, and create Cases and a Classification system for this most discrete unit of analysis. Then add all possible Attribute Values to these Cases. If needed, you can create Cases and Classification systems for other units of analysis later. The rationale for this will become clearer as you work with different Case Types in your study and see how much easier it is to later bundle them together or 'roll them up' rather than to separate them out or 'break them apart'.

Using Attributes for comparison

In Chapter 3, you were introduced to the idea that you can use a Coding Query (pp. 96–97) to find all of the passages of data that were coded at multiple Nodes. Thus, you could find all the passages where any participant talked in *Positive* terms (a subnode under *Valence*) about *Real estate development* (a subnode under *Consequence*), or, by changing the Nodes in the Query, how much and in what ways *Real estate development* was seen to be a feature of *Community change*.

Attributes can be used similarly in a Coding Query, but to answer a somewhat different question. By combining a Node with an Attribute Value in a Coding Query, you can find just what was said by *Educators*, or by *Newcomers to Down East*, or by those in their *40s*, about specific Nodes such as *Real estate development*, or *Community change*. But Attribute Values invite comparisons! When you are thinking about this kind of data, what you really want is to directly compare different demographic groups (*Educators* and *Nurses*; or *Newcomers*, *Mid-term*, and *Long-time residents*). You might be curious about what they said regarding an experience, an attitude, or about issues raised in the study. Does it differ by occupation? Is it influenced by length of residence? Is it impacted by level or type of experience? How do verbal reports of an experience match up with participants' ratings of that experience? And for convenience, you want to make these comparisons in a single operation.

So, although you can incorporate an Attribute Value into a regular Coding Query, you will almost always use a Crosstab or, possibly, Matrix Coding Query when your query involves Attribute Values. Each of these can produce a table in which project items (usually a Node or multiple Nodes) define the rows of the table, and the Values of an Attribute define the columns. The cells in the table essentially comprise a series of Coding Queries. These data are presented in tabular form with counts of Coding References (or optionally, Cases) in each cell, but you can also open each cell with a double-click to show the actual text (or video, audio, pictures, etc.) resulting from the particular combination of a Node and an Attribute Value (Figure 5.5).

Person	Gender = Female (47)	Gender = Male (71)	Total (118)
Ecosystem services	5	3	8
Environmental change	22	15	37
Environmental impacts	2	8	10
Habitat	11	3	14
Landscape	17	17	34
Renewable energy	0	0	0
Water quality	51	73	124
Total	108	119	227

<Files\\Interviews\\Barbara> - § 5 references coded [16.53% Coverage]

Reference 1 - 4.82% Coverage

The biggest change that I'm aware of is the sense – I think that now there's the sense the commercial fishing as a livelihood is dying as a viable option. And I know – I think that that is a change since 30 years or 35 years ago. I don't remember that being sort of this sense of doom. For me that's the most profound. That's a huge thing that I think is very sad. And that has to do with – that's such a complex situation -- the water quality and also the overharvesting and tearing up of the bottom – all these different things that are factors.

Reference 2 - 0.22% Coverage

pressure on water quality

Figure 5.5 Using a Crosstab Query to view data sorted by Attribute Values

On the one hand, the numeric output from a Crosstab or Matrix Coding Query provides a basis for comparative pattern analysis where it can be seen how often different groups report particular experiences or attitudes. Is one's gender associated with a different pattern of responses to a crisis situation? Do those with a different history of association with Down East have different ideas about real estate development in the area? On the other hand, comparison of the text for a particular Node for those in different groups allows you to see in what way different groups report particular experiences, and so has the potential to reveal new (or previously unobserved) dimensions in those data. It might also raise further questions about *why* this group talked about this topic or issue differently from another group. This strengthening of the comparative process is one of the more exciting outcomes of using these techniques.

We will suggest using Crosstab and Matrix Coding Queries for other kinds of analyses later (in Chapters 6 and 7). The Matrix Coding Query offers additional set-up options and refinements that are not needed now and so, in this chapter, we will focus on showing you how to use the Crosstab for comparative purposes with Attribute Values.

Using Sets to manage data

In Chapter 2, we suggested there can be times when you need to bring groups of Files together with Sets. The two most common situations where this occurs, and the way in which Sets provide a solution, are:

- When the same person is interviewed on more than one occasion, all interviews will be added to the same Case and given Attribute Values describing the person. But, whether the text in that Case corresponds to the first, second, or third time of interview cannot be recorded as an Attribute Value as it applies to only some of the Files in the Case. The solution is to create Sets of Files in addition to the Cases. One of these Sets will contain the Time 1 interviews for all Cases, another all the Time 2 interviews, and a third all the Time 3 interviews.
- In some projects with complex Cases, Files might be of different types. For example, in a study about children with ADHD (attention deficit hyperactivity disorder), the children, their parents, their doctors, and their teachers were all interviewed. In addition to their interviews, the participants sometimes provided photographs and drawings. All of these Files were collected together for the Case (the child with ADHD), so children could be compared according to the Values associated with each Case (e.g., *Medication A* or *Medication B*). But, sometimes it would also be useful to differentiate whose opinion was being given (e.g., the parents', doctors', teachers', or the child's own). Do these different players in the children's worlds have similar or different opinions about the initial diagnosis? To ask this question, the researcher can create Sets for each of the kinds of people involved in the children's lives – either to allow comparisons, or perhaps to limit (scope) a Query about some other kind of association to just a Set (e.g., *Teachers*).

Sets in NVivo are highly flexible tools. They can comprise Files, Nodes, Cases, or any combination of these. Any of these items can be in more than one Set, because Sets hold shortcuts to items, rather than the actual item. Furthermore, because Sets contain shortcuts to items such as Files, changes in the actual item (e.g., coding or edits) are immediately reflected in the Set(s) to which the item belongs. Sets are usually treated as a single (composite) item, but in some situations, items within them will be treated separately. This latter capacity is primarily of importance when a group of conceptually linked Nodes, which might be arranged in different hierarchies, are brought together as a Set – something we shall discuss further in relation to Queries (Chapter 7).

SECTION 5.3: CASES AND CLASSIFICATIONS IN NVIVO

NVivo terms used in this section

Attribute

Auto Code

Case

Classification

Crosstab Query

Set

Value

Creating a Classification (or two)

We are starting at this point because most methods of making Cases assume that you have already created a Classification. This, in turn, assumes that you have already decided what types of Cases you have in your project and, therefore, how you are going to classify your Cases.

━━━━━━━━━━ **5.a.** ━━━━━━━━━━

Create a new Case Classification

⇒ *Ribbon*: **Create > Case Classification.**
⇒ Name the Classification > **OK / Done.**
⇒ We suggest you do *not* choose to use one of the predefined Classifications because they have predefined Attributes and Values that are unlikely to match your study.

Your new Case Classification will be listed in the *List View* (as in Figure 5.4) as well as in the *Navigation View* in the Case Classifications folder.

Creating Cases

Cases can be created as you import Files, although we do not generally recommend it as it is unlikely you will remember you did so (and wonder how the Cases appeared later). Alternatively, they can be created in one (or more) of the following ways, based on your circumstances.

- Creating Cases directly from your list of imported Files:
    - Where participants are separately interviewed on one occasion only, single Files will be assigned to separate Cases, with each Case coding just one File.
    - Similarly, if you have a single report only from each of several companies, then each company's Case will refer to just one, whole File.

- Creating Cases by coding groups of Files (selected in *List View*) to a Case:
    - Where you collected data of different types for the same person (e.g., interview, photograph, video).
    - Where you collected data at different times for each participant, such as an interview at Time 1 and an interview at Time 2.

- Creating Cases by coding sections of a File, using Auto Coding, a Text Search Query, or interactive coding.
    - If your project contains a File that has more than one Case in it, such as a focus group transcript or a multi-person interview, you can Auto Code the relevant sections of the File to each Case using identified names or initials above or at the beginning of each paragraph where they start speaking (as noted in Chapters 2 and 4).
    - In some circumstances you can run a Text Search Query to hunt for unique names, spread to the paragraph, and create a Case from this data (Chapter 4).
    - If you cannot Auto Code or use a Text Search Query, use the strategy for coding you have been using all along, such as dragging and dropping relevant text into a Case (Chapter 3).

We will use text-based Files in our examples to help you understand Case creation for these circumstances. For additional instructions on creating Cases from multimedia data, turn to Chapter 9 (pp. 275–276). If you have a survey (mixed qualitative and quantitative data recorded in a spreadsheet), turn to Chapter 6 (pp. 177–181) to see how you can use an Auto Code Wizard to make Cases from each row of that data.

━━━━━━━━━ **5.b.** ━━━━━━━━━

Create Cases from imported Files (one File per Case)

⇒ *Navigation View*: **Data > Files > Select** the Folder with your Files.
⇒ *List View*: **Select** Files **> Right-click > Create As > Create As Cases > Select** the location for these Cases > **OK.**

- Optional: Create a Folder for your new Cases and move them into this Folder.

Combining multiple Files into a single Case

⇒ *Navigation View*: **Data > Files > Select** the Folder with your Files.
⇒ *List View*: Use **Shift + click** or **Ctrl + Click / Cmd + Click** to select all the Files relating to a single Case from that Folder **> Right-click**.

  o **Code > Cases > OK > Name** the New Case **> OK.**
  o **Code Files > At New Case > Name** the Case **> Done**.

If the Case already exists:

⇒ **Select** the existing Case and the new data will be added to it **> OK**.
⇒ **Select** At existing Nodes or Cases **> Select** the word 'Cases' on left side (do not tick) and tick the Case on the right side **> Select.**

  o All selected Files will be assigned to that Case (Figure 5.6).
  o If the Files are in different Folders (e.g., because they contain data of different types), you will need to code the Files from each Folder in separate steps.

Figure 5.6   Coding multiple Files to a New Case (Windows)

(Continued)

(Continued)

If several Cases have already been created from each separate File (or an additional Case through Auto Coding from part of a shared File) when just one is what is wanted, then use **Cut / Copy** and Merge (Chapter 3, p. 89) to combine the duplicated Cases into a single Case holding all of the relevant data. Mac users will need to go back and delete the original.

Making Cases from sections of a File

Using participant names above or at the beginning of a paragraph

⇒ *Navigation View*: **Data > Files > Select** the Folder with your Files.
⇒ *List View*: **Select** the File or Files with multiple (uniquely named) Cases within them **> Right-click > Auto Code.**
   o The Auto Code Wizard will open **> Speaker name** (Figure 5.7) **> Next > Enter** each speaker name, followed by **Enter** (Figure 5.8) **> Next >** identify a **Classification** (Figure 5.9) **> Finish.**
   o **By Speaker... >** Auto Code Panel will open (Figure 5.10) **>** Complete the sections in the panel **> Auto Code.**

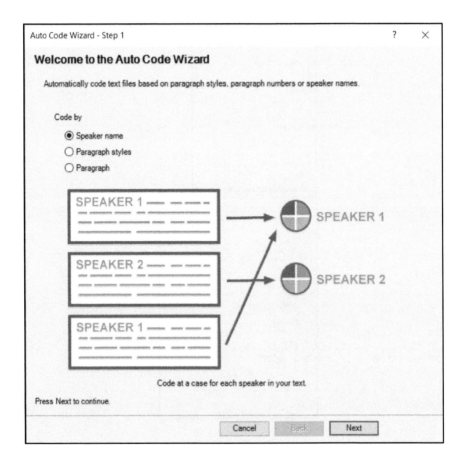

Figure 5.7 Selecting a method for Auto Coding (Windows)

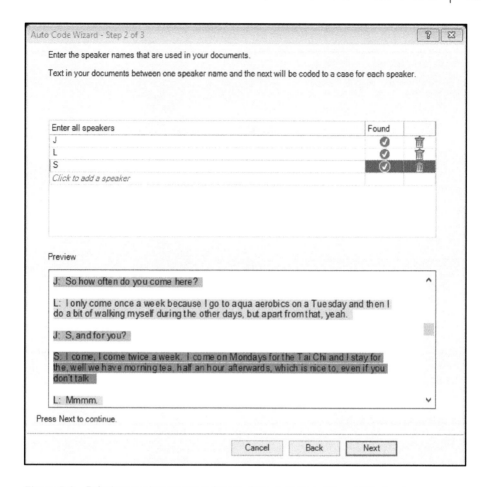

Figure 5.8 Entering speaker names in Step 2 of the Auto Code Wizard (Windows)

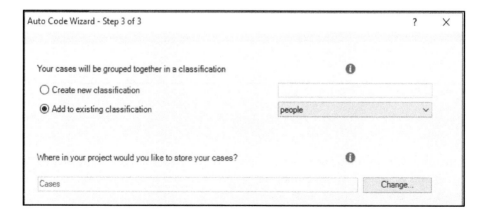

Figure 5.9 Identifying the Case Type (Classification) and location for the new Cases in Step 3 of the Auto Code Wizard (Windows)

(Continued)

(Continued)

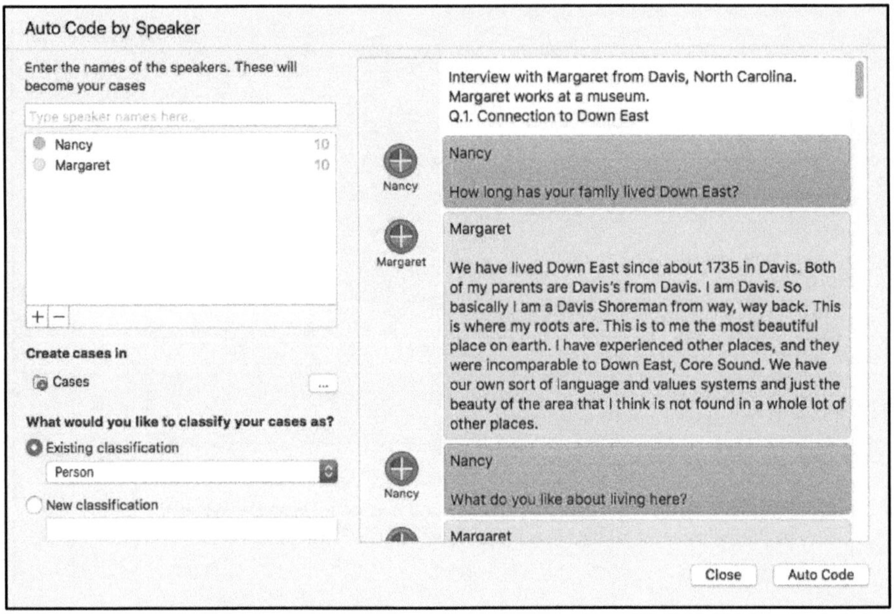

Figure 5.10   The Auto Code by Speaker panel (Mac)

Classifying the Cases

At several points along the way during these steps, you were either forced to add a Classification to the Case, or you had the option to do so. In either event, you can check that it worked, or assign the Classification.

⇒   *Navigation View*: **Cases > Cases**.
⇒   *List View*: **Select** a Case > **Right-click > Classification >** your Classification should be checked, or you can assign the Classification here by **Selecting** the correct option.
   o   Use your Shift key to select all of the Cases if you want to assign them to the same Classification.

Two ways to add Attributes and Values to Classified Cases

Now that your Classification and Cases are set up, we will walk you through the steps to add Attributes and Values to a Classification, and assign Values to Cases, so you will then be able to compare subgroups in your sample.

There are two primary ways to create Attributes and Values in the software:

- Step by step inside the software. This is the best way to start if you are new to the software as it helps you understand the processes that are involved. Also, you will use this method if you decide to infer Attribute Values from within your sources while coding their thematic content.

- Import an Excel or SPSS file with all of the data – a useful and efficient way to do it if (a) you already have the data in Excel or SPSS; or (b) you have a large number of Cases and/or Attributes (e.g., more than 20 Cases and more than five Attributes). Even if you intend to import from Excel or SPSS, it might be helpful for you to follow the step-by-step process for a few Files first, so you understand how the various components of the Project connect and work together.

5.c.

Create Attributes and add Values, step by step

Create Attributes with Values

⇒ *Navigation View*: **Cases > Case Classifications > Right-click** on the Classification you created earlier **> New Attribute**.

The **New Attribute** dialogue box will open (Figure 5.11)

⇒ Provide a short **Name** for the new Attribute. Add a **Description** if needed for clarity.
⇒ Select a data **Type** for the Values of the Attribute.
⇒ Most Attribute Values will be Text, as that includes any combination of letters and numbers, or ranges of numbers, such as 20–29, 30–39. If the Attribute comprises numeric values only, then choose Integer (whole numbers) or Decimal to ensure that they can be correctly sorted. Date values can be entered in local format with

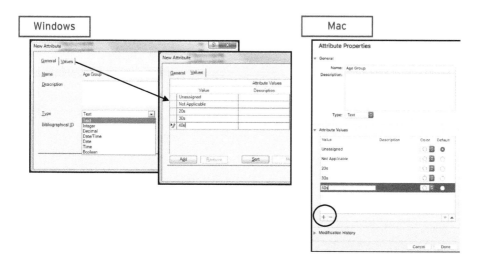

Figure 5.11   Adding an Attribute and Values in Windows (left) and Mac (right)

(Continued)

(Continued)

day, month, and year, so if you want to record years only, then use Integer. A Boolean attribute can assume two values only (e.g., Yes, No; True, False). If you are uncertain which type to select, choose Text because this type will accommodate any alphanumeric combination.

⇒ **Select** the tab for Values at the top of the dialogue.

⇒ You will see two Values already listed: these are assumed to be valid options for any Attribute and they cannot be removed. The default Value is set at Unassigned, and in general you should leave this as the default.

⇒ Use the **Add / +** button on the bottom left to create new rows so you can type in the Values you need for this Attribute. When you are finished, click on **OK / Done**. Further Values can be added later, if necessary.

Add Values to the Cases

⇒ *Navigation View*: **Cases > Case Classifications > [your Classification] > Right-click > Open Classification Sheet.**

⇒ *Navigation View* : **Cases > Case Classifications.**

⇒ *List View* : **Double-click** [your Classification] **> Click** on **Classification Sheet** tab.

⇒ The Classification Sheet (Figure 5.12) will open in *Detail View*, with your Cases in the rows, and the Attributes you have created as the columns. Currently all the Values will be listed as Unassigned.

⇒ *Detail View*: **Click in a cell of the Classification table / Click on the search icon for a cell of the Classification table** and select an appropriate Value from the drop-down list for that cell. If the Value you want does not exist, double-click in the cell and overtype Unassigned with your new Value, followed by **Enter**. The new Value will be added to your list and made available for other Cases with the same Classification.

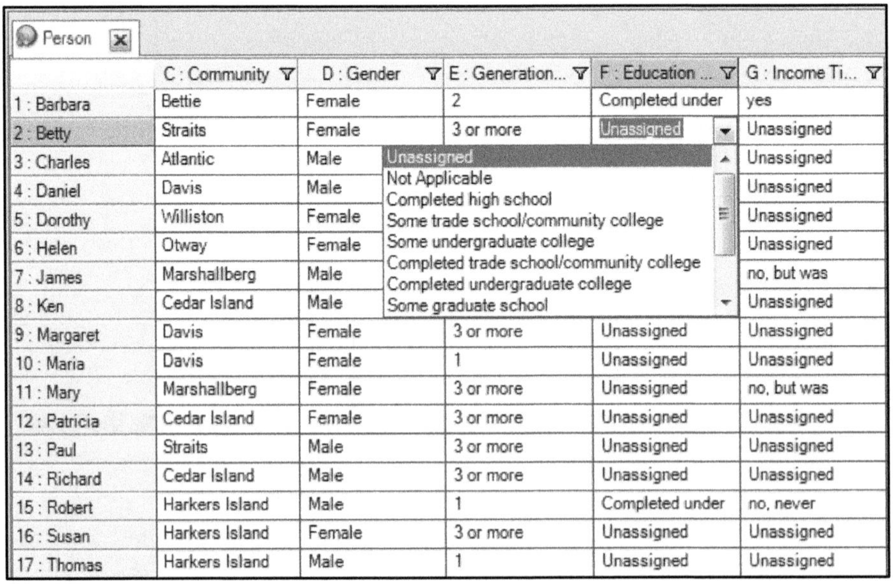

	C : Community ▽	D : Gender ▽	E : Generation... ▽	F : Education ... ▽	G : Income Ti... ▽
1 : Barbara	Bettie	Female	2	Completed under	yes
2 : Betty	Straits	Female	3 or more	Unassigned ▼	Unassigned
3 : Charles	Atlantic	Male	Unassigned ▲		Unassigned
4 : Daniel	Davis	Male	Not Applicable		Unassigned
5 : Dorothy	Williston	Female	Completed high school		Unassigned
6 : Helen	Otway	Female	Some trade school/community college ≡		Unassigned
7 : James	Marshallberg	Male	Some undergraduate college		no, but was
8 : Ken	Cedar Island	Male	Completed trade school/community college		Unassigned
			Completed undergraduate college		
			Some graduate school ▼		
9 : Margaret	Davis	Female	3 or more	Unassigned	Unassigned
10 : Maria	Davis	Female	1	Unassigned	Unassigned
11 : Mary	Marshallberg	Female	3 or more	Unassigned	no, but was
12 : Patricia	Cedar Island	Female	3 or more	Unassigned	Unassigned
13 : Paul	Straits	Male	3 or more	Unassigned	Unassigned
14 : Richard	Cedar Island	Male	3 or more	Unassigned	Unassigned
15 : Robert	Harkers Island	Male	1	Completed under	no, never
16 : Susan	Harkers Island	Female	3 or more	Unassigned	Unassigned
17 : Thomas	Harkers Island	Male	1	Unassigned	Unassigned

Person ✖

Figure 5.12   Classification Sheet with Attribute Values for interview participants (Windows)

When you are done, check one or two of your Cases to see that the Values are added:

⇒ *Navigation View* : **Cases > Case Classifications > Select** [your Classification].
⇒ *List View* > **Click** the + (**plus** symbol) next to a Case to show the list of Attribute Values.
⇒ *Navigation View* : **Cases > Case Classifications.**
⇒ *List View* > **Click** the Triangle next to your Classification.
⇒ **Click** the Triangle next to the Case to show the list of Attribute Values for that Case.

Import a Classification Sheet to create and apply Classifications, Attributes, and Values

You can achieve all the steps outlined above by setting up a table of data and importing that table.

- Windows users can use an Excel spreadsheet, SPSS database, tab-delimited txt, or csv file.
- Mac users must use a tab-delimited txt or csv file, usually created in and saved from a spreadsheet such as Excel or Filemaker.

Data imported in this way will become Attribute Values of Cases for a single Classification. It can be imported from either Excel or SPSS. If the data file is in an alternative program (e.g., Access, Stata), we recommend opening it and saving it as an Excel file as a first step. If your Excel file contains variables that you are unlikely to use in association with your qualitative data, make a copy of the file and delete the extraneous variables before importing (you can always add them and reimport that or an additional file later if you change your mind). SPSS provides you with options to retain Value Labels (which you will want in NVivo) and to select the Variables you want to retain when you Save As a new file.

The File will have a similar structure to that shown above in Figure 5.12, but with the Classification name added to the top of the first column.

- Case names go in the first column.
- If using Excel, Attribute names will be in the first row. (For SPSS, Attributes will adopt your variable names.)
- Cell A1 in Excel, the label for the Cases column, must contain the Classification name for the Cases in the table.
- The order in which Cases are listed is not important, but their names must exactly match those in your NVivo project.
- Cells hold data that will become Attribute Values (e.g., *Male*, *Over 60*, etc.). Text labels, numbers, or dates/times are entered in each cell, with one value only in each cell. In SPSS, value labels should be defined and used. Blank cells are OK if a value is not known.

5.d.

Importing Attribute Values for Cases from Excel, SPSS, txt or csv

⇒ *Ribbon* : **Import: SPSS** or **Classification Sheet.**
⇒ *Ribbon* : **Data: Classification Sheets.**
⇒ *Import wizard*: **Step 1**: Use **Browse** to find the Excel or SPSS file **/ Select** the tab-delimited text file or csv file **> Open > Next.**
⇒ *Import wizard*: **Step 2**: Check you are importing Case **Classification** data.

  o   Create a new Classification (e.g., *Person*) or import into an existing one.
  o   Tick all three boxes:

    ☐   **Create new attributes if they do not exist**. This tells NVivo that you want to create the attributes listed in the first row of your table.
    ☐   **Update the classification of existing items**. This will connect the Cases listed in the table with the Classification identified.
    ☐   **Replace Attribute Values of existing files or cases**. If you are adding to or correcting any existing Attribute Values, even if all Values are Unassigned, this is required to overwrite the existing cells. Checking this box will never remove entire Attributes from the system: it simply changes Values in existing cells to match those in the table.

⇒ *Import wizard*: **Step 2** for **SPSS / Mac users** > **Classification** > Choose to **Create new classification** or **Import into existing classification** > **Next.**
⇒ *Import wizard*: **Step 3**:

  o   **Excel:** Choose between the first two radio buttons to match the case name structure in your Classification Sheet (**As names** or **As hierarchical names**) – usually **As names** (e.g., *Barbara*). If you have created hierarchical lists or sub-folders under Cases and you choose **As names,** then you also need to use the **Select** button to indicate the exact location of these names, e.g., **Cases > People.** If you choose **As hierarchical names**, the full path for each Case will need to be specified in the table you are importing (e.g., Cases\\People\\ Interview Participants\Barbara).
  o   **SPSS:** Identify (a) the location for the Cases in your NVivo project and (b) the variable name for the column that records the Case names in SPSS.
  o   **tab-delimited text:** The full path for each Case will need to be specified in the table you are importing (e.g., Cases\\People\\Interview Participants\Barbara). Providing you have classified the cases and created at least one Attribute (no Values), you can obtain a ready-made table with the Case paths by right-clicking on the Classification to Export.

⇒ *Import wizard*: **Step 3**: Uncheck **Create new cases if they do not exist** unless you are deliberately trying to create cases that don't already exist in the Project. The danger of leaving this option checked is that you will accidentally create 'empty' Cases you do not want, especially if you are importing classification data from a larger statistical file **> Next.**
⇒ *Import wizard*: **Step 4**:

  o   **Excel:** Change the default options for dates, times, and decimal symbols, if necessary, to match your data **> Finish.**
  o   **SPSS:** Check **Create attribute values using value labels > Finish.**
  o   **Import.**

Review your classification data

⇒ *Navigation View*: **Cases > Case Classifications.**

⇒ **Double-click** [your Classification name].
⇒ *List View:* **Double-click** [your Classification] **> Click** on **Classification Sheet** tab.
⇒ A table set out like your spreadsheet will open in *Detail View*, allowing you to quickly check if your data have imported as you expected.

o Check for any rows (Cases) in your Classification Sheet where all Values are Unassigned. Is this because they were not entered in your Excel spreadsheet, or because you did not write the name exactly as it is in NVivo, and so the Values for that Case did not import? If the latter, correct the error in the table, and reimport.

o If you make corrections inside NVivo (e.g., on reading the transcript for a Case), be sure to make the same correction in your Excel or SPSS data file in case you have need to import it again.

Report on Attributes and Values (Windows only)

For later analyses, particularly for subgroup comparisons using the Matrix Query, and also for writing up your methodology, it can be useful to have a report that tells you how many Cases there were for each of the Values of your Attributes. This will allow you to better plan for comparisons of subgroups and assess the results you obtain. It makes a difference, for example, when 6 males and 6 females have talked about *trust*, to know that you had 12 males in your sample and 8 females.

5.e.

Case Classification Summary Report (Windows only)

⇒ *Navigation View*: **Output > Reports > Case Classification Summary Report > Double-click** to open.
⇒ *Filter Options*: Check each to reveal what options are offered and **Select** (a) which Classification, (b) which Cases, and (c) which Attributes you want the report to cover **> OK.**
⇒ *Ribbon*: **Report >** Optionally uncheck **Thumbnails** and **Report Map** if the additional space is needed to see the main (middle) panel with the report.
⇒ *Detail View*: **Right-click** on the main panel to **Print** or **Export Report Results.**

Using Crosstab with Attributes for pattern and comparative analyses

The Crosstab provides a rapid overview of the pattern of responses for Nodes across selected Attribute Values. It presents a comparative display showing how many in each subgroup of the sample (such as *Male/Female; Senior/Middle/Junior;* etc.) talked about particular topics or themes, and it provides access to the underlying text so it can be seen how different subgroups talked about these things.

5.f.

Running a Crosstab Query with Attributes

⇒ *Ribbon*: **Explore / Query** > **Crosstab**. The Crosstab Query panel will open in the *Detail View* (Windows: Figure 5.13; Mac: Figure 5.14).

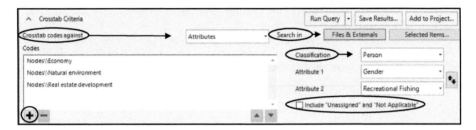

Figure 5.13   Crosstab Query interface (Windows)

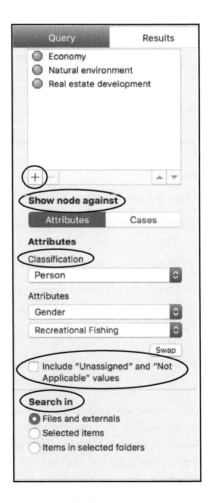

Figure 5.14   Crosstab Query interface (Mac)

⇒ *Detail View*: **Crosstab Criteria > Crosstab codes against / Show node against > Attributes** (the default).

⇒ Add Nodes (or other Codes) to the rows of the Crosstab in one of two ways:

    o *Navigation View*: **Codes > Nodes > Select** [your Nodes] and then drag from the *List View* to the **Codes / Nodes** box in the **Crosstab Criteria** dialogue; or

    o *Detail View*: **Crosstab Criteria >** Click the **+ (plus** symbol) at the bottom left of the **Codes** panel > **Select Project Items (Nodes** will be selected already, as a default).

    o Check the boxes next to the specific Nodes, or check **Automatically select descendent codes** and then select the Node at the top of the hierarchy (tree or subtree) of Nodes you want in your Crosstab. **OK / Select**.

    o Use the **- (minus** symbol) to remove any unwanted selections.

⇒ Select Attribute Values for the columns of the Crosstab:

    o *Detail View*: **Crosstab Criteria / Attributes > Classification >** choose which Classification you will work with.

    o Select the **Attribute** within that Classification (usually one) using the drop-down menu. The Values of this Attribute will define the columns for the Crosstab. If a second Attribute is selected, the Values for the second will be shown for each value of the first.

    o Tick if you want to **Include "Unassigned" and "Not Applicable" values**.

⇒ *Detail View*: Check options at the top right / bottom of the **Crosstab Criteria** dialogue:

    o **Crosstab Criteria > Search in**: Choose whether you want all **Files and Externals, Selected Items** (particular Files, Nodes, Cases, or Sets), or all files within **Selected Folders** to be included in the analysis.

    o **Add to project / Save Query** allows you to store the specification for the Crosstab so that you can run it again at a later time, for example, if you add to or change your data in some way, or for a different Folder of Files or Selected Items.

⇒ **Run Query**.

    o **Save Results** will store the results for future reference. Saved Results will not be updated if your data change.

⇒ *Ribbon*: **Crosstab Tools >** Refine the display using options in the **Cell Shading, Layout, Column Headers**, and **Label Format** groups (Figure 5.15).

⇒ *Detail View*: **Results** tab > Refine the display using options in **Show results as, Show cell values as, Transpose, Heat map, Table headers** groups (Figure 5.16).

⇒ *Detail View*: **Double-click** on a cell in the Crosstab to see the text associated with that combination of Node and Attribute Value (and see Chapter 7 for additional information).

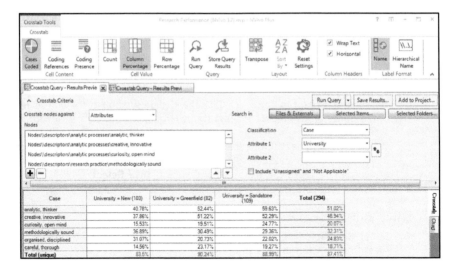

Figure 5.15 Crosstab Query Results Display, showing cell content options selected from the *Ribbon* (Windows)

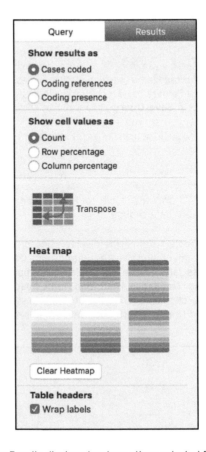

Figure 5.16 Crosstab Query Results display, showing options selected from the Results tab (Mac)

Results open in the *Detail View*, below the Crosstab specification panel. Figure 5.15 shows the Crosstab resulting from comparing the frequency with which academics from different universities use some descriptions for high-performing researchers. The total N for each Attribute Value is shown in brackets in the column header, and column percentages show the proportions of the sample who had the Attribute Value in that column who were coded with each of the row Nodes. Thus, in Figure 5.15, 40.78% of the 103 people at New University suggested that high-performing researchers were strongly analytic or deep thinkers, compared to 52.44% of the 82 respondents from Greenfield University and 59.63% of the 109 respondents from Sandstone University. The Total (unique) row indicates the proportion of the sample for that column with passages coded at any one or more of the listed Nodes (this can be useful if the Nodes selected are all from a common thematic group).

5.g.

To show results as a chart (Windows only)

⇒ *Detail View*: **Select** the Chart tab at the far right side of the display.
⇒ *Ribbon*: **Crosstab Tools > Chart**: Change the **Type** of Chart using the arrows at the right to show the full range > **Click** to select.
⇒ We recommend using a **Grouped Column** chart for displays involving Nodes by Attribute Values (Figure 5.17). Values shown are determined by the last selections on the Crosstab display.

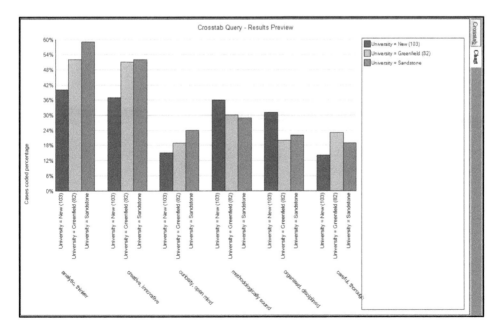

Figure 5.17 Grouped column chart displaying results from the Crosstab Query shown in Figure 5.15 (Windows)

Reporting the results of a Crosstab Query

Often you will do nothing more with a set of Crosstab Query results than review them on screen, and maybe make a few notes or jot some ideas for follow up. If the results warrant it, however, a table with the numeric results can be exported either to Excel, SPSS, or as a text file **(Right-click** > Export Crosstab Results / Share > Spreadsheet).

Alternatively, if you double-click on a cell you can copy the text and paste it into Word, where you can add a summary of cell contents to supplement the numbers already there (see Bazeley 2013: Chapter 9, for examples of summary tables and more on comparative analyses). Making notes or summaries in this way prompts you to think about and deal with the results as they are generated, when they will mean most to you. It also saves a lot of time and paper and avoids the risk of your being daunted by large volumes of results texts at a later stage.

Make Sets of Cases for scoping Queries

You might want to create a Set that you can use, for instance, to scope a Query to a subset of your data. You can make a Set from your *List View* of items, such as your list of Files (**Select** the items > **Right-click** > **Create As** > Create As Set / Set > **Name** the Set > OK / Done).

Windows users can also make Sets based on Attribute Values (e.g., a Set of all Females) with the Group Query (or Advanced Find). Group Query provides the most straightforward and efficient method for most purposes. Advanced Find offers additional options, including (a) the possibility of specifying a range of specific values when defining the Set, and (b) providing an option to save the results as a Search Folder rather than a Set. (A Search Folder saves the specifications for the Find so that results are readily updated if more Cases are added.)

──────────── **5.h.** ────────────

Using Group Query to construct Sets of Cases according to Attribute Values (Windows only)

⇒ *Ribbon:* **Explore** > **Group.**
  ○ **Look For** > **Items by Attribute Value.**
  ○ **Scope** > **Select** > **Case Classifications** > **[your choices]** > **OK** (Figure 5.18).
  ○ **Range** > **Select** > **Selected Items** (or **Selected Folders**) > Choose **[your Cases]** > **OK.**
  ○ **Run.** The resulting display will show all Values for each selected Attribute. Expand a value to see the Cases that have that value.

⇒ *Detail View:* **Select** the Cases for an Attribute Value. **Right-click** > **Create As Set** > **Name** the Set > **OK.** Values can be grouped (e.g., Years into Decades) by selecting Cases for more than one Value at the same time.

Resulting Sets are listed in *Navigation View*: **Search** > **Sets.**

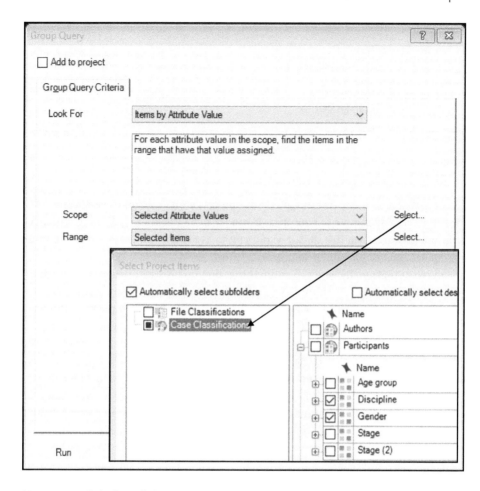

Figure 5.18 Selecting Attribute Values in a Group Query (Windows only)

SECTION 5.4: CHAPTER 5 TAKEAWAYS

■■■■■■■ Key points from this chapter ■■■■■■■

o Cases are your units of analysis and each Case will pull together all the qualitative and all of the quantitative or demographic data for that unit (e.g., an interview participant).

o The Classification system is a three-tiered hierarchy (although it does not look like it inside the Project):

Classification > Attribute(s) > Values. These three tiers are mutually interdependent.

o You might have more than one Case type such as *People* (with Cases for *Dorothy*, *Susan*, *William*) and *Organizations* (with Cases for *Hilltop Elementary*, *Mapleton Elementary*, and

(Continued)

(Continued)

Cityside Elementary). If you do, you will have multiple (equivalent) Classification systems as well.

o Attributes and their Values are used primarily for making comparisons across the qualitative data, e.g., for comparing what people of different ages say about *Trust*, or *Real estate development*.

Tips, challenges, and warnings

- As we say with so many features, pilot your process with Cases and Classification Sheets on a small sample of your data. If you try to handle these tasks in big batches without piloting them first, it can be difficult to assess if it worked properly and it can be challenging to implement solutions.
- In NVivo, it is generally easier to group things up into broader categories rather than break them apart. So, if you think you might have Cases and Classification systems at multiple levels (e.g., *Students*, *Classrooms*, *Schools*, *States*), start with the most discrete unit and set up the system for this kind of Case (e.g., *Students*) and Classification System (e.g., *Student*). Once you have it up and running, it is generally easier to create the other kinds of Cases and Classification Systems.
- Do not nest your Cases for *Participants* (*Dorothy*, *Susan*, *William*, etc.) in a hierarchy underneath the Case of which *Organization* (*Hilltop Elementary*, etc.) to which they belong. These are different units of analysis and you will find they are easier to manage according to their Case type, not according to the conceptual map of the setting.
- File Classifications are used to store general information about your Files, such as interview date, interviewer, and location of interview. They are generally not used to hold Case information. The process for making File Classifications is directly parallel to that for Case Classifications. Most Projects do not require the use of both File and Case Classifications, and since Case Classifications are more flexibly used, Case Classifications are suggested if there is a question about which to use.
- One way of setting up a table outside of NVivo for your Case Classification Sheet is to export a file populated with Cases from NVivo (this avoids typos in Case names). Firstly, create a Classification inside NVivo (p. 145), then create your Cases and Classify them (pp. 146–150) and add one Attribute (without Values). To export your sheet, go to *Navigation View*: **Cases** > **Case Classification** > Right-click on the Classification > Export Classification Sheet / *List View*: Right-click on the Classification > Export.

Videos and online resources (https://study.sagepub.com/jackson3e)

Help files

- *File*: Help.
- *Menu bar*: **Help > NVivo Help.**

Search for any of the following:

- Automatic coding techniques
- Cases
- Classifications
- Classification sheets
- Classify cases
- Create cases automatically
- Create cases manually
- Create case classifications
- Work with attribute values
- Work with crosstab query results

Practice questions

1 In your Project, what are your Case Types?
2 What Attributes might be relevant to your study (e.g., *Age, Gender, Ethnicity*)?
3 What is your plan for collecting them?
4 Will you predetermine the Values, or allow participants to self-identify and later develop subgroups (e.g., *Cuban-American, White, Latino, Black, African-American, Caucasian, White*)?
5 Could some (or all) of the Classifications, Attributes, and Values emerge during coding instead of being determined a priori? Why or why not?
6 Construct a Classification Sheet that provides the information you know you want to collect for a few of your Cases. Is there other data you would like to add to this table? If so, is there a way of finding this data and adding it to your Classification Sheet?
7 How do you plan to use Attribute Values and/or Cases in your Queries? (See Chapter 7 for additional ideas.)

6

Section 6.1: Introduction to surveys and mixed methods   166

Section 6.2: Conceptual grounding in surveys and mixed methods   167

Section 6.3: Surveys and mixed methods in NVivo   175

Section 6.4: Chapter 6 Takeaways   194

SURVEYS AND MIXED METHODS

The utilization-focused evaluator works with intended users to include any and all data that will help shed light on evaluation questions, given constraints of resources and time. Such an evaluator is committed to research designs that are relevant, rigorous, understandable, and able to produce useful results that are valid, reliable, and believable. The paradigm of choices recognizes that different methods are appropriate for different situations and purposes. (Patton, 2008: 466)

SECTION 6.1: INTRODUCTION TO SURVEYS AND MIXED METHODS

Tools in NVivo can be used to support the integration of varied types of qualitative and quantitative data and analyses in mixed methods research, including surveys with both closed- and open-ended questions. Mixed methods research has gained broad recognition as a third major methodological approach since the turn of the century, following on from and combining elements of quantitative and qualitative approaches. Increasing adoption among those in the wider social science community has fostered development of theory and strategies – and software tools – to scaffold and facilitate analysis of mixed methods data.

In this chapter you will

- Discover what is distinctive about mixed methods.
- Learn how NVivo supports mixed methods.
- See how to import and manage survey data in NVivo.
- Learn to import statistical data files into NVivo.
- Find out how to combine mixed forms of data for complementary analyses.
- Discover how to combine quantitative and qualitative data for a range of different comparative analyses.
- Learn how to transform qualitative coding into quantitative variable data and export it for different types of statistical analyses.
- Consider ways to visualize mixed data.
- Learn the importance of not losing touch with qualitative data that is used as a source for quantitative analyses.

Other chapters with related materials
Chapter 5: Cases, Classifications, and comparisons

Chapter 5 helps you think conceptually about what a case is in your research with details about working with NVivo Cases and associated Attributes. This is foundational for mixed methods analyses.

Chapter 7: Querying data

The structure of your mixed methods NVivo Project is likely to influence and be influenced by the use of Queries. Therefore, having a general sense of the different Queries and what they can do might help you think through your approach to mixed methods in NVivo.

Chapter 10: Twitter, Facebook, YouTube, and web pages

Social media data presents interesting, new opportunities in mixed methods research. Some social media data also imports in a spreadsheet format, so the techniques learned with mixed methods data will also be of benefit with the social media data.

SECTION 6.2: CONCEPTUAL GROUNDING IN SURVEYS AND MIXED METHODS

Mixed methods as a methodological approach

Researchers in both sciences and social sciences have been using quantitative and qualitative data together in their investigations, reports, and in mixed form surveys for a long time – well before doing so was recognized or named as a particular methodological approach (Maxwell, 2016). Purposefully integrating different data sources and methods during data analysis has a lesser history, however, and many mixed methods researchers report difficulty in 'bringing together the analysis and interpretation of the quantitative and the qualitative data and [in] writing a narrative that linked the analyses and interpretations' (Bryman, 2007: 10). Lack of established strategies and tools to support them for all but the simplest forms of data integration have contributed significantly to this problem, but with the growing popularity of mixed methods, developers of qualitative software have increasingly turned their attention to ways in which their software can also support mixed methods research.

'Mixed methods studies are those in which more than one source or type of data and/or more than one approach to analysis of those data are integrated throughout the study in such a way as to become interdependent in reaching a common theoretical or research goal' (Bazeley, 2010: 432). Integration, defined here as interdependence between the different approaches and methods used in a study, is the key to mixed methods research. Purposeful interdependence between methodological approaches means there is a 'two-way exchange of information and inferences ... during the design and analysis processes of a study, without which the component parts cannot fully function in meeting the overall study purpose' (Bazeley, 2018: 8).

Mixed methods researchers argue that there is a net gain to this approach because a more comprehensive, generalizable, deeper, and/or insightful analysis of the topic being investigated will result than would be provided by use of a qualitative or quantitative approach alone. NVivo supports exchange and integration of qualitative and quantitative data during analysis in three principal ways.

- Material from different types of sources (e.g., transcripts, videos, images, documents, statistical reports, social media posts) relating to the same topic or issue can be readily brought together for complementary analysis.
- Qualitative data coded to Cases can be linked with quantitative data for the same Cases (e.g., particular people, organizations, or sites), to facilitate comparative analyses for quantitatively defined subgroups (based on genders, roles, scores on a test, level of development, etc.) or varied contexts (e.g., times, locations).
- Qualitative codes (e.g., *renewable energy, water quality*) can be transformed into and exported as variable data, allowing for conversion to or combination with a statistical database, thus extending the possible range of analyses.

Integration does not just happen at analysis stage. Planning for integration, as well as for analysis, needs to occur as a project is being designed, so that data are appropriately collected and managed in ways that will support integration and analysis of those data. For example, if different sources of data are designed to be linked for each case, then it becomes necessary to ensure all Files are identified or have a common identification that will allow the different Files for each Case to be matched. Researchers planning a mixed methods project are likely, firstly, to find it is helpful to use visual models (Maps) to assist in both conceptualizing the project and in setting out how the project will be conducted. Secondly, memoing to track links between methods is especially important in a mixed methods project as part of an audit trail for the project. Connections and insights generated through writing enrich the 'conversation' between methods along the way.

Data for a mixed methods project

Interviews and other qualitative sources are usually one part of the data mix in a mixed methods project, to be combined with a variety of categorical and statistical data types. Projects might use more than one type of qualitative data, including short answers from surveys, field notes, interviews, videos, web pages, or newspaper articles. Documents such as company reports, administrative records, school grade reports, or reports of statistical analyses could also, potentially, be included as source Files in a mixed methods project. All these data will be content coded, as described in Chapter 3, using a common set of Nodes for all sources. Most will also be assigned or coded to Cases in the project.

Demographic data, categorical survey responses, scaled data from questionnaires, test scores, administrative or financial data, or data specifying locations, dates, or times can all be linked to the coded qualitative data already stored in (or later added to) the Cases. These descriptive and quantitative data can be recorded as Attribute Values for each Case while you are working in NVivo, or they can be imported all at once from Excel or SPSS (see Chapter 5, pp. 153–154). Any coding applied to the qualitative data intersects with the Attribute Values for that Case, allowing, for example, for analysis of the relationships between values of a quantitative variable (e.g., scores on a test) and coded text (e.g., about how the child felt about that subject and doing that test).

Structured surveys and questionnaires containing both closed questions (with pre-categorized and/or scaled response options) and open-ended questions are one of the most common ways in which mixed data are gathered (Bryman, 2006). When a pre-categorized (checkbox) response to a question is followed up with a request to respondents to provide comment, explanation, or illustration for their answer, these open-ended responses add supplementary, illustrative information. They also assist the researcher in interpreting what the associated closed-response options really meant to the survey respondents. The flexibility of the coding system in NVivo means detail in the comments is readily coded into Nodes representing emergent themes, as well as being (automatically) sorted by the question asked. Text identified by these Nodes is then linked to responses to demographic, categorical, or scaled questions for each Case, stored as Attribute Values.

The web and social media provide new forms of data to contribute to mixed methods projects – even though, like surveys, the data comes in through a single method. Social media such as Twitter, Facebook, and YouTube, downloaded and imported using NCapture, have a similar structure to a survey database. Fields such as *number of retweets* or *number of likes* are numeric; other fields, such as *location*, are categorical; while open-ended fields such as the *tweet* or the *post* provide qualitative data. Because NVivo is able to help capture these data and transform them into a spreadsheet-style structure, they can be managed and analysed using similar tools. (Details about working with social media, specifically, can be found in Chapter 10.)

Conflicting responses regarding harassment and discrimination

In a self-report questionnaire about discrimination experienced by female physicists, respondents provided both categorical (yes/no) responses and written examples and comments to questions about being treated differently, being harassed, or experiencing discrimination at various stages of their student and work careers. Queries were used to sort the examples and comments for each of these according to whether the respondent gave a yes or no response to the categorical questions, to provide a participant-based understanding of what constituted harassment and discrimination. When is harassment (or discrimination) 'acceptable', that is, not felt to be sufficient to warrant a yes response? How is this different from harassment that is considered unacceptable? Of particular interest were inconsistent responses, where a similar example might be used to illustrate both yes and no categorical responses. Answers to all these questions could be explored in the kinds of explanations given, and also using associated statistical data pointing to the demographic characteristics of those giving conflicting responses.

Analysing mixed methods data

In the context of this chapter, NVivo has a range of features and tools that contribute to complementary analyses of qualitative and quantitative data, and to comparative and transformative analyses that further integrate those data, regardless of whether the different forms of data were imported from separate sources or together in a survey. Procedures used in

NVivo, illustrated by visual examples, for the types of analyses outlined here are provided in Section 6.3.

Complementary analysis strategies supported by NVivo

Complementary strategies are those in which data from different (types of) sources that relate to the same topic or issue, collected either sequentially or at the same time, are brought together for analysis (Table 6.1). This basic mixed methods strategy allows for the different data to mutually inform and/or build on each other to provide a fuller picture of the topic being investigated.

Table 6.1 Complementary analysis strategies

Analysis strategy	Data/sources	NVivo tools
Review coded data from all Files for a particular topic or each aspect of an overall topic, regardless of data type, to create and report on a comprehensive picture of that topic or issue.	Data from multiple (i.e., any) File types.	Coding and retrieval. Show Attribute Values in Coding Stripes as an option when reviewing (Windows only). Use a Concept Map or Memo to record what is learned.

Dimensions, conditions, and consequences of wellbeing

As part of a study on the relationship between health and wellbeing, Pat was interested to know how older women understood wellbeing. She had data from interviews, surveys, picture elicitation data, and free listing responses, as well as literature. Data from all these sources were coded to identify components of wellbeing. Considerable time was spent reviewing, recoding, and regrouping the combined data in the Nodes, 'playing around' with these until they 'made sense.' Pat then put these Nodes into a Concept Map. Rearranging them helped her to identify that some were dimensions of wellbeing (capacity to engage, forward orientation, social connection/attachment, and autonomy/independence), while other Nodes were seen to be more about conditions affecting wellbeing (e.g., economic security, physical health), or consequences of wellbeing (e.g., self-care). Evidence supporting this arrangement came from literature, interviews, and surveys, in combination.

Consider what is reported on a topic in Files of different types, e.g., compare interview data with field notes and/or statistical summary data with a view to finding commonalities, while also noting differences.	Coded data in Files of different types.	*Windows users:* Save (Folders of) Files of different types as Sets. Use a matrix to view data from these for particular Nodes. Alternatively, use an adapted Framework Matrix for side-by-side viewing.

Comparative analysis strategies supported by NVivo

Comparative analyses are a core mixed methods strategy that combine quantitative data for Cases with the qualitative data coded to those Cases (Table 6.2). They show if, how often, and in what ways the coded qualitative data might vary for subgroups that are defined by Values of demographic or other categorical or numeric variables. These kinds of analysis serve a variety of purposes, including (but not only) descriptive reporting for subgroups, validation of scales, and identifying dimensions within concepts.

Table 6.2 Comparative analysis strategies

Analysis strategy	Data/sources	NVivo tools
Compare and contrast distribution and content of qualitative data based on Attribute Values, coded contexts, or Sets, for purposes as outlined above.	Coded case data; linked categorical or scaled data.	Crosstab or Matrix Coding Query and associated Charts, using Codes and Attribute Values or Sets.

Comparing wellbeing among different groups of people

In Pat's study of wellbeing and health for older women, the way in which the women describe wellbeing (in general, and for themselves) can be compared, for example, for those who live alone or with family, for those who experience different levels of economic security, and for those who score at different levels on the World Health Organization (WHO) scale of wellbeing.

Compare distribution and content of qualitative data based on newly created Attribute Values.	Text and other non-numeric data.	Attributes; Crosstab and associated Charts.

Generating Attribute Values from qualitative coding

A study was designed to better understand and provide for safe travel from home to work for adults with a range of communication and mobility issues. In interviews, family members and employers discussed the level of mobility of these adults as they journeyed from home to work: they could be highly mobile (i.e., few transportation issues), somewhat mobile (i.e., some sporadic difficulties), or problematically mobile (i.e., consistent difficulties). These characteristics, developed initially through qualitative analysis as Codes, were turned into Attribute Values for the purpose of comparing how members of these three groups talked about a range of travel and other experiences, coded in other rich, qualitative Nodes.

(Continued)

(Continued)

Analysis strategy	Data/sources	NVivo tools
Combine qualitative and quantitative data to create blended variables and use these for comparisons within both statistical and qualitative data.	Text and other non-numeric data.	Attributes; Crosstab or Matrix Coding Query.

_____ **Spinal injury patients' desire** _____
for and access to services

In Lynn Kemp's (1999) PhD study of the community service needs of people with spinal injuries in New South Wales, she found a mismatch between need and care delivery. While her quantitative data revealed a desperate shortage of community services, the qualitative data spoke of people feeling ambivalent about whether they would access services they had most complained about not having. In her quantitative database, she combined Nodes reflecting people's feelings about services (exported from NVivo) with a variable that reflected their current use of services. This created a four-category variable that blended use of and desire for services. Subsequent quantitative analyses using this variable suggested that the qualitative ambivalence to services was the response of the people with spinal injuries to the apparently arbitrary distribution of community services, despite these being legislatively mandated to be allocated according to need. Lynn then added the blended use-desire variable to the qualitative Project as an Attribute and used it in combination with Values for service satisfaction scales to compare respondents' qualitative responses about the beneficial and detrimental effects of services. When re-analysed qualitatively, the quantitative arbitrariness of service provision was, in fact, not so arbitrary. Services were allocated on the condition that persons with spinal injuries adopted life plans which met the expectations of service providers, demonstrated by being not too independent, nor too dependent, and by showing suitable levels of gratitude and humility.

Transformative (conversion) analysis strategies supported by NVivo

Qualitative Nodes can be converted into quantitative variables, a process referred to as transformation in the mixed methods literature. These variables can be created as dichotomous (binary, 0/1) scores based on the presence or absence of each code for each Case (or File), or as a measure based on the frequency with which a Node is used within a Case. These variables can then be used in a statistical program for further analyses. Whenever such variable data are used, check back to the qualitative data on which the statistics were based, for further insights and deeper understanding of the statistical results obtained.

The following includes just some samples of what can be done using transformative strategies (Table 6.3). Use these as a basis for imagining other possibilities to suit your own needs. This is an area of work that is currently undergoing rapid development, prompted in part by the explosion of big data.

Table 6.3 Transformative analysis strategies

Analysis strategy	Data sources	NVivo tools
Obtain frequency counts for codes, showing how many sources or passages are coded by each. Use as part of descriptive reporting for a study, or as background information in an appendix.	Coded qualitative data.	List View display Node Summary Report (Windows only) Group Query (Windows only)
Make numeric and relative (%) comparisons of differences in distribution of coded text in Nodes for subgroups of the sample (based on Values of an Attribute).	Coded Case data with Attributes.	Crosstab

Positive and negative emotions during early and late stages of a career

Researchers, at different stages of their career, experience positive and negative emotions to varying degrees. A Crosstab of emotions by career stage (earlier/later) in the *Researchers* data shows that a higher proportion of later career researchers talk about being excited by or gaining satisfaction from engaging in research than for early career researchers. And for those few who talked about negative emotions, it would appear that uncertainty gives way to stress or anxiety as careers develop.

Export coded qualitative data for statistical analysis (assuming sampling is adequate), using frequencies, comparisons, regressions, etc. to supplement qualitative with quantitative analyses or to compare and contrast results from different approaches to analysis.	Coded qualitative data. Cases and/or Files.	Crosstab of Codes against Cases. Matrix Coding Query with Cases or Files in rows, and Codes in columns. Export displayed data from either Crosstab or Matrix to Excel or SPSS.

Judges' decisions and compensation paid for accidental injuries

In a study of court awards of compensation to be paid by insurers for injuries received from motor vehicle accidents, the primary data were judgments made by the judge or arbitrator deciding each case. The primary analysis was designed to derive an understanding of the process of judges' decision-making about compensation in these cases, but because the amount awarded was known, it was possible also to test how relevant particular considerations were in determining the amount of the award. Where the text of the judgment included discussion relating to, say, the veracity of the plaintiff, the regularity of his or her previous employment, the nature of the injury, whether the medical assessments were those of a treating doctor or one brought in especially by the insurance company, or whether there was conflicting medical evidence presented, that part of the text was coded at appropriate Nodes in NVivo, regardless of where it occurred in the document.

(Continued)

(Continued)

The presence or absence of such coding for each Case then could be exported to Excel or SPSS as dichotomized values and added to the variables already there (which included some facts about the court case and, critically, the amount awarded). Statistical testing could then be used (once data from a large, consecutively drawn sample were aggregated) to assess whether these considerations, either singly (using t-tests) or in combination (using multiple regression or, possibly, qualitative comparative analysis), were associated with the level of compensation paid.

Visualize patterns of association between sources or between Nodes using Visualizations based on exploratory multivariate analyses.	Sources and/or Nodes.	*Windows users*: Cluster and Multidimensional displays and associated statistics.

Cluster analysis of literature based on word similarity

Imagine you wanted to gain a preliminary view of whether the academic and professional literature in your project dealt with the same issues and in similar ways. A cluster analysis of those literature Files, based on word similarity, shows whether or not the Files fall neatly into two main clusters, based on the language used in relation to the topics covered. Later, when they have been coded, you could cluster them on the basis of the similarity of their coding, to see whether the two groups actually do cover different issues, or whether any apparent differences were more to do with the way the issues were expressed in the two different literatures.

Apply exploratory multivariate analysis techniques to exported data using SPSS or another statistical program, including cluster analysis, multidimensional scaling, or correspondence analysis.	Exported coded source or case data (as above); exported Crosstabs or Matrices based on intersections of Nodes.	Matrix Coding Query: Export displayed data to Excel or SPSS for further analysis.

Characteristics of high-performing researchers

Pat explored the association between the 29 descriptors given by academics to the way high-performing researchers worked (e.g., persistent, creative, strategic) and the outcome of performance (products, reputation, impact) that was mentioned at the same time. Data were coded in NVivo with frequency of association (intersections) between the two sets of Nodes identified using a Matrix Coding Query. These frequencies were transferred to SPSS and correspondence analysis was used to visually display the associations between these two sets of factors (Bazeley, 2018).

SECTION 6.3: SURVEYS AND MIXED METHODS IN NVIVO

NVivo terms used in this section

Attribute

Chart

Classification

cluster analysis

Crosstab

Dataset

dendrogram

Matrix Coding Query

survey

Value

Importing and managing mixed data files

Mixed methods projects typically embrace multiple types of Files, representing different types of data, as outlined earlier. The process for importing most types of non-numeric data such as pdfs and transcripts (Chapter 1), multimedia (Chapter 9) and social media (Chapter 10) are similar.

Management systems are especially important when dealing with mixed File types. It is strongly recommended that each type of File is stored in its own dedicated subfolder within the Data > Files area, as shown in Figure 6.1. Not only does this provide visual clarity, it facilitates selection of files with similar structural characteristics for scoping when running Queries or other processes.

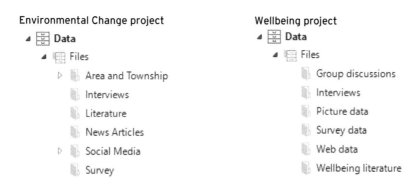

Figure 6.1 Examples of Folder structures for projects with multiple File types

Importing demographic and quantitative variable data for Cases

Demographic and other quantitative variable data play an important part in most mixed methods studies. These will be set up in your project as Attributes for Cases, where relevant Attribute Values will become associated with the qualitative data in each Case. Attributes can be set up interactively in NVivo or imported from a table in Excel or SPSS. Instructions for doing it either way were provided in Chapter 5.

Importing and managing survey data

Survey data containing both open- and closed-ended questions (e.g., Figure 6.2) can be imported from an Excel spreadsheet. Windows users can also download an online survey directly from SurveyMonkey or Qualtrics.

In NVivo, a structured survey or questionnaire is imported as a Dataset. A Dataset typically contains both qualitative (open-ended) and quantitative (numeric or categorized) fields, set out in a spreadsheet. Data for Cases are entered in rows, one case per row, while columns define fields for the data being entered in response to particular questions. In the example in Figure 6.2, Column A lists the names of the Cases, while other columns

A1		f_x Respondent						
Down East Survey Responses.xlsx								
A	B	C	D	E	F	G	H	I
Respond	The natural environment Down East is	The water quality Down East is	Commercial fishing Down East is	Township	Generations Down East	Pace of development	Age	Gender
DE046	beautiful, clean, full of life, rare on the East coast, the main attraction, even for the local people	apparently very good	an important way of living, heritage and generations handed down to family as well as making and mending fish nets and decoys for hunting	Straits	1	about right	52	Male
DE047	Special environment for wildlife + hearty people	still in good shape	almost gone	Smyrna	3 or more	about right	42	Female
DE048	one of the most scenic in the world	clean and inviting	dying, fuel prices, foreign competition, encroachment by fishermen from other state (FL), and lack of customers for custom made fishing boats are hurting the comm. fishermen.	Sea Level	1	too fast	49	Male
DE049	not polluted & is clear + clean.	of good reproductive quality for marine life.	in danger, Fuel costs and markets there seems to be plenty of seafood.	Marshallberg	1	too fast	56	Female

Figure 6.2 Survey data, prepared using an Excel spreadsheet[1]

---

[1]For convenience when entering and viewing data in Excel, select columns that will contain text data then **Right-click > Format Cells > Alignment tab > Wrap text**.

match questions that were asked. Cell entries in Columns B–D contain short verbatim text responses to structured questions. Cell entries in Columns E–I contain demographic information relating to each case. Columns might be used also to include numeric codes or text labels selected in response to pre-categorized questions; 0/1 data indicating selection of an alternative from a list; or a score from a scaled test, rating, or visual analogue scale. Potentially, also, text cell entries might contain summarized contents from longer interviews, perhaps including pithy quotes.

When the survey is imported, Cases are created for each participant, with each person's open-ended responses coded to their Case and their closed responses recorded as Attribute Values for their Case – thus qualitative and quantitative data are recorded together in a Case for each person. In addition, all responses for each open-ended question are Auto Coded to a Node for that question. These are collected together in a tree in the Nodes area, under the survey title.

Auto Coding qualitative survey data (NVivo Plus only)

The *Survey Import Wizard*, for those who have NVivo Plus, offers an additional step in which participants' responses to the open-ended questions are Auto Coded into thematic groups and responses are coded as expressing positive or negative sentiment. These Auto Coding tools are optional and we advise they should be used with caution. Coding can be checked and modified afterwards, but as a general rule, as qualitative researchers, we have found that human coding is more valid. See Chapter 4 for additional information on Auto Coding.

━━━━━━━━━━ **6.a.** ━━━━━━━━━━

Importing a survey prepared in Excel (Windows)

⇒ *Ribbon*: **Import > Excel.**

⇒ **Browse** to locate the Excel file **> Open > Next**. The *Survey Import Wizard* (Figure 6.3) will open. **Step 1** of the wizard provides information only **> Next**.

⇒ *Survey Import Wizard*: **Step 2**: **> Check data format.**

  o Check the number of rows used for question headers (e.g., SurveyMonkey typically uses two; in Excel, you would normally have just one).

  o Check the format of your dates and times, if you have them (hover for additional information) **> Next.**

⇒ *Survey Import Wizard*: **Step 3**: **> Manage your survey respondents**. This step creates Cases for your respondents.

  o Choose where you want to store your Cases. Cases can be already existing, or new, but all will need to be in the same location (in a Folder, or under a parent Case).

  o Indicate which column in your survey data identifies the Cases.

(Continued)

(Continued)

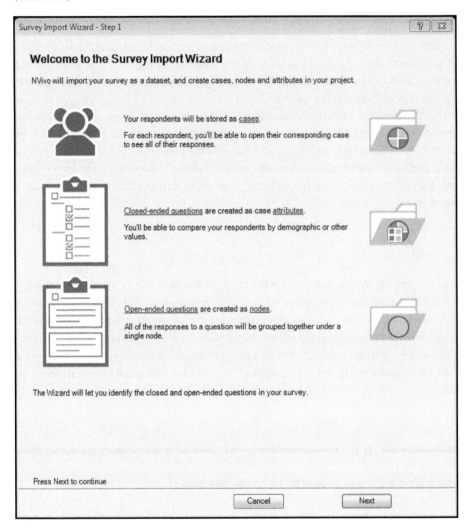

Figure 6.3 The *Survey Import Wizard*

o Indicate the Case Type of the Cases (as explained in Chapter 5): are you creating a new Classification for them or using an existing one? **> Next**.

⇒ *Survey Import Wizard*: **Step 4**: Check that NVivo has correctly identified which questions in your survey are open-ended (qualitative) and closed-ended (quantitative), as shown in Figure 6.4. NVivo allows you to scan the first 25 cases to check your choices.

o Data from open-ended questions will be stored in a Folder (with the same name as your survey) under Nodes.

o Data from closed-ended questions will become Attributes of Cases **> Finish** (if you are in NVivo Pro).

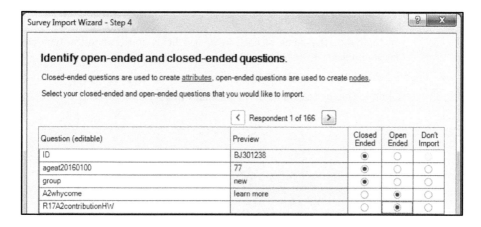

Figure 6.4   Choosing question type in Step 4 of the *Survey Import Wizard*

⇒   NVivo Plus users:

 o   **Step 5**: (NVivo Plus only) > **Auto Code Themes and Sentiment** (Figure 6.5) > **Finish.** NVivo will then show you the progress of your import.

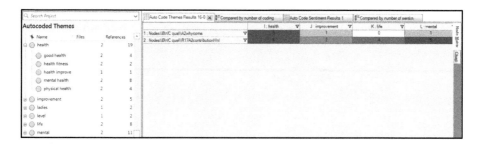

Figure 6.5   Nodes and Matrix display of results from Auto Coding themes related to wellbeing (NVivo Plus)

Importing a survey prepared in Excel (Mac)

⇒   *Ribbon*: **Data > Import Dataset > Select** the file > **Open.**

⇒   *Import Dataset Assistant*: **Step 2 of** 5 (if you only have 1 sheet in your workbook, this step will be skipped and the remaining steps will be 2 of 4, 3 of 4, etc.).

 o   **Select** the worksheet you want to import > **Next.**

⇒   *Import Dataset Assistant*: **Step 3 of 5**.

 o   Check the format of your dates and times, if you have them.

 o   **Tick** First row contains field names > **Next.**

⇒   *Import Dataset Assistant*: **Step 4 of 5** (Figure 6.6).

 o   Check that NVivo has correctly identified which questions in your survey are Classifying (quantitative) and which are Codable (qualitative). NVivo allows

(Continued)

(Continued)

you to change the name of each field, skip fields and change the type of Classifying fields. Examine the first 25 cases, to check your choices **> Next.**

⇒ *Import Dataset Assistant:* **Step 5 of 5.**

o Option to change the **Name** of the Dataset **> Import.**

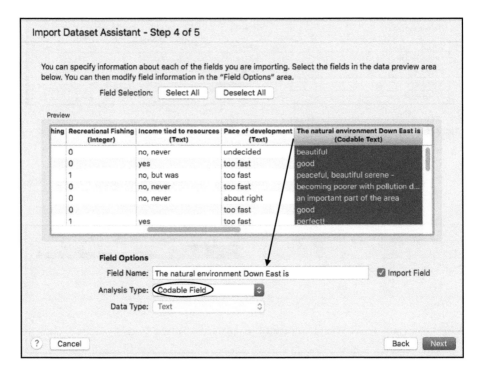

Figure 6.6 Choosing question type in Step 3 of the Import Dataset Assistant (Mac)

If you are working in the Mac version, you might need to take additional steps to create a Node for each open-ended question and to create Cases and a Classification sytem. We provide these steps in the online resources (https://study.sagepub.com/jackson3e).

Importing survey data from SurveyMonkey or Qualtrics (Windows only)

⇒ *Ribbon:* **Import > Import Survey > From SurveyMonkey/Qualtrics.**
⇒ You will then be asked to provide your login details to continue.

Once you have located your file, the *Survey Import Wizard* will open and you can continue to work through the wizard as for Excel (above).

Viewing and (interactively) coding survey data in NVivo

⇒ *List View:* **Double-click** [your survey file] to open it.
⇒ *Detail View:* Use the tabs on the right margin to display the information in **Table** or **Form** view.

Coding of the qualitative content can be carried out in this view, but we find it is easier to do it by coding on from either the stored Cases or from the stored responses to each question:

- if the focus of the survey was to understand each Case, then go to *Navigation View*: **Cases > Cases > [your subfolder]** and click to see the Cases in the *List View*. Work through each Case, coding each one's responses to all of the open-ended questions.
- if the focus of the survey was on a series of separate issues covered by the questions, go to *Navigation View*: **Codes > Nodes > [your survey folder]** and click to see the questions in the *List View*. Work through each question, coding the responses to that question from all respondents.

NVivo tools for integrated mixed methods analysis

Many of the tools you regularly use in NVivo are also of assistance in mixed methods and survey analyses. These include Code retrievals, the Matrix Coding Query, and several of the visualizations that are available. The Crosstab, which you met in Chapter 5, is an additional tool provided specifically to support mixed methods. Methods for using these tools to support the types of integrated mixed methods analyses outlined earlier (in Section 6.2) are described below.

Node retrievals for complementary analyses

Simple code retrievals (as described in Chapter 3, pp. 155–160) provide valuable data for complementary analyses because they bring data together from any or all of your Files, regardless of what type of source they represent, for any topic of interest that is represented by a code. Associated display options can sometimes assist interpretation.

━━━━━━━━━━ **6.b.** ━━━━━━━━━━

Using Node retrievals in a complementary mixed methods analysis

Nodes are retrieved in the usual way, but Coding Stripes can be displayed to show additional complementary data.

Retrievals with complementary Case or Node data

⇒ *Navigation View*: **Codes > Nodes.**
⇒ *List View*: **Double-click** on a Node to open it in *Detail View*.
⇒ *Ribbon*: **Node Tools / View**. Use **Coding Stripes > Nodes Most Coding** to show intersecting Nodes and Cases as you work through the retrievals; or
⇒ *Ribbon*: **Node Tools**. Use **Coding Stripes > Coding Density Only >** hover over the grey bar in the Coding Stripes area to see the intersecting Nodes and Cases.

(Continued)

(Continued)

Retrievals with complementary Attribute data (Windows only)

⇒ *Ribbon*: **Node Tools**. Use **Coding Stripes > Selected Items > Case Classifications > Select** a Classification from the right side of the dialogue to limit which Attribute Values are shown > **OK**.

Record what you have learned

⇒ *List View*: **Right-click** on the Node > **Memo Link > Link to New Memo >** provide a **Name >** OK **/ Done**.
⇒ Record what you learn from reviewing that topic and its associated data. Use See Also Links (Windows only, Chapter 1, pp. 30–32) to connect an insight with the quote or other item that prompted it.

Joint displays for complementary and comparative analyses

Joint displays, recently popularized as an integrative mixed methods strategy by John Creswell and associates (e.g., Guetterman, Fetters, & Creswell, 2015), are a variation on the types of summary tables or comparative matrices researchers have been constructing historically, using pencil and paper or a spreadsheet. Different types of data are juxtaposed in order to detect both convergence and difference across those different sources for particular thematic categories.

Technically, a Matrix Coding Query can provide the kind of information sought in a joint display, but the contents of each cell in the matrix have to be viewed one cell at a time, and there is no facility within the software for summarizing or printing the contents of matrix cells. Creating a useful and printable joint display requires using a workaround[2] based on the Framework Matrix tool.

6.c.

Constructing a joint display using the Framework Matrix tool (Windows only)

Create Cases for the Files

Create Cases for the Files you want to use in your joint display, if they don't already exist; or, to compare groups of Files of particular types (such as are stored in Folders):

⇒ *List View*: **Right-click** on the Folder or on selected Files **> Create As Set** > **Name** it **> OK**.
⇒ *Navigation View*: **Search > Sets > [your new Set] > Right-click > Create as Code** (save to a new Folder in the **Cases** area to keep these separate from your regular Cases).

Create the Framework Matrix

⇒ *Ribbon*: **Create > Framework Matrices > Name** your new Framework Matrix.

---

[2]At the time of printing. This could change in the future.

    o   **Rows** tab > **Select** the **Cases** made from Files (or groups of Files).
    o   **Columns** tab > **Select** the **Nodes** you want to compare across > **OK**.

Show the intersecting content

    ⇒ *Detail View*: **Click** in any cell to activate the **Framework Matrix** tab in the *Ribbon*.
    ⇒ To show the intersecting content in any cell:

       o   *Ribbon*: **Framework Matrix > Associated View > Cell Coding**.
       o   **Click** in any cell to see the intersecting content in the Associated Data panel on the right.

Fill cells with intersecting content

To fill the cells with content, you have two options:
    ⇒ Work through and type in your own summaries (Figure 6.7); or
    ⇒ Fill with all intersecting content. (*Beware*: this is likely to create a very large table.)

       o   *Ribbon*: **Framework Matrix > Auto Summarize > OK**.

Export the table

    ⇒ *Detail View*: **Right-click > Export Framework Matrix** (to Excel).
    ⇒ In Excel, select the matrix > **Copy > New Sheet > Right-click > Paste (Transpose)** to obtain a classic Joint Display.

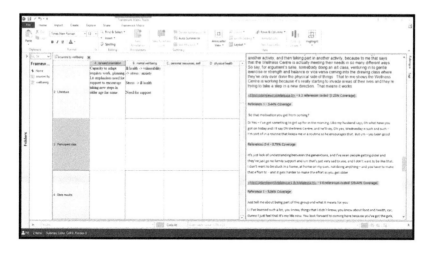

Figure 6.7 Using a Framework Matrix to construct a Joint Display

Crosstab for pattern and comparative analyses involving Attribute Values

The Crosstab was introduced in Chapter 5 (pp. 155–160) as a means of obtaining a rapid and flexible overview of the pattern of responses for Nodes across selected Attribute Values. It shows which subgroups of the sample (i.e., those defined by particular Attribute Values) talked about selected topics or themes, how much they said, and, if a Cell is double-clicked, what they said. The *Ribbon / Options panel >* **Results** accompanying the display indicates the form of the results being shown – whether counts of Cases, percentages of passages, etc., as described in Chapter 5 (pp. 156–159).

Subgroups considered in a Crosstab might be based on demographic values or responses to closed-ended questions, stored as Attribute Values. For a mixed methods project, they might also be based on Values of a ranked or scaled (numeric) Attribute, such as scores on a test, or ratings of an experience (Figure 6.8). The Crosstab then combines the qualitative and quantitative data in its display, with the qualitative data for each selected Node separated and sorted to allow for comparison of that coded data across the Values of the selected Attribute. As always, data are initially presented as counts to facilitate identification of patterns, but then a double-click on a cell reveals the qualitative data for that cell. Windows users can also view results in a Chart (Chapter 5, p. 159).

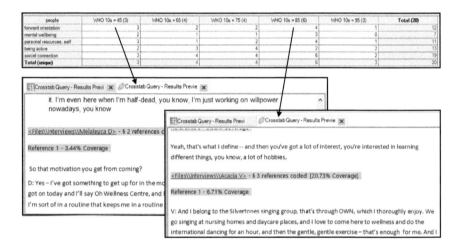

Figure 6.8 Crosstab combining qualitative text with quantitative scaled data

Note: Nodes in this table depict some of the ways in which older women talk about wellbeing, with responses compared based on their scores on the WHO wellbeing index.

Crosstab to transform coding for export as variable data

The Crosstab can be used also to rapidly transform qualitative coding into variable data for Cases, to export directly to Excel or SPSS for statistical analysis, or to add to existing demographic or other variable data in SPSS for further analysis.

━━━━━━━ **6.d.** ━━━━━━━

Transforming Codes using a Crosstab

Set up the data in a Crosstab

⇒ *Ribbon:* **Explore / Query > Crosstab** (Windows: Figure 6.9; Mac: Figure 6.10).
⇒ *Detail View:* **Crosstab Criteria > Crosstab codes against /** *Options panel >* **Query > Show node against > Cases.**

⇒ Add **Codes** to the Crosstab (drag or click +).
⇒ Add **Cases** to the Crosstab (drag or click +).
⇒ **Crosstab Criteria / Crosstab Query > Search in >** Choose options for where to search.
⇒ **Run Query**.
⇒ *Ribbon*: **Crosstab Tools /** *Options panel* **> Results > Select** options for what is counted (**Coding References** or **Coding Presence**) and how these are shown (**Counts**).

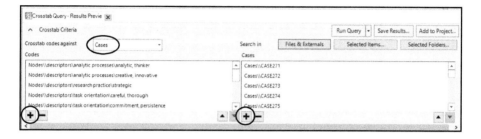

Figure 6.9 Crosstab specifications used for transformation of coding to variable data (Windows)

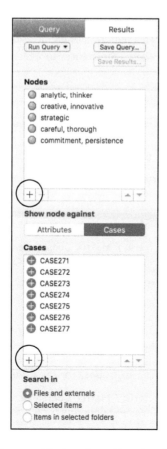

Figure 6.10 Crosstab specifications used for transformation of coding to variable data (Mac)

(Continued)

(Continued)

Export the data

⇒ *Detail View:* **Right-click** > **Export Crosstab Results** / *Detail View Top:* **Share Button** > **Select** your preferred **File type** (Excel or SPSS /Spreadsheet or SPSS), and **Save /OK**.

Coding Presence will be converted to 0/1 codes in an exported SPSS file.

Matrix Coding Queries for pattern and comparative analyses

The Matrix Coding Query is one of the most versatile analysis tools in NVivo for mixed methods researchers because of its unique capacity to combine multiple forms of both qualitative and quantitative data in a great variety of ways. Like the Crosstab, it facilitates comparisons of qualitative data for subgroups of the sample that are defined by Attribute Values and it can be used to generate variable data from coding, but the options provided by the Matrix Coding Query for pattern searches and transformation of data extend those provided through the Crosstab. We will provide basic instructions for using this tool with Nodes (in Windows and Mac) and Sets or Search Folders (Windows only), and then follow this with a list of the variations that are possible, with the circumstances in which each of these variations could be useful.

━━━━━━ **6.e.** ━━━━━━

Run a Matrix Coding Query

⇒ *Ribbon:* **Explore** / **Query** > **Matrix Coding**. A set-up panel will open in *Detail View* (Figure 6.11).

Select Nodes for Rows in the Matrix

⇒ *Detail View:* **Matrix Criteria** / **Matrix Coding Search Criteria** > Click the **plus** symbol at the bottom-left of the **Rows** panel > **Select Items**.

  o In the **Select Project Items** dialogue, click on the word **Nodes** (do not check the box!).
  o Check the boxes next to the Nodes you want in your Matrix Coding Query > **OK / Select**.

⇒ Use the **minus** symbol to remove any unwanted selections.

Select project items (e.g., Sets – or Nodes) for the Columns in the Matrix

⇒ *Detail View:* **Matrix Criteria** / **Matrix Coding Search Criteria** > Click the **plus** symbol at the bottom left of the **Columns** panel > **Select Items**.

  o In the **Select Project Items** dialogue > click **Nodes** or **Sets** (do not check the box!).
  o Check the boxes next to the specific Nodes or Sets you want in your Query > **OK / Select**.

⇒ If Sets are selected: Click on the first (Collections) icon at the bottom-right of the Columns panel to check the options for displaying Sets. The default is to show each Collection as a single item, using one column for each Set.

⇒ Use the **minus** symbol to remove any unwanted selections.

⇒ *Detail View*: Check options at the top right of the **Matrix** dialogue:

   o **Matrix Criteria / Matrix Coding Search Criteria > Search in:** Choose whether you want all **Files and Externals, Selected Items** (particular Files, Nodes, Cases, or Sets), or all items within Selected Folders to be included in the analysis.

   o **Add to project / Save Query** allows you to store the specification for the Matrix Coding Query so that you can run it again at a later time, for example, if you add to or change your data in some way, or for a different Folder of Files or Selected Items.

⇒ **Run Query**.

View and refine Matrix Query results

⇒ *Ribbon*: **Matrix Tools / View > Node Matrix** > Refine the display using options in the **Cell Shading, Cell Content**, and **View** groups (Figure 6.11).

⇒ *Detail View*: **Double-click** on any cell to see the associated text.

⇒ **Save Results** will store the results for future reference (located in *Navigation View*: **Search > Query Results**). Saved Results will not be updated if your data change.

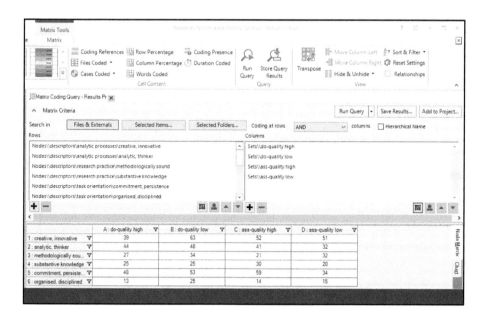

Figure 6.11 Using a Matrix Coding Query with Sets (Windows)

Note: Sets in this analysis were created from Cases that were assigned ratings that fell into the uppermost and lowest quartiles for the importance of quality (compared to 7 other characteristics) when doing research and for assessing research performance. Nodes selected for the analysis were those often used by those participants to code descriptions of researchers demonstrating quality in their research.

Options for selecting Row and Column content in a Matrix Coding Query

For primarily qualitative analyses, where you want to explore the pattern of association between one set of Nodes and another set of Nodes (see Chapter 7, p. 209):

- Nodes in rows, Nodes in columns, to find the pattern of association between groups of Nodes (e.g., Aspects of the *natural environment* by *Attitudes*).

For mixed methods comparative analyses:

- Nodes in rows, Attribute Values in columns (this option is more commonly carried out using a Crosstab).
- Nodes in rows, Sets (Windows only) in columns.
- Nodes in rows, Nodes representing a different aspect of the coding structure (e.g., context, inputs, outcomes) in columns.

	analytic, thinker	creative, innovative	strategic	careful, thorough	commitment, persistence
CASE271	1	1	0	0	0
CASE272	1	1	1	1	1
CASE273	1	1	0	0	0
CASE274	1	1	1	1	0
CASE275	0	1	1	1	0
CASE276	1	1	1	0	0
CASE278	0	1	1	1	0
CASE279	1	1	0	1	0
CASE28	0	1	1	1	0
CASE280	0	1	0	1	1

(a) Case by variable table (presence/absence of code for cases)

	commitment...	organised, ...	strategic	methodologi...	technical skill	substantive ...	analytic, thi...
commitment, persist...	133	20	8	7	4	15	27
organised, disciplined	20	74	8	7	4	7	16
strategic	8	8	63	5	4	7	12
methodologically so...	7	7	5	96	12	19	37
technical skill	4	4	4	12	44	6	9
substantive knowled...	15	7	7	19	6	86	33
analytic, thinker	27	16	12	37	9	33	151

(b) Similarity matrix (frequency of co-occurrence between Nodes)

	creative, innovative	careful, thorough	commitment, persistence	finisher	problem solver
impact	52	13	11	14	18
product	8	1	9	15	5
reputation	4	3	8	7	11

(c) Pattern matrix (frequency of co-occurrence between Nodes)

Figure 6.12 Matrix data based on qualitative coding for export from NVivo for use in statistical analyses

Note: Examples are from data in which academics described the characteristics of high-performing researchers. (Source: Bazeley, 2018: 185, Figures 8.1, 8.4, and 8.3.)

To generate transformed data for export to statistical software for further analysis:

- Cases in rows, Nodes in columns, to generate a case by variable table for descriptive or inferential statistics (e.g., Figure 6.12a: this can also be created using a Crosstab).
- Files in rows, Nodes in columns, also to generate a source by variable table for descriptive or inferential statistics.
- Nodes in rows, the same Nodes in columns, to generate a (reflected) similarity matrix for cluster analysis or multidimensional scaling (e.g., Figure 6.12b).
- Nodes (e.g., describing an outcome) in rows, Nodes (e.g., describing input) in columns, to generate a pattern matrix as a basis for, say, correspondence analysis (Figure 6.12c).

Variations in how rows and columns are combined in a Matrix Coding Query

The default in the Matrix Coding Query dialogue is to search for **Coding at rows AND columns** (Figure 6.13), which, for mixed methods analyses, is what you will almost always want, and always when Attribute Values, Sets, or Case Nodes are part of the Query. This means, for the examples above, in any particular cell, NVivo will find text that matches both the Node (or Case) for that row AND the Set (or Node) for that column (a Boolean intersection). In Windows, this option can be changed so that the finds meet alternative criteria, such as differences or proximities. Because these options are more relevant to qualitative analyses than to mixed methods analyses, they will be described more fully in Queries (Chapter 7, 210–211, 225).

Figure 6.13   Selecting the operator for combining rows and columns

Should I use a Matrix Coding Query or Crosstab?

The Matrix and Crosstab tools serve overlapping but slightly different functions. The Matrix Coding Query offers a greater range of options and functions than the Crosstab, but for analyses involving Attribute Values in particular, the Crosstab offers speed, convenience, and vital attribute information not available in the Matrix. The differences are outlined in Table 6.4 to help you make a decision about which to use.

Table 6.4   Comparison of Crosstab Query and Matrix Coding Query

Crosstab Query	Matrix Coding Query
Limited options as to what is included (Codes by Attribute Values; Cases by Codes).	Items that can be included in either or both rows and columns include Files, Cases, Nodes, Attribute Values. Windows users can also use Sets.
Rapid processing.	Processing of large matrices can be slow.

(Continued)

Table 6.4 (Continued)

Crosstab Query	Matrix Coding Query
Provides counts, totals, and proportions based on the size of the relevant sample.	Provides counts and proportions based on finds (not on the size of the sample).
Allows only for Boolean intersections of rows and columns (AND).	*Windows only*: Allows for full range of Boolean (AND, OR, NOT) and proximity (NEAR, PRECEDING, SURROUNDING) operators to combine rows and columns.

Visualizing coded data in multivariate displays (Windows)

Exploratory multivariate analyses are used in mixed methods research because they do not have the same sampling and data requirements (e.g., normality of distribution) as regular statistical analyses (Bazeley, 2018: Chapter 9). They can be useful for revealing structure within data, including underlying dimensions. Although statistics are available, multivariate analyses are most valued for their visual displays which use spatial geometry to present the patterns and relationships found in the data.

Cluster Analysis (Windows only), as one of the forms of multivariate analyses provided in NVivo, identifies and groups similar items in your data sources (Files) or in coded text (Nodes) and presents the results in visual form. In providing a visualization of the structure of the data, it allows you to gain some distance to supplement your thematic understanding arising from close reading of your Nodes (Guest & McLellan, 2003). NVivo's clustering tool

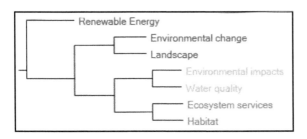

Node A	Node B	Pearson ▽
Nodes\\Natural environment\Water quality	Nodes\\Natural environment\Environmental imp	0.484135
Nodes\\Natural environment\Habitat	Nodes\\Natural environment\Ecosystem service	0.452668
Nodes\\Natural environment\Water quality	Nodes\\Natural environment\Environmental cha	0.442685
Nodes\\Natural environment\Environmental ch	Nodes\\Natural environment\Ecosystem service	0.40437
Nodes\\Natural environment\Landscape	Nodes\\Natural environment\Environmental cha	0.400106
Nodes\\Natural environment\Environmental im	Nodes\\Natural environment\Environmental cha	0.392465
Nodes\\Natural environment\Water quality	Nodes\\Natural environment\Ecosystem service	0.383477
Nodes\\Natural environment\Habitat	Nodes\\Natural environment\Environmental cha	0.377993
Nodes\\Natural environment\Habitat	Nodes\\Natural environment\Environmental imp	0.329755

Figure 6.14 Dendrogram and associated statistics based on clustering Nodes by word similarity (Windows)

assesses similarity based on either (a) the similarity in the frequency with which the top 100 *words* are used in the selected Files or are found in data coded with the selected Nodes, or (b) the similarity in the frequency with which the same *codes* have been applied to the text or images in those Files or Nodes. Similarity can be assessed in different ways, with NVivo using Pearson correlation as a default method (see Figure 6.14). The similarities are then presented as a horizontal or vertical dendrogram – a diagram which shows which of the selected Files or Nodes were most similar, then groups them based on a progressive reduction in the number of clusters created (Figure 6.14). These displays are accompanied by a list of the statistical measures of association (e.g., correlation coefficients) between all pairs of items in the display. Results are conditional on which Files or Nodes are selected for the analysis, as well as the measure selected for assessing similarity, and will vary if these vary (Hair, Black, Babin, & Anderson, 2010).

In NVivo these similarities between Files or between Nodes can also be shown mapped, using similar metrics, in a multidimensional scaling (MDS) process in two- or three-dimensional space (Figure 6.15). The primary value of MDS is to allow the user to detect dimensions underlying similarities in the data. These are detected from the way in which the Files or Nodes vary across, say, each of the horizontal or vertical dimensions of a display, with the user rotating the display until they feel confident in interpreting the pattern they are seeing. Visual clusters (groupings) of the points in the display might also be evident.

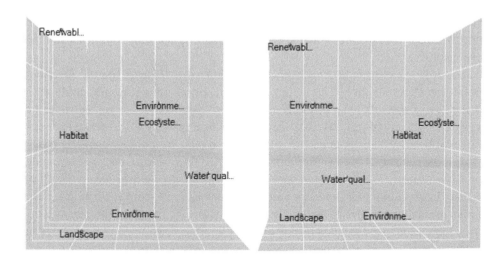

Figure 6.15 Three-dimensional cluster diagrams, based on clustering Nodes by word similarity (Windows)

Clustering or dimensionalizing data based on similarities in words used or in coding is generally best used in an NVivo project in an exploratory manner to provoke ideas, rather than as explanatory evidence of association – there are so many factors and choices that are potentially influencing the results obtained (especially where coding is involved). Other methods of exploring the data can then be used to investigate those associations in more depth. Note also that the clustering and dimensionalizing results that are produced by NVivo are likely to be different from those that would be obtained if data are exported to a statistical program; the units of analysis being compared will be different and the processes chosen for measuring similarity and for agglomerating (building) clusters may also be different. Statistical programs, additionally, provide measures of stress or goodness of fit of the models shown.

Figure 6.14 shows a simple example from NVivo, created from a Cluster Analysis of the *Nodes* used for coding data about different aspects of the natural environment in the *Environmental Change* Project, based on the words found in any of the coded material. Clearly this diagram suggests that renewable energy was spoken about very differently than other aspects of the local environment (perhaps it belongs elsewhere in the coding system?). The display suggests links that might be followed up by examining the text at those Nodes (available as a right-click option from the display) or by running a Coding Query to review intersecting text.

A summary of the correlation coefficients used to create the dendrogram is also provided, accessed via a tab on the display, also shown in Figure 6.14 (columns can be sorted by clicking on the header row). If you examine the statistical summary for the cluster analysis, you will see that *Water quality* is closely linked with *Environmental impacts* and is drawn to show that, but it is almost as closely linked with *Environmental change*, which is drawn in a different cluster. In cluster analysis, the presence of quite close links can be hidden by higher-level links. Nevertheless, Guest and McLellan (2003: 189) argue that 'cluster analysis provides a useful alternative [to MDS graphs] as it presents data in clearly defined clusters in two-dimensional space, rendering a quick and easy visual tool for interpretation'.

The alternative of using MDS to view the associations in 3D space has the advantage that it affords the possibility of seeing a third dimension, thus revealing clusters not necessarily apparent from the dendrogram. Different perspectives are gained when the mouse is used to rotate the 3D MDS map, shown in Figure 6.15. The relative statistical associations between *Water quality*, *Environmental impacts*, and *Environmental change* become more evident (along a vertical dimension) than they were in the 2D dendrogram, with *Water quality* positioned between the other two on the vertical dimension. Note also how the positioning of *Landscape* and *Habitat* changes markedly, for example, when the dimensional perspective is changed, indicating that they share commonality on one vertical dimension, but are much further apart on another when the image is rotated on a vertical axis.

6.f.

Cluster Files or Nodes for a multidimensional display (Windows)

Cluster Files

⇒ *Navigation View*: **Data > Files**.
⇒ *List View*: **Select** Files for clustering (Files need to be in the same Folder).
⇒ **Right-click > Visualize > Cluster Analysis of Selected Items**.

Cluster Nodes

⇒ *Navigation View*: **Codes > Nodes**.
⇒ *List View*: **Select** Nodes for clustering (Nodes can be in different trees, but need to be at the same hierarchical level).
⇒ **Right-click > Visualize > Cluster Analysis of Codes or Cases**.

Modify the display (the display must be open in **Detail View***)*

⇒ *Ribbon*: **Cluster Analysis > Options > Clusters** > Change the number of clusters shown to improve the readability of the display.
⇒ *Ribbon*: **Cluster Analysis > Select Data** to change the display to a clustering based on **Coding similarity** rather than **Word similarity**.
⇒ *Ribbon*: **Cluster Analysis > Type**. Change the display from a dendrogram to a **3D Cluster Map** and experiment with rotating the MDS display using the mouse.
⇒ *Detail View*: **Double-click** on an item in any display, to open it.

Overall options for gaining a multidimensional perspective on your data (with some cautionary notes) include:

- Cluster sources or Nodes on the basis of word similarity in NVivo. Words included in your stop list will not be included in the calculations.
- Cluster sources or Nodes on the basis of coding similarity in NVivo. In this, NVivo is looking at what other Nodes any of the requested Nodes are coded at, and is also looking for similarities in the distribution of those.
- Cluster the words generated from a Word Frequency Query.
- Export a case by variable table (from a Crosstab or Matrix Coding Query of Cases by Nodes) to Excel or SPSS. Run cluster analysis of the variables (Nodes) based on similarity in their distribution across the Cases (this is a more traditional format for data to which cluster analysis is applied than that used in NVivo), or alternatively cluster the Cases on the basis of similarities in patterns of coding.
- Create a similarity matrix in NVivo by adding the same list of Nodes to both the rows and the columns of a Matrix Coding Query. Export the matrix to SPSS or via Excel to a similar statistical program to run MDS based on the similarity matrix (Bazeley, 2018).

Overall, then, you have two broad choices of strategy in approaching these kinds of tools:

- Because these visualizations are quick and easy to generate in software like NVivo (and can be fun to play with), use them there primarily as a way of sparking ideas, without putting too much weight on the results obtained. If these visualizations lead you to explore some aspect of your data that then becomes profitable for your analysis, it is the evidence you gather in that further exploration that will support your conclusions, rather than the clustering or other visualization.
- You can engage in an extended statistical endeavour, using the evidence gained through the calculations done either by NVivo or a follow-on statistical analysis (e.g., in SPSS) to build a case for a conclusion – but if you are going to do so, then you will

need to have a much more thorough understanding of what you are doing with the particular approach you choose to take, and you will need to further support your conclusions with additional analyses.

Guest and McLellan (2003: 198–199) wisely concluded:

Cluster analysis can be both a useful and a powerful tool, but its use must be tempered with common sense and in-depth knowledge of the raw data. Interpretation is only as good as the procedures that precede it (i.e., code development and application), and applying structure to an unfamiliar data set will have little meaning for even the most seasoned researcher. Used properly and solidly grounded in the data, cluster analysis can help provide meaningful structure to QDA and thematic interpretation.

SECTION 6.4: CHAPTER 6 TAKEAWAYS

━━━━━━━━ Key points from this chapter ━━━━━━━━

o Tools to assist in the analysis of mixed methods data (including surveys) are provided by NVivo. These include:

- The ability to import and work with multiple diverse types of data files within the one project.
- Tools for importing and managing survey and social media datasets, as well as regular text sources and attribute data.
- The capacity to manage complex data, including cases constructed from multiple and/or partial data files.
- Linking of qualitative and quantitative data through the addition of numeric attributes to case data.
- Regular and special tools to facilitate complementary, comparative, and transformative analyses of mixed data, including Crosstabs and the Matrix Coding Query.

o The Crosstab rapidly counts Cases and Coding References for comparative or transformative displays and exports, but has a limited range of inputs.

o When it comes to mixed methods analyses, the Matrix Coding Query is a best friend for comparative and transformative analyses. It is versatile with regard to both input data and output content. It combines both qualitative and quantitative data.

o Both Crosstabs and Matrices provide both quantitative and qualitative data to both summarize and elaborate on results obtained. Anyone using the numbers from these displays must also check the text to ensure that the numbers are used meaningfully.

Tips, challenges, and warnings

- Whenever you generate results in a mixed methods analysis, immediately review those results and write about what you learn from them. Be very selective in saving results of Crosstabs and Matrices, in particular, for later review. They will make most sense to you at the time you generate them, and it is very easy to end up with a very large number of saved Matrices that will not be meaningful or useful to you at a later time. Furthermore, saved results will not update if you make a change in your data (save the Query instead).

- Efficient data management is critical to successful conduct of a mixed methods project. Learn to make effective use of Folders, Cases, Attributes, and Sets to manage different elements within your Project.
- When case counts are displayed in a Crosstab (or Matrix result), in order to test the null hypothesis of no difference between different groups (as defined in the columns) for the Nodes shown in the rows, there are two points to consider:

    o Testing has to be conducted for each row separately, i.e., you cannot run a chi-squared test across the whole table. This is because the Nodes in the rows are not mutually exclusive (the same data could be coded at more than one of the selected Nodes).

    o To test a single row using the chi-squared statistic, you need to use the number of Cases with each of the Attribute Values as the expected values, as shown in the header bar of the table. Alternatively, if you use a Compare Proportions test, you will need to calculate what *proportion* of Cases has each of the Values used based on the *N*s in the column headers.

When importing survey data

- You cannot add or edit fields in a Dataset after it has been imported, but:

    o you can annotate them, e.g., if you find an error you want to correct;
    o you can change an Attribute Value after it has been assigned to a case (annotate the survey file to note the change);
    o you can add additional data to the same cases by importing a second dataset (or other sources) and coding it to the same Case(s).

- Auto Coding from a new survey will be added to previous Auto Coding results unless the names of the existing folders have been changed.

Using displayed results from Crosstabs and Matrix Coding Queries

- Always give thoughtful consideration to the purpose for which you are using the output when selecting the cell content (usually Coding References or Cases) for the display and associated Charts.
- Percentages in Crosstabs are calculated very differently from those in Matrix Coding Queries. The latter are useful only if you are interested in comparative character-based counts of volume of text.

Help files

- *File*: Help.
- *Menu bar*: **Help > NVivo Help.**

Search for any of the following:

- Cluster analysis diagrams
- Crosstab query
- How are cluster analysis diagrams generated?
- Matrix coding query
- Qualtrics
- SurveyMonkey
- Surveys and datasets

Practice questions

1   What advantage does NVivo offer for researchers using mixed methods, compared to working 'by hand', with Excel, or with a statistical program?
2   If you are collecting data from different types of sources for the same cases, what options do you have for managing those sources in NVivo?
3   If you do follow-up interviews with people who have answered a survey, what steps (inside and outside NVivo) do you need to take to effectively link and compare the two sets of responses?
4   If you are exporting case data for statistical analysis, when might you use dichotomous case counts, and when might you choose volume counts (number of Coding References or Words Counted)?
5   Why is it important to return to the qualitative data after conducting a comparative or transformative (statistical) analysis of the data?

7

Section 7.1: Introduction to Queries   200

Section 7.2: Conceptual grounding in Queries   201

Section 7.3: Working with Queries in NVivo   217

Section 7.4: Chapter 7 Takeaways   232

QUERYING DATA

All models are wrong; some models are useful. (Box, Hunter, & Hunter, 2005: 440)

SECTION 7.1: INTRODUCTION TO QUERIES

In earlier chapters, we introduced some of the Queries at times when they could be helpful. It is a good idea to get into the habit of checking and rechecking the associations in your data as you progress, rather than waiting until the end to 'test' the associations. As with any quantitative or qualitative analysis, your results will only be as good as is allowed by the combination of your:

- skill in coding, linking and reflecting within the Project;
- ability to ask relevant questions (to guide your choice of Queries);
- capacity to interpret – and challenge – the output.

This chapter begins with a discussion of ways to explore your data with an interrogative mindset, developing questions for which Queries and other tools will be useful. Then we help you think comprehensively about the Queries available in NVivo, so you will be better able to turn to them when you need them. We also discuss the Framework Matrix tool in NVivo, which technically is not a Query but certainly acts like one.

In this chapter you will

- Think about what you are aiming for in your Project.
- Review the range of Queries available in NVivo, and the features they have in common.
- Try different strategies for developing theory based on case analysis and/or associations between Nodes.
- Learn how to build reports to suit your needs.

Other chapters with related materials

Chapter 2: Designing an NVivo Project

Using NVivo's ability to focus on Folders, Sets, Cases, and Values will facilitate efficient and effective use of Queries. Review Chapter 2 to get a handle on how the structure of your Project will influence the efficiency with which you can run some Queries.

Chapter 4: Advanced coding

You will likely want to create Node hierarchies while being mindful to use 'vista' Node structures and avoid 'viral' ones. Vista structures will be especially helpful in running Matrix Coding Queries. Other aspects to consider from Chapter 4 that might influence your use of Queries and Query Results include the amount of context to code and the use of Word Frequency Query and Text Search Query to create Nodes.

Chapter 5: Cases, Classifications, and comparisons

Chapter 5 helps you construct Cases in NVivo. This area of the software is especially helpful if your research involves additional design complexities such as the examination of change over time, or requires the comparison of subgroups.

SECTION 7.2: CONCEPTUAL GROUNDING IN QUERIES

The analytic journey

Start your analysis with a question, a concept, a puzzle, and explore from there. Write as you go, and small questions will build into bigger ones. Explore, test, check back into your data and into your disciplinary literature, building up until you reach an integrated picture. The secret to analysis is in asking questions of the data, and then thinking through how you might pursue ways of answering them from the data. If you have stalled in the approach you are currently using, go back to the methodological literature seeking fresh stimulation. Read other studies using the same methodology, even if they are on an entirely different topic, for further ideas on strategies to use. Read theory and wonder how it might inform your study. Check out Part III of Richards (2015), Parts 3 and 4 of Bazeley (2013), and Chapter 11 of Miles, Huberman, and Saldaña (2014) for a wealth of practical strategies for searching, querying, displaying, and seeing your data as you seek to move your project forward and bring it to a conclusion. Bazeley (2013), in particular, addresses the issue of how to move forward if you reach the point of saying 'I've coded all my data. Now what do I do?' by proposing a three-step 'describe, compare, relate' process to apply to each of the categories or concepts you have developed.

Working with one Node at a time, write a description of what you found out about that concept or category. Then, compare how different Cases or subgroups talk about it, asking questions all the time to challenge the data. Use questions such as, 'What is it about this group that led them to respond differently?' to prompt ideas about relationships in and across your data. Use Queries to check those out. By the time you complete this with a selection of your Nodes, you are starting to build a web of understanding and the beginnings of theory.

By now, you should have a strong sense of where you are heading, what you are expecting to achieve, what questions your project will answer, and what will bring it all together. Outcomes of your work with your NVivo Project might include:

- 'Thick description' – a term popularized in the ethnographic writing of Geertz (1973) to convey deep understanding of a culture or experience. Thick description goes beyond details of spoken content to include wider semiotic analysis and attention to context. It is more than simply reporting what you observed or what your participants said.

- Theory development – qualitative analysis is typically described as being an inductive process. Your focus, as a theory builder, is to work at identifying and making sense of the patterns and relationships in your data; theory will not emerge on its own. Theory is often small and local to start with; as your work extends and grows, so will your theoretical sophistication.
- Theory testing – less frequent as a primary goal for a qualitative project. NVivo's Query tools do allow, however, for extensive testing of hunches or hypotheses which have been brought to the Project or developed within it.
- Practical application – in policy analysis, situation analysis, needs analysis, or program evaluation.

Going further into theory building

We recognize that talking about theory or theory building can seem slightly daunting to some researchers. The thought that your data and the analysis of them has to use, contribute to, and make sense of or build theory can halt the research process altogether. We can think about theory in terms of connecting ideas, and this seems far less daunting. Everyone can use, develop, and generate ideas. (Coffey & Atkinson, 1996: 140)

Essentially what you are looking for in developing theory is to specify patterns and relationships between concepts. Theory supports explanation or prediction. 'The acts involved in [developing theoretical sensitivity] foster seeing possibilities, establishing connections, and asking questions. ... When you theorize, you reach down to fundamentals, up to abstractions, and probe into experience. The content of theorizing cuts to the core of studied life and poses new questions about it' (Charmaz, 2006: 135). The question now is: How can you use your coding system and the Queries provided by NVivo to move toward your destination?

Starting from Nodes, building associations

By now you should be well practised in applying strategies for reviewing concepts stored at Nodes. In this section, we encourage you to push your thinking about using your Nodes and applying or modifying tactics (including Queries) you learned in earlier chapters to find answers to your research questions.

[T]he move from coding to interpretation involves playing with and exploring the codes and categories that were created. ... categories can be retrieved, split into subcategories, spliced, and linked together. Essentially, the codes and categories you have selected should be used to make pathways through the data. (Coffey & Atkinson, 1996: 46)

Choose a Node which appears to be quite central to your current thinking about your topic. This might be selected because it is common to many Files, or because it frequently appeared as a focal point in Maps, or because you wrote extensive Memos about it. Then play with some of the following activities:

- Review the Node – reading through, writing a Description, recording any further ideas and questions prompted by it in a Memo, refining the coding.
- Provide the Node with a job description (What is its purpose? How is it meant to achieve that?) and then subject it to a performance review.
- View it with Coding Stripes visible. Depending on the Node, you might choose to view Stripes for all Nodes, or refine your view to selected Coding Stripes (e.g., for people referred to in this context, or a set of consequences).
- Chart a Node to examine the distribution of data across your Files (Chapter 3, pp. 93–94).
- View it with a Hierarchy Chart of Nodes to see the other Nodes coded to the same data. *List View*: Identify a Node > **Right-click > Visualize > Hierarchy Chart of Nodes Coded at This Node**.
- Run a Coding Query (Chapter 3, pp. 96–97) to check more precisely any apparent relationships, or a Matrix Coding Query (Chapter 6, pp. 186–189; and 7, p. 223) to explore possible differences associated with contextual factors or conditions or outcomes.
- Create a Project Map (Chapter 1, pp. 26–32) and place this Node at its centre. Ask to see associated items and ask yourself what other Nodes (or other Project items) should be linked to it? Write about what you are learning. If a question arises as you are writing, explore or check it immediately.

Repeat these processes for other Nodes which appear to have a potentially central role in your project. If you have a number of Nodes that focus around a core idea, try creating what Lyn Richards termed a 'dump Node' with them – perhaps more formally referred to as a metacode.

- Copy each of them and merge into a new Node, or if they are in a concept-based Set, right-click to create the Set as a new Node.
- You might add in the results of some Text Search Queries and Word Frequency Queries (Chapter 4, pp. 126–130) as well, just to make sure you have all possible aspects included.
- Scan the contents of that larger Node to gain a sense of its overall 'shape' and dimensions (perhaps use a Word Frequency Query scoped just to that Node to help). Uncode any clearly irrelevant passages. Now scan it again, showing Coding Stripes for the original set of Nodes. Do your original Nodes adequately reflect the dimensions of this broader concept?
- Try using this new metacode in a series of Crosstabs or Matrix Coding Queries with Attribute Values and with other Sets of Nodes. See how it varies depending on who is the source of the comments, or the conditions under which they arise, what strategies are being applied, or what the consequences are. This may confirm your original subcategories, or it may reveal a new way of seeing (new dimensions in) this concept. Understanding what brings about the different realizations of a phenomenon helps to create understanding of the phenomenon itself (Peräkylä, 2004).

Again, repeat these processes for other Sets or metacodes which also have a potentially central role in your project. Which Nodes (original single Nodes, or metacodes) still 'stand up' (have the best explanatory power) after going through these examination processes? These are categories that will move you forward in your analysis as you look for ways they, with their dimensions, might link together to provide an interpretive description, enriched understanding, comprehensive model, or explanatory theory, supported by data. Using all of these approaches to analyse your data will help you better understand and more appropriately use NVivo's cadre of Queries.

Understanding the Queries

When you run a Query, NVivo searches through your data to locate all the text references, picture regions, and media extracts that meet the criteria of your inquiry. The different types of Queries have a common architecture, but they allow you to construct and find data to answer the unique questions arising in your Project. Before we deal with specific instructions, however, we will review the general function and capabilities of Queries in NVivo according to three groups:

- Word or phrase Queries
- Theory-building Queries
- Administrative Queries

The distinction we make between these three groups is largely heuristic, however, as the word or phrase Queries can be used to build theories and the theory-building tools can be directed toward clerical tasks. We begin our orientation to Queries with a brief description of each and examples of the visual displays that each produce, to help you see how they might assist your analysis. This description is designed to give you an overview without distracting you with all of the clicks and options that we provide later in the chapter.

Word or phrase Queries

Word-based Queries search the text material in the Project for specific words or phrases. There are two types of these in NVivo: Word Frequency Query and Text Search Query.

Word Frequency Query overview

A Word Frequency Query catalogues the words used most often in the data or a subset of the data; it is a popularity contest among words (Figure 7.1). Researchers usually use the Word Frequency Query to explore or map words used in the data, and this tool is often used as part of content analysis. One visual is the Word Cloud which visualizes the top 50 words: the larger the word in the Word Cloud, the more often it appeared within the Query Results (notice the column for Count in Figure 7.1). You can double-click on a word in the list or the visualization to see all of the words in context (bottom half of Figure 7.1) and save this material as a Node if you wish.

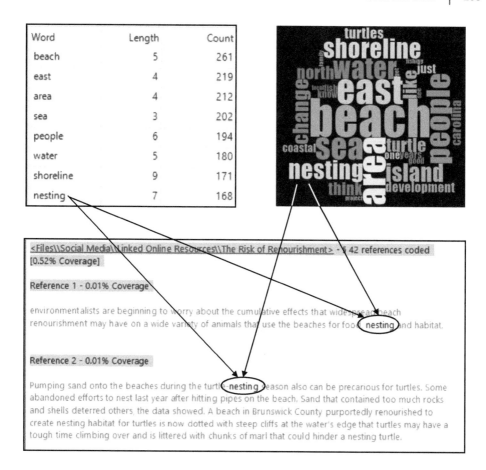

Word	Length	Count
beach	5	261
east	4	219
area	4	212
sea	3	202
people	6	194
water	5	180
shoreline	9	171
nesting	7	168

<Files\\Social Media\\Linked Online Resources\\The Risk of Renourishment> - § 42 references coded
[0.52% Coverage]

Reference 1 - 0.01% Coverage

environmentalists are beginning to worry about the cumulative effects that widespread beach renourishment may have on a wide variety of animals that use the beaches for food, nesting and habitat.

Reference 2 - 0.01% Coverage

Pumping sand onto the beaches during the turtle-nesting season also can be precarious for turtles. Some abandoned efforts to nest last year after hitting pipes on the beach. Sand that contained too much rocks and shells deterred others, the data showed. A beach in Brunswick County purportedly renourished to create nesting habitat for turtles is now dotted with steep cliffs at the water's edge that turtles may have a tough time climbing over and is littered with chunks of marl that could hinder a nesting turtle.

Figure 7.1 Word Frequency Query with visualization

A few ways you might use the Word Frequency Query:

- Create a Set (Chapter 5, pp. 160–161) of your Files that represents one of your subgroups and run this Query only on the subgroup.
- Compare the Word Clouds of two different Folders or Sets (e.g., compare literature with interviews, or Time 1 with Time 2).
- See if some of the interview questions tend to generate responses with different kinds of words (e.g., thoughts, feelings, actions).
- Examine the different kinds of language a participant uses when he/she is in an individual interview versus a focus group.
- After running another Query, run a Word Frequency on the Query Results to see the kinds of words commonly found in this material.

Text Search Query overview

A Text Search Query searches for words or phrases you specify in the data or a subset of the data; it is a purposeful hunt, not a popularity contest (Figure 7.2). Researchers usually use this when they are aware of key terms or phrases and want to locate all related data (often nouns like *Island* or *Fishing boat*). Unlike the Word Frequency Query that presents a list of words, this provides a single window with all References that satisfied the criteria (top half of Figure 7.2). One visual is the Word Tree that presents recurrent phrases in a branching structure (known as key-word-in-context – KWIC).

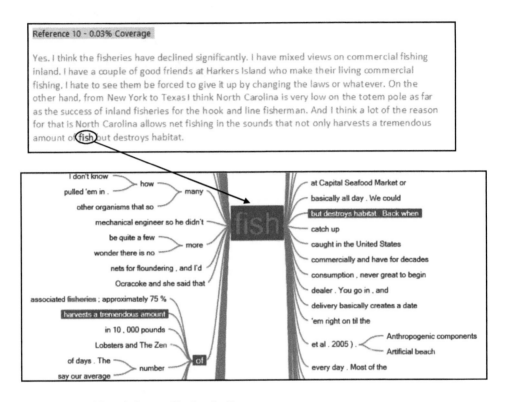

Figure 7.2 Text Search Query with visualization

A few ways you might use the Text Search Query:

- Double-check the interactive coding you did with a Text Search Query.
- Combine a Text Search Query with a Coding Query (using AND NOT) in a Compound Query (Windows only).
- Because you became aware of a concept late in a study and cannot go back through the data due to time constraints, craft a Text Search Query to help you look for the concept in the Files already coded.
- Run a Text Search Query on a subgroup (Folder or Set) in your data and compare the Word Tree to another subgroup.
- Run a Text Search Query and use the Word Tree to check out keywords that precede or follow the central word; right-click on a keyword preceding or following the central word to run another Text Search Query that narrows down the search on that phrase.

- Use a Text Search Query to explore the frequency of a phrase instead of individual words, looking both across and within Files.

Theory-building queries

Theory-building queries help you explore the relationships among items in the NVivo Project and are the most likely among the Queries to lead you toward a rich interpretation of the data. These Queries include the Crosstab Query, Matrix Coding Query, Coding Query, and (Windows only) Compound Query.

Crosstab Query overview

A Crosstab Query shows you a table of Cases or Attribute Values by Nodes. Researchers tend to use this Query when they want quick access to the data coded to Nodes, separated by Attribute Values (Figure 7.3). It presents a fairly straightforward comparative display but requires that you have Cases in your NVivo Project, and a Node or File Classification System in your Project (Chapter 5). Unlike a Matrix Coding Query, the Crosstab Query makes it easy to enter two Attributes of interest at the same time and provides the number of Cases for each Attribute Value as well as the totals for each column and row. While some of these elements of the Crosstab Query make it appealing, the Matrix Coding Query allows you to enter more types of Project items in the columns and rows (e.g., Files and Sets). After running a Crosstab Query, double-click on a cell to see the qualitative data. Windows users can instantly turn the Query Results into an interactive chart. If you are looking for a Cases by Nodes format in which the cells can be populated with the intersecting text, see our concluding instructions on the Framework Matrix (which technically is a kind of Note in NVivo, not a kind of Query).

Person	Gender = Female (40)		Gender = Male (64)		Total (104)
	Recreational Fishing = No (21)	Recreational Fishing = Yes (19)	Recreational Fishing = No (23)	Recreational Fishing = Yes (41)	
Economy	20	18	22	41	101
Natural environment	21	19	23	41	104
Real estate development	20	18	22	39	100
Total (unique)	21	19	23	41	104

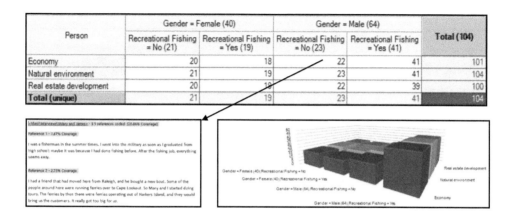

Figure 7.3 Crosstab Query with visualization

A few ways you might use the Crosstab Query:

- Look at the interaction of two Attribute Values after running them separately to compare the Results.
- Generate a Crosstab of all Nodes by all Cases to obtain a comprehensive overview of the prevalence of Nodes in each Case.
- Run a Crosstab with two Attribute Values and use the 'Selected items' button to first select one subset of the data (e.g., *Time 1*) and then run it again on another subset of the data (e.g., *Time 2*).
- Compare the prevalence of a topic across representatives of a particular subgroup to identify topics that, although present, are the focus of particular people within the subgroup.

Matrix Coding Query overview

In a Matrix Coding Query, a wide range of items in the Project can be paired via the rows and columns of a table without necessarily requiring the construction of Cases or a Classification system. The items can be Files, Nodes, Cases, Sets, and even Query Results. Double-click on a cell to see the qualitative data. Windows users can instantly turn the results into an interactive chart (Figure 7.4) and both Windows and Mac users can export the table into other programs (e.g., Excel) to create charts. While the diversity of potential items in the Query make it appealing, the Crosstab Query provides the number of Cases for each Attribute Value as well as counts for each cell, column, and row. The Matrix Coding Query does not. The Crosstab Query also makes it easier to run two groups of Attribute Values in the same Query (e.g., *Male* or *Female* as well as whether a participant fishes *Recreationally* or not, as in Figure 7.3). Additional examples of differences between the Crosstab Query and the Matrix Coding Query are provided in Chapter 6 in Tables 6.1, 6.2 and 6.3.

	A : Positive	B : Mixed	C : Negative	D : Neutral
1 : Real estate development	112	13	131	1
2 : Infrastructure	8	3	20	0
3 : Policy, management	8	3	12	0
4 : Natural environment	93	15	95	10

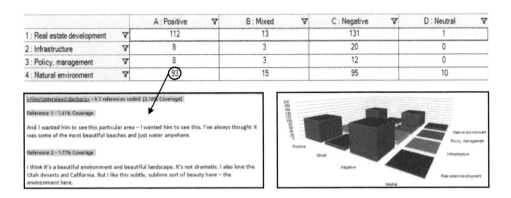

Figure 7.4   Matrix Coding Query with visualization

A few ways you might use the Matrix Coding Query:

- Generate a Matrix Coding Query of all Files by all Nodes to obtain a comprehensive overview of the prevalence of Nodes in each File.

- Compare Nodes by Sets of Files to examine prevalence of coding by a characteristic other than an Attribute Value (e.g., your Sets for *Time 1*, *Time 2*, and *Time 3*).
- Run Nodes by other Nodes to observe the coding at pairs of Nodes. Windows users can run multiple iterations with different kinds of Boolean operators (AND, OR, NOT) and Proximity parameters (NEAR, PRECEDING, SURROUNDING).
- Take your *Memorable quotes* Node and run it against all other Nodes to contribute to your write-up, being careful not to cherry pick your results.
- Run Attribute Values by Node Sets (Windows only) to generate more refined Sets from the content in each cell.
- Run Attribute Values by other Attribute Values to facilitate the creation of a Set of Files that represent the interaction of two Attribute Values. These Sets can be used in subsequent Queries.

Coding Query overview

A Coding Query finds text or other data in response to a single, sometimes complex question involving multiple Nodes and/or Attribute Values. Often constructed to test an idea that emerged during analysis, the Coding Query can be used to examine the connections between just a few items or a large number of them.

This Query can overcome the practical limits of the number of project items that interact in the cell of a Crosstab Query (practical maximum of four in a cell) or a Matrix Coding Query (practical maximum of three in a cell). While five or more may seem like a lot of items, some researchers want to ask one very complicated question using different types of Boolean logic in a single inquiry. For example, what do (1) fathers (2) over 50 years of age say about

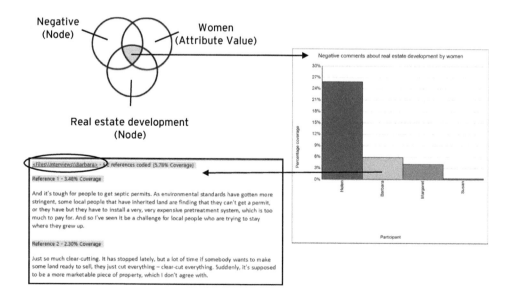

Figure 7.5 Coding Query with visualization

(3) future hopes for their (4) sons, but only if the fathers are (5) single and (6) not employed in the commercial fishing industry. You can chart the results in several ways if you save the Query Results, including prevalence of results by File (Figure 7.5). The Venn diagram on the top left of Figure 7.5 is not available in NVivo but inserted to help you visualize the example of an intersection of three elements (two Nodes and one Attribute Value).

A few ways you might use the Coding Query:

- To explore very particular associations between two Nodes, perhaps based on a hunch recorded when coding.
- To look for coding in Node A or Node B that is also in Node C.
- To answer associations suggested by the review of a Crosstab Query or a Matrix Coding Query but that cannot be tested by these Queries.
- To examine the intersection of three or more items but only when specific Attribute Values are also true.
- To further explore the results in the cell of a Crosstab Query or a Matrix Coding Query when the data in the cell seems to be at odds with your knowledge of the data and the Project.
- To look for data that has not been coded.

Compound Query overview (Windows only)

A Compound Query identifies qualitative data within the Files (Nodes or text strings) near or adjacent to other qualitative data (other Nodes or text strings). Researchers often use this to loosen the restriction of a strict Boolean intersection to look at data within a user-defined distance within the File. Some also use it in a narrative analysis to find the kinds of language that occur before or after other language. For example, find the word *fisheries* near the words *policy* or *policies*, as long as they are within 50 words, reporting both finds and text in between (Figure 7.6). Users can also look at the closeness (in the File) of any combination of the following, in any of the File types that can be imported into NVivo:

- Text strings
- Nodes
- Coding Query Results

You can chart the Query Results in several ways, including frequency of results by File.

A few ways you might use the Compound Query:

- You run an intersection of two Nodes with a Coding Query because you suspect they have a relationship, but encounter few Query Results. You decide to run these two Nodes again in a Compound Query but ease up the restriction so they do not need to be intersecting, but simply near each other.
- In an online chat room, you want to trace the beginnings of conversations that you coded. For example, you coded some conversations as *Contested* and others as *Agreeable*.

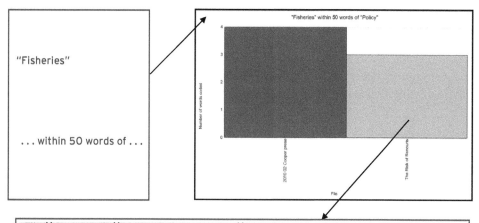

"Fisheries"

... within 50 words of ...

"Fisheries" within 50 words of "Policy"

<Files\\Social Media\\Linked Online Resources\\The Risk of Renourishment> - § 3 references coded

The North Carolina Marine **Fisheries** Commission, the state's major regulatory agency on marine **fisheries** issues, outlined the potential dangers in November 2001 and declared in a **policy** statement that 'the array of large-scale and long-term beach alteration projects currently being considered for North Carolina constitutes a real and significant threat to the marine and estuarine resources and **policies**' of the state. Scientists note that the mole crabs, coquina clams and other creatures that live in the sand in the surf zone are a critical part of the food chain.

Figure 7.6   Compound Query (Windows only) with visualization

You already have a sense of the words/terms that can lead to such discussions in this context and now you want to test for those relationships.

- You are looking for a passage you read weeks ago but cannot find it. You do remember a keyword in the passage, and that it was near the only passage you coded to a specific Node. Search for the word and the Node within a reasonable distance.
- You want to do a highly focused Query on a few keywords found in some Nodes in order to retrieve some specific quotes.
- You want to check the thoroughness of your coding by seeing what a search for keywords in a Node will find across all your Files, as long as that find is *not* already coded at the Node.

Administrative Queries

Administrative Queries are a little less likely to provide immediate interpretations of your data but can help you take stock of the NVivo Project. They might also be a critical step in the ongoing process of interpreting the data because you can use them to generate data, questions, or issues to explore further. These are the Group Query (Windows only) and the Coding Comparison Query.

Group Query overview (Windows only)

A Group Query finds items that are associated with other items in your Project and presents output in the form of lists (groups). Researchers usually use this to double-check the structure of the Project or to gather items in order to put them into a Set. Instantly view the Query Results in a connection map. Figure 7.7 shows the Nodes that are coded at two Files.

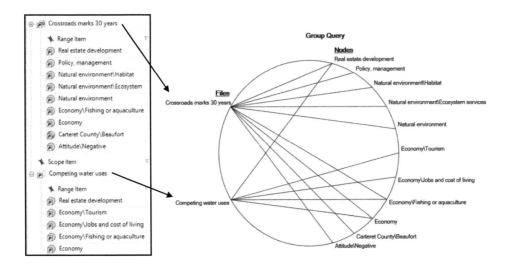

Figure 7.7 Group Query (Windows only) with visualization

A few ways you might use the Group Query:

- Find a list of Nodes coding another Node or a File.
- Create a list of Files coded to a Node.
- Generate a list of See Also Links in a Node or File.
- Generate a list of Files with a particular Attribute Value.
- Find the Nodes that are coded to a particular Case then use these in a Concept Map, with Connectors, to think about what you have learned from the Case.

Coding Comparison Query overview

A Coding Comparison Query compares the coding of two coders (or two groups of coders). The Query Results provide a kappa score and an agreement score for each unique pairing of Files and Nodes. It can help develop coding reliability among the team because of the ability to instantly access and discuss the qualitative data through the Query Results. Or, it can measure progress regarding coding consistency. Coding Stripes by User (coder) can be turned on within a Node (or File) to see the initials of the coders and where they agreed and disagreed. Figure 7.8 shows the output and the presence of the *Habitat* Node in *Barbara's* File by User.

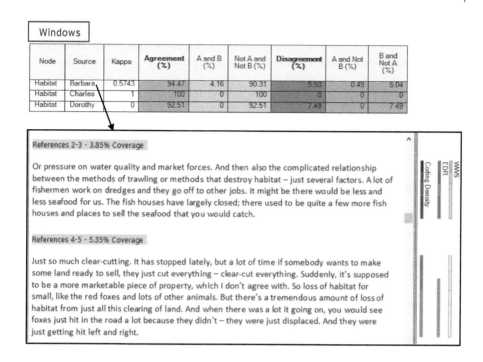

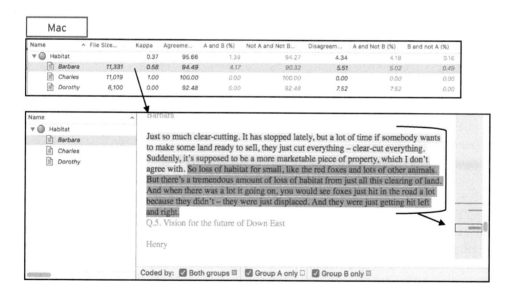

Figure 7.8 Coding Comparison Query with visualization

A few ways you might use the Coding Comparison Query:

- See how your early coding compares to the coding of one of your teammates before you progress too far into the Project.

- Use the Query to provide feedback when training new members of the team.
- Use the differences in coding to refine your Node Descriptions and examples.
- Have a colleague code data and see if you are in agreement about your observations of the data.
- Compare the coding you did to the first transcript in the beginning of the research with the way you code it later after you are more familiar with the data (create a new User Profile and code the file again to compare yourself at two time points).

Applying Queries to within-case and cross-case analysis

Some Projects will focus around one Case, but even where there are multiple Cases, one of the reasons for taking a qualitative approach is to develop a deep understanding of each of those Cases. Eventually, however, you might bring them together in either cross-case or variable-oriented analyses. It is through practical experience with multiple Cases, over and above knowledge of general theories and rules, that one gains nuanced understanding of a topic and its related issues (Flyvbjerg, 2004). Whether or not you would describe your project as a Case study, the methods of within-case and cross-case analysis are foundational to a range of methodologies from phenomenology through to programme evaluation (Bazeley, 2013).

The purpose of within-case analysis, as noted above, is to develop a deep understanding of a particular Case. Any Query can be set up to run within a single Case by moving the default **Search In** option off **Files and Externals** to **Selected Items**. For example:

- Use a Coding Query to review what a Node looks like within a particular Case, for example if you need to explore a deviant or negative Case to see how and why it is different.
- Search for text within a Case to determine whether or how a particular person used a particular expression.
- Use a Matrix Coding Query to undertake within-case comparisons or to look for within-case associations of Nodes, for example to explore changes over time.

If you have been writing a summary or building a Map of each Case as you completed your initial coding of it, then this is a really good time to read through those summaries or to review those Maps, in a sense treating these now as your data – noting recurring themes, odd discrepancies, or significant concepts. Now you are indeed ready for cross-case analysis! The dual goals of multi-case (or cross-case) analysis are succinctly expressed by Miles and Huberman:

> One aim of studying multiple cases is to increase generalizability, reassuring yourself that the events and processes in one well-described setting are not wholly idiosyncratic. At a deeper level, the aim is to see processes and outcomes across many cases, to understand how they are qualified by local conditions, and thus to develop more sophisticated descriptions and more powerful explanations. (1994: 172)

Whereas analysis based on groups of Cases (comparing those with a different Attribute Value, or all the responses to situation X compared to situation Y) gives an averaged result, in cross-case analysis the comparative focus is on the individual Cases, with their unique-ness preserved. Analyses involving cross-case analysis involve using either Crosstab, Matrix Coding Query, or Framework Analysis. We discuss each of these in turn.

Cross-case analysis using a Matrix Coding Query or a Crosstab Query

Set up your Matrix Coding Query or Crosstab Query with the required Cases in the rows, and Nodes in the columns (or Sets, if you are using Windows). If you want to refine your analysis by comparing what has been said or what happens at different time phases in the life of an organization, or through repeated interviews with the same participants, use time-based Nodes or Sets to identify the columns in a matrix (with Cases in the rows). By scoping the Query to a particular Node, you will have a comparison of how each case progressed over time for that par-ticular issue/topic. Thus, with cross-case analysis using a Matrix Coding Query, you are able to:

*   Compare Cases on a specific factor, and then refine to consider an additional dimension such as time/phase.
*   Examine and determine the significance of patterns of association in Nodes, for example, seeing how many (and which) Cases have one or other or both of two Nodes present (or three or four), and then reviewing the text at those Nodes on a case-by-case basis. Use the filter button on a column in the matrix results to sort the 'hits' on a particular item, and then view the other Nodes to which those Cases were coded.
*   Generate a coding table for Cases that can be exported as a case-by-variable matrix for use in a statistics program.

Cross-case analysis using Framework Matrices (Windows only)

As you now know, the Matrix Coding Query and the Crosstab Query generate tables with numbers, although you can double-click on any cell to access the qualitative content of a single cell. In contrast, Framework Matrices provide a table wherein the qualitative content occupies the cells across the entire table (Figure 7.9). You can ask NVivo to populate the cells with intersecting content, or you can use this as a data distillation strategy and work with it to include only the key quotes or a summary of intersecting content in the cells. This table can also be exported for further manipulation, analysis, or presentation.

This unique aspect of the Framework Matrix makes it a great tool for cross-case analysis because Cases can occupy the rows and thematic Nodes can occupy the columns. Cases can be displayed sorted by Attribute Values. You can either generate a table that is empty so you can summarize the intersecting content for each cell (which will be shown to you in the panel at the right), or you can have NVivo generate the table for you with all of the intersect-ing content already visible in the cell (Figure 7.9).

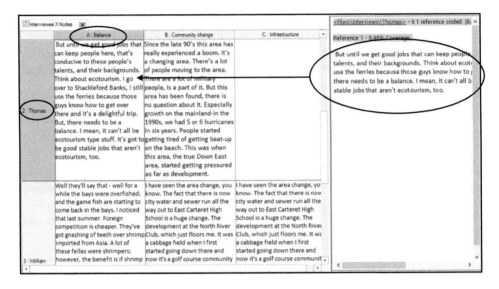

Figure 7.9 Framework Matrix cell content using the Auto Summarize feature

Keeping track of conclusions

Saving the Results is not enough to get you through your analysis, nor is printing off endless text reports from your data. These are ways of deferring thinking, and the mounting volume will quickly prove daunting. Make a practice of immediately recording what you learn from each investigation, even if it 'doesn't produce anything', because nothing is always something. Making these records as you go will save you enormous amounts of time in three ways:

- You will not find yourself running the same Query again because you forgot what the output indicated.
- Recording what you learned from the Query will prompt you to ask further questions, and so facilitate your searching and analysis process.
- The record provides the basis for your write-up. It is always easier to start writing results when you have something already written down, regardless of how 'rough' it is.

Record your emerging understanding in a special Memo in NVivo, where you can create See Also Links to the evidence that supports that understanding. Alternatively, if you are close to the end of your analysis, create a document with results in Word, and use headings liberally to identify the bits and pieces of ideas you are recording. Drop your ideas, notes, and quotes under a heading, and use the headings to navigate in your document. When you think you are done on that topic, try turning them into prose.

Visual displays

Throughout this section of the chapter we incorporated visualizations to help you understand the Queries and to provide a sample of some of the visual output. We have not exhausted all of the options, in part because visual displays and tools are used both separately from and in association with Queries. Visual summaries of data in charts, graphs, and diagrams, generated from other parts of the Project (e.g., the *List View*: **Right-click** on a **Node > Visualize**), help us see patterns and relationships in data. Creating a visual Map clarifies our understanding of who or what is involved, their relationships and their relative importance, and perhaps even causal pathways. Visualization strategies assist throughout a project – from design through working with data to later analyses and in presenting results. Therefore, be sure to explore some of the available visualizations outside of this Queries chapter as you continue to make sense of your data.

Iterative searching

When you save the Results of your Queries as a Node (or Nodes), they can be reflected upon and used iteratively in further Queries. You might start with a simple question, perhaps about the level of association between two categories, but then go on to seek further clarification or detail.

- Is it true for everyone?
- Does it depend on some other factor also being present?
- What characterizes the cases where this is not true?

In NVivo, you can repeat the Query using a different scope to see whether this association holds only for some subgroups in your Project. Or, you can use the saved Results from a first Query as one of the items in a subsequent Query. As you progress with your Project and grow in sophistication in using the Query tools, you will be able to make your questions increasingly targeted, detailed, and specific – providing your Node system and Project structure allow it.

SECTION 7.3: WORKING WITH QUERIES IN NVIVO

NVivo terms used in this section

Query

Query Results

Report

Scope/scoping

Visualization

Queries and Query Results

Before you get started, observe that each Query has two main components:

1 The Query: the customized language you use to ask a question.
2 The Query Results: the data NVivo presents to you after you run a Query.

When you go to *Navigation View*: **Search > Queries** you will find the subfolders for **Queries** and **Query Results**. The Queries folder contains the Query specifications you have crafted and saved so you can use them later. The Query Results folder contains the saved, fixed-in-time output created by running the Queries. The Sample Project provides examples of each of these items in respective folders.

Your task is to point to the data in your Project that can help answer your question (craft the Query), and NVivo's contribution is to select and sort the data for you (generate Query Results). This is often accomplished with a degree of complexity which would be prohibitively cumbersome when working manually. Effective Queries and informative Query Results depend on the quality of your data. Therefore, this portion of the NVivo Project will quite likely depend on the quality of your research questions, methodology, reflective thinking (hopefully captured in Memos), coding, and perhaps the construction of Cases and a Classification System. You will use NVivo's Search capabilities to investigate this information and then interpret it in relation to your questions – the answers will not come ready-made.

───────── **7.a.** ─────────

To create and Run a Query

⇒ *Ribbon*: **Explore / Query** > **Select** the Query you want to run.
⇒ Enter the criteria from one of the following **Queries > Run Query**.

See the section after the last Query (Coding Comparison Query, later in this chapter) for more information on saving Queries and handling Query Results.

Windows

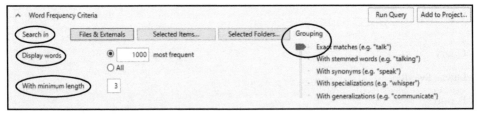

Mac

Figure 7.10 Word Frequency Query interface in Windows (top) and Mac (bottom)

Options for entering Query criteria

Word Frequency Query

A popularity contest among words (Figure 7.10):

- See Figure 7.1 for sample output.
- See Chapter 4 (pp. 127–128) for this Query in a more specific context.

━━━━━━━ **7.b.** ━━━━━━━

Word Frequency Query interface

This is a wide net and captures question numbers, participant names, etc. You may instruct NVivo to ignore words by adding them to the Stop Words List (for both this and the Text Search Query):

⇒ *File*: / *Menu bar:* **File > Project Properties > General** tab **> Stop words**.

You should look at the words already in this list by default, which includes conjunctions, pronouns, etc. Delete any that you would like to appear in your word-based Queries (e.g., *because* and *if* can be useful if you are looking for causal relations). The customization is only set for the current Project, but you can save it in a document and paste it into other Projects if you wish.

⇒ **Search in**: By default, NVivo will look in all of your Files and Externals.

  o **Selected items**: Allows you to scope the Query to a smaller area of the Project, including Files, Nodes, Sets, etc.

⇒ **Display words**: Allows you to set the number of words or Select All.
⇒ **With minimum length**: Allows you to set a number for the minimum number of characters in order to eliminate short words.
⇒ **Grouping / Finding matches**: Allows you to combine similar words, such as words with the same stem.
⇒ **Run Query**: Generates the output in the bottom half of the *Detail View*.

  o Note the tabs on the right margin **/ above the Results** in the *Detail View* to access the Word Cloud, etc.
  o **Right-click** on a word in the list or any of the visuals **> Create As Code / Run Text Search Query (and see next Query for additional information)**.
  o **Double-click** on any word in the Result to go to the data and investigate further.
  o **Right-click** on any word in the list or any of the visuals **> Add to Stop Words List**.

⇒ After you run the Query, see other available options in the *Ribbon*: **Word Frequency Query**.

Text Search Query

A specific hunt for words or strings (Figure 7.11):

- See Figure 7.2 for sample output.
- See Chapter 4 (pp. 129–130) for this Query in a more specific context.

Windows

Mac

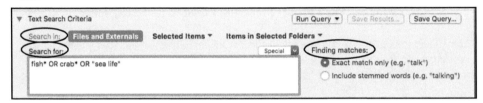

Figure 7.11 Text Search Query interface in Windows (top) and Mac (bottom)

━━━━━━━━ **7.c.** ━━━━━━━━

Text Search Query interface

⇒ **Search in**: By default, NVivo will look in all of your Files and Externals.

  o **Selected items**: Allows you to scope the Query to a smaller area of the Project, including Files, Nodes, Sets, etc.

⇒ **Search for**: Allows you to add any words or phrases using quotation marks for phrases.

  o See information at the beginning of the Word Frequency Query section regarding Stop Words, as they apply here as well.

⇒ **Special**: Provides operators such as the spanning wildcard (*) and alternator (OR), but once you learn these you can simply type them into the window yourself.

⇒ **Spread to**: automatically selects additional material around the word or phrase for inclusion in the Result (you can also do this later).

⇒ **Find / Finding matches**: Allows you to combine similar words, such as stemmed words, synonyms, specializations, and generalizations.

⇒ **Run Query**: Generates the output in the bottom half of the *Detail View*.

  o Note the tabs on the right margin **/** above the Results in the *Detail View* to access the Word Tree, etc.

⇒ After you run the Query, see other available options in the *Ribbon*: **Node.**

Crosstab Query

A table of Cases or Attribute Values by Nodes (Figure 7.12):

- See Figure 7.3 for sample output.
- See Chapter 5 (pp. 155–160) and Chapter 6 (pp. 183–186) for this Query in a more specific context.

Windows

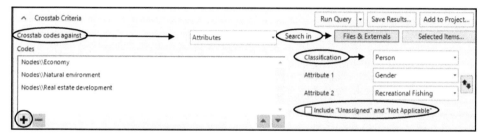

Mac

Figure 7.12 Crosstab Query interface in Windows (top) and Mac (bottom)

7.d.

Crosstab Query interface

⇒ **Crosstab codes against / Show node against**: By default, the columns of your Crosstab will be Attribute Values but you can select Cases if you prefer.

⇒ **Search in**: By default, NVivo will look in all of your Files and Externals.

  o **Selected items**: Allows you to scope the Query to a smaller area of the Project, including Files, Nodes, Sets, etc.

⇒ **Plus symbol**: Takes you to the Select Project Items window to identify the rows of your Crosstab. Or you can drag them into the relevant panes from *List View*.

⇒ **Classification**: When you select the Classification of interest, you can further identify either one or two Attribute Values.

⇒ **Include "Unassigned" and "Not applicable"**: Tick this box if you want to see the potential impact of missing data.

⇒ **Run Query**: Generates the output in the bottom half **/ left half** of the *Detail View*.

  o Note the tabs on the far right side of your screen to access the Chart.

⇒ The Results of the Crosstab present a Case count by default but you may change this to Coding References by right-clicking on any cell > **Cell Content / Show Results As** > Coding References.

⇒ **Double-click** on a cell to see the intersecting material.

⇒ After you run the Query, see other available options in the *Ribbon* : **Crosstab / Results tab on the far right.**

Windows

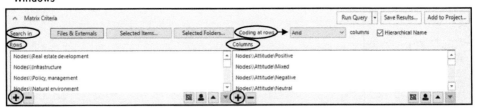

Mac

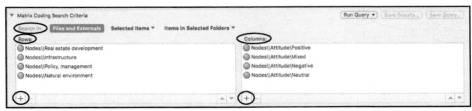

Figure 7.13 Matrix Coding Query interface in Windows (top) and Mac (bottom)

Matrix Coding Query

In a table format, you can run almost any Project item by any other Project items (Figure 7.13).

- See Figure 7.4 for sample output.
- See Chapter 6 (pp. 186–189) for this Query in a more specific context.

7.e.

Matrix Coding Query interface

⇒ **Search in**: By default, NVivo will look in all of your Files and Externals.

    ○ **Selected items**: Allows you to scope the Query to a smaller area of the Project, including Files, Nodes, Sets, etc.

⇒ Rows **plus** symbol and Columns **plus** symbol: Allows you to choose Select Items (or Select Attribute Values) > in the Select Project Items window to identify the rows and columns of your Matrix Coding Query.

⇒ **Coding at rows:** Allows you to change the default logic of AND (intersection) to Or, Not, Near, Preceding, or Surrounding.

⇒ **Run Query:** Generates the output in the bottom half of the *Detail View*.

    ○ Note the tabs on the far right side of your screen to access the Chart.

⇒ See other available options in the *Ribbon*: **Matrix / View > Node Matrix.**

Coding Query

Finds text or other data in response to a single, sometimes complex question involving multiple Nodes and/or Attribute Values (Figure 7.14):

- See Figure 7.5 for sample output.
- See Chapter 3 (pp. 96–97) for this Query in a more specific context.

Windows

Mac

Figure 7.14 Coding Query interface in Windows (top) and Mac (bottom)

7.f.

Coding Query interface

⇒ **Search in**: By default, NVivo will look in all of your Files and Externals.

 o **Selected items**: Allows you to scope the Query to a smaller area of the Project, including Files, Nodes, Sets, etc.

⇒ **All**: Indicates that all of the lines of criteria in the entire Query must be true (think of it as an intersection). This can be changed to 'Any', which instructs NVivo to retrieve data if it satisfies any of the lines of criteria (think of it as a union).

⇒ For the individual lines in the criteria:

 o **Coded at**: Can be changed to Not Coded At.

 o **All Selected Codes or Cases**: The default option indicates that all of the items within the line must be true (Boolean AND). This can be changed to 'Any Selected Code or Case' (Boolean OR) or 'Any Case Where' (which allows you to identify an Attribute Value instead of a Code or Case).

 o **Three dots (...)**: Allow you to select the items > **OK.**

 o **All of these nodes:** The default option indicates that all of the Nodes within the line must be true (Boolean AND). This can be changed to 'Any of these Nodes' (Boolean OR) or 'Any Case Where' (which allows you to identify an Attribute Value instead of a Code or Case).

 o The Arrow: Allows you to select items > **Select.**

⇒ **Plus symbol** and **minus symbol**: Add another line of criteria or remove a line of criteria.

⇒ **Run Query**: Generates the output in the bottom half of the *Detail View*.

⇒ Note the tabs on the far right side of your screen to access the Chart and Summary.

⇒ See other available options in the *Ribbon*: Node.

Windows

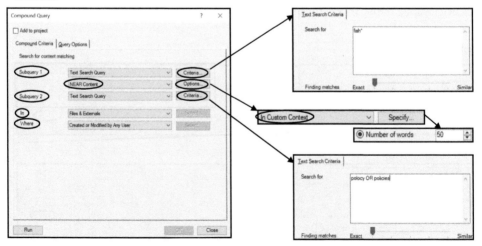

Figure 7.15 Compound Query interface (Windows only)

Compound Query (Windows only)

Identifies qualitative data within the Files (Nodes or text strings) near or adjacent to other qualitative data (other Nodes or text strings) (Figure 7.15):

* See Figure 7.6 for sample output.
* See Chapter 8 (pp. 252–253) for this Query in a more specific context.

━━━━━━━━━ **7.g.** ━━━━━━━━━

Compound Query interface (Windows only)

⇒ Subquery 1 and Subquery 2:

    o   If the desired content field is text, leave the default at **Text Search Query > Criteria** and enter the text.

    o   If the desired content field is a Node or Coding Query Result, change the default to **Coding Query > Criteria**. Use the **Simple** tab to identify an item or multiple items. Use the **Advanced** tab to run a more complex operation. (The interface is very similar to the Coding Query interface described earlier.)

⇒ **NEAR Content**: Can be changed to **PRECEDING Content, SURROUNDING Content, AND, OR,** or **NOT.**

    o   **Options**: If using **NEAR** or **PRECEDING** , this allows you to specify the **Proximity** (such as **Custom Context**) and to **Specify** a range (if relevant). Also tick the boxes for the data you want to **Retrieve > OK.**

⇒ **In**: By default, NVivo will look in all of your Files and Externals.

    o   **Selected items**: Allows you to **Select** a portion of the Project in which to search, including Files, Nodes, Sets, etc.

⇒ **Where**: Provides options for the Users you want to include in order to further scope the portion of the Project in which to search. This option is rarely used.
⇒ **Run**: Generates the output in the *Detail View.*
⇒ See other available options in the *Ribbon*: **Node.**

Group Query (Windows only)

Finds items that are associated with other items in your Project and presents output in the form of lists (groups) (Figure 7.16):

* See Figure 7.7 for sample output.
* See Chapter 9 (pp. 278–279) for this Query in a more specific context.

Windows

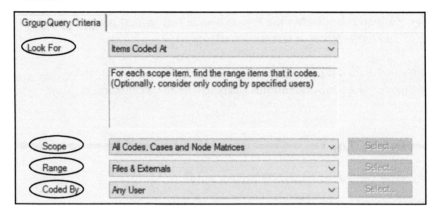

Figure 7.16 Group Query interface (Windows only)

7.h.

Group Query interface (Windows only)

⇒ **Look For**: Provides seven options of the type of list. Experiment to find the one you want but the common options are:

    o **Items Coding** (e.g., a list of the Nodes coded to each selected File).

    o **Items Coded At** (e.g., a list of the Files coded to each selected Node).

⇒ **Scope**: Limits the items to include.

⇒ **Range**: Limits the kind of items retrieved in the list.

⇒ **Coded By**: Select data coded by particular team members (only available in **Items Coding** and **Items Coded At**).

⇒ **Run**: Generates a list of items satisfying the criteria in the bottom half of the *Detail View.* Each list can be saved as a Set.

    o Note the tabs on the far right side of your screen to access the Connection Map.

Coding Comparison Query

Compares the coding of two coders (or two groups of coders) (Figure 7.17).

- See Figure 7.8 for sample output.
- See Chapter 11 (pp. 333–335) for this Query in a more specific context with additional information about interpreting the output. We strongly encourage you to review this additional material in Chapter 11 if you think you want to use the Coding Comparison Query.

Windows

Mac

Figure 7.17   Coding Comparison Query interface in Windows (top) and Mac (bottom)

7.i.

Coding Comparison Query interface

⇒ **User Group A and User Group B**: Allows you to choose one or more Users to compare with one or more other Users.

   o   When selecting a group of users instead of a single user, NVivo treats their coding as though it was conducted by one researcher.

⇒ **Scope / Search in**: By default, NVivo will look in all of your Files and Externals.

   o   **Selected items**: Allows you to scope the Query to a smaller area of the Project, including Files, Nodes, Sets, etc. Other options are also available.

⇒ **At / Coded At**: Determines the Nodes you want to include.

   o   **Selected Nodes**: Select / Arrow allows you to scope the Query to a subset of Nodes. Other options are also available.

⇒ **Calculations based on**:

   o   The character level.
   o   Optional levels: Character, sentence, or paragraph.

⇒ **Run**: Generates the output in the *Detail View*.
⇒ To compare the coding of a Node at a File:

   o   Double-click on a row.
   o   Tick Show coding comparison content and select a node.

Saving Queries and saving Query Results

Saving Queries

The Query and its Results do not automatically save or update, which may sometimes present a reason to save them, and sometimes a reason to simply preview them. Saving a Query can be helpful if you think you might run it again. For instance, you added *Sue's* third interview to the project yesterday, and the Query you created a month ago is looking in the third round of interviews for *Juan, Laura, Muriel, Petra,* and *Richard.* If you saved the Query, you do not need to construct it all over again. You can return to the saved Query and simply include *Sue's* third interview along with everyone else's.

7.j.

Saving the Query to your Project

To save the Query so you can run it later without having to reconstruct it:

> ⇒ *Detail View:* **Add to Project / Save Query** > provide a **Name** and **Description** > **OK / Save Query**.

If you closed the Query and want to save it to your Project:

> ⇒ *Ribbon:* **Explore / Query** > **Last Run Query** to re-open and save it.

Modifying your saved Query

The Query has a permanent location in your Project unless you modify or delete it:

> ⇒ *Navigation View:* **Search > Queries.**
> ⇒ *List View:* **Right-click** on the Query > **Open Query / Open.**

Saving Query Results

Results of Queries are provided in preview mode by default, which means the Results will appear on the screen but will disappear when you close them. You might receive a message when you save the Project that 'Preview query results will not be saved'. This is usually not a problem because you can run the Query again. Generally speaking, the Query Results are intended for rapid perusal and then deletion. However, some might warrant saving as a way to log and review your trajectory in the Project, because they are a particularly important set of Results that you will want to refer to when writing things up, or because they deserve to be in your coding system. As you work with a few Queries, you will become more comfortable with your decision to save either the Queries or the Results or to leave the defaults and let them 'disappear' after you are done with them.

Saving the Query Results to your Project

Outside of your Project

You can Export the results from any of the Queries to save them elsewhere on your computer:

> ⇒ *Detail View:* **Right-click > Export / Share...**

Inside your Project

You can save the Query Results from most of the Queries and store them inside the Project, with the exception of the Word Frequency, Group, and Coding Comparison Query Results.

⇒ *Detail View*: **Save Results** (or sometimes via the **Query Options** tab in the Query or in the *Ribbon*: Query/Store Query Results).
⇒ *Navigation View*: **Search > Query Results**.

This location provides a fixed-in-time view of your data. If you wish to modify your Results, you will need to either (a) rerun the Query with changed specifications, or (b) copy and paste the Result into your Node system. Because the output is then stored in a Node, you will be able to add or remove coding from it.

Framework Matrices (Windows only)

We will outline the basic instructions for you on running a Framework Matrix, but there are also extended descriptions and instructions available in the NVivo Help.

━━━━━━━ 7.k. ━━━━━━━

Creating and filling a Framework Matrix

Creating the framework

⇒ *Ribbon*: **Create: Framework Matrix.**
  ○ Provide a Name and Description.
  ○ **Rows** tab: **Select** the **Cases** you want to examine. (Optionally **Select attributes to sort the rows by > Select** the **Attribute**.)
  ○ **Columns** tab: **Select** the **Nodes** you want to examine.
⇒ **OK.**

You are looking at an empty table with the rows and columns specified. When you click in a cell for any Case, the column on the right-hand side of the screen will be populated with all the data for Case. This will allow you to read through and create a summary in the cells even if the data have not yet been coded for that Case. If your data are coded, then you can choose to show only the Node data that intersects with the Case for the selected cell.

Show intersecting content

⇒ *Ribbon*: **Framework Matrix > Associated View > Cell Coding.**

(Continued)

(Continued)

Adding your summaries

⇒ **Select** the first cell for which data are available. Read through the data for that cell, and type a summary into the cell. Continue to create a summary in each cell for which you have data.

Create a link between your summaries and the quotes

⇒ **Select** a passage from the data that supports your summary statement > **Right-click > Copy.**

⇒ **Select** the part of the summary you wrote > **Right-click > New Summary Link.** Clicking in the pink highlighted link in the text (at any time) will activate the link, illuminating the associated passage with yellow highlight.

Automatically fill the cells with intersecting content

⇒ *Ribbon*: **Framework Matrix > Auto Summarize.**

Export (e.g., for printing)

⇒ *Detail View*: **Right-click > Export Framework Matrix.**

NVivo stores the summaries you create for each cell, so that if you use the same combination of any Case by Node as part of another Framework Matrix, it will auto fill with that summary. This means that any changes you make to that summary will transfer across the previous and future Framework Matrices in which that cell combination occurs.

When data are sorted by Case, in addition to seeing common patterns, you can readily identify instances where individuals go against a trend. These Cases might be outliers on a statistical measure, deviant Cases in qualitative terms, or Cases where there is an apparent contradiction in the data from the different sources (Bazeley, 2013; Caracelli & Greene, 1993; Miles & Huberman, 1994). Whichever of these situations applies, they warrant focused attention, as it is often through exploration of such Cases that new understanding is gained.

Creating and customizing reports

NVivo provides a range of export options and standard report formats for those times when you need to have something exported or printed from your NVivo project. *Windows users*: We do not propose to give a full digest of standard Report options here (*Navigation View*: **Output > Reports**), as they are very adequately covered in the NVivo Help, but instead offer a couple of pointers to things you might consider – and avoid(!) – when working with Reports.

In many situations you are able to print or export your work directly from the *List View* or *Detail View*. We suggested this, for example, for listing Nodes; for exporting the text of a Node with Annotations and See Also Links as endnotes; for printing, copying, or exporting Matrix tables; and for copying or exporting Charts and Maps. What we will consider here is how to filter, run, and view a predefined Report.

With the predefined Report options that are provided by NVivo, it is intended that you shape them to suit your particular needs by using the optional filters. If you simply select and run one of these reports without filtering, you are likely to generate a very large amount of useless information.

7.I.

Using a predefined Report (Windows only)

To see a description of what any predefined Report provides:

⇒ *Navigation View*: **Output > Reports.**
⇒ *List View*: **Right-click on a Report > Report Properties.**

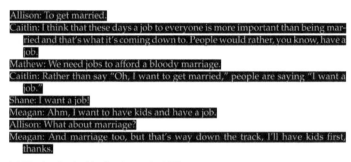

Allison: To get married.
Caitlin: I think that these days a job to everyone is more important than being married and that's what it's coming down to. People would rather, you know, have a job.
Mathew: We need jobs to afford a bloody marriage.
Caitlin: Rather than say "Oh, I want to get married," people are saying "I want a job."
Shane: I want a job!
Meagan: Ahm, I want to have kids and have a job.
Allison: What about marriage?
Meagan: And marriage too, but that's way down the track, I'll have kids first, thanks.

(a) Text selected in the imported File

<Internals\\Warr QI 2005 focus groups> - § 1 reference coded [0.35% Coverage]

Reference 1 - 0.35% Coverage

Allison: To get married. Caitlin: I think that these days a job to everyone is more important than being mar- ried andthat'swhatit'scomingdownto. People wouldrather,youknow,havea job. Mathew: We need jobs to afford a bloody marriage. Caitlin: Rather than say "Oh, I want to get married," people are saying "I want a job." Shane: I want a job! Meagan: Ahm, I want to have kids and have a job. Allison: What about marriage? Meagan: And marriage too, but that's way down the track, I'll have kids first, thanks.

(b) Reference tab view of coded text

(c) PDF tab view of coded text (Windows)

Figure 7.18 Filter options in a Case Classification Summary Report (number of Cases with each Attribute Value) (Windows only)

Alternatively, a description of each is provided in Help.

Filtering and running a Report

When you select a Report in *List View*, a dialogue such as that in Figure 7.18 will open, listing the fields of the report for which you can select data.

⇒ Click in a checkbox next to Field.
⇒ Look at the options under Comparison and Select for Values to help understand what filters are available > make your selections accordingly > **OK.**

When a Report opens in *Detail View*, it can be cramped and difficult to see, especially if you have your *Detail View* on the right-hand side of the NVivo window. Either change your *Detail View* to the bottom of the window and/or remove the map and preview panes:

⇒ *Ribbon*: **Home > Detail View > Bottom.**
⇒ *Ribbon*: **Report > Uncheck Report Map and/or Thumbnails.**

SECTION 7.4: CHAPTER 7 TAKEAWAYS

━━━━━━━━ **Key points from this chapter** ━━━━━━━━

o There are three types of queries in NVivo:

- Word-based Queries (Word Frequency and Text Search).

- Theory-building Queries (Crosstab, Matrix Coding, Coding, Compound).
- Administrative Queries (Group and Coding Comparison).

However, these distinctions are heuristic and designed to help you understand them conceptually.

o Each Query has two main components:

- The Query: the customized language you use to ask a question.
- The Query Results: the data NVivo presents to you after you run a Query.

o Examining the visual output of each Query can help you better understand the capabilities of a Query (this is why we began the chapter with the output).

o Visualizations are available for many of the Query Results, but you can also use visualizations to examine other parts of the Project outside of Queries (i.e., to chart the Files coded to a Node).

Tips, challenges, and warnings

- Learn the conceptual overview of the Queries so you understand what they can do, but do not try to memorize the clicks. It is more important to recognize when a need for one of them arises. You will learn how to click through a Query when you need it.

- Write up your observations about your Query Results – you should not assume that they speak for themselves.
- Examples of all Queries are in the Sample Project. Poking around in those examples might help you understand how to construct one and what to expect from the output.
- If you never save your Queries or your Query Results, it is possible you will get lost or end up in a learning loop while trying to create a Query that meets your needs. Consider saving query specifications for further use or modification (you can delete them later), and be sure to keep a record of all results obtained.
- Interesting findings will not tumble out of your data when you get to Queries at the end. If you wait for this to happen it is a sign that you are not reflectively thinking while you are coding. It is also a sign that you do not have any Memos.
- In a Framework Matrix, any changes you make to a cell summary will transfer across the previous and future Framework Matrices in which that cell combination occurs.

Help files

- *File*: Help.
- *Menu bar*: **Help > NVivo Help.**

Search for any of the following:

- Coding query
- Compound query
- Crosstab query
- Framework matrix
- Group query
- Manage query results
- Matrix coding query
- Text Search query
- Word frequency query
- Work with crosstab query results

Practice questions

1 Articulate one hypothetical example from each Query that might pertain to your research.
2 How would you rank the Queries in order of importance to your research?
3 How would you rank the Queries in the order of the chronology you anticipate using them?
4 What visuals will be helpful for you as you think through your data?
5 What visuals might be helpful in communicating your results to an audience?

8

Section 8.1: Introduction to literature reviews and pdf Files   236

Section 8.2: Getting grounded in literature reviews and pdf Files   237

Section 8.3: Literature reviews and pdf Files in NVivo   246

Section 8.4: Chapter 8 Takeaways   253

LITERATURE
REVIEWS AND
PDF FILES

The use of too many or nonselective references is an indication of poor scholarship and an inability to separate the central from the peripheral. (Bloomberg & Volpe, 2008: 57)

SECTION 8.1: INTRODUCTION TO LITERATURE REVIEWS AND PDF FILES

Reference material of many kinds and from a variety of sources plays a part in most research projects, including a qualitative project. NVivo's suite of tools is very useful for working with this type of data. You can Code, reflect on, write Memos about, and Query reference material just as you do with an interview, focus group, or pictures. To assist this process, you can import pdf Files, your bibliographic database (EndNote, Mendeley, RefWorks, or Zotero), and online articles downloaded with the assistance of NCapture (a browser add-on that is a companion to NVivo; see Chapter 10, pp. 293–295). While NVivo is not a substitute for the referencing functions provided by a bibliographic program, it does provide many benefits:

- A rapid way of bringing the literature you have been gathering and reading into your Project.
- An ability to refine your analysis of that literature and quickly access relevant material when you are writing your review or report.
- Word or phrase Queries to find keywords in your literature and your notes.

In this chapter you will

- Consider the ways you might work with reference material within NVivo.
- Discover the potentials and pitfalls of importing and working with pdf Files in NVivo.
- See what options NVivo provides for importing reference material from a bibliographic database and from web pages.

Other chapters with related materials

Chapter 1: Where to begin?

Memos and Links help keep track of ongoing ideas and threads of connections in your data and this is often where a good portion of your analytical work can be developed and tracked. Be sure to use Memos and Links as you think through the literature.

Chapter 3: Coding foundations; Chapter 4: Advanced coding

You will use the same basic skills to manage your Nodes and Node hierarchies that we discussed in Chapters 3 and 4, including coding, uncoding, merging, aggregating, using Coding

Stripes, etc. You will likely want to create Node hierarchies while being mindful to use vista Node structures and avoid viral ones.

Chapter 7: Querying data

Having a general sense of the different Queries and what they can do might help you think through the structure of your literature review. If you have not yet done so, get acquainted with Queries by running a Word Frequency Query and a Text Search Query and consider turning these Query Results into Nodes.

Chapter 10: Twitter, Facebook, YouTube, and web pages

The NCapture browser add-on that helps you collect social media data and web pages could be useful during your literature review. This tool sometimes captures web pages as pdf Files and so you might use it to collect online articles.

SECTION 8.2: GETTING GROUNDED IN LITERATURE REVIEWS AND PDF FILES

The role of literature in your project

Because a literature review is your current focus, this might be the first chapter you explore in the book. While we will cover the basics of handling pdf Files and thinking about your literature here, you might turn to other chapters periodically to see how to Code, Link, and Query. Many of the technical aspects of using these tools in NVivo with a pdf File are handled similarly for both an interview transcript and a journal article. Therefore, we focus in this chapter on issues that are unique to pdf Files and literature reviews and frequently point you to other chapters, so you can customize your learning about NVivo in the context of a literature review.

Practical approaches to a literature review using NVivo

Beginning a project by reviewing what is already known on the subject of your research is a well-established practice. However, as Bloomberg and Volpe (2008) illustrate, the timing of a review of the literature is likely to vary, depending on the methodology you are using in your research. Inductive approaches such as phenomenology and grounded theory sometimes delay the literature review until during, and after the data collection process. Even in these traditions, however, there is evidence that reviewing the literature is a source of stimulation and/or sensitization and that this can occur throughout a project (e.g., Charmaz, 2006; Corbin & Strauss, 2008; Silverman, 2010). Traditions that often incorporate a literature review early in the research include any qualitative study with a focus on hypothesis testing, as the hypotheses are almost always connected to prior work.

In a research-oriented literature review you will usually look for three types of information:

- substantive (topic-based);
- theoretical;
- methodological (how did those studying this topic do it).

Published and online literature has the potential to play multiple roles in a qualitative project, whether or not you use NVivo:

- to build a framework for your research design and analysis;
- to familiarize you with common concepts and potential themes in the subject area;
- as a source of contrast, for comparison with your data;
- to frame the debates (or camps) in your field of study;
- to establish a corpus of material that you will return to again and again because it is a core area of research for you.

In a practical vein, working with notes from literature or other archival materials in an NVivo Project can be a good place to start developing skills and ideas using NVivo. NVivo can be of great benefit because it can assist you in moving from rough notes to an organized review.

- Academic researchers are generally accustomed to this approach for their scholarly research and in preparation for human-subject review processes.
- Researchers in evaluation and public policy settings often conduct a review of the literature to prepare grants or bids.
- Consumer and market researchers might want to access available information on prior approaches to similar studies or on market trends that might influence data collection and analysis.

Most academic and student researchers now have access to electronic databases of articles through their university or college libraries. Typically, they will also have access to bibliographic database software to store citation details for their reference material, with EndNote being one of the most common. Any researcher who has not started storing their reference information using bibliographic software is strongly advised to do so. Even if you only use it at a basic level, it is usually well worth the cost and the effort to learn enough to set up your reference library. NVivo will not duplicate the functions provided by your bibliographic software. Rather, it is designed to supplement them by facilitating searching, coding, reflecting, writing, and analysis using your literature. Data of this type can be imported at any time during your research, and there is no problem importing further sets of reference material during your analysis.

A few guideposts along the way that might be more relevant to researchers in academic settings:

- Determine early on if you are conducting a review of great breadth in order to conduct a broad survey of the literature, or a deeper dive into a corpus of materials relevant to your study. Or, you might engage in a creative combination of the two, either concurrently or sequentially. It is especially helpful for doctoral students to clarify this with supervisors or committee members as the assumptions about the purpose and process of the literature review often remain unarticulated and can therefore create miscommunications.

- When in doubt, place an emphasis on relevance over volume when it comes to a literature review. While the plethora of digital materials available might necessitate this by default, we encourage new scholars to realize that a literature review is a subjective process full of judgement calls. You will need to weigh the relevance of literature based on your interests, your research design, and the credibility (or lack thereof) of certain literature to your audience, particularly those who will be assessing your work.

- While engaged in your literature review, remember that there are things to pay attention to besides theories, methodologies, and conclusions. You might pick up tips along the way that you want to borrow: the use of particular visuals to clarify a research design, scenarios or historical events that might prompt interview questions, tactics for arguing about logical connections in the research design, customized presentation of findings for different audiences, etc.

- Consider revisiting the literature throughout the study as the rest of your data informs the literature you should attend to.

- During the write-up of your research, weigh the advantages and disadvantages of integrating the literature into your narrative rather than keeping it separate. Or, use a traditional chapter for the literature review but then weave the key issues into the remaining narrative.

Using published material as primary data

For some researchers, the literature represents the core of their collected data and they do not intend to go into the field to collect interviews, observations, etc. We have worked with researchers doing innovative research with newspaper articles, blogs, web pages, company reports, poetry, and novels – a near infinite variety of published material. These documents are often analysed for trends and patterns over time or across various File types.

Media and newspaper articles in a public relations campaign

Jannet Pendleton, at the University of Technology, Sydney, used media releases and newspaper articles as her primary sources of data for her doctoral study of the public relations campaign conducted by a pharmaceutical company to have a newly developed (and expensive!) vaccine added to the recommended list for childhood immunization in Australia. Using NVivo, she was able to trace the development of the campaign over time, and the way in which materials contained in media releases from the company, especially human interest stories, were incorporated more or less directly into subsequent newspaper articles.

The overwhelming amount of information now available to both academics and practitioners has led to increasing adoption of meta-analyses, systematic reviews, and metasyntheses of the literature (Barnett-Page & Thomas, 2009; Dixon-Woods, Agarwal, Jones, Young, & Sutton, 2005). Researchers can use NVivo to filter, condense, and extend what has been learned through all those individual studies.

Linking, coding, organizing, and thinking about the literature

A bibliographic database will allow you to search for keywords, write notes, and sort and group your reference material. However, bringing that literature into NVivo has the potential to add value through use of its more sophisticated memoing, linking, coding, and querying tools. After your first experiment of using NVivo for a literature review, you might lament, like many of the rest of us, 'Why didn't I do this sooner?' – particularly if you find yourself repeatedly hunting for key passages that are especially relevant to you. Each time you use this material, you see something slightly different as your research evolves. Now you can track this evolution through Nodes and Links and return to the original, relevant material with ease and efficiency. You can thereby double-check your assumptions and revisit the way you used this material in prior iterations without thumbing through pages of your prior manuscripts.

Annotations, Memos, and Links

Just as we detailed regarding the use of Annotations, Memos, and Links in Chapter 1 (pp. 27–33), you can use these tools to mark-up and create a trail of your ideas as you work with pdf Files. You will find these tools especially helpful as you take a rich, deep dive into key pieces of your literature.

Annotations can be used to:

- Clarify acronyms or jargon.
- Identify a citation in an article that has a newer edition available for review.
- Briefly reflect on an internal inconsistency in logic.
- Indicate where you have stopped reading as a virtual bookmark. This makes it easier to pick up when you are ready to resume reading.

Memos and See Also Links can be used to:

- Jot notes about the underlying assumptions in a passage.
- Briefly articulate reasons why a methodology or theory is inadequate or exemplary in a study design.
- Note when an expository claim is delivered as though it was based in evidence.
- Keep a record of the search terms and parameters you used to find literature, so you can update your materials or revisit them if you become aware of gaps.

- Track the way citation errors across Files perpetuate inaccurate understandings of original material.
- Keep a running account of places where you see gaps or omissions in the narrative.
- Generate a list of lingering questions that are inspired by literature you read.
- Track the literature that you considered but is not related directly to your research and you plan to omit. This will help you establish boundaries around your research and keep you from accidentally reviewing it a second time.
- Collect examples of the way other scholars handled their data that are appealing to you and you want to consider borrowing. This could include the framing of the content area, formulation of research questions, unique combinations of methodologies and theories, and innovative output or findings.
- Keep track of books you want to consider buying and literature cited by scholars that you want to add to your reference management software.

Nodes and coding

All of the tactics for generating Nodes and reflecting on Node hierarchies from Chapters 3 and 4 also pertain to an NVivo Project that contains literature. As a starting point, instead of thinking about harnessing the unique capabilities of NVivo, you might simply mimic the way you mark passages while you read. To do this, the labels or brief comments you scribble in the margins are candidates to become Nodes (although some of them might be Annotations or See Also Links). Also, as we described in Chapter 3, a single passage is likely to have multiple meanings and you should code it to all Nodes that are relevant. Later you will be able to run a Coding Query (Chapters 3 and 7) to look at relationships among your Nodes, or between Nodes and Attribute Values.

Transparency in qualitative research

In Kristi's study of qualitative researchers' conceptualization of transparency in the qualitative research process, she wanted to examine the degree to which discussions of transparency were implicit (use of the term with no attempt to define it), simple (a brief definition or explanation of the term), or explicit (elaboration regarding dimensions of transparency such as the purpose, ways to achieve it, or potential problems with pursuing transparency). As she reviewed articles in her NVivo Project, she gave each pdf an attribute value of implicit, simple, or explicit, in order to be able to run a Matrix Coding Query on these values by whether they used QDAS or not.

Consider using Nodes to track elements in the literature that are unique to your topic. These include ethical issues, historical accounts of the evolution of thought in an area, guidelines/

standards for practice, conventional ideologies, innovative scholarship, professional associations, and scholars' projections for the future. These could also be Nodes that emerge from data collection through other means, such as interviews, but you might want to consider coding them in the literature as well. There are no rules about the Nodes you should create, so be innovative. We have seen Nodes for *Articles to review, Books to buy, Misquoted,* and *References to double-check.*

Revisiting Node hierarchies

NVivo can also be especially helpful when looking across the articles for patterns through the construction of Node hierarchies. Queries can be subsequently used to examine relationships in these hierarchies.

Three Node hierarchy examples in a literature review

1 Pat has a Project that comprises pdf articles as well as abstracts and notes made while reading mixed methods literature (much of it pre-dated being able to readily access electronic pdfs or to link those with EndNote) in which she coded material relating to the paradigm debates in mixed methods research, as well as other topics and issues. Because each File has a date Attribute (year of publication), it is possible to sort the coded material on paradigm debates, for example, by decade (or a shorter period if desired), to trace changes in the way researchers have written about that issue.

2 Kristi has a project comprising pdf articles about qualitative researchers' understandings of the advantages and disadvantages of using QDAS. While some of the articles claim to be research-oriented, they contain considerable references to expository materials from other authors. Therefore, to more accurately distinguish 'research findings' from 'expository literature', she created a Node for each type, and while reading the articles she coded the referenced material to the appropriate location. After doing this, she ran a Matrix Coding Query on the Benefits and Problems of using QDAS (two columns) by whether the literature cited was Research or Expository (two rows). By doing so, it became evident that when researchers wrote about potential problems with QDAS in their articles, they consistently cited a single expository article by Coffey, Holbrook, and Atkinson (1996) rather than any actual research that confirmed these potential problems.

3 In Wickham and Woods' (2005) article documenting their literature review process for their doctoral theses, they identify several benefits of using NUD*IST (now NVivo). One benefit was the way their coding of the literature pointed to gaps in the research in order to develop pertinent research questions. One of these students coded literature to a Node for the *Role of Government*, and after reviewing these roles became aware that 'government social responsibility' was a missing strand. This concept was included as a question to be addressed by the research.

In Chapter 4 (pp. 107–110), we discussed the differences between viral and vista coding structures. You should review that chapter if you have forgotten the difference between them in order to avoid the former and pursue the latter. In addition to the suggestions for Node hierarchies in Chapter 4 (pp. 118–120), we add the following branches to consider, specifically geared toward the process of coding your literature:

- Topic: The topic you are studying with child Nodes related to this topic.
- Theories: Using child Nodes that represent the various nuances or distinctions in these theories.
- Methodologies: Child Nodes can be used to track specific ways of collecting and handling data.
- Subgroups: A hierarchy for various subgroups of researchers with different views might help you distinguish how people in *Group A* and *Group B* talk about the topic and code material that seems to defy the boundaries of these groups or tries to identify similarities among them.
- Article structure: The typical structure of a research article with child Nodes for the various structural features in the article (this is analogous to a hierarchy based on the questions in an interview guide).
- Reading lists: Create Nodes for 'must read' and 'would like to read' and code references as you come across them that you feel you must read and those you would like to read. That way, you can keep a track of your reading list in NVivo. Simply uncode from the relevant list once you have read it.

Queries in a literature review

As we indicate throughout this book, the various Queries in NVivo can be used to look at patterns across your coding. When focusing on literature as data, the Queries can help in diverse ways. They might help early on in the design of your research or closer to the end of your analysis when you compare your findings with existing publications. For example, you could run a Word Frequency Query (Chapter 4, pp. 126–129; Chapter 7, pp. 204–205; 219) and develop a Word Cloud for each of your child Nodes under *Theory*. This Query helps you investigate the kind of language used by researchers who use specific theories. The Query Results of other investigations could also yield interesting patterns. You might run a Matrix Coding Query (Chapter 6, pp. 186–189; Chapter 7, p. 208) of what people say about *Group A, Group B, Group C* (Nodes) by whether or not the statements are published in a *Newspaper*, a *Pamphlet*, or an *Academic journal* (Attribute Values). This Query could help you identify an association between the groups and forms of publication that are favourable or unfavourable to the views promoted in these camps.

Miscellaneous recommendations

You will also find that you can apply the tactics for handling Files and Nodes in innovative ways that suit your analysis of the literature. For instance:

- Use Node Colours creatively. If you are conducting research that combines two theories, use one Colour for Nodes directly related to theory A (e.g., yellow), another Colour for theory B (e.g., blue), and a third Colour (e.g., green) for any Node that applies to both theories. This will allow you to visually track the coding via a customized *List View* of your Nodes (Chapter 4, pp. 89–90) or by viewing your Coding Stripes by these Colours (Chapter 3, p. 83).
- Use Sets as an alternative structure for sorting your literature (Chapter 2, pp. 56–59). If you also gather literature in waves, consider Sets for *Wave 1, Wave 2, Wave 3* to track your process. Or, if you want to quickly sort literature according to your degree of immersion in a particular File, create Sets for *Briefly reviewed, Not reviewed, Reviewed* and move Files into these Sets as you work your way through the literature.
- Create a Concept Map (Chapter 1, pp. 25–26) that represents the assumptions, primary concepts, and/or theory of change used in a key piece of literature.
- NVivo Plus users can consider using the Relationship tool in NVivo to develop a Network Sociogram of the way scholars refer to each other. Or, to trace the influence of a particular author. See the blog by di Gregorio (2018) for additional information: https://www.qsrinternational.com/nvivo/nvivo-community/the-nvivo-blog/extending-your-literature-review-with-nvivo-11-plu

Formatting pdf Files

Shortly we will show you how you can import pdf documents as part of your bibliographic database, but sometimes you will have pdf Files that are stored independently of that database. This section will cover issues faced in dealing with these pdf Files.

There are several formatting issues you should keep in mind:

- If you highlight text in your pdf using Adobe Reader (or similar) before importing it, those passages will remain highlighted when you import the pdf.
- Comment markers attached to the text remain visible after import, but the comments are not.
- Pencil marks and text boxes on the text will be visible, but they can only be selected with the Region selection tool.
- If you have been annotating articles in your bibliographic package, you will see an icon where there is a comment/annotation, but the text in the comment will not be imported into NVivo.
- When viewing pdf material in a Node, none of the added markers are visible in the Reference view. We will show you how to jump to the pdf from this location, but it can become cumbersome to do so with large volumes of data.
- You might also import notes you have stored in Word files, in OneNote, or in Evernote. For guidance on importing from and working with OneNote or Evernote notes or pages, search for OneNote or Evernote in the NVivo Help, where the alternatives for selecting parts or all of your pages to import are very adequately described.

- NVivo supports the import of Outlook email messages as msg Files. The emails are imported as pdf Files and attachments are also included. The tools you learn for coding, linking, and querying pdf Files will also be relevant to these emails. Additional information can be found in the NVivo Help.

We suggest that you store literature in one or more folders separately from other Files in your Project. Create one if you are happy to have it all together, or more than one if you want to separate items. You might want to organize data by their format (of the two outlined above), by the type of material they contain (e.g., web pages, industry reports, peer-reviewed articles), or by some other characteristic. The issue of where to store pdf files in your Project can be especially important now that web pages collected with NCapture (Chapter 9) are converted into pdf files when they are imported. The symbol for a pdf file in NVivo is the same regardless of whether the File is a web page or an article. Therefore, the storage location and naming convention you provide to these Files might influence your efficient management of the data. The Files can be easily imported directly into these folders or moved to them later.

Pdf Files can be in either of two formats, with different implications for how you work with them.

1   *As normal text:* Most downloaded pdf files will appear as normal text (or text and images) that allow you to code content in the usual way such as dragging with your mouse pointer. This means they are optical character recognition (OCR) Files. However, irregularities in the layout of the original document, such as tables or figures can affect the way this material appears in a Node or is exported. Scanned data might also appear this way, if it has been scanned to pdf rather than scanned as an image. OCR can also be used with scanned handwritten responses.

2   *As an image:* Some scanned and downloaded pdf material will appear more like an image, as if the page has been photocopied or photographed. One of the hints that you are working with this format is if you cannot select ranges of characters within text when viewing it as a pdf in Adobe Reader before you import it. In some cases, you can convert a scanned image to text using OCR software before you import it (there are some free OCR conversion programs available on the web). Mac users have an extra tool that converts Files to OCR after import (*Detail View:* **Recognize text**). As an alternative, you can select text by Region to associate the data with Nodes and Links, just as you would work with a picture File (see Chapter 9). You will not be able to use Word Frequency or Text Search Queries in this type of File, and their appearance in Nodes or when exported will be similar to those for pictures.

As we recommend with so many other tools in NVivo, pilot your material with a small subset first, and test memoing, linking, annotating, coding, querying, and exporting with those Files.

SECTION 8.3: LITERATURE REVIEWS AND PDF FILES IN NVIVO

NVivo terms used in this section

Annotation

Compound Query

Link

Memo

Node

Region selection

Text selection

Importing pdf Files, selecting text, and coding

In this section we focus on traditional literature Files such as articles, chapters, and reports. In most circumstances, Files follow format type 1, above. These Files can be annotated, linked, and coded like other Files, as described in earlier chapters. Additional issues that arise with web pages are covered in Chapter 9.

━━━━━━━━━━━━ **8.a.** ━━━━━━━━━━━━

Import pdf Files

⇒ *Ribbon*: **Import: Files > Select** the File(s) **> Open > Import.**
⇒ *Ribbon*: **Data: PDFs > Select** the File(s) **> Import.**

Selecting text for coding in a pdf File (format type 1)

You will be able to select text for drag-and-drop coding or coding using the right-click menu in the normal way for both regular text in paragraphs and for text in articles with columns (Chapter 3, pp. 80–81). Depending on the File and circumstances, however, you may find some specific issues arise in relation to selecting text and viewing it when coded.

- If your text selection runs across a page break, it is likely to include the footer and header text.
- When you select text in a pdf File in NVivo you will often notice that there is a space between lines and sometimes between the words in the text (Figure 8.1). If your mouse

pointer lands on that space when you go to drag the passage to a Node for coding, it will change to a cursor rather than pointer, and when you click to drag, the original selection will be lost.

- *Windows users*: Text selection is unstable under some circumstances. In particular, if you have to scroll your Node list to locate a second Node, the selection is lost (use right-click to code to multiple Nodes at once as an alternative).
- When working with tabbed text (e.g., where speakers are set apart from what they say) or text with line numbers, you might not be able to select material correctly (Figure 8.2a). This material might not show up correctly in the Reference view of a Node, either, so you should switch to region coding for that passage, as for format type 2 (see below).

In general, you will be working with regular paragraphs of text, and you should not experience significant difficulties in selecting, coding, or viewing it.

Viewing coded text from a pdf source (format type 1)

Standard paragraphs of pdf text do not pose any issues with regard to viewing coded material. Depending on the nature of the File, however, you may find that when you view what you have coded, the text on the page is not sequenced as you expect. This warning will apply if you look at the Reference tab view of the coded text for non-standard paragraphs of data, as spacing and line breaks in the original are likely to have been reconfigured to some degree. Figure 8.2 illustrates these alternatives, with text involving multiple short lines of speech. *Windows users*: If this creates a problem, the safer option for viewing is to select the PDF tab, where coded text will be shown in its page context.

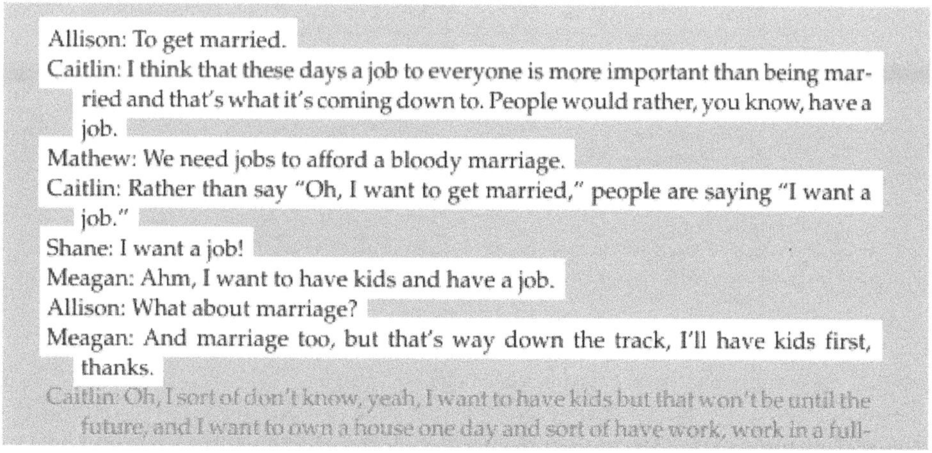

Allison: To get married.
Caitlin: I think that these days a job to everyone is more important than being married and that's what it's coming down to. People would rather, you know, have a job.
Mathew: We need jobs to afford a bloody marriage.
Caitlin: Rather than say "Oh, I want to get married," people are saying "I want a job."
Shane: I want a job!
Meagan: Ahm, I want to have kids and have a job.
Allison: What about marriage?
Meagan: And marriage too, but that's way down the track, I'll have kids first, thanks.
Caitlin: Oh, I sort of don't know, yeah, I want to have kids but that won't be until the future, and I want to own a house one day and sort of have work, work in a full-

Figure 8.1 Selection and retrieval of text in a pdf File

Source: Warr (2005).

Coded text with line numbers, and sometimes tabbed text (for speakers), is reordered when seen in the Reference tab view (Figure 8.2b), rendering that view not useful if line numbers are needed. The PDF tab view is better (Figure 8.2c), although on those not-so-common occasions where you might wish to code text on to further Nodes while viewing it in a Node, you will need to select it from the original File, as you will not be able to select a line number with its adjacent text from either this or the Reference view in a Node.

(a) Text selected in the imported File

1	Allison:	To get married.
2	Caitlin:	I think that these days a job to everyone is more important than being
3		married and that's what it's coming down to. People would rather, you
4		know, have a job.
5	Mathew:	We need jobs to afford a bloody marriage.
6	Caitlin:	Rather than say "Oh, I want to get married," people are saying "I want a
7		job."
8	Shane:	I want a job!
9	Meagan:	Ahm, I want to have kids and have a job.
10	Allison:	What about marriage?
11	Meagan:	And marriage too, but that's way down the track, I'll have kids first,
12		thanks.

(b) Reference tab view of coded text

1 2 3 4 5 6 7 8 9
10 11 12
Allison: To get married. Caitlin:
I think that these days a job to everyone is more important than being married and that's what it's coming down to. People would rather, you know, have a job.
Mathew: We need jobs to afford a bloody marriage. Caitlin:
Shane: I want a job!
Meagan: Ahm, I want to have kids and have a job. Allison: What about marriage?
Meagan: And marriage too, but that's way down the track, I'll have kids first, thanks.

(c) PDF tab view of coded text (Windows)

1	Allison:	To get married.
2	Caitlin:	I think that these days a job to everyone is more important than being
3		married and that's what it's coming down to. People would rather, you
4		know, have a job.
5	Mathew:	We need jobs to afford a bloody marriage.
6	Caitlin:	Rather than say "Oh, I want to get married," people are saying "I want a
7		job."
8	Shane:	I want a job!
9	Meagan:	Ahm, I want to have kids and have a job.
10	Allison:	What about marriage?
11	Meagan:	And marriage too, but that's way down the track, I'll have kids first,
12		thanks.

Figure 8.2   Selection and retrieval of text in a line-numbered pdf File

There is one further potential limitation with pdf sources that you need to understand. If you copy and paste text from a pdf into a Word document, you will notice, in some circumstances, that there will be paragraph breaks at the end of each line.

- In NVivo, the effect of these paragraph breaks is to remove the opportunity to meaningfully view the paragraph surrounding a segment of coded data from inside a Node (*Detail View*: **Right-click > Coding Context > Broad**). Instead, view the context of a coded passage using the PDF tab which will show the full page as context, or use Open Referenced File (*Detail View*: **Right-click > Open Referenced File**).
- Paragraph breaks at the end of each line will also impact your ability to run a Compound Query (Windows only) that looks for words or Nodes that co-occur within the same paragraph (NEAR options). It will not affect your ability to locate passages coded by Node *x* AND Node *y*.

Importantly, however, pdf text can be coded and retrieved, if care is taken, in one form or another that will allow for review and for most if not all the analysis options you are likely to want to use. Additionally, a Word Frequency Query and Text Search Query will work with text in these pdf Files.

8.b.

Coding by Region

⇒ *Navigation View*: **Data > Files**.
⇒ *List View*: **Double-click** on the pdf (Figure 8.3).
⇒ *Ribbon*: **PDF > PDF Selection > Region**.
⇒ *Detail View*: **Selection Mode > Region** symbol.
⇒ **Select** the text.
⇒ Code via drag-and-drop or right-clicking, as you would for text (Chapter 3, pp. 80–81).

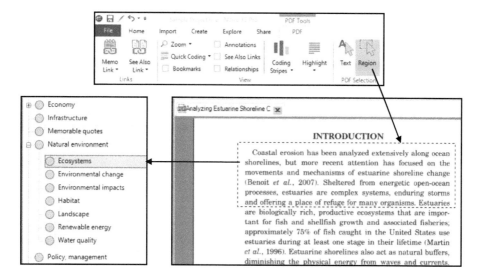

Figure 8.3 Selection and coding of a region in a pdf File

Selecting a region for coding in a pdf File (format type 2)

When a pdf File is not available in OCR or cannot be converted to OCR, it will import as a pdf but behave in NVivo like a picture. Material will be coded with the Region selection tool.

- Also use this approach if you wish to select a table or a figure within any pdf File.
- *Windows users*:
  - o Annotations and See Also Links are applied to the Region, just as they are for pictures (Chapter 9, pp. 266–268).
  - o In a Node, the text will show as coordinates for a Region in the Reference view; in the PDF view they will appear in a similar way to retrieved pictures, as a highlighted area within a page.

Using reference material from bibliographic software

When you import literature from bibliographic software, NVivo will place

- attached files into a designated folder under *Navigation View*: **Data > Files**;
- the citation for any references that do not have attached files into *Navigation View*: **Data > Externals**;
- abstracts, and any notes you have recorded, into a Linked Memo that is attached to the File or External for that reference.

Other fields in the bibliographic software (e.g., publication year and author) will be recorded by NVivo as Attributes of the File, with specific Values attached to each File. This is one of the few occasions in NVivo where you are likely to make use of File Attributes for comparative analyses, rather than Case Attributes. If you want to import the original pdf (or Word) Files as you import the reference information, make sure that:

- you have attached Files to all your selected entries in your bibliographic software;
- the attached Files are in the locations pointed to within the bibliographic software;
- that this location will be available as you import the database into NVivo.

━━━━━━━━━━━━━━ **8.c.** ━━━━━━━━━━━━━━

Importing literature from a bibliographic database

Preparing to export from your reference manager

Select the references you want from your reference database, to import into NVivo. Your selection might be based on a keyword, a combination of keywords, or some other sorting feature of that software. If you are unsure how to select references, check the Help files in your bibliographic software.

Exporting

Export the references you want from your bibliographic software in a format that will be recognized by NVivo. These are:

⇒ EndNote - export as .xml and keep the .xml file in the same folder as the .enl file in order for it to pick up the relative links to all of the pdfs.
⇒ RefWorks - export as .ris

o Files attached using the RefWorks 'attachment feature' cannot be exported with the .ris format.

⇒ Zotero - export as .ris
⇒ Mendeley - export as .ris

NVivo will recognize already imported references and provide options for ignoring or updating those.

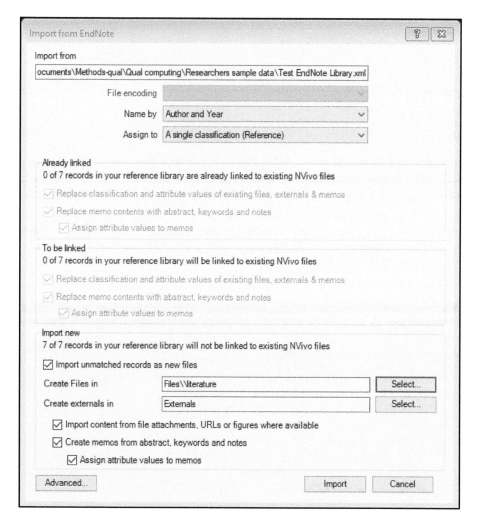

Figure 8.4 Selecting options in the import dialogue for reference material from EndNote (Windows)

(Continued)

(Continued)

Importing your literature in NVivo

⇒ *Ribbon*: **Import / Data > Bibliographic Data > Select** your exported reference manager file.
⇒ The import dialogue in Figure 8.4 will open.
⇒ Change the default for **Name by** to **Author and Year**. This is so that the author and year of publication will show in the Node at the top of each coded passage – the kind of information you will need when writing up from your literature. NVivo will add the database record number for the source to the name, as well, to assist with Cite While You Write functions.
⇒ Keep the **Assign to** as **A single classification** – unless you want to create multiple classification sheets, with one for each type of worksheet (publication) you have included in your bibliographic database.
⇒ Note where NVivo is going to locate the files, and modify to your preferred location.
⇒ Unless you recorded the abstracts or made notes, or the original articles are attached to the reference, then you will only be able to use the metadata (which tends to be less useful than using both the metadata and the qualitative data).

Viewing, coding, and analysing your reference material

Reference material imported from EndNote, Zotero, RefWorks, or Mendeley, and the attached Memos, can be viewed, coded, annotated, and linked in the usual ways, subject to the above provisions regarding pdf Files. Notes and abstracts in Memos as well as original Files (e.g., articles) will have Attributes attached to them, allowing for their use in Queries.

You could run a Compound Query (Windows only) to find words near each other because you remember they appeared in a pdf but cannot remember which one. You want to find that File because it has other information of interest.

━━━━━ **8.d.** ━━━━━

Compound Query (Windows only)

For this example, we use the *Environmental Change* sample Project to look for a File in which the calculation of shoreline change is discussed.

⇒ *Ribbon*: **Explore > Compound**.
⇒ Subquery 1: **Criteria >** enter a string (e.g., *calculat**) **> OK**.
⇒ NEAR Content: **Options >** Change 'Overlapping' to 'In Custom Context' **> Specify >** number of words (e.g., 99) **> OK > OK**.
⇒ Subquery 2: **Criteria >** enter a string (e.g., *shore**) **> OK**.
⇒ **Run**.
⇒ You find the article and can investigate further (Figure 8.5).
⇒ If you want to save this Query to run it again later:

  o *Ribbon*: **Explore > Last Run Query > Tick** Add to Project **> Name** it **> OK**.

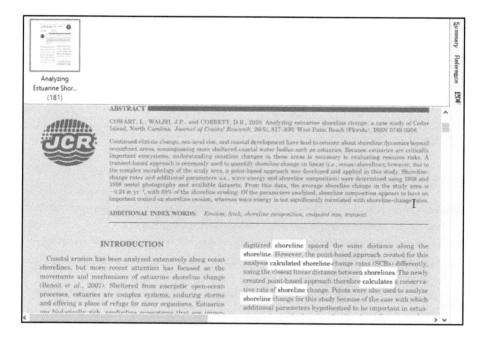

Figure 8.5 Compound Query Results (Windows only) in the *Environmental Change* Project

If you wish to compare content over time, you are likely to need to combine years of publication into Sets of years (e.g., decades). You can do this with Advanced Find using the Advanced tab to set multiple criteria when you need to get, say, all references including and after (>= value) 1980, but before (< value) 1990. If you are constantly updating your references, then save the result as a Search Folder rather than a Set, because Search Folders update when you use them to reflect that further Files have been added to your Project.

SECTION 8.4: CHAPTER 8 TAKEAWAYS

▬▬▬▬▬ Key points from this chapter ▬▬▬▬▬

o Most of the tools you will use to code and write about the literature are discussed in other chapters but in this chapter we try to help you think about these tools differently.

o You will probably use Nodes to think about your literature, but some of them are likely to be different than the Nodes you will create to code other data such as interview transcripts.

o pdf Files can be imported easily but you are likely to prefer it if they are in OCR format.

(Continued)

(Continued)

o You can code images and tables in pdf Files via the Region selection tool, which you will also use if you are coding pdf Files that are not in OCR format.

o pdf Files can also be imported as part of a bibliographic database, where additional information such as the year of publication will be converted by NVivo into Attribute Values.

Tips, challenges, and warnings

- Import your literature in different formats and pilot a few activities, particularly coding, to make sure you will get what you need from the Project.
- Do not import material from your reference manager if it does not have an associated pdf File unless the reference has other substantive qualitative data, such as an abstract or notes you want to code.
- Text in a pdf File initially seems to behave like text in a Word document. A few differences warrant a pilot with pdf Files as you might choose instead to save selected parts of a pdf as a Word File.
- Reference managers can grow quickly. Be selective about what you import so that chaos does not reign in your NVivo Project.
- If you have a huge amount of reference material to import, consider keeping it in a separate project (although this means you can't directly link the literature to your other data).

Help files

- *File*: Help.
- *Menu bar*: **Help > NVivo Help.**

Search for any of the following:

- Classify files
- Documents and PDFs
- Emails
- Links
- OneNote Online
- Queries
- References from reference management tools

Practice questions

1   What is the purpose of your literature review?

2   Are you conducting a broad survey of many items, a deep dive into the relevance of a smaller subset of the literature, or some other approach? Why?

3   When will you attend to the literature? Are there moments when you want to revisit it later?

4   What are some Nodes or Node hierarchies you think you will create to facilitate your literature review?

5   What Attribute Values or Sets might you consider to filter and sort ideas in the literature?

6   What are some of your favourite ideas from that chapter that you want to use in your literature review?

9

Section 9.1: Introduction to pictures, audio, and video 258

Section 9.2: Conceptual grounding in pictures, audio, and video 259

Section 9.3: Pictures, audio, and video in NVivo 263

Section 9.4: Chapter 9 Takeaways 281

WORKING WITH
MULTIMEDIA FILES

The computer can assist, by holding a myriad threads, exploring the sticky links to other catego-ries, by allowing the exploration of many patterns and the building of one web on another, and by testing the strength of the resultant fabric. But the task of theory discovery remains for the human researchers; the questions are theirs, the combinations of categories specified by them. (Richards & Richards, 1994: 170)

SECTION 9.1: INTRODUCTION TO PICTURES, AUDIO, AND VIDEO

Changes in the way we communicate, interact, and collect information through various media have brought with them a need to analyse such data in new ways. The emerging ana-lytical approaches that are fuelled by and which generate non-text data are pushing many researchers to rethink the way they inquire, analyse, and disseminate findings. NVivo allows you to import and work with pictures, audio, and video files, much to the delight of the visual researcher. Because you can, however, does not mean you should. We explain both the benefits, and the caveats, to working with non-text (multimedia) data.

In this chapter you will

- Find out about the way technology (especially the digitization of information) has changed our understanding and management of data.
- Learn the benefits and challenges of using non-text data in your research.
- See how to prepare, import, and transcribe (if relevant) pictures, audio, and video.
- Learn how to link, annotate, and code pictures, audio, and video.
- Discover options for exporting pictures, audio, and video to open in Word or as html.

Other chapters with related materials

Chapter 1: Where to begin?

Memos and Links help keep track of ongoing ideas and threads of connections in your data and this is often where a good portion of your analytical work can be developed and tracked. Be sure to use Memos and Links as you think through your audio, video, and pic-ture data.

Chapter 7: Querying data

Having a general sense of the different Queries and what they can do might help you think through the structure of your Nodes with audio, video, and picture data. Experiment with your coding and with some of the Queries to get an idea of how the material will look when it appears in Query Results or when it is exported.

Chapter 10: Twitter, Facebook, YouTube, and web pages

Windows users will find that YouTube videos behave just like other videos, although YouTube videos are not actually imported into your Project. Learning how to access this data with NCapture might give you additional ideas about how to use YouTube videos in your research.

SECTION 9.2: CONCEPTUAL GROUNDING IN PICTURES, AUDIO, AND VIDEO

The promises and perils of non-text data

The capacity of NVivo to allow you, as a researcher, to represent, manage, analyse, and report non-text data offers both possibilities and limitations. Most of the tools in NVivo, particularly those we describe in this chapter, are designed to do much more than package a few key images or sounds for the purpose of presenting findings. But, if that is all you need, NVivo will do that for you too, using simpler tools such as pictures embedded into text sources, or Hyperlinks to sound bites or video clips. The key is understanding, methodologically, why you might want to use this material and then using NVivo to support your preferred approach. Failing to assess and pilot your options is likely to lead you into handling non-text data in ways that are unnecessarily cumbersome or problematic.

Why use pictures, audio, or video as data?

Much current qualitative practice includes the collection of text or the transformation of data into text via field notes, audio or video transcripts, and other written materials. However, as Ochs (1979) described in her work on transcription as theory, the act of transcribing data (turning other forms of information into text) can carry with it some hidden assumptions. In her classic example, Ochs explains that when analysing the talk between adults and children, it is a common convention in her community of practice to place the text of the adults in the left-hand column of the page and the text of the children in the adjacent right-hand column of the page, with sequential turn-taking back and forth from left to right. This common convention may lead researchers to presume, more often than is warranted, that the adults are leading the conversation. In fact, as Ochs explains, in many instances the children lead the adults. To track these assumptions, researchers might turn to audio or video data either independently or alongside text data. This allows researchers to see or hear information that is unavailable, concealed, or unknowingly modified by the act of transcription.

An additional reason to turn to non-text data is that some research questions simply cannot be adequately investigated with text and require pictures, audio, or video. A study of sarcasm in executive meetings at a company's headquarters provides an example. To examine the use of this very specific form of humour in the management of power and position among executives, access to synchronized audio and/or video data allows for a far more intricate study. Gestures such as eye-rolling and audible inflections that are associated with sarcasm can be included in the analysis. Or, if you want to study the way movie marketing reifies notions of racism and sexism, consider a study of newspaper advertisements for action movies in the 1980s, where the images of hero, villain, and victim are examined for their location in the advertisement and their associated demographic characteristics: the fair-skinned, female likely victim on the bottom left-hand side of the image, the villainous, dark-skinned man tormenting her in the middle, and the heroic musculature of her white hero swooping in from above to save her.

As another rationale for using these forms of data, some researchers claim that the handling of non-text data creates a more intimate relationship between the researcher and the subjects and thereby improves the rigour of the study. For example, Pink (2001) argues that the visual ethnographer who collects and investigates the sounds and images of her participants is invited more explicitly to empathize with their sensations. She acknowledges that while researchers may not be able to feel or experience the exact same things as the participants, seeing and hearing the data regularly may allow researchers to become more contextually aware of the physical and emotional realities of research participants.

Why not use pictures, audio, or video?

Before moving on to the detail about how to import, manage, and code such data, a few caveats are warranted about the allure of multimedia Files. There is no doubt that a vivid photograph, compelling sound bite, or graphic video clip can be used effectively to supplement textual information for the purposes of creating vignettes or presenting findings. The use of these types of media is fairly common, even when the primary data are in textual form, because they stimulate our auditory and visual senses and help us understand social settings. However, even with these reasonable discussions of the benefits of using media data, researchers should use caution given some of the issues about the fidelity with which such data are represented, manipulated, and reported in QDA software (Silver & Patashnick, 2011). The issue you should address early on is whether non-text media should become an important data source, or simply an adjunct to text or a way to communicate findings.

Our assessment is that coding media such as the audio of an interview is a mistake if you are confident that the transcripts, alone, will answer your research questions. While NVivo allows you to code streaming audio and video Files, an NVivo Project with 20 interviews will quickly become very tedious to manage, because you will review the material over and over as you code, Memo, Link, run Queries, and examine output. You will soon be reminded of one of the reasons why we became literate: reviewing the transcript is much faster than listening to or watching the recorded audio or video. NVivo does allow for a helpful compromise via the simultaneous examination of audio or video and the associated transcript, so you should consider the use of non-text data. We see a red flag, however, when we are contacted by new qualitative researchers who want to use their picture, audio, or video data, without exactly knowing why. Sometimes they are simply hoping to avoid transcription, which is probably one of the worst reasons to use non-text data. This suggests it is time to pause, to review some of the literature that discusses methodological issues in the analysis of non-text data, and to pilot the procedures. You might also reconsider your impulse to use non-text data if:

- you simply find visual data more exciting than text;
- the use of media sounds 'cool';
- a photograph is of global interest such that you do not need to code pixels of the image and can therefore embed it in a text document instead of importing it in a picture format such as a jpeg or pdf;
- ethical considerations prohibit the public dissemination of media files either because of the risk of damage through revealing a participant's identity, as expressed in your human-subjects guidelines or your commitment to handling the data honourably;
- leaving the data in media form will present practical problems in disseminating the results to the intended audience or limit the venues through which you can publish them;
- you have massive amounts of media files that could become cumbersome to manage in an NVivo Project. (NVivo does allow you to store media files outside the project. However, you will need to manage these data as part of your Project, too.)

Using pictures in your research

Pictures might be photographs, or they could be drawings, maps, computer graphics, handwriting samples, flow charts, architectural designs, company logos, or quilt patterns. This genre of data can be collected in any digital format if you plan on linking to them externally with a Hyperlink (Chapter 1, p. 33). Or, you need to collect this data in one of the supported formats if you want to import them, add other Links, and code the images. We provide a few ideas next, to get you thinking about their potential for use in your research.

Image-elicitation techniques are used when the researcher wants to collect participant perceptions on a predefined image or set of pictures. The images are usually determined before data collection and may be used for a wide range of research purposes, including:

- supplementing interview questions with visuals to help prompt the respondent;
- determining the most appealing brand images for a specifically targeted audience;
- collecting a series of word associations for particular images (similar to a Rorschach test);
- assessing participant recall of the elements in the image after allowing them to review the image before it is taken away.

In the spirit of participant-directed research projects such as action research, individuals might use cameras to collect data prior to their interview:

- homeless children taking snapshots of the people and places that provide comfort;
- athletes photographing the objects that play a critical role in their training;
- farmers taking photographs of the various stages when they tend to their crops;
- octogenarians capturing the locations where they volunteer.

In addition, drawings or graphics might be produced during the interview process to help participants work through their understandings and communicate these to the researcher verbally, including:

- an organizational diagram of power relations in a corporation that is produced by participants while they discuss their mentors and advocates;
- a diagram of family ties associated with a mother's description of the role of religion in her relationships with family members;
- a drawing of a car crash and a report of the injuries associated with an accident;
- a creative, visual representation of educational barriers and the resources required by a non-traditional student to overcome them.

Images might also be used to augment other types of data in your project. In some instances, you may be aware of the relevance of such data prior to starting your research. In others, you may not realize the relevance until you are immersed in the research or learn what you can do with images with the assistance of NVivo. These images are not typically provided by the respondents but collected in response to their participation. The types of images that can serve as supplements can vary widely, including:

- images of buildings or locations that were described by participants as welcoming, dangerous, peaceful, etc.;
- aerial photographs of a region that are compared with the participants' discussions of their perceptions of changes in the geography of that region (see the photographs in the *Environmental Change* Project);
- street maps of a neighbourhood to supplement interview transcripts with blind students about the obstacles they encounter when navigating to their school in this neighbourhood;
- magazine advertisements for the clothing items associated with school cliques after hearing various students' discussions about the values or identities associated with this attire.

The diversity of picture formats, the reasons you might use or collect them, and the role you and your respondents have in creating them point to the applicability of images in addressing a wide range of research questions.

Using audio and video Files in your research

Audio can capture a wide range of sounds and conversations, such as emergency phone calls with a fire department, radio transmissions from fishing vessels, candidate debates, and even bird songs in the Amazon. Video offers exciting possibilities to those engaging in community or behavioural research, where context and action can 'speak' more loudly than words. Providing a video camera to participants in the research so that they can film episodes of their own lives and communities changes the perspective from which the data are seen (Mitchell, 2011). As with pictures, this genre of data can be collected in any digital format if you plan on linking to it externally with a Hyperlink (Chapter 1, p. 33). You can also import a range of these file formats into NVivo.

▬▬▬▬ Video narratives of chronic illness ▬▬▬▬

Michael Rich and his colleagues had adolescents with chronic illness create video narratives that included tours of home and neighbourhood, interviews with family and friends, daily activities, and daily diaries in a study designed to have patients teach clinicians about their illness experiences (Rich & Patashnick, 2002). Working over a decade ago with 500 hours of video data, the researchers experienced limitations in computing capacity and in qualitative software that have now been overcome in a technical sense - although the question of simply working through the sheer volume of data remains.

Video may be required when the audible record cannot address the research questions as in our earlier example of sarcasm in team meetings. They can also be retained along with the sound to augment the analysis, even though you are not sure if you will need the video. For example, you are studying the decibel difference between television dramas and television advertisements and want to see and hear participants discuss their reaction to this decibel change.

SECTION 9.3: PICTURES, AUDIO, AND VIDEO IN NVIVO

NVivo terms used in this section

Embedded files

Hyperlink

Log

Node

Not-embedded files

Picture Region

Playhead

Region selection

See Also Link

Timeline

Transcript row

Three technical options with pictures

If you are convinced pictures will play a role in your research, you have three options for managing them technically. These options are to use a Hyperlink, embed the image in a text

File, or import the image as a standalone File. Before you commit yourself, you should probably pilot all three to determine the best fit. Determining the best option is likely to depend on several issues: the relevance of these data to your primary research questions, the degree to which you need to analyse discrete portions of the image, your personal style, and the amount of data you will be managing.

Create a Hyperlink

In Chapter 1 we described how to create a Hyperlink in NVivo that allows you to connect a specific spot, such as a sentence in an interview, with a File that has not been or cannot be imported into NVivo. If a picture has a logical connection to one of your text documents (e.g., a map someone drew can be associated with their interview transcript where they discuss the map), follow our instructions in Chapter 1 (p. 33) to create a Hyperlink from the interview transcript to the picture and see if this will meet your needs.

- Advantages:
    - The ability to keep the item external so it does not take up space in the Project.
    - Storage of the linked files in locations where you already have them nicely organized (hopefully!).

- Disadvantages:
    - The potential for links to be broken if you move either the Project or the linked images (although you can link them again later).
    - The inability to code the picture.
    - The inability to export picture content out of the Project because it does not actually exist in the Project.

Embed in an imported text-based File

Simply embed your picture as an illustration in a Word document (Insert > Pictures) and then import this File into your NVivo Project. You may then Link, code, and Query according to the instructions in Chapters 1, 3, 4, 5, and 7).

- Advantages:
    - The picture can be managed in a familiar text document.
    - The picture is immediately present in its relevant context.
    - Code the entire picture.
    - The picture can be exported as an integral component of the File, in both docx and html formats.

- Disadvantages:
    - You cannot code portions (pixel regions) within the picture and must instead code the entire picture.
    - Annotations and See Also Links can be added only to the picture as a whole.

Import as a standalone File

The third option, importing the picture as a standalone File, allows you to treat the data quite intricately because it allows you to code pixel regions of the image as well as record and code associated text in a log. The remaining information about images in this chapter pertains to this third strategy, as it is by far the most complex.

- Advantages:
  - The most detailed way to code and link images.
  - An ability to choose whether to code a region of the image, the text associated with the region, or both.

- Disadvantages:
  - When one of the other strategies will suffice, this approach can be unnecessarily cumbersome to manage because there are more technical issues to handle.
  - If you code an image with this strategy, coded regions can be exported efficiently from the Project only in html format. This is in contrast with the option above to embed it in a File, which provides both docx and html export options.

Importing the picture, creating a log, and adding Links

After saving the picture in one of the recognized formats (bmp, gif, jpg, jpeg, png, tif, tiff), import the File in the same way as for a text-based document (Chapter 1, pp. 26–27). You will also use this same strategy for audio and video data. Before you import any of these different data types, however, consider whether you want to store them in their own Folder, within the Files area. If so, then create the additional Folders before you start importing them (Chapter 2, pp. 54–55).

Once they are imported, you will find that most of the tools you have learned to use with text can also be applied to pictures and other multimedia Files with just a few slight variations to accommodate differences in methods of selecting what is to be linked or coded.

- Region code pictures in the same way as for scanned text, or images and tables in a pdf File.
- Use Annotations or the log of a picture to comment on what is happening in a selected region of the picture. The log can be coded, whereas an Annotation always remains linked to the picture, so the content of the Annotation cannot be coded.
- Link specific parts of a picture to part of another imported File.
- Create a series of sequenced pictures, for example, by using a series of See Also Links to entire items (Windows only).

Additionally:

- Folders or Sets of pictures can be custom displayed in the *List View* as thumbnails, to create a gallery presentation on a topic or theme (Windows only, Figure 9.1).

Figure 9.1 Thumbnail display of Files (Windows only)

While the instructions to follow will focus on linking and coding pictures, many of the strategies apply also to audio and video Files and so these commonalities will not be repeated when we discuss them.

View an example

The *Environmental Change* Project makes extensive use of picture data. Look in the *Navigation View*: **Data > Files** subfolders under Area and Township to see photographs and geographical information systems (GIS) data. Click on the number identifying a log entry to see the part of the picture to which it refers (it will be highlighted with a shade of purple – see shading in Figure 9.2).

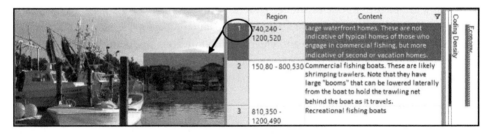

Figure 9.2 A picture Region with an associated log and Coding Stripe

Turn on the Coding Stripes (*Ribbon*: **Picture > Coding Stripes**) to see the coding applied to either or both the Picture and its log.

9.a.

Importing, viewing, annotating, and linking a picture

Import and examine Properties of a picture

⇒ *Ribbon*: **Import > Files / Data > Picture** > locate the File(s) > **Open > Import**.

⇒ *List View*: **Right-click** on the **File > Picture Properties / Get Info > Picture tab** to access metadata such as the date the photo was taken, aperture, and exposure time.

View and adjust your picture

⇒ *List View*: **Double-click** on the **File**.

⇒ **Click to Edit / Tick** Edit.

⇒ *Ribbon*: **> Edit**.

⇒ You can now adjust the **Brightness & Contrast**.

⇒ Rotate the image 90 degrees **Right** or **Left**, for instance.

    o   The area allocated to the image versus the log (described next) can be adjusted with a double-headed arrow on the vertical line separating these areas.

    o   On the bottom right-hand side of the NVivo window you will also see a slide bar that allows you to zoom in or out on the image.

    o   On the bottom left-hand side of the NVivo window you will also see two magnifying glasses that allow you to zoom in or out on the image.

Writing about a picture

If you would like to write notes about some or all of the image, this can be accomplished with a log, an Annotation, or a Memo Link.

Enter a log

⇒ *Detail View*: **Right-click** in the **picture** > make sure the **Edit** icon is illuminated. If not, select it to turn it on.

⇒ **Click** in the picture and **drag** your cursor diagonally to create a Region and **release your Click** (Figure 9.3).

⇒ Inside the **Region > Right-click > Insert Row with Region**.

⇒ The log locates the region (using pixel coordinates **/ using diagram**) and you can **add text** in the Content field (Figure 9.3).

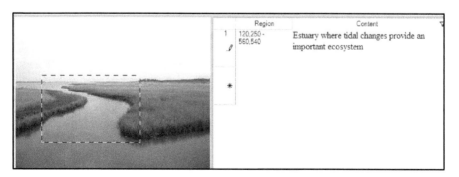

Figure 9.3   Picture with a newly inserted log entry

⇒ Select the number next to any row to illuminate the associated portion of the picture.

(Continued)

(Continued)

Add Annotations or Links to the image or log

To add a Memo Link, Annotation, or See Also Link to the picture or log, follow the instructions in Chapter 1 (pp. 27–33) and treat the selection just as you would text from an interview transcript. In brief:

Memo Link

⇒ *Detail View*: **Right-click** anywhere in the **picture** or **log > Links > Memo Link > Link to New** (or **Existing**) **Memo**.

Annotation (Windows only)

⇒ *Detail View*: **Select** a portion of the **picture** or **log > Right-click > New Annotation**.

See Also Link to an entire item (Windows only)

⇒ *Detail View*: **Select** a portion of the **picture** or **log > Right-click > Links > See Also Link > New See Also Link**.

See Also Link to specific content (Windows only)

⇒ *Detail View*: **Select** a portion of the **picture** or **log > Right-click > Copy**.
⇒ Go to another **File,** such as an interview, article, or another picture and **Highlight** the passage that is related to this part of the **picture**.
⇒ **Right-click > Paste As See Also Link**.
⇒ Alternatively, **Select** content from another **File** and **Copy** it, then return to **Select** a place in the picture or log > **Right-click** and **Paste As See Also Link**. (See Chapter 1, pp. 30–32 for additional information about See Also Links.)

Coding a picture or log

You can code a picture and its log in much the same way as you code a transcript (drag-and-drop, right-click, or select recently used Nodes from the Quick Coder). See Chapters 3 and 4 for details about coding text and working with Nodes. The difference from coding other text is in the way parts of the picture or log are selected for coding, and how they appear in a Node.

Coding picture Regions

⇒ *Detail View*: **Click** in the picture and **drag** your cursor diagonally to create a Region and **release your Click** (Figure 9.3).
⇒ **Drag** this Region of the picture to any **Node**, or **Right-click** to **Code**.

Coding the log

⇒ Code part of the text in a log row (for images, audio, or video) as you would for any other text.

⇒ To code an entire log row (instead of just a portion) **>** **Select** the **number /**
diagram to the left of the row > **drag** this number to the **Node** (or **Right-click**
and code).

Viewing a coded picture and log in a Node

Viewing a coded picture

⇒ *Navigation View*: **Codes > Nodes**.

⇒ *List View*: **Double-click** on a Node that is coded with picture data.

  o See the pixel coordinates of the image in the **Reference tab** (the default Node
  display).

  o To see the picture (Figure 9.4): on the right margin of the Node display, switch to
  the **Picture tab**.

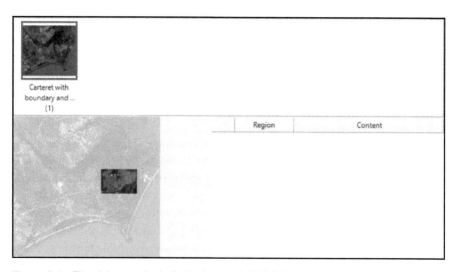

Figure 9.4 The picture content of a Node open in *Detail View*

Viewing a coded log

⇒ Coded text from a log entry will appear in your Nodes along with other text
References.

Adding images to Cases

In Chapter 5 we walked you through the conceptualization of Cases, Classifications, Attributes,
and Values. These are often used to track demographic characteristics, usually for the purpose
of comparing subgroups in the data. Return to Chapter 5 for conceptual grounding if these are
unfamiliar to you, where you will also find detailed instructions for creating and managing
them. Any type of qualitative data you can import into NVivo can be associated with a Case.

For example, if your Cases represent people and one of the Case Types in your Project is *engineers*, you could ask engineers to bring along photographs of customized tools they use. After you import these photographs into your Project, you might be examining just the picture, just the log rows associated with the picture where the engineers discuss the specific features of the tools, or both. These pictures and/or their associated log data would then be included in the Case for the particular engineer who uses the tool (assuming your Cases are people). Alternatively, your Cases could be types of tools or sites where different tools are used. Tactics for coding pictures to Cases parallel the ones used with text (see Chapter 5, pp. 146–148). Once you create the Cases, you can add Attribute Values to them, just as you would any other Case.

Importing and managing audio and video files

As with pictures, the audio and video data can be in any format if handled with a Hyperlink that connects a location inside the NVivo Project to the externally located File (Chapter 1, p. 33). However, if you want to import these data, it must be in a recognized format (Windows: mp3, m4a, wma, wav, mpg, mpeg, mpe, mp4, avi, wmv, mov, qt, 3gp, mts, m2ts; Mac: mp3, m4a, wav, mp4, avi, mov). In addition to these formats, you must have the necessary codecs installed on your computer (Windows only). A codec is a programming term that is a contraction of the phrase 'coder-decoder'. In NVivo, these programs facilitate transmission, storage, playback, and editing of audio and video Files. There are literally thousands of codecs, and if you are unable to import or play an audio or video File in NVivo even if it is one of the supported formats, it is likely that you need to check the codecs on your computer. The NVivo Help provides instructions for investigating the codecs on your computer in the event you need to locate one for installation.

Because audio and video Files can be very large, and therefore influence the performance of a project, NVivo allows for smaller files (up to 40MB) to be either embedded in the NVivo Project or stored in another location. Larger files have to be stored outside the project. As you work with your media, the interface in NVivo is identical whether media are embedded or not embedded. When the File is not embedded, the software creates a seamless link between the Project and the externally located File. The critical factor with Files that are not embedded is ensuring that, if the Project is moved, these Files travel with it and the File paths (the links from NVivo to the videos) retain their integrity. Although audio and video are used quite differently in the field methodologically, they are handled technically very similarly in NVivo (the screens look identical but the audio does not have an image). The following screenshots and instructions will focus on video, but the instructions apply equally to audio.

━━━━━━━━━━ **9.b.** ━━━━━━━━━━

Importing audio or video Files

Import audio and video Files in the same way as you import pictures or text data. Then check to see whether the File is embedded or stored elsewhere.

⇒   *List View*: **Right-click** on the **File** you just imported > **Video Properties / Get Info**.

⇒ **Select** the **Video tab**. If your media file is under 20MB, you will see it was imported as an embedded file. If it is 20MB or larger, it was imported as a not-embedded file.

    o   At any time, you may alter the status of Files up to 40MB as embedded or not-embedded by changing the Video Properties of the File.

You can change the options for your project to modify the size of files that will be embedded (up to 40MB) when you import them (*File:* **Options > Audio/Video**). If you move a not-embedded File and break the link, you will receive an error message when opening it from inside NVivo. Fear not, however, because as soon as you re-establish the link by updating the file location, all of your coding and Links will jump back into position.

Playing media

When you open a video File inside NVivo, you see both a timeline (the audio waveform) and the video playback. In your research you might make use of both of these features. The variations in the waveform give an indication of rising and falling volumes that potentially tell you about, for example, the progress of an argument, or the rise in distress of a caller to the emergency line. The video, of course, reveals gestures, facial expressions, and actions that are not accessible any other way. Video was used, for example, to analyse children's play activity during assessments in a study involving early intervention with families at risk (Kemp et al., 2011). The time and kind of attention given to objects associated with literacy (such as books) compared to other play materials was a focus of one related sub-study.

If you click in the *Detail View* of an open video, the video playback appears at the top of the screen in the *Ribbon* / bottom of the video (Figure 9.5).

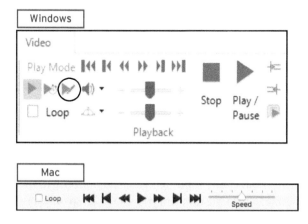

Figure 9.5 The Playback group in the *Video Ribbon* (Windows) and the Player controls (Mac)

In the Playback group you can play, pause, start, jump to another location, and change the speed and volume of the playback, much as you would when managing audio and video outside of NVivo. If you are familiar with them, use your shortcut keys or see the NVivo Help for a list of keyboard shortcuts.

9.c.

Playing media

⇒ *List View:* **Double-click** to open your video.
⇒ *Ribbon:* **Video > Play/Pause.**
⇒ *Detail View:* **Player controls > Play symbol.**
⇒ *Detail View:* Watch the playhead move across the timeline (Figure 9.6).
⇒ **Select > Stop / Pause symbol.**
⇒ You can place your cursor on the playhead and **drag** it to any point along the timeline to a different segment > **Play/Pause.**

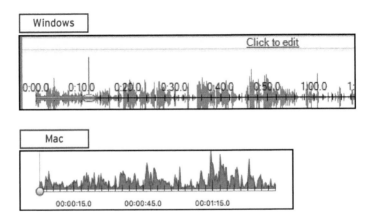

Figure 9.6 The playhead moving across the timeline of an audio or video File in Windows (top) and Mac (bottom)

Transcribing media files

Many issues surrounding transcription were discussed in Chapter 2, and a few were noted earlier in this chapter. Before you dive into transcription, consider those issues carefully, test different options, and develop a plan for your preferred strategy. If you plan to code directly to the audio or video timeline, rather than transcribe, you can skip to the subsequent section on coding – but remember our earlier warning that coding directly to the media timeline is not likely to save you time in the long run, and you should do so only for clear methodological reasons.

If you do transcribe, you can do so directly within NVivo, or as noted earlier, you can prepare a transcript outside of the software and import it later. QSR also provides a transcription service and as the technology changes, you will find changes to this service. Consult the NVivo Help for the most updated options.

Transcribe to the level of detail that suits you (see Chapter 2), answering these questions before you begin transcribing:

- Do you need every utterance (uhm, ah, hmm-mmm)?
- Do you need to indicate pauses or overlapping speech?
- Are there gestures you want to capture and record as part of the transcript?
- Will you be able to answer your research questions if you simply summarize rather than transcribe verbatim (especially given you have the parallel video)?

If you want to transcribe outside of the software, search NVivo Help for 'Audio and video transcripts' so that you format the data correctly to allow synchronization with the media File.

If you transcribe inside the software, NVivo will accommodate your transcription machine foot pedals and keystrokes for start, stop, etc. Alternatively, you can use the software interface to provide commands while you transcribe. Either way, you need an orientation to the *Video Ribbon* or *Audio Ribbon*.

9.d.

Transcribing in NVivo (Windows)

⇒ In the *Video Ribbon*, Playback group, you will see Play Mode with three different settings (Figure 9.5). You are currently in Normal play mode with a green triangle illuminated.

⇒ To transcribe, you will need to **Select** the Play Mode on the right that is probably greyed out (circled in Figure 9.5). To access and use it:

○ *Detail View*: If it is available, **Select** the **Click to edit** bar just above the timeline of your audio or video.

○ From the Play Mode options, **Select** the **Transcribe icon** (circled in Figure 9.5).

○ **Adjust** the **speed** and **volume** of the playback to suit your needs.

○ Move your playhead to the location where you want to begin transcribing and click **Play/Pause** (or use your keystrokes or foot pedal).

○ A transcript row appears to the right of the media where you can begin typing next to the Timespan (Figure 9.7).

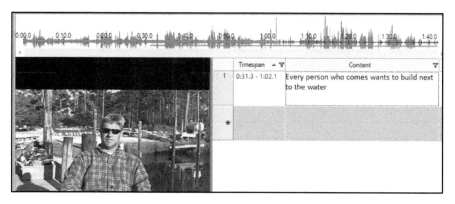

Figure 9.7   Entering a new transcript row (Windows)

(Continued)

(Continued)

⇒ Click **Pause** (or use your keystrokes or foot pedals) to remain in the same row while you correct, retype or catch up.

○ Click **Play** to start again.

⇒ Click **Stop** and then **Play** to create a new row.

Transcribing in NVivo (Mac)

⇒ *Detail View*: **Tick** the Edit box of your audio or video.

⇒ **Adjust** the **speed** of the playback to suit your needs at the bottom of the audio or video.

⇒ Move your playhead to the location where you want to begin transcribing **> click +** at the bottom of the transcript area to create a new transcript row where you can begin typing (Figure 9.8).

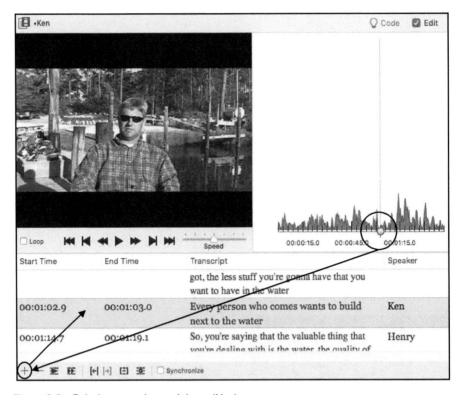

Figure 9.8 Entering a new transcript row (Mac)

⇒ Click **Player control symbols** to correct, retype, or catch up and **Pause** when transcript row is complete.

⇒ *Menu bar*: **Analyze > Media > Apply End Time**.

⇒ Click **+** to create a new transcript row.

Your decision about when to create a new row or stay in the existing row depends on your analytical goals. You will be able to code either selected text within the transcript row, or select the number next to the row to code the entirety. Some researchers create a new row for each speaker to allow Auto Coding for Cases. Others divide data into similar lengths, or identify meaningful episodes within the media based on the content. *Windows users*: Each time you create a new row it appears at the top of the *Detail View* for easy access, but the rows will sort themselves by timespan and you can play the media chronologically whenever you like. After you pilot a few minutes of transcription, go to the *Video Ribbon*: **Play Mode > Synchronize** (the triangle/stopwatch icon between the Normal and Transcribe modes in Figure 9.5) / tick Synchronize in the Transcript and selection controls. While you are in the Synchronize mode, the transcript will scroll into view as the media plays.

Links in media Files (Windows only)

To add Memo Links, Annotations, See Also Links, and Hyperlinks directly to the media or a Row adjacent to the media, select as you would for other types of data, such as transcripts, and follow the same steps (Chapter 1, pp. 27–33) To add Links to the media timeline, select material the same way you would for coding (see below).

Adding audio or video to Cases

Entire media Files can be coded as Cases by employing the usual strategies (as outlined in Chapter 5). If a File includes more than one speaker, however, you are likely to want to code portions of the File to different Cases. This could be achieved interactively but will be much easier to do if the transcript is structured so each speaking turn is in a new row. This will allow for Auto Coding based on a custom field added (as a column) to the transcript to identify the speakers.

━━━━━━━━━━ **9.e.** ━━━━━━━━━━

Using custom fields and Auto Coding in a media transcript (Windows)

Add a custom field

⇒ *File*: **Project Properties > Audio/Video** tab.
⇒ **Custom Transcript Fields > Select** the **Audio** or **Video** tab and use the **New** button to add new fields.
⇒ Enter a name, such as **Speaker > OK**. Any fields that you add will be applied to all media of that type within this project.
⇒ *Detail View*: See the new field in the video or audio transcript.

Auto Code speakers to create Cases

⇒ *List View*: **Select** your audio or video File **> Right-click > Auto Code**.
  ○ NVivo Plus users: **Select** Use the style or Structure **> Next**.

(Continued)

(Continued)

⇒ **Select** the Available Transcript Field containing your Case names (e.g., Speakers) and use the **arrow** to move right, under Selected Transcript Fields.

⇒ Identify the **Location** and **Name** for where the Cases are to go > **Finish**.

⇒ You can now classify your Cases and add Attribute Values to them, just as you would any other Case. (See Chapter 5 for more details.)

Coding media files

As with the picture data, you can code either the media or the transcript, or both.

━━━━━━━━━ **9.f.** ━━━━━━━━━

Coding a media file

Coding the transcript

⇒ *Detail View*: To code the transcript, use your right-click or drag-and-drop options as you would any text (Chapter 3, pp. 80–82). As with pictures, **Select** a row number to code the whole transcript row.

Code the media timeline as media clips (Windows)

You have two options for selecting portions of the media timeline for coding:

⇒ *Detail View*: If you know the time range you want to select (because it has already been transcribed or because you just played it), **click and hold** on the timeline where you would like the episode to begin, and **drag** as far as you need.

   o   Your cursor is marking off a blue box around the selected range.
   o   **Release** and your box is complete.

⇒ *Media Ribbon*: **Click** to Start Selection or Finish Selection as the media plays. Again, a region in the timeline will be marked off with a blue box.

Now that you created a blue box to identify the range, you are ready to code:

⇒ *Detail View*: Place your **cursor inside the blue box** and code as you would normally (**drag-and-drop**, **right-click**, etc.)

Code the media timeline as media clips (Mac)

If you already know the time range you want to select because it has already been transcribed:

⇒ *Detail View*: With Synchronize ticked, **Click** in the transcript row and a blue box will appear in the timeline.

⇒ Place your **cursor inside the blue box** and code as you would normally (**drag-and-drop**, **right-click**, etc.).

You have two options for directly selecting a portion of the media timeline for coding:

⇒ *Detail View*: **Click and hold** on the timeline where you would like the episode to begin, and **drag** as far as you need. Your cursor is marking off a grey area around the selected range.

⇒ *Detail View*: **Transcript and selection controls > Click** Start Selection and Finish Selection symbols as the media plays. Again, a region in the timeline will be marked off with a grey area.

  o *Detail View*: Place your **cursor inside the grey area** and code using **right-click** or **Code button**.

Viewing coded media

⇒ *Navigation View*: **Codes > Nodes**.

⇒ *List View*: **Double-click** on a Node that contains media data.

⇒ *Detail View*: You are in Reference view and so you will see only the time range identified (alongside any text you coded at the Node). To see the range of media and play it:

  o Go the right side of the *Detail View* and choose the appropriate tab (**Audio** or **Video**).

  o *Media Ribbon*: **> Play**. The episodes or clips coded at that Node will play consecutively.

  o **Double-click** on the blue Hyperlink above the time range to play the media in the File.

Viewing Coding Stripes for images, audio, and video

Coding Stripes were introduced in Chapter 3 (pp. 83–86) as a way of checking the coding you were applying to text. With images and media Files you can use Coding Stripes to see a visual of your coding, but with a new feature for Windows users – Shadow Coding Stripes. Figure 9.9 shows the Coding Stripes and the Shadow Coding Stripes in Max Coltheart's interview in the *Researchers* Project.

Turning on Coding Stripes (*Ribbon*: **Video** or **Audio > Coding Stripes**) will provide a visual of where and how you have coded the actual media timeline (solid, horizontal stripes below the timeline). Use your right-click menu to access additional viewing (and coding) options.

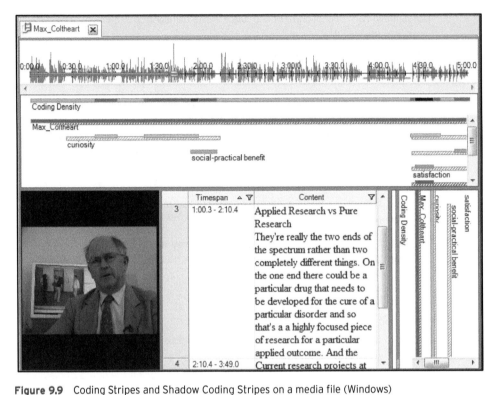

Figure 9.9 Coding Stripes and Shadow Coding Stripes on a media file (Windows)

Note: Interview with Professor Max Coltheart, Federation Fellow and Professor of Cognitive Science, Macquarie University. Used with permission.

Windows users:

- See stripes next to the transcript rows (solid, vertical stripes to the right of the text).
- Also see hatched stripes. NVivo calls these hatched stripes Shadow Coding Stripes.
- The horizontal Shadow Coding Stripes below the timeline indicate that a portion of the transcript row was coded during this range.
- The vertical Shadow Coding Stripes to the right of the text indicate that a portion of the video was coded during this row.

Run a Group Query (Windows only) to collect media into a Set

Another way to look at your coding and think about the relevance of the patterns is to run a Group Query to gather media Files that have been coded to a Node or multiple Nodes.

--- **9.g.** ---

Run a Group Query (Windows only)

For example, in the *Environmental Change* Project you could find all the audio and video Files that have been coded to *Real estate development* and *Natural environment*. After you find the Files, you can instantly turn them into a Set of *People who talk about Real estate development and Natural environment*. You can use this Set in a subsequent Query pertaining to only these people.

⇒ *Ribbon*: **Explore > Group**.

⇒ Look for: **Items Coding**.

⇒ Scope: **Change** Files and Externals to Selected Items **> Select >** tick the boxes next to your audio and video interview Files (e.g., *Betty and Paul, Helen, Ken*) **> OK**.

⇒ Range: **Change** to Selected Items **Select >** tick the boxes next to the Nodes (e.g., *Real estate development* and *Natural environment*).

⇒ **Run**.

⇒ Right-click on the File names to **Create As > Create As Set > Name** the Set **> OK** (Figure 9.10).

o The Set will be stored in *Navigation View*: **Search >** Sets.

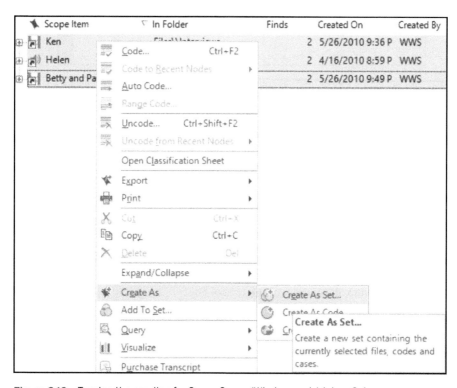

Figure 9.10 Turning the results of a Group Query (Windows only) into a Set

⇒ **Select** the Connection Map tab on the right to visualize the connections (Figure 9.11).

(Continued)

(Continued)

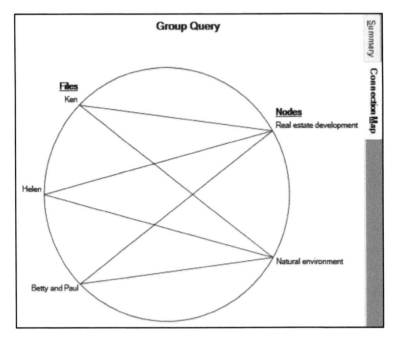

Figure 9.11   A Connection Map of the Files coded to *Natural environment* and *Real estate development*

If you want to save this Query to run it again later:

⇒   *Ribbon*: **Explore > Last Run Query > Tick** Add to Project **> Name** it **> OK**.

Exporting non-text data

After you link and code your picture, audio, or video data to your satisfaction, you can export or print it in several ways, depending on the type of File.

━━━━━━━━━ **9.h.** ━━━━━━━━━

Export from the *Detail View*

⇒   *Navigation View*: **Codes > Nodes** (or **Data > Files**).
⇒   *List View*: **Double-click** on a Node (or File).
⇒   *Detail View*: **Right-click > Export > Export Node** (or **Export File**).

- o **Entire Content**: The contents of the File or Node will be saved as an html file, with tabs for Summary and Reference views and also for each type of content (e.g., text, video, pdf, picture). Coded passages from pdf sources will also show as highlighted regions within the context of the relevant page.
- o **Reference view / File Format:** The contents of the File or Node will export as a Word file (defaulting to docx, but with other options) showing coded text and pdf passages. For coded image, audio, or video Files, you will see only the pixel coordinates, time stamps, or the coded log or transcript rows, and not the image or the video contents. Coded passages from pdf Files will also show as highlighted regions within the context of the relevant page. A pdf coded as text shows as text, but regions just show coordinates.

Export from the *List View*

⇒ *Navigation View*: **Codes > Nodes** (or **Data: Files**).

⇒ *List View*: **Right-click** on a Node (or File) **> Export > Export** (Node or File).

SECTION 9.4: CHAPTER 9 TAKEAWAYS

▬▬▬▬▬▬ Key points from this chapter ▬▬▬▬▬▬

Pictures, audio, and video can be used in different ways during the research:

- o Having participants capture or develop materials prior to or during an interview.
- o Using non-text data as an elicitation technique during an interview.
- o Following up after an interview, observation, etc., to collect images that reflect participant observations.
- o Having participants create media diaries as part of the research process.

- o Using media recordings to understand not just what was said but how it was said.
- o The issue you should address early on is whether non-text media should become an important data source, or simply an adjunct to text or a way to communicate findings.

Tips, challenges, and warnings

- Coding media such as the audio of an interview is a mistake if you are confident that the transcripts, alone, will answer your research questions.
- Experiment with the different ways to use non-text data because there are many options and you want the one that is the least cumbersome but will still get you to the answers to your research questions.
- If you have pictures, run a small pilot where you import some as embedded images in a Word File and others as image data (jpeg, pdf, etc.). Code, create Cases, run Queries, and export data to see what happens to the data during these phases. It will help you decide how to handle pictures.

- When sourcing a recording device, choose one that creates files in a format that NVivo recognizes. You can usually convert audio or video files into NVivo recognized formats but it's much easier if you don't have to.

Help files

- *File*: Help.
- *Menu bar*: **Help > NVivo Help**.

Search for any of the following:

- Audio and video transcripts
- Create audio or video transcripts
- Export files or nodes
- Import audio or video transcripts
- Pictures
- Play audio and video

Practice questions

1   If you are still in the design stage of your research, what are some creative ways you could incorporate non-text data that you were overlooking because of your focus on text?
2   What are the potential advantages of adding this data?
3   What are the potential disadvantages of adding this data?

10

Section 10.1: Introduction to Twitter, Facebook, YouTube, and web pages   286

Section 10.2: Conceptual grounding in Twitter, Facebook, YouTube, and web pages   287

Section 10.3: Twitter, Facebook, YouTube, and web pages in NVivo   292

Section 10.4: Chapter 10 Takeaways   303

TWITTER, FACEBOOK, YOUTUBE, AND WEB PAGES

The basic premise of social network analysis is that relationships cannot be discretely quantified as units of measurement; that is, the relationship between two individuals must always be seen within the context of all the other relationships those individuals engage in (either shared or separately). (Eyman, 2015: 103)

SECTION 10.1: INTRODUCTION TO TWITTER, FACEBOOK, YOUTUBE, AND WEB PAGES

Twitter, Facebook, YouTube, and web pages should not be overlooked as sources of data for your study. A wide variety of research questions can be answered by exploring communication in the online environment. You can look at the way various companies present themselves online to the public, how viewers make judgements about talent show performers, or how support groups construct distributed communities to provide ongoing encouragement. Alternatively, these data might serve as a supplement to the types of data we have discussed in other chapters. For example, you might unexpectedly want to capture a web page because one of your interview participants mentioned curriculum guidelines that she found on a web page. Or, she might mention a Twitter hashtag that was popular on campus recently and was part of a social movement. NCapture is a free browser extension for Internet Explorer or Google Chrome that will collect this data with just a few clicks, so you can import it into NVivo. You will then be able to code content, Link, follow embedded Hyperlinks, and use Queries with this material.

In this chapter you will

- Consider why you might incorporate Twitter, Facebook, YouTube, and web pages in your research.
- Learn the mechanics of installing and using NCapture to collect data from Twitter, Facebook, YouTube, and web pages.
- See the limitations of the volume and type of data collected from these platforms.
- Discover how to Memo, Link, code, and Query this data inside NVivo (which sometimes entails pointers to other chapters).

Other chapters with related materials

While you might find all the material related to your current needs in this chapter, you should also consider these other chapters that contain closely related information:

Chapter 6: Surveys and mixed methods

When possible, it is likely that you will want to import social media data as a Dataset in NVivo. Datasets in the form of surveys are covered in Chapter 6, where you will find details about how to code and run Queries on Datasets.

Chapter 8: Literature review and pdf Files

NVivo converts web pages and some Facebook pages into pdf Files during import. You might want to write about or code the text and images in these pdf Files and we provide details about how to do so in Chapter 8.

Chapter 9: Working with multimedia Files

NVivo handles YouTube videos the same way it handles non-embedded video Files. In Chapter 9 you will find additional information about transcribing, coding clips, and handling other technical details surrounding these videos.

SECTION 10.2: CONCEPTUAL GROUNDING IN TWITTER, FACEBOOK, YOUTUBE, AND WEB PAGES

A working understanding of social media

Platforms like Facebook, Twitter, and YouTube operate in constantly changing digital, commercial, and social landscapes. Do not assume other people share your understanding of social media; rather, articulate your definition as this has an impact on the boundaries and focus of your research. Some researchers view any online platform that allows individuals to interact with one another as a social media site. This means that blogs, wikis, and any other digital interface using Web 2.0 capabilities could qualify as social media.

We prefer the definition of social media proposed by McCay-Peet and Quan-Haase (2017). They say that social media platforms are:

> Web-based services that allow individuals, communities and organizations to collaborate, connect, interact, and build community by enabling them to create, co-create, modify, share, and engage with user-generated content that is easily accessible. (p. 17)

As scholars like Fuchs (2017) have noted, this definition still begs several questions:

- What is a 'community?'
- What does it mean to 'interact?'
- What does it mean to 'share?'
- Who or what is a 'user?'
- What does it mean to be 'easily accessible?'

Your research will likely benefit from early attention to the answers to these questions or a stated intent to focus on these questions as part of your study. Furthermore, your specific research questions will direct you to different data or unique aspects of this data. The examination of cyberbullying is likely to attend to different characteristics of a social media platform than the effectiveness of a holiday sale campaign by a retailer.

Social media examples

Mohameden, Alkhairi, Issa, Mohameden, and Yuvienco (2017) qualitatively analysed the top 20 YouTube videos on "rheumatoid arthritis" and assessed the information according to whether it was useful or misleading. With only 20% of the videos coming from health care organizations or professionals, the researchers determined that YouTube lacked high-quality information for rheumatoid arthritis patients. However, because YouTube is frequently accessed by patients, the researchers recommended that professional health care organizations continue to use YouTube while modifying their engagement in two ways: (1) by providing more oversight in the production of agency-sponsored educational materials; and (2) by engaging with the creators of popular videos to correct misleading or inaccurate information.

Twitter to assess and improve emergency management

Merchant, Elmer, and Lurie (2011) suggest that emergency management communities might be in a better position to coordinate appropriate resources by contributing to and observing social media platforms like Twitter.

Twitter and women's health

In their research on the role of social media in promoting women's health education, Bahkali et al. (2015) analysed 5,167 tweets from followers of a Saudi-based Twitter account to promote women's health. Results provided a breakdown of the type of information sought by women and indicated that Twitter followers showed an increased level of health awareness and comprehension, as compared to their awareness before following the account.

Facebook page from a bookseller

Sagun and Luyt (2017) conducted an analysis of Facebook posts on an independent Singaporean bookstore, BooksActually, to find out how they present facets of print culture. The findings showed that the Facebook page blurs the dichotomy between the cultured and popular circuits of the book trade. The implication is that booksellers can potentially reach out to both circuits, which contradicts conventional wisdom.

Structural features of different social media platforms

One of the most notable features of YouTube, Twitter, and Facebook is the different ways the user agreements establish the public or private status of user contributions and other user information. For example, Twitter hashtags are searchable on the internet and YouTube is accessible whether or not you have your own YouTube channel. This makes the data on these platforms 'more public' than Facebook in some respects. Facebook requires that a request be accepted before an account holder's posts can be viewed by another account holder.

Facebook also provides an array of constantly changing privacy settings that determine the types of information (e.g., profile details) that are accessible to different classes of people in the Facebook world (e.g., the public, Facebook friends, and Facebook friends of friends). These structural features are established by the parent companies of the platforms. They also undoubtedly influence the dynamics of the contributions by users and exchanges among them. Your research questions and methodology should reflect this.

Theoretical and methodological terrain

The application of existing approaches to analysis

In *Digital Rhetoric*, Eyman (2015) explains that longstanding approaches to analysing discourse cannot simply be applied in cookie-cutter fashion to data from Twitter or Facebook. One key difference is the incredible volume of information available which is produced in a constant flow through social media. Isolating a conversational thread becomes nearly impossible because of the way individuals dip into and out of this platform, sometimes as readers and sometimes as contributors. Eyman (2015) argues that Twitter is perhaps the most difficult platform in which to trace a thread to its origins because of the way this platform provides a 'continual stream rather than a discrete conversation' (p. 76). Furthermore, because of the geographic distribution of communities of users, it is challenging to observe the nuances of their fluid participation. As Paulus, Jackson, and Davidson (2017) argue, 'these digital realities are neither simply mirrors of physical realities nor an extension of them' (p. 753).

Simultaneous and sequential use of multiple platforms

To complicate these methodological and theoretical matters, users also spread their own participation over multiple platforms. In addition to Twitter and Facebook, some also engage with others via Instagram, Qzone, Weibo, etc., or a specialized online forum that focuses on one of their interests. Because many platforms enable users to repost information from another platform, it becomes difficult to assess the role of a single platform in the exchanges among members. As McCay-Peet and Quan-Haase (2017) note, the fluid movement of individuals around these virtual communities is problematically absent in the research on and with social media.

Virtual and physical worlds

The degree to which you decide to separate or connect social media to physical events and realities presents another choice. If you are studying flash mobs as a social movement or disaster relief efforts after an earthquake, you will need to establish boundaries around the social media data and other data. What kinds of conversations on Twitter or Facebook do you want to examine regarding the coordination of such an event? Those before, during, and after? Or, only at a single time point? Why? You will also need to consider how the actual event influences and is influenced by the social media platforms in which it is discussed. It could be important to consider the relationship between these physical and virtual worlds in your analysis and to define the parameters of these relationships.

Researcher orientations

As a final issue to consider in your research, McCay-Peet and Quan-Haase (2017) claim that there is often an inadequate description of the disciplinary orientations of researchers in published literature on social media. This hides the ways particular orientations might influence the analysis of the data. We agree and add that the theoretical and methodological frames with which you define the research problem and research questions will also influence how you handle your social media data in NVivo. The study of an online community of chess players at a college is one example. From a discourse analysis perspective, your Nodes are likely to focus on parts of speech, pronouns, and discursive strategies such as hedging, coaching, or endorsing. You might extensively use Memos and See Also Links to track the experiences of individual members and the metaphors they use to describe these experiences. In contrast, a critical race theory applied to this same social media data might lean you toward a focus on the power and political economy of the social media platform, itself. This kind of analysis is more likely to attend to the way individuals use social media to reproduce or challenge social structures. Memos and See Also Links with this approach are more likely to include members' perceptions of bureaucratic practices within the institution, while Nodes might focus on critical incidents and impact of chess club rules.

Ethical considerations

Trust and safety

Trust and safety in online environments also sometimes reflect diverse views and practices among users. On one hand, engaging with strangers on a potentially faceless, online forum can initially feel safe and anonymous during the interaction. This is particularly true when individuals can join with pseudonyms or nicknames. However, this feeling can quickly turn to exposure and a violation of trust when posts are used for research purposes or distributed outside of the core group, even if it is 'public'. On the other hand, because of the ability to join anonymously, participants sometimes are not vetted and could be 'trolls', individuals who post inflammatory material simply to create conflict and undermine the group. These issues surrounding trust and safety influence the veracity of the data as well as the processes for gaining trust and entre as a researcher.

Consent

The terms and conditions agreed to by users of Facebook and Twitter provide information about the way in which their content can be used by the company who owns the platform and by other users. Based on the fact that using a hashtag makes a tweet public, Townsend and Wallace (2016) argue that informed consent is not necessary for use in an academic article. Nonetheless, as Williams, Burnap, Sloan, Jessop, and Lepps (2017) discovered, the expectations of privacy and consent vary widely among individuals who participate in the same social media platform. Furthermore, four in five individuals in their study expected to be asked for consent regarding the use of their data for research purposes, regardless of the terms within the user agreement.

Privacy

Byrne (2017) reflects on the implications for ethical practice with a unique, geographically bounded platform like Yik Yak (now defunct). Yik Yak set a parameter of a 5-mile radius to promote interactions among individuals who lived near one another. This platform was popular from 2014 to 2016 at college and university campuses in the USA. Despite the innovative use of rotating icons representing an individual across threads on Yik Yak, the patterns of writing and additional information available often revealed identities to some members, particularly when they knew each other in their physical communities. With a platform that is specifically designed to help users stay in touch with local issues and perceptions (e.g., Nextdoor, a social media platform for neighbourhoods), there is a much greater chance for users to identify one another. The diversity of user agreements and wide-ranging perception regarding consent, privacy, and data-sharing result in a complex combination of issues with social media data.

Our task in this chapter is not to tell you how to approach your social media data. However, we argue that use of social media data requires you to reflect on a wide array of issues before you begin analysis with NVivo. Our intent is to help you and your audience avoid the erroneous assumption that the data speaks for itself or that social media is simply an extension of non-digital cultures and contexts. On one hand, you will be guided by your definition of social media, research questions, and methodology. On the other hand, you will be faced with the potential of an unprecedented volume and unique flow of communication via social media. Furthermore, the information you collect will be constrained by the structural features of the individual platform. Combined with the diverse views of users regarding privacy and consent and the potential mismatch between these views and platform user agreements, the use of social media presents a host of issues. As a result, Williams et al. (2017) recommend that all researchers who use social media engage in a customized risk assessment to determine potential user harm resulting from the use or publication of social media content.

Web pages that do not have user-generated content

We include web pages in this chapter regardless of whether they support user-generated content or not. We do so primarily because the NCapture tool used to collect social media data can also be used to capture any web page, which is then converted to a pdf. NVivo does not assist you in the analysis of web traffic, page scripts, or server logs as part of the larger trend in web analytics. However, the capture of a web page might be useful to answer questions around, for instance, the way various political rivals are using branding strategies on their web pages or social media channels to distinguish themselves from their competitors. Analysing web pages within NVivo can provide insights about how a site has changed over time (necessitating multiple captures); the match between the objectives of the site and the symbols or information available within it; the use of text, visualizations, and other elements to craft a consistent message; or the prominent elements, confusing aspects, and useful pages as described by a visitor to the site.

▬▬▬ Web pages in a palliative care project ▬▬▬

Kristi worked on an initiative in a palliative care project in Colorado involving doctors, hospices, and hospitals who had a goal of improving the coordination of end-of-life care between these service providers. Assessment of whether this had been achieved or not involved examining how frequently each website provided a link to one of the other organizations, and how accurately and thoroughly they explained the services of the other organization. Being able to capture and code the content of each organization's website facilitated this evaluation.

In the next section, we will show you how to access and work with Twitter, Facebook, YouTube, and web pages in NVivo. Although working with this online data in NVivo offers interesting opportunities, our advice is to tread carefully, testing all alternatives before you commit to capturing and analysing a large volume of material.

SECTION 10.3: TWITTER, FACEBOOK, YOUTUBE, AND WEB PAGES IN NVIVO

NVivo terms used in this section

Attribute

Capture

Case

Classification

Dataset

Link

NCapture

Node

Sociogram

Value

Installing NCapture

NCapture is a browser extension provided with NVivo for the purpose of capturing web-based data using Chrome or Internet Explorer for analysis within NVivo. When you open one of these search engines (depending on the choices you made during the NVivo installation) you should see the NCapture button in the toolbar (Figure 10.1).

Search NVivo Help for NCapture if you are having any problem with the installation of or access to NCapture. Sometimes the extension is installed but not visible, and in other instances you might need to find the free download because you declined the offer to install it when you installed NVivo.

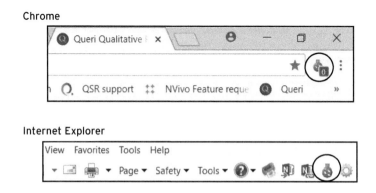

Figure 10.1 NCapture icon showing in the Chrome menu (top) and Internet Explorer Command bar (bottom)

Capturing and Importing Twitter and Facebook data

The Application Programming Interface (API) regulates the volume and type of information you can download from Twitter and from Facebook and is determined by the social media company. This will play a critical role in the material you can collect. For example, API parameters can be influenced by subscription services that provide additional options for the volume and type of material you can collect. In Twitter, the API governs two aspects: (1) the *search API*, used to retrieve past tweets matching your criteria (within the available search window that is also determined by the API) and (2) the *streaming API*, used to subscribe to new tweets matching your criteria, as soon as they are available. To understand the limitations, you should check current information about the specific API.

At present, the Facebook API only permits you to download posts from a group if you are the administrator. You might want to set up your own Facebook private group as a data collection tool to generate a group discussion which you can later analyse in NVivo. In addition, you should be aware of the following:

- News Feed: Your default view is usually the News Feed which you can only capture as a pdf.
- User: You can only capture a User wall as a pdf.

- Page: You can capture wall posts for a page as a Dataset (note that the user name will not be captured). You can also capture the web page containing the Page as a pdf File.
- Public Group: If you are the Admin of a public group, you can capture public group posts as a Dataset or the web page as a pdf. Otherwise, you can only capture public group posts as a pdf.
- Private Group: You can only capture private group posts as a pdf file.

You might want to develop a plan for regularly collecting new material as it is posted; when you import, NVivo defaults to a checkbox at the bottom of the *import wizard* with the instruction to **Merge matching social media datasets (including previously imported)**.

10.a.

Capturing Twitter and Facebook data

⇒ Go to the web page and select the NCapture browser extension (Figure 10.1).
⇒ Depending on what you capture, you will encounter an interface for a Dataset or for a pdf (Figure 10.2).

Figure 10.2 Capturing a Twitter hashtag (left) and Twitter home page (right) with NCapture

⇒ Add a **Description** for the item and a **Memo** if you wish. Both will be imported and both can be added or modified later.
⇒ **Code at nodes**: Add Nodes for coding if you wish, although the entire File will be coded at these Nodes.

    o You might wait to code the File, because you will be able to code all or part of it later, after import.

⇒ In Chrome: **Capture**. The default download location is **Downloads**.
⇒ In Internet Explorer: **Save** in either the default location or **Browse > Select** a location > **Capture**.

Importing Twitter and Facebook data

After capturing the material, return to your NVivo Project.

⇒ *Ribbon*: **Import / Data > NCapture**.

⇒ If you do not see the name of the page you captured > **Select** Browse **/ Click** on the arrow to identify the correct folder.

⇒ **Select** the captures to import by choosing one of the three radio buttons **/ clicking** on All captures not previously imported and **ticking** the desired captures **> Import** (Figure 10.3).

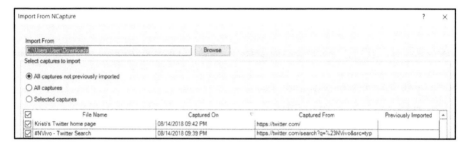

Figure 10.3   Selecting an NCapture file to import

⇒ *Navigation View*: **Data > Files**.

⇒ *List View*: **Double-click** on the imported File.

Handling Twitter and Facebook as you would other data types inside NVivo

Twitter

- If you capture information from your own page, the data will be imported as a pdf and you will follow our guidelines for pdf Files from Chapter 8 (p. 246).
- If you go to an organization's page or search for a hashtag, the material will be captured and imported as a Dataset with one Tweet per row.

  o Metadata such as the number of retweets will also be collected and can be converted into Attribute Values.

  o Follow our guidelines for analysing survey Datasets in Chapter 6.

Facebook

- You can code the post, picture captions, and comments as you would code text in other Datasets (Chapter 6).
- Picture links are included in their own column in the Facebook Dataset.

  o   The pictures are located in a subfolder in *Navigation View*: **Data > Files**. NVivo created this folder for you during import.
  o   All of the imported pictures can be handled as you would any picture (Chapter 9, pp. 265–269).

Cases and Classification systems

NVivo does not Auto Code rows into Cases or create an associated Classification System for your Dataset. If you want to use these features to handle the comments and replies, you will need to take a few additional steps.

■ 10.b. ■

Auto Code into Cases and Nodes

  ⇒   *Navigation View*: **Data > Files**.
  ⇒   *List View*: **Right-click** on the Dataset > **Auto Code** (Figure 10.4).

  o   NVivo Plus users will first need to **Select** 'Use the style or structure'.

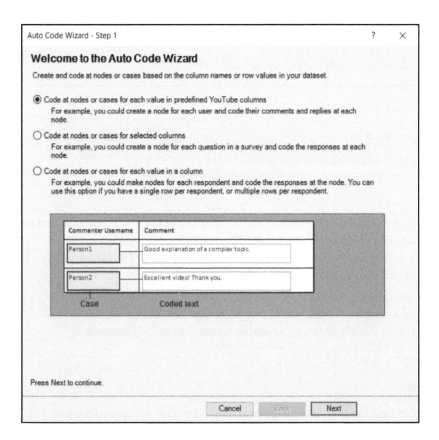

Figure 10.4   Auto Code Wizard

⇒ **Create at nodes or cases for each value in predefined Twitter/Facebook/ YouTube columns > Next**.

⇒ Step 2: Leave defaults to create Cases by **Username** and **Hashtag > Next**.

⇒ Step 3: Leave the default locations for **Nodes** and **Cases > Finish / Auto Code**.

Viewing your Cases

⇒ *Navigation View*: **Cases > Cases**.

⇒ *List View*: **Username (Twitter)** (you will see a list of Cases).

    ○ **Double-click** on a **Case** to see the tweets for that user.

    ○ **Right-click** on a **Case >** ○**Case Properties / Get Info > Attribute Values** to see the **Name** and **Location** (if available). Later you can **Classify Nodes from a Dataset** (see the NVivo Help for 'Automatic coding in datasets') if you want to add other Attribute Values to this Case.

Visualizations of social media Datasets (Windows only)

After importing social media as a Dataset, you will notice several tabs in the *Detail View* (Figure 10.5), including some visualizations that vary slightly by social media type.

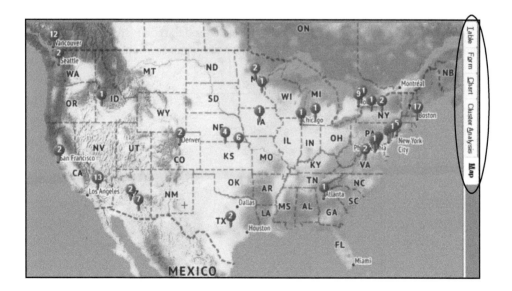

Figure 10.5 *Detail View* with a Map of a social media Dataset

Note that the geographical Map for Twitter, Facebook, and YouTube data is based on the profile of the user, not the location they occupied when they submitted a comment, reply, post, or tweet. After viewing the default Chart or Cluster Analysis, see the *Ribbon* for additional tools to modify the type of data or type of display. NVivo Plus users can also visualize Twitter networks as a Sociogram based on retweets and mentions.

All of the possibilities for memoing, linking, coding, and searching this social media Dataset parallel those detailed in Chapter 6. This means, for example, you can open the File and code the data. You can also run a Word Frequency Query (Chapter 4, pp. 126–129; Chapter 7, pp. 204–205; 219) or a Text Search Query (Chapter 4, pp. 129–130; Chapter 7, pp. 205–207), or use Attribute Values in a Matrix Coding Query (Chapter 6, pp. 186–189; Chapter 7, p. 208).

Importing and handling YouTube videos and comments (Windows only)

YouTube videos cover a diverse array of topics and make it a rich source of data. In addition to the videos, themselves, you can analyse the comments associated with videos to assess the way viewers respond to them. In Chapter 9 we explored the qualitative analysis of videos. Many of the observations, tips, and warnings from that chapter apply here, so you should read it if you have not yet done so. In sum, we encourage the analysis of video data only when it is an appropriate match to your research questions and we encourage you to consider transcribing data when your research questions can be answered without focusing on the visual content of streaming video. You should also consider the possibility of synchronizing a transcript with the video for a simultaneous look at the data in both forms.

You can choose to capture only the video, or the video and the comments (Figure 10.6), by following the same steps provided earlier to capture Twitter and Facebook data.

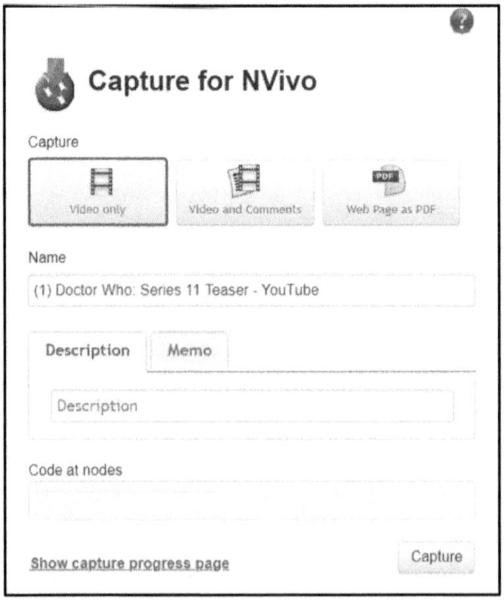

Figure 10.6   Collecting a YouTube video with NCapture

Importing YouTube material

YouTube videos are not imported into your Project, which is a restriction set by YouTube. Videos are accessed through a link that goes directly to the YouTube website, so you must be connected to the internet to access the video with NVivo. Although the video is not embedded in your Project, you can treat YouTube videos like any other video, with just a few, relatively minor exceptions:

- You cannot display a waveform.
- You cannot adjust the playback speed.
- The video size always scales to fit the player window.

Other than these exceptions, you can use all the tools we identified in Chapter 9 (pp. 271–275) to play, transcribe, Memo, Link, code, and search your videos.

YouTube comments

In addition, if you chose to capture the comments associated with a YouTube video, they will be imported into a unique folder in NVivo, along with the Video and any replies to the posted comments. However, unlike the video, the comments and replies are directly imported into your Project and do not require internet access. The comments import as a separate File in NVivo as a Dataset, as we described earlier with Twitter and Facebook data.

YouTube Cases and Nodes

As with Twitter and Facebook Datasets, NVivo does not Auto Code rows into Cases or create an associated Classification System for YouTube data. If you want to use these features to handle this social media data, follow the associated steps in Figure 10.4. All of the possibilities for memoing, linking, coding, and searching this social media Dataset parallel those detailed in Chapter 6, and all of the possibilities for handling the videos parallel those detailed in Chapter 9.

Capturing, importing, and viewing web pages

When you capture and import a web page, NVivo converts it to a pdf File. If you want to make sure you can distinguish an NVivo File that started as a pdf (such as an online article) with a File that is converted to a pdf (such as a web page), consider creating different folders for the storage of this material. Once a page is converted to pdf, you cannot edit it. If you want to analyse part but not all of the material, you might consider copying and pasting the relevant text and pictures into Word as an alternative to downloading the page with NCapture. This will allow you to 'tidy up' the layout (and remove unwanted text) so that selection of text for coding is no longer a problem.

10.c.

Capture a web page

⇒ Open the web page you want to capture.
⇒ **Select** the NCapture button (Figure 10.1).
⇒ The NCapture window opens, indicating that the web page will be imported as a pdf (Figure 10.7).

Figure 10.7 Collecting a web page with NCapture via Internet Explorer

⇒ **Select** 'Article as PDF' if you are viewing an online article and wish to exclude unnecessary content such as advertisements and links to other articles.
⇒ Add a **Description** for the item and a **Memo** if you wish. Both will be imported with the web page and both can be added or modified later.
⇒ **Code at nodes**: Add Nodes for coding if you wish, although the entire page will be coded at these Nodes.
  o You might wait to code the page because you will be able to code all or part of it later, after import.
⇒ In Chrome: **Capture**. The default download location is **Downloads**.
⇒ In Internet Explorer: Save in either the default location or **Browse > Select** a location **> Capture**.

The entire web page will have been captured, beyond what was immediately visible on the screen (i.e., the capture is not limited to what will fit on a single page). These will be saved as .nvcx files, which NVivo will later use to reconstruct the Files as pdfs in your Project.

Import and view a web page

⇒ *Ribbon*: **Import / Data > NCapture**.

⇒ If you do not see the name of the page you captured > **Select** Browse **/ Click** on the arrow to identify the correct folder.

⇒ **Select** the captures to import by choosing one of the three radio buttons **/** clicking on **All captures not previously imported** and ticking the desired captures **>** **Import** (Figure 10.8).

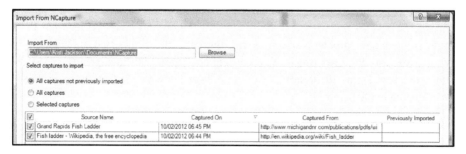

Figure 10.8 Selecting an NCapture file for importing as a web page

⇒ *Navigation View*: **Data > Files**.

⇒ *List View*: **Double-click** on the imported File (Figure 10.9).

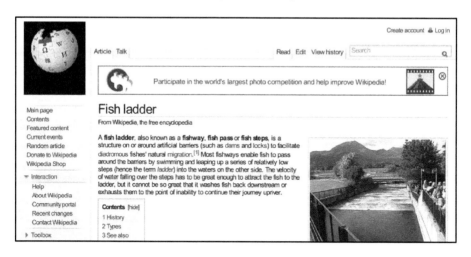

Figure 10.9 A web page converted into a pdf and opened in NVivo

Handling web pages inside NVivo

Linking and writing about web pages

In Chapter 8 on pdf Files and literature reviews, we discussed handling a pdf with Memos and Links in NVivo. While web pages seem to be a very different type of data, you can manage these as you would any other pdf in NVivo. We encourage you to review Chapter 8 for additional guidance but, in brief: Memo Links, Annotations, and See Also Links can be applied as you would in other text and picture Files. In addition, Hyperlinks within the web page will convert to NVivo Hyperlinks (and so can be accessed using **Ctrl + click**).

Coding web pages

If your web page is set out with text and images in frames and boxes rather than in neat columns, you will have problems selecting text, similar to those discussed in Chapter 8 (primarily an issue for Windows users). As a consequence, you will have problems also with viewing coded text. Figure 10.10 provides an example of a downloaded web page, to illustrate the points being made below.

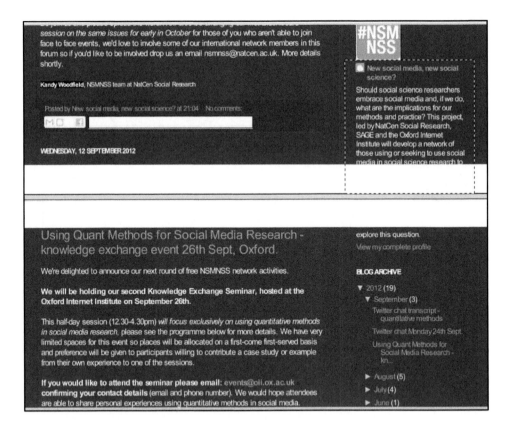

Figure 10.10 Web page captured and imported into NVivo

Note: Downloaded from http://nsmnss.blogspot.co.uk/ on 30 September 2012.

Text selected and coded within a section on the left-hand side of the downloaded page can be viewed in the *Detail View* of the Node relatively well in Reference tab as well as the PDF tab. If you try to select text in a column on the right-hand side of the page in order to code, you are likely to include a large section of text from the left-hand column as well. This is particularly so if there is a break between lines in the text you are trying to select. When you view your text in the Reference tab of the *Detail View*, the additional text from the left-hand column will be inserted between the sections of the text you intended to code.

For example, using the page in Figure 10.10, when selecting the text on the right beginning with 'New social media, new social science?' (as text), the date at the bottom left of the page followed the heading, and then – because the paragraph ran across a page break – the whole of the article on 'Using Quant Methods' was selected at the same time and, in Reference view, was inserted before 'explore this question'.

- While you can move smoothly across page breaks inserted into the web page by NVivo when viewing the source document, this does not happen when viewing coded text in the PDF view of a Node. In that view, you will jump from one page to the next, sometimes losing continuity in the process (page breaks in NVivo are based on regular page lengths, not content).
- Selecting by Region rather than Text will solve selection problems to some extent – as long as you don't want your selection to cross an NVivo page boundary (see the selected region around the same right-hand-side article in Figure 10.10), and, of course, your only option then for viewing the coded data in a Node is through the PDF tab.

SECTION 10.4: CHAPTER 10 TAKEAWAYS

━━━━━━━ Key points from this chapter ━━━━━━━

o Social media platforms have different positions regarding the public and private status of user contributions. Facebook requires users to request access to the pages of other users, while Twitter and YouTube do not.

o Social media data presents complexities around ethics that pertain to diverse understandings of public and private spaces as well as consent.

o Methodological issues to consider with social media data include: sequential and simultaneous use of multiple platforms, the relationships between virtual and physical worlds, and the disciplinary orientations of the researchers.

Tips, challenges, and warnings

- Stay up to date on the APIs of your social media platforms.
- Plan for periodic capture of social media data over time, according to your research design.
- Consider what you want to do with this data after analysis and how you will present or communicate findings. A conference presentation with sample clips will likely be quite different from a published paper.

- Think about the kinds of web pages that might be relevant for your research and consider including a plan to use them at the design phase.

Help files

- *File*: Help.
- *Menu bar*: **Help > NVivo Help.**

Search for any of the following:

- Automatic coding in datasets
- Datasets
- Documents and PDFs
- NCapture
- Surveys and datasets
- Twitter data

Practice questions

1   In your research, what is the relationship between physical worlds and virtual ones?
2   How will your area of expertise or your field of study (education, health, linguistics, etc.) influence the way you approach online data such as social media and web pages?
3   What is your plan for handling ethical issues in your research?
4   Run a pilot of the kind of online data you want to collect. Capture it and import it into NVivo and use Nodes, Links, Memos, Cases, Attribute Values, Maps, and other tools to examine the data. What did you learn from this pilot?

11

Section 11.1: Introduction to teamwork   308

Section 11.2: Conceptual grounding in teamwork   309

Section 11.3: Teamwork in NVivo   317

Section 11.4: Chapter 11 Takeaways   335

TEAMWORK

People often cannot see what they take for granted until they encounter someone who does not take it for granted. ... A radical statement of this would be that information is only information where there are multiple interpretations. (Bowker & Star, 2000: 291)

SECTION 11.1: INTRODUCTION TO TEAMWORK

Whether you are in a small team working on a Project with limited scope (such as a pair of students in a qualitative methods course analysing a few interviews) or a large, geographically dispersed team analysing hundreds of items from different regions, you will find many helpful tips in this chapter for planning and conducting team-based qualitative research. While the process will bring unique challenges, one of the wonderful benefits is that the process forces researchers to discuss and track observations, options, and decisions that often go unarticulated when they work in isolation. This tends to unearth some of the assumptions in a study that lie below the surface, and the analysis often benefits from the resulting excavation. Much of what you will find in this chapter is related to the importance of communication as well as the strategies you can use to monitor and change the analytical activities of the team. While there are tools in NVivo that are specifically designed to support team research, others are multi-purpose and their implications for team research may not yet have occurred to you. Because most of these tools are described elsewhere in the book, you will encounter many pointers from this chapter to other locations for additional instructions.

In this chapter you will

- Explore practices that can guide your work as a team.
- Consider some of the issues that might influence how you code as a team.
- Understand the arguments for and against reliability testing for qualitative coding.
- Learn the options for storing (and accessing) a team Project.
- Develop strategies for communicating as a team in NVivo.
- Explore NVivo's tools to track team member contributions in NVivo.
- Learn how to combine copies of Projects if you are not using NVivo for Teams.

Other chapters with related materials

Chapter 1: Where to begin?

Memos and Links help keep track of ongoing ideas and threads of connections in your data. They also facilitate team communication and help team members build ideas and conceptual frameworks. Be sure to use Memos and Links as you think through the data and your team process.

Chapter 2: Designing an NVivo Project

Managing teamwork usually entails the use of Folders, Sets, and other structural components of a Project. In Chapter 2 you were acquainted with these aspects of the Project and you will want to incorporate them into your team process as early as possible.

Chapter 3: Coding foundations; Chapter 4: Advanced coding

As a team, you will use the same basic skills to manage your Nodes and Node hierarchies that we discussed in Chapters 3 and 4. This includes coding, uncoding, merging, aggregating, using Coding Stripes, etc. You will also likely want to create Node hierarchies while being mindful to use vista Node structures and avoid viral ones.

SECTION 11.2: CONCEPTUAL GROUNDING IN TEAMWORK

A team by any other name

When researching teamwork, you will find definitions as simple as 'work done by several associates with each doing a part but all subordinating personal prominence to the efficiency of the whole' (Merriam-Webster, https://www.merriam-webster.com/dictionary/teamwork), or explanations that are more explicit about the dimensions of teamwork: 'A team is a small number of people with complementary skills who are committed to a common purpose, performance goals, and approach for which they are mutually accountable' (Katzenback & Smith, 1993: 45). Regardless of your definitions, the customizable nature of qualitative research, diversity among researchers, and the unique dynamics of interpersonal relationships, often make qualitative team research feel unpredictable. This is true even for researchers with extensive experience in using qualitative methods.

■ Dedication to the team effort ■

While facilitating an NVivo training with a group of researchers in early childhood education, Kristi asked, 'before we finalize the NVivo training agenda, who here will be working in a research team?' With a mischievous head-tilt and raised eyebrows, one of the researchers looked over to a colleague and said, 'it depends on what you mean by TEAM'. The recipient of the look said, 'By "team", I mean ME!' and they both laughed. This first wave of chuckles was generated by the friendly banter between two colleagues, but there was a second wave of smiles and laugher from everyone in the room, nudged by a collective realization that an engaged room of talented qualitative researchers are unlikely to achieve perfect agreement on anything, let alone a definition of teamwork. With this awareness, several researchers shrugged their shoulders with an air of acceptance and smiled as if to say, 'there are as many definitions of teamwork as there are teams, but this doesn't stop us from dedicating ourselves to the team effort'.

As part of the teamwork process, it is important to acknowledge that there is no blueprint for the perfect team. Structural factors related to team member contributions and availability will drive, to some extent, the use of particular strategies and tools. However, within this milieu, there are creative and improvisational moments that can shift the dynamics of the team or the focus of the task at hand.

Getting ready for teamwork

If you are new to managing a team of qualitative researchers, you may have a general sense that multiple perspectives about the analytical process can add tremendous strength to an investigation. What you may not yet know is that qualitative research in teams, with all of the benefits, can be very challenging. One problem is the potential for inexperienced qualitative researchers to apply expectations from quantitative research where role differentiation and division of labour are much clearer, and tasks are more easily separated across data collection, entry, analysis, and reporting. Fidelity to the original design is perhaps the most important principle in such a quantitative study, wherein the hand-off points and products are relatively standardized and predictable.

In qualitative research, this type of division of labour can be dangerous. There may be compelling reasons to change the research plan as the project proceeds and many components (depending on your methodology) can be modified. Examples include:

- Interview guides
- Site selection and sampling procedures
- Coding structures
- Modes of analysis
- Theoretical frameworks
- The research questions

In qualitative research, therefore, it is critical that any differences in roles among the team members are constructed with multiple opportunities to work together, communicate, and document successful procedures. Processes can be modified if they begin interfering with (or fail to further) the analysis, or it is realized a better approach is possible.

Research ethics and politics in a qualitative team

While ethical practices are not unique to teams, the collective responsibility team members have in protecting participants brings unique dimensions and practices that can be employed to promote ethical qualitative team research. MacQueen et al. (2008) identify several sources of explicit guidance regarding team-based qualitative research: formal ethical standards are provided by review boards for research involving human subjects; guidelines for conduct established by professional associations help identify and manage issues that are related to a particular community of practice. To these we add local behaviours and practices that are more closely related to micro-politics than ethics, per se. These include institutional reward structures, authorship agreements, and other factors that usually fall outside formal ethical standards or guidelines. Nonetheless, these might influence team member actions and subsequently affect the research.

Formal ethical standards and guidelines for conduct

A frequently identified set of ethical principles across qualitative and quantitative research designs involving human subjects comes from the *Belmont Report* (National Commission, 1978). The report established three guiding principles:

- *Respect for persons*: Primarily through the recognition of individual autonomy and the protection of individuals with reduced autonomy (such as children).
- *Beneficence*: Maximizing benefits and minimizing harm.
- *Justice*: The equitable distribution of research costs and benefits.

A contemporary frame for ethics in qualitative research emphasizes two characteristics that are unique to qualitative research: (1) the intimacy of the endeavour, because qualitative research reduces the distance between researchers and participants when compared to experimental and quasi-experimental designs, and (2) the open-ended unfolding of the process, because the participatory approach cannot be fully predicted prior to implementation (Howe & Dougherty, 1993). This intimacy and open-endedness requires considerable vigilance by the qualitative researcher who seeks to handle relationships in the field in an honourable manner (Howe and Moses, 1999). It also warrants a reconsideration of the traditional ethical principles of the *Belmont Report*, which are more applicable to quantitative research.

We extend these reconsiderations of qualitative research ethics to posit that just as there is increased potential emphasis on intimacy between the researcher and the participants in qualitative research, there is also a potential increased intensity of closeness among team members that adds complexity to ethical decisions, as compared to solo research.

- A team member could be forced to choose between the autonomy of one team member over another.
- The pursuit of justice with research participants could threaten justice within the team.
- Members of a team might argue about definitions of benefits and harms for participants in ways that go unacknowledged by the lone researcher.

The challenges and rewards of pursuing ethical principles and guidelines can take on new dynamics in the qualitative team context. Therefore, team qualitative research and associated ethical practices are different than for quantitative research and raise additional issues beyond those faced by researchers who work independently.

Local politics and pressures

We suggest paying attention to local politics and pressures in team qualitative research because some values and patterns of behaviour can influence the efficacy of the team. Intentional usurpation of credit that should have been given to another teammate, nefarious ladder-climbing by downplaying someone else's abilities, or prioritizing sycophantic skills over research skills can all harm the research in team contexts. However, far more often we observe political problems in team research because values or priorities that seem clear to one member are not always so obvious to others. These do not come from intentional ill will and are simply part of the complex fabric of human interaction. Teammates might differ in terms of:

- definitions of consensus (and processes for achieving it);
- preferences for working independently (or under direction);
- the value ascribed to various rewards for their contributions (or perception of fairly distributed consequences for sub-par work);
- commitment to positive outcomes for participants in the research (or prevention of negative outcomes);
- the importance of efficiency in team tasks (and navigating the tensions that can occur when efficiency and quality are at odds among team members).

These and many other assumptions alongside the implicit and explicit pressures from peers and supervisors can both negatively and positively influence the unfolding dynamics of the team and the work of individual members.

Even the issues that appear most mundane can have consequences. As Tilley and Powick (2002) discovered in a qualitative study of eight individuals hired to transcribe tapes in university research, there were, at a minimum, three factors that influenced transcription:

1 The challenges faced by the transcribers in completing their work.
2 Transcription decisions made in the moment.
3 The effects of the transcriptionist's degree of investment in the research.

The dynamics of a team can easily influence these factors, and your reflexive team Memos can be used to track these issues and to support a healthy team. While an extensive exploration of the ethics of team research is outside of the scope of this chapter, we encourage teams to attend to specific agenda items at team meetings to discuss, prioritize, and honour the ethical and political priorities of the research, including attention to relationships among team members.

Clarity of purpose in all team research activities

The purpose(s) may change as your team research progresses, but failing to have a clear goal can lead to a blind, mechanistic analysis. By constantly asking yourself 'What is the purpose of this activity?' and by asking your fellow teammates to also clarify their perceptions of purpose, teams are less likely to wander into unproductive data management at the expense of analysis. In teams there can also be a dangerous tendency for individuals to trust that others on the team understand what is going on in the grand scheme of the project, even though the current activity seems unproductive. This can lead to a great deal of wasted time and effort. We tend to see this most often when the entire team convenes after data is collected, rather than during construction of the design, although we understand that sometimes the team is unable to convene until midway through the collection or analysis.

Piloting processes to determine if they are effective for the team

Team size, geographic dispersion, volume and variety of data, and duration of the research all contribute to the complexity of storing and analysing data and of coordinating the team research process. Beyond the design of the project and choice of methods, specific questions for teams to consider include:

- What experience does each researcher have with qualitative methods, with the research setting, or with NVivo?
- What decision-making models (e.g., consensus, democratic vote, or team leader directives) are in play to guide team progress?
- How can the geographic dispersion of the team be managed?
- What work will be done independently, in pairs, or in groups?
- What is the time frame for the analysis (including interim deadlines)?
- What kind of access do team members have to the software?
- Who is responsible for reporting and what do they need to produce?

Always consider making small steps first by piloting your proposed processes. This will give you an opportunity to modify them without the pressure of getting it perfectly right the first time.

Creating Memos to log the pilot activities, the lessons learned, and the current procedures are important steps for most teams. Examples include:

- protocols for data collection, cleaning (e.g., reviewing inaudible portions of tapes), and storage;
- role clarifications or job descriptions;
- coding structures and definitions, along with examples and counter-examples;
- ideas proposed by team members and decisions made regarding these proposals;
- timelines or benchmarks for the phases in the research process;
- minutes of meetings;
- emerging models or hypotheses.

In addition, it can be helpful to keep a log of decisions as they evolve over time to help keep everyone mindful of the progress made. If relevant, pay special attention to the issue of researchers rotating in and out of the team. A training binder helps initiate new researchers in the unique aspects of the research and could contain the items listed above and other training tools.

Facilitating the strengths of team members

Differences among the team may relate to practical tasks like recruiting participants, coding, and organizing Project backups. Ideally there is a match between the things people like to do, what they are competent to do, and what needs to be done, but this is not always so. It takes a good team leader, or existing collaborative dynamics, to appropriately manage these strengths. Practical skills may be identified during team member selection, but sometimes these skills do not become apparent until the group is together and working on the research. When leaders identify and acknowledge individual strengths early, they help keep team members motivated and engaged. As processes unfold and individuals gain skills, these strengths may shift. Continuous attention to these changing contributions is an important part of managing the team and potentially modifying the distribution of tasks.

Coding as a team

Our experience indicates that most teams vastly underestimate the time needed to meet and discuss the various ideas and differences among team members, especially in the early stages of the coding process. In some instances, teams would be better off coding as a group in the initial stages in order to begin moving forward on firm footing. This helps the members address and discuss diverse views before these differences become liabilities instead of assets to the project. While coding together may seem cumbersome at first, it could save hundreds of hours in the long run. We know of a few teams that are less constrained by deadlines and budgets and code all of the data in pairs or groups because of the rich discussions this promotes. Memos generated from the insights developed during these partnerships are sometimes more valuable than the Memos researchers write in solitude.

Work distribution

There is no magic number associated with the hours per day or week that lead to researcher burnout (too much time) or distance (too little time). Being mindful of the potential to fall into either trap will help you guard against unproductive coding:

- It is likely better to have three team members who can work on the data at least twelve hours a week rather than nine team members who can only allocate four hours per week.
- It is likely better to have four members who can work on the data 25 hours a week rather than two people who can allocate 50 hours per week.

If you plan on dividing up the work, a team member can either code different documents (e.g., interviews 6–10 of 20), different sections of the interview (e.g., questions 1–3 of 12), or different themes within the interviews (e.g., all the Nodes about education versus all the Nodes about health).

- With the first choice, researchers gain comprehensive knowledge of a subset of the participants, but not all of them.
- With the second choice, researchers become content experts in an area of the protocol, but may not have a good sense of any participant's holistic experience.
- With the third choice, researchers become experts in an area of the Node structure, but also broadly read of all the data.

In practical terms, it is easier to build consistency between coders by coding to parent Nodes first, and then taking a second pass at the data to refine these into more discrete child Nodes.

- Pushing for consistency may inhibit inductive coding, however, and is less common when coding through the constant comparative method or phenomenology, for example.
- Beware of the potential to create purely descriptive Nodes when using deductive coding strategies and continue to revisit the ways you might engage in rich interpretation of the data.

Benefits and potential problems of 'proving' reliability

Many teams are understandably concerned about tracking and managing differences in the way individuals see and interpret meaning in the data. Lyn Richards' (2009) activity for naming Nodes (described in Chapter 3, pp. 75–76) is also useful for locating and discussing team differences in interpretation. Ask team members to:

- review a portion of the data;
- identify the items or issues they find interesting;
- articulate why they find them interesting.

By comparing the responses from team members, researchers become aware of different perspectives and eventually gain clarity on the interpretive lenses within the team.

Teams generally strive for consensus in coding and some write their plans for becoming reliable and measuring coding reliability into their research plan or grant proposal. Establishing coding reliability is especially useful when transcripts will be allocated to different researchers and the team wants to ensure that differences in coding are a reflection of differences in the data rather than differences among researchers. When pursuing coder reliability, early variation or vagueness in coding is purposefully clarified and corrected by the time final analyses are undertaken. Additionally, categories developed should make sense to an external observer, to those who provided the data, and/or to those for whom a report is being prepared.

In line with our earlier statements about the influence of local politics and pressures among teams, Sanders and Cuneo (2010) explore facets of coder reliability related to the relationships among team members.

We explore three aspects of social reliability during team coding: explicit team knowledge, implicit team suppositions and assumptions, and explicit and implicit emotionality. Inter-coder reliability is not merely a methodological and scientific issue, but also a social one. Researchers [working in teams] ignore it at their peril. [Abstract]

Part of the reason we recommend that team members code together in early stages of the research is to help surface and address some of these implicit and explicit aspects of coder reliability.

Taking time to work through these issues is important, because teams that rush to coding reliability might be sacrificing validity along the way. Furthermore, in some rare circumstances, reliability may be a lower (or non-existent) priority because diversity in coding is highly valued. For some researchers, the strength of the analysis and the clarity and comprehensiveness of the evidence carry more weight than a statistical (quantitative) measure of reliability, because reliability testing for inter-coder agreement does not inevitably add to the strength of your conclusions.

━━━━━━━ Prioritizing validity over reliability ━━━━━━━

In a study of African-American girls attending an after-school programme on science, the principal investigator delegated coding of classroom transcripts to two graduate students. One was a self-identified white female, and the other was a self-identified black female. Instead of training these students to code according to an established framework, the principal investigator asked both students to code according to the issues they observed in the data that related to the primary research question: what factors contribute to self-perception as a 'scientist' among the young, African-American girls in the programme? The only directive was to pay attention to the way the identities of the girls may have changed over the course of the study, all of the girls having begun with the self-proclaimed stance that they were not interested in science.

The white student focused attention on the structure of the course activities and the actions of the innovative instructor (who used collaborative curriculum design, active learning, and unstructured classroom discourse). The black student identified a range of discursive strategies the girls used to experiment with their identities as scientists. While both approaches to coding contributed to answering the research question, they did so from particular, socially constructed vantage points that the principal investigator wanted to leverage in the analysis. This generated a rich interpretation of identity development in the programme and fostered an expansive (rather than narrow) view of the data. Because an expanded, non-standardized view of the data that considered multiple angles was the primary purpose of the research, the approach was well suited to the task.

Regardless of the degree to which you pursue coder reliability, track your process so you can later take your audience through your main steps. The assistance of detailed Memos about the team processes could be critical. Memo contents could include clarifications, revisions to your approach, efforts to confirm patterns, and the strategies you used as a team to make decisions about Nodes and Descriptions. These should be supported with evidence from the data.

SECTION 11.3: TEAMWORK IN NVIVO

NVivo terms used in this section

Annotation

Coding Comparison Query

Coding context

Combining Projects

Map

Memo Link

Node

Password

Project copy/ies

Project Log

See Also Link

User

Training together on the Project

If NVivo skills are not already available in the team, find a trainer, such as one of those who have contributed to this book. Consider requesting customized training with your data. Enlisting the assistance of a trainer will help identify issues that are unique to your project and help you begin the process of developing guidelines for your team. This is especially important if team members are also new to qualitative research.

- If possible, hold your training when you start to collect data. By doing this you can more easily reap the benefits of some tips for preparing the data before all of the responses are collected.
- If data have not yet been collected, generate a page of a transcript for five imaginary participants based on the research questions and the interview protocol; for example, have team members interview each other for a few minutes as a role-play activity prior to the training session.
- Regardless of whether you do it before or after data collection, customized NVivo training that is framed by your research design will help you move forward and keep you from wasting time. Learning the software as a group will help you determine which work practices and software tools are the most relevant for your research.
- In the process, you are also likely to resolve many of the project set-up and management issues that result from the kind of complex data arrangements that often accompany team projects.

Because qualitative team research with NVivo can take so many different forms based on the answers to these questions, perhaps the most important advice we have regarding this endeavour is to pilot each planned activity using NVivo. Much of this piloting will occur early on, but you will need to test new activities throughout the research as you move to each new stage.

Options for storing and accessing a team Project

Your team Project can be stored and accessed in one of three ways:

1   As a single Project accessed by each team member at different times (i.e., with no simultaneous use).
2   Using multiple copies of a Project such that each researcher has his or her own copy, working independently and perhaps simultaneously until it is time to combine them into one Project.
3   As an NVivo for Teams (Windows only) Project where multiple researchers can access the same Project at the same time if they choose to do so.

If you have only one licence for NVivo, and you want individuals to code independently, your team will work in a single Project and the researchers will access the Project at different times. The Project will reside on a single computer – either in a research office or on a portable laptop – and individuals will schedule time to work on this computer.

If the dynamics of the Project require that multiple researchers work simultaneously, you must either make multiple copies of the Project for use on separate computers or purchase NVivo for Teams (Windows only). When working in multiple copies of the Project, several rules must be followed in order to eventually reintegrate the different work among the team members into one Project. If you intend to use this strategy, we strongly recommend that you read the section of this chapter on *Combining Projects* very carefully before you begin (and the material between here and there might also be important to you). Working back and forth between the Windows and Mac versions is possible but not recommended for teamwork, as some work done in one version can be lost in the other. Additionally, all researchers need to be using the same version of NVivo, including recent service packs. The primary benefit of working in multiple copies is the ability to meet rapidly approaching deadlines with the simultaneous coding and analysis efforts of team members. The primary limitation is the problem created when individual researchers edit the contents of shared Files (e.g., by fixing typos) so the merged Projects contain unmerged duplicate Files (and we have seen a few research teams weep and start over in this circumstance). Following a few simple rules from the outset can prevent this problem.

Alternatively, in order to support the work of multiple researchers working simultaneously, you can purchase NVivo for Teams (Windows only). This software allows multiple researchers to work in the same Project (located on a server) at the same time with no worries about the consequences of editing files. When one researcher is editing the contents of an interview, it will be unavailable to other researchers (to either code or edit). As soon as the interview is returned to 'read only' status (which means you can still code the Files but you cannot edit the contents), it is available for multiple researchers to examine or code.

Identifying which of these strategies to use (with points to take into consideration summarized in Table 11.1) is one of the first decisions you need to make when using NVivo for a team project.

Table 11.1 Choosing a Project storage and management strategy

Points to consider	Single Project	Multiple copies	NVivo for Teams
You are most likely to use this strategy in a team if ...	You have only one licence for the software. You want to avoid the potential problems of merging Projects. You will not be purchasing NVivo for Teams.	You have multiple licences for the software. Your team members need to work simultaneously. You will not be purchasing NVivo for Teams.	Your team members need to work simultaneously. You want to avoid the potential problems of merging Projects.
Can I edit the text while I work?	Yes	No	Yes
Can we work simultaneously?	No	Yes	Yes
Can we code differently and track who did what?	Yes	Yes	Yes
Do we need to make backup copies?	Yes	Yes	Yes (they can be scheduled to run automatically).
Can we use different versions of NVivo?	Not applicable, since you are working in a single Project.	Only if you convert any work done in an older version of the software to the newer version before merging.	No. All Users must be in the same version.
What basic rules do I need to follow?	Change the Application Options to 'Prompt for user' when you launch NVivo so that User actions are correctly tracked.	Unless each researcher works exclusively with different internal sources, do not allow editing of the text of those internals until after the projects are merged. Ensure the User is being correctly recorded for each working session in each copy of the Project.	You may edit and code as you wish. If another researcher is editing a File, it will not be available to you until they finish editing. Users will need to log in, to access the Project.
What Help files will assist me?	Teamwork	Teamwork. Merge projects or import items from another NVivo project. Save and copy projects.	About NVivo for Teams

Before moving on to the tools in NVivo designed specifically for teams, we revisit some tools already discussed in earlier chapters and show how to adapt these for team research.

Creating a Project shell for sharing among team members

As you work through the rest of the information in this chapter, create a 'shell' for your Project to set up a framework for data management and team communication and to pilot some of the activities. In order to reduce redundant work, especially if you plan on working in multiple copies of the Project, think through all of the set-up activities you can accomplish in a single Project to include in this shell before it is copied. For example:

- Create Folders for your Files, if relevant (e.g., by wave or data type) (Chapter 2, pp. 55–56).
- Import one or more Files (Chapter 1, pp. 26–27), depending on how the work of coding is to be distributed among team members.
- Create as much of your Node structure as possible, including Node Descriptions, colours, etc.
- Develop a Classification System and Cases (or a plan for creating them when you are ready) (Chapter 5).
- Create a Node for each coder. Later, each researcher may create provisional Nodes under their own name as a way of proposing new Nodes without creating a chaotic coding structure (Chapter 4).
- Create a Memo for each researcher where they can later track their particular questions, issues, and insights (Chapter 1, pp. 27–29).
- Create a Memo called 'Teamwork in NVivo' as a protocol document based on early team discussions (subject to further review and comment by individual researchers later).
- Create and maintain an archive folder on a server or external drive to store backup copies of the Project (see below).

Using NVivo's tools to facilitate team communication

In Chapter 1, we detailed:

- Tools for recording thoughts about ongoing analysis
- Logging changes made in the Project
- Linking between items

Here we provide suggestions for ways to make use of these strategies to facilitate communication in a team project.

Use colours to flag things for team members

In Chapter 1 you learned a little about the use of colours to identify Project items. Teams might find this tool useful as a way of tagging and sorting items according to researcher.

If Pat is assigned ten transcripts to code that do not fall in alphabetical order in the list of Files, and Kristi is to code another ten, we can allocate a colour to each User's interviews to help us distinguish our allotted interviews. This strategy can be useful also to flag Memos created by different researchers.

Memos and Reports/Exports

Memos are an important tool for analysis, but they are also important for keeping track of team guidelines, decisions, activities, benchmarks, proposals for changes, issues for the next team meeting, etc. Make and save regular Reports and/or exports of these Memos and of your Node lists with Descriptions (Chapter 4, pp. 114–116). This will help keep the team from wandering back over earlier decisions without a clear purpose or rationale. In general, Reports and Memos also serve as helpful references when you write up your methods, because they map the trajectory of your decisions and your use of the tools in NVivo. Have one of the researchers take responsibility for maintaining these records.

The issue of tracking Node Descriptions often emerges in team research. If you are working in multiple copies of the Project, you need a strategy for tracking Node Descriptions (which essentially serve as your Codebook) when aggregating copies of the Projects. It is a mistake to have individual researchers make changes to the Node Descriptions in their copy, because NVivo will only retain the Node Descriptions from one Project when they are combined. One option for tracking recommended changes in the Node Descriptions is to have a Memo for each researcher where she or he can add recommendations for changes that will be reviewed at team meetings (and after the Project copies have been merged).

Memo Links

In addition to any of these 'standalone' Memos, a team can also benefit from linking Memos to either Nodes or Files for the purpose of creating helpful summaries for one another. Because it could take weeks (or months) for each team member to read through all of the data in each File or Node in a very large project, this process of creating Memo Links (Chapter 1, pp. 29–30) can help the team efficiently discuss the patterns in the data. When managed effectively, this allows researchers to obtain a broad view of the entire corpus of data while also allowing each researcher to become an 'expert' in a subset of the data.

See Also Links

As team members interact with the data and develop questions, ideas, or things they want to discuss later with other team members, the See Also Link inside a Memo (Windows only; Chapter 1, pp. 30–32) can be a helpful component of effective communication. For instance, you might write the following inside a Memo called, *Coding questions and recommendations*: 'I am unclear if this quote should go into *loyalty* or *trust*, and I'm wondering if we need to change the definition of *loyalty* so that it always involves an action or behaviour, while *trust* always involves a thought or feeling without a specific action.' By pasting the quote as a See Also Link in the Memo, you place all ideas for discussion in one location, with links to the quote(s) in the data. If team members are working on one computer, they can then be reviewed by each team member as they work, or the points for discussion can be brought to a team meeting or principal investigator for review, either by:

- exporting or printing the Memo with See Also Links as endnotes (see Chapter 1, pp. 30–32) and distributing it before a meeting; or
- using a projector to display your Project with the various suggestions and making changes as needed.

Use See Also Links to:

- point to locations that clarify your request for changes in Node Descriptions;
- flag places that you want to discuss because the passage is unclear or because you disagree with your teammate's coding;
- ask the researcher who conducted the interview for clarifying context;
- propose evolving theories or hypotheses to your teammates and direct them to specific examples or ask them to identify counter-examples.

Annotations (Windows users)

Because Annotations in the Mac will not merge across Projects, the advice in this subsection applies to Windows users only. Consider using Annotations to help make your teammates aware of context (Chapter 1, pp. 27–28). For instance, you conducted the interview and are coding the transcript as a first pass through the data. One of your interviewees says, 'It's like that awesome donation we had in year one of the programme. It breathed new life into the entire organization and everyone seemed more willing to cooperate and to compromise.' You know the donation was a $50,000 gift from a former participant of the programme. This is a piece of information that may have come from another interview or simply from your contextual knowledge of the setting, but your teammates do not know this. You could add an Annotation to 'donation' that says, 'A $50,000 gift from Gloria, a former participant of the programme.' Mindfully adding Annotations to help clarify these quotes for your teammates will help them better understand and interpret the data when they encounter your interviews.

Using Annotations in NVivo raises two additional issues for teams:

- Unless the researchers go to *Navigation View*: **Notes > Annotations** (with the *Detail View* closed or on the bottom) it is not evident who wrote an Annotation. Make sure each researcher initials (and perhaps dates) his/her Annotations in the event it becomes important to quickly ascertain the author.
- Later we will provide a warning that team members working in copies of Projects should never edit the text (e.g., transcripts, picture logs, etc.). Adding an Annotation

is not the same as editing the text. Therefore, it is safe for different researchers to add different Annotations to the same document (such as an interview) in their own copies of the Project. Thus, they also provide a safe way to note corrections to the text. They will all be transferred into the single File later.

Maps

In Chapter 1 we walked you through the creation of a Mind Map (pp. 23–24) and a Concept Map (pp. 25–26) to begin representing ideas and expectations. When working in a team, Maps can be an effective way of accomplishing two things at once.

- Maps can hone the ideas of different researchers on the team regarding the related concepts, causal relationships (if relevant), and factors at play in the study.
- When a diverse range of perceptions are at play among team members, mapping can be an efficient visual way of presenting, exploring, and assessing the various ideas. For some learning and communication styles, this is an effective way for teams to share and explore alternative explanations.

The thorny issue of how much context to code

When teams are trying to promote coding consistency among team members, the amount of contextual information to code is a frequently debated topic. Some researchers prefer coding more discrete passages and others code broadly, to include context. There are three issues to consider early in the team coding process (and you may need to revisit them as the analysis unfolds):

1 the need to ensure that all team members similarly understand what is meant by 'passages' ('meaning units' or 'Coding References') for coding purposes;
2 the information that NVivo will retrieve when you run Queries with an AND (intersection) operator;
3 the mechanics of the Coding Comparison Query, because this Query yields a lower score for agreement if coders select different amounts of context when they code.

Regarding the first issue, there is a unique dynamic in teamwork regarding the ease of understanding the coded portions that have been removed from context. To the coder who read and coded the transcript, a brief fragment may make sense when reviewing a Node, but a researcher who did not code this data may be unclear about the meaning and lament the lack of context. In Chapter 3 (see especially Figure 3.10) we explained how, with a right-click of the mouse button, you are able to see either the immediate context of a coded passage (e.g., the remainder of the paragraph) or you can jump to the File to see the passage highlighted in its original File. For the former option, the additional context will be temporarily incorporated into the *Detail View*, as greyed-out material.

- If seeing it as temporary context is not sufficient and you want to retain some or all of the context around the coded portion, then select and code in your usual way (e.g., drag-and-drop the additional context into the Node). It will then show as coded text in the Node.

The second issue to consider regarding context is the implication for searches involving the intersection of Nodes (i.e., Coding Queries and Matrix Coding Queries, using AND). A Query result can be empty if Coding References are too short, or it can include unhelpful intersections where References are too long (where the tail end of coding for one Node connects with the start of coding for another). Pilot some Coding Queries early in the process so you can make more informed choices as a team about how much context to include.

The third issue regarding coding context is the impact of coded context on the Coding Comparison Query, which we detail in the final section of this chapter. When two researchers code independently and one codes the first two sentences in the paragraph to *trust*, but the other codes all four sentences to *trust*, the Coding Comparison Query will report the discrepancy, and report lower kappa and agreement scores because one coder applied the Node to approximately twice as much data (unless you are in the Mac version and using a parameter other than 'character'; more on that later).

Keeping track of who did what: Passwords, Users, and Logs

Before discussing the mechanics around coder reliability and the Coding Comparison Query, we first attend to the NVivo tools designed specifically with teamwork in mind.

─────── **11.a.** ───────

Passwords

Passwords can be added to specific Projects to allow for Read/Write access or Read Only access.

⇒ *File:* / *Menu Bar:* **File** > **Project Properties** > **Passwords**.
⇒ If you enter a **Read/Write Password**, you will also enter a **Read Only Password**.
⇒ You will be asked for the Password the next time you open the Project.

Recording Memos and tracking Users

⇒ With a Memo such as *Teamwork in NVivo* open and in edit mode, add the date and time **(Ctrl / Cmd + Shift + T)** to track the chronology of ideas about team protocols, and write something about your team process (e.g., 'We need to identify someone to manage the backup of our Projects.').
⇒ Close the *Detail View* and look at the columns that are visible in the *List View* (Figure 11.1).

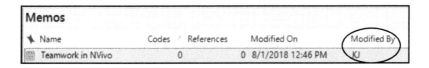

Figure 11.1 *List View* of Memos with *Detail View* closed or on the bottom

This is your first glimpse of NVivo's ability to track researchers. This list is available for every type of item in the *List View* of your project (Files, Nodes, Attributes, Sets, Queries, Maps, etc.). Windows users: We describe ways you might want to customize this list in Chapter 3 (pp. 89–90).

Identifying Users

If you are working on a solo copy of the Project, on your own computer, ensure that it is correctly registering you (and not the administrator) as the User each time you open the software. If you work on a shared computer, the default setting that does not prompt for the user on launch should be changed (Figure 11.2).

⇒ *File*: **Options** / *Menu Bar*: **NVivo12 > Preferences > General tab > Prompt for user on launch** (check the box).

Subsequently, each time a researcher launches the software on the computer they will be asked to provide their login name and initials.

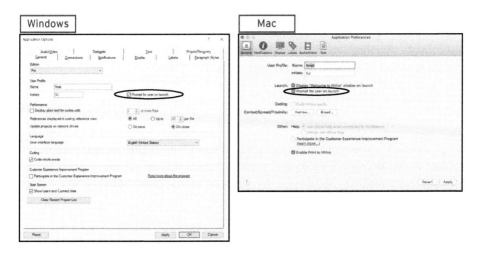

Figure 11.2 Setting the Application Options to 'Prompt for user on launch' in Windows (left) and Mac (right)

The setting to 'Prompt for user on launch' should be changed whether or not you have added Read/Write or Read Only password access (described below), because the User names and initials are requested when the software is launched and before opening a particular (potentially password protected) Project.

- Exit the software completely and launch NVivo again if you are switching Users on the same computer. Closing and reopening a Project while the software remains open will not activate the request for the User.
- If a team member has accidentally entered a different name or initials on different occasions, you can remove one of their User names and replace it with their other User name. Because this will change all the coding in the system done under either of those names and allocate it to the single User, it is wise to make a copy before following these steps to combine Users.

11.b.

Combining Users

⇒ **File > Project Properties > Users.**
⇒ **Click a name > Remove > Select a user** (who will replace the User being removed) **> OK / Replace > OK.**

Note that if Sylvia Blake and Sadik Botros both enter SB as their initials, you will have problems distinguishing authorship of work that is identified on screen using only initials. If this is a risk, the team leader should determine the name and initials for each team member to use prior to initiating work in the Project. In addition, if two or more Users code the same passage to the same Node, the Reference count (but not the actual text) is duplicated. To obtain accurate reference counts when you have multiple Users, make a copy of the Project and merge the work of all of the Users by removing all but one.

Project Logs (Windows only)

Although the User names and initials in the *List View* will provide researchers with information about recent changes, they do not track each independent action in the software. A Project Log where researchers can trace these actions can be created for any NVivo Project. This allows you to:

- track the specific activities of individual researchers;
- identify the exact time and date that an error occurred (e.g., SB deleted an important Memo accidentally!) with the hope that you can reincorporate this item into your project from one of your backup copies.

Be aware of two limitations to the Project Log:

- The Log will describe a specific event (e.g., on 02/03/2019 10:24 AM, Henry coded a passage to the *Balance* Node), but it will not provide the source or the exact passage. In this regard, it is much more of a log (aptly named) than an audit.

- The Log is not interactive, so while you will obtain a history of events, you cannot use the Log to access specific Project items to make rapid changes or corrections to them.

━━━━━━━━━━ **11.c.** ━━━━━━━━━━

Turn the Project Log on or off (Windows)

⇒ *File:* **Project Properties > Write user actions to project event log** (check or uncheck).

To see the Log entries (or to clear the Log) (Windows):

⇒ *File:* **Open Project Event Log** (or **Clear Project Event Log**).

Keeping track of different copies of projects

At the end of Chapter 1 (pp. 30–34) we walked you through the steps for saving backup copies of your Projects if you are not using NVivo for Teams. If you plan on merging different copies of Projects later, we have a few additional recommendations about keeping track of your copies. Things tend to go much more smoothly when one person is in charge of this process and sets up some housekeeping rules.

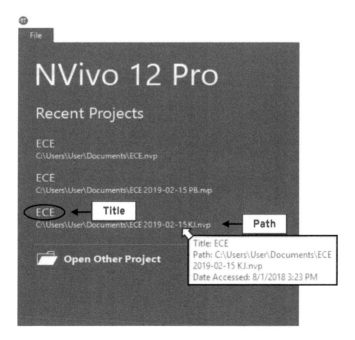

Figure 11.3 The initial window showing an original Project and copies with Title and Path

We recommend naming duplicate copies of the Project in the following way: project title, date, researcher. So, for instance, if an early childhood education project with the title ECE is being distributed to Pat and Kristi for coding:

- Pat will receive   ECE 2019-02-15 PB
- Kristi will receive   ECE 2019-02-15 KJ

In addition to helping Pat and Kristi differentiate successive versions of the projects, this naming convention will help the Project manager distinguish different Projects during the merge.

Figure 11.3 shows that for a single Project, the Title (which is registered in NVivo) will be different from the Path name (which you see in your list of files in Windows Explorer or the Mac Finder). If you hover over a Title or Path in the initial NVivo Window without clicking on the Project, the date last accessed is also visible.

If you would prefer to have your project Title match the end of the Path name (which sometimes avoids confusion among team members) then you can change it by opening the copy of the Project and changing the Title without causing problems for merging.

──────── **11.d.** ────────

Manually matching the Project Title and Project Path

⇒ **File > Project Properties > rename the Title > OK > Save** the Project (Figure 11.4).

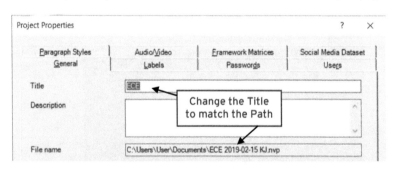

Figure 11.4 Changing the Project Title to match the Project Path (or File Name) (Windows)

You will find it important to develop a system for how team members should label their own backups. Detail this system in the Teamwork Memo, and then ensure that everyone is following that procedure. The approach will vary depending on which of the methods you are employing for managing the Project. Projects should be backed up at least once each working day, and although you might delete some of your old backups, keeping a few of them from critical junctures could help you write about your methods.

Preparing to combine Projects

If you are working in a team with the Project spread across several computers, you should combine copies early in the Project to test the process to make sure it will serve your needs later, and to take stock of the way multiple coders are approaching the data. Then, you will combine Projects once coding is completed in order to undertake comprehensive Queries and produce final reports.

The basic rules for importing one Project into another

All Project items (Files, Nodes, Sets, Queries, Maps, etc.) are considered when one Project is imported into another, even if one copy of the Project has the item but the other does not. Projects are likely to have some combination of common and unique items. (*Windows users*: Unless you specifically ask for duplicate items to be ignored or added to the project as separate items, NVivo will combine them wherever possible. *Mac users*: You cannot ask for duplicate items to be ignored or added to the project as separate items.) Combining Projects is very easy, provided researchers are aware of some basic rules, which we provide in this subsection. Know these rules before you start copying and working in separate Projects, because failure to follow these rules may result in an inability to combine Projects successfully.

When you combine Projects you will open one (which we call, the master), and then import the other (which we call the auxiliary) into the master. Your immediate task is to decide which is the master and which is the auxiliary. If you have more than two Projects to merge, only one is the master and all of the others are auxiliaries. The remainder of this section will help you prepare for the process and help you make the decision on which Project should be the master.

Files and Nodes

Files and Nodes in Project A and Project B will merge as long as three conditions are met:

1   The Nodes and/or Files have the same name.

- The Node *Positive* in Project A is also called *Positive* in Project B.
- The File *Susan* in Project A is also called *Susan* in Project B.

2   The Nodes and/or Files are in the same hierarchical location with the Projects.

- *Positive* in Project A and *Positive* in Project B are under the same parent Node, such as *Valence*.
    - o   If the Node *Positive* in Project A is under *Valence* but in Project B it is under *Attitude*, the two Nodes will not merge. This is fairly easily resolved later as you can manually merge two or more Nodes after the Projects have been combined, although this can become tedious if it happens often.

- *Susan* in Project A and *Susan* in Project B are in the Files folder, but …

  - If *Susan* in Project A is directly under Files but *Susan* in Project B is under a customized folder called *Interviews*, the two Files will not merge. This is a much more significant problem than having two Nodes that do not merge, because the coding of two separate Files cannot be combined within a Project in the way Nodes can be merged. Therefore, it is important that one of the first things you check after a Project is imported is that the Files were merged properly.

3   The third condition applies to all Files in the Project. The two copies of the interview for *Susan* in the different Projects will merge only if each copy contains the exact same text characters.

- It is therefore critical that none of the researchers edit any of the text Files that are held in common across the copies of the Project. Researchers may code as differently as they like, but they must not edit the text in any Files to be merged.
- If a researcher working in Project A finds the word 'dove' in *Susan's* interview, and changes it to the correct word, 'love', but the researcher in Project B does not, the two versions of *Susan* will not merge, even though the Files have the same name, are in the same hierarchical location, and have the same number of characters.

To ensure the Files are not edited while researchers work in Project copies, explain this problem of editing text to all team members early in the process. Because the 'Click to edit' bar is quite visible in the *Detail View* when a File is open, this is especially important. We suggest training researchers to use an Annotation or a See Also Link in a Memo to note any editing errors they find in the text, which can then be corrected once the Project is fully and finally merged.

Other Project items and their Properties

While the Nodes and Files are the primary concern for most teams when Projects are merged, it is also helpful that NVivo adds any item that is unique to the auxiliary into the master. In addition to Files and Nodes, this includes Classifications, Collections, Queries, Reports, and Maps. Furthermore, several Project Properties from the auxiliary project will be added as well, such as customized fields for audio or video transcripts.

The issue is more complicated when items with different properties exist in the master as well as the auxiliary. Examples include colours, Node Descriptions, and whether Nodes are Aggregated (Chapter 4, pp. 120–121) or not. For instance, the Descriptions of Files, Nodes, etc. in the master Project will be retained, but none of the auxiliary item Descriptions will be incorporated. The master also trumps the auxiliary regarding the settings to Aggregate or not to Aggregate the Nodes, the application of colours to Project items, the Stop Words List (Chapter 7, pp. 219–220), and other tools. *Windows users*: If Sets with the same name exist in both Projects, NVivo will import all Set members from the auxiliary Project into the same named Set in the master Project. *Mac users*: Sets, Annotations, Queries, and Result Nodes are not imported. For a complete list of the way NVivo identifies and reconciles conflicts in the master and the auxiliary, see the book's online resources (https://study.sagepub.com/jackson3e).

Combining Projects

We are assuming at this point that you are choosing to import the content of one whole Project into another to combine the work of team members.

Final preparation

Before you combine Projects, first create an archive folder for all the Projects you will be combining by making copies and putting them in a safe place where they will not be altered. This is especially important for the Project that will become the master, as it will be changed. All others, by default, will be auxiliaries.

11.e.

Import the auxiliary Project

⇒ Open the master Project that will be the foundation for the new, combined project.
⇒ *Ribbon*: **Import / Data > Project > Project to import > Browse** > locate the project you want to import > **Open**.
⇒ Tick the **All (including content)** option if you want to add all items in the auxiliary Project to the master.
⇒ Select **Options**. Choose how you want to handle duplicate items - to **Merge into existing item** or **Create new item**. The default to merge items is by far the most common need.
⇒ **Import**.

When the process is complete, a Report will open describing the items that were or were not imported. Do not be too dismayed regarding Items Not Imported in the Report, because if an item already exists in the master, it is not imported. Your main concern will be to check that additional content in the auxiliary Project has been added to the master (e.g., whether the coding Pat did to *Positive* was added to the coding Kristi did to *Positive*).

Check the import worked as intended

First, check that all Users have been imported (*File*: / *Menu bar*: **File > Project Properties > User**s). Then, you may do one or more of the following as a double-check with Project items:

- Look in your Files to make sure none of them was duplicated. Be careful of ignoring the subfolders, where duplicates can often hide.
- Open a Node and turn on Coding Stripes by User (*Ribbon*: **Node > Coding Stripes > Selected Items** > tick the box next to **Users > OK**).
- Check your Classification System contains the correct Attributes and Values. As an extra check, you might also go to the Properties of one of your Case Nodes to make sure the Attributes for that Case are correctly assigned.

- Examine your Sets to see if all the members are identified as expected.
- Look in your Queries to see what has been added and organize them in subfolders if needed.

Be aware that if a Project manager engages in activities such as manually merging Nodes in the new Project, her initials will appear in the *List View* as the researcher who most recently modified an item. She will also be listed as the researcher who created the item if she creates a new Node and merges existing items into that new Node. Fortunately, the Coding Stripes for Users adjacent to the text of the newly merged Nodes retain the initials of the original coders.

Comparing coding with the assistance of NVivo

NVivo provides ways to visualize the coding done by the team and also contains a Query designed to compare the coding of two researchers. You will use different strategies, depending on whether you want to:

- see how different coders are working, as a basis for discussion about coding strategies; and/or
- check if there is a sufficiently high level of agreement (inter-coder reliability) between different coders.

Coding Stripes by User (Windows only)

In Chapter 3 (pp. 83–86), we showed you how to examine your coding with Coding Stripes. If you logged on as different Users in the same Project or you merged Projects, you can also turn on Coding Stripes according to User. This visualization can facilitate conversations among the team about choice of Nodes, the Node Descriptions, and the coding context selected for particular References.

━━━━━━━━━━━━━━━ **11.f.** ━━━━━━━━━━━━━━━

View coding by different Users with Coding Stripes (Windows only)

⇒ *Navigation View:* **> Data > Files.**
⇒ *List View:* **Double-click** on a File.
⇒ *Detail View:* **Click** on some text so NVivo knows you are active in the File.
⇒ *Ribbon:* **Document > Coding Stripes > Selected Items >** check **Users.**

You will be shown the equivalent of a coding density bar for each User, allowing you to hover to see what Nodes each used (if any) for the adjacent passage of text (Figure 11.5). If you are using this method to review or assess commonality of coding strategies, it is critical that you hover over the different Users' Coding Stripes to see what actual Nodes have been coded, as the stripe might appear the same, but the Nodes coded might be different.

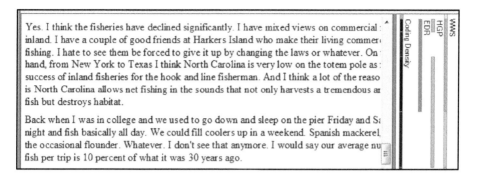

Yes. I think the fisheries have declined significantly. I have mixed views on commercial inland. I have a couple of good friends at Harkers Island who make their living commerc fishing. I hate to see them be forced to give it up by changing the laws or whatever. On hand, from New York to Texas I think North Carolina is very low on the totem pole as success of inland fisheries for the hook and line fisherman. And I think a lot of the reaso is North Carolina allows net fishing in the sounds that not only harvests a tremendous ar fish but destroys habitat.

Back when I was in college and we used to go down and sleep on the pier Friday and Sa night and fish basically all day. We could fill coolers up in a weekend. Spanish mackerel, the occasional flounder. Whatever. I don't see that anymore. I would say our average nu fish per trip is 10 percent of what it was 30 years ago.

Figure 11.5   Coding Stripes showing the work of three coders on a File (Windows only)

Using a Coding Comparison Query

After considering our discussion of the advantages and disadvantages of coder reliability earlier in the chapter, you may wish to use the tools in NVivo that are explicitly designed to compare the work of different coders. This pursuit presumes that you have established a coding structure, trained researchers on the coding process, engaged in some group coding or practice coding, and are now ready to pilot a Coding Comparison Query. You will need to identify a File and select a range of data within it (e.g., several pages) that all researchers in the team have coded or will code. We recommend selecting a small portion of the data first, in the event there are problems with the technical process of merging projects or running the Coding Comparison Query. If things run smoothly, you can do it again on a larger portion of the data. See Chapter 7 (pp. 226–227) for detailed instructions on running this Query and then see the next subsection on interpreting the Query Results.

Windows

Code	File	Kappa	Agreement (%)	A and B (%)	Not A and Not B (%)	Disagreement (%)	A and Not B (%)	B and Not A (%)
Habitat	Barbara	0.5743	94.47	4.16	90.31	5.53	0.49	5.04
Habitat	Charles	1	100	0	100	0	0	0
Habitat	Dorothy	0	92.51	0	92.51	7.49	0	7.49

Mac

Name	File Size...	Kappa	Agreeme...	A and B (%)	Not A and Not B...	Disagreem...	A and Not B (%)	B and not A (%)
▼ ◯ Habitat		0.37	95.66	1.39	94.27	4.34	4.18	0.16
📄 Barbara	11,331	0.58	94.49	4.17	90.32	5.51	5.02	0.49
📄 Charles	11,019	1.00	100.00	0.00	100.00	0.00	0.00	0.00
📄 Dorothy	8,100	0.00	92.48	0.00	92.48	7.52	7.52	0.00

Figure 11.6   Statistical output from a Coding Comparison Query in Windows (top) and Mac (bottom)

Coding Comparison Query Results

A portion of the output for a Coding Comparison Query in the *Environmental Change* sample data is shown in Figure 11.6. The coding of *Effie* (User A) and *Wanda* (User B) for the single Node, *Habitat*, is compared across each of three Files (*Barbara*, *Charles*, and *Dorothy*).
Results include:

- **Kappa** – a value of 1 indicates perfect agreement (identical coding), 0 (or less) indicates no better than chance (or worse than chance).
- **Agreement (%)** – overall level of agreement between coders (a combination of the next two columns).

  o   A and B (%) – the percentage of units in the File coded by both coders.
  o   Not A and Not B (%) – the percentage of units in the File not coded by either coder.

- **Disagreement (%)** – overall level of disagreement between coders (a combination of the next two columns).

  o   A and Not B (%) – the percentage of units in the File coded by A but not coded by B.
  o   B and Not A (%) – the percentage of units in the File coded by B but not coded by A.

Visual output from the Query

- Double-click on any line in the statistical output. NVivo will take you directly to the File so you can examine the Coding Stripes for that particular Node by those Users (Figure 7.8).
- Click on a Coding Stripe to see the exact characters coded. This allows you to see easily and specifically where two people are coding similarly or differently, to provide a basis for discussion.

To interpret the statistical results, it is important to understand that the unit of measurement for kappa and percentage agreement in Windows is the text character (or equivalent small unit in media). Researchers cannot currently change this default in Windows (to expand the parameters to a sentence or a paragraph, for instance). This is part of the reason the kappa in *Barbara's* interview is so low (0.57, in Figure 11.6). In the Mac version, the researcher can select between character, sentence, and paragraph to loosen the restrictions on agreement. To explain both the kappa and the agreement scores, consider the scores from *Barbara's* data in NVivo Windows.

The results obtained for *Barbara's* File lead us to question why the (Cohen's) kappa score is so low, given the high agreement score. While the agreement score is based on a combination of where the coders agreed to apply the Node and where they agreed not to apply the Node, the kappa only considers data where some coding for the relevant Node is present. Because *Effie* and *Wanda*, for *Habitat* in *Barbara's* document, agreed on just over half of the coded data for that Node across the whole interview, the kappa is 0.57 and suggests a failure to achieve a high level of reliability – but 90% of *Barbara's* File was not coded by either of them, and so they achieved a quite high agreement score.

Apart from difficulties occasioned by the very fine level of assessment (the text character) used in these calculations in the Windows version, there are other difficulties related to the qualitative nature of the data regardless of whether you are using NVivo in Windows or Mac:

- The kind of detailed coding differences shown in the statistical output do not necessarily impact the final interpretation of the data, which, as we noted earlier, should depend on patterns across the entire body of data.
- If a coding structure contains so many discrete Nodes that very few References from a File are coded to any single Node, the agreement score may be artificially high just because of all the text that is not coded to the Node.
- Coding reliability is a concept borrowed from quantitative research in which only coded data are considered. The idea of including what is not coded as part of the measure of the percentage of agreement is an alternative, but not widely recognized or published.
- Use great caution on using an average agreement (or kappa) across multiple Nodes and Files, because, unlike quantitative research, several factors make it difficult to standardize:
  - Not all Nodes are created equal. Some Nodes are much more important to the analysis than others and there is no way to weight the importance of more interpretive Nodes versus more descriptive Nodes.
  - There is also no way to know during early stages of confirming coder reliability which Nodes will be more important in the final analysis.
  - Not all Files are the same size and not all coders do the same amount of work.

Because of the inherent diversity, we advise against averaging scores across lines of output in the Query Results. An alternative for the purpose of summarizing the output in this Coding Comparison Query is to identify the percentage of Nodes that fall above or below a certain score. What is more important, however, is to convey how the team revisited the data for the Nodes with the lowest scores. In the end, having considered all this information on the numbers in the Coding Comparison Query, we think reviewing the Coding Stripes for particular Users in specific Nodes and Files is its most appropriate use (a feature that is currently only available in Windows). Using the Query allows researchers to identify potential problem areas, and then drill in for further examination to enhance the process of discussing, revising descriptions, and coming up with additional guidelines for coding as a team. Most teams seem to find this more helpful than the numbers provided by the kappa or the percentage agreement.

SECTION 11.4: CHAPTER 11 TAKEAWAYS

Key points from this chapter

- Teams are very diverse and vary from study to study. There are no blueprints for success.

- Communication and planning are critical components of team qualitative research.

o Ethical considerations in team qualitative research are not simply an extension of ethics for the lone researcher.

o There are several options for storing a Project depending on the configuration of your team and your access to the software.

o You might make use of special tools in NVivo that are designed for team research (e.g., Users, Passwords, Coding Comparison Query).

o You might consider the implications (or alternative uses) for other tools in the software (e.g., Memos, Links, Annotations, colours, Maps) because you are now operating in a team.

o You might find the Coding Comparison Query more useful for generating conversations and examining your ideas than measuring reliability.

Tips, challenges, and warnings

- If you are new to the software, to qualitative research, or to conducting this research in teams, it will be easy to make major missteps without the guidance of a mentor or expert.
- Consider allocating time and budget to training the team in the use of NVivo and getting ongoing access to a consultant or trainer who can help you through hurdles during the analysis.
- Political problems and interpersonal conflicts in qualitative team research usually occur because values or priorities that seem clear to one member are not always so obvious to others.
- Reserve meeting time for process issues (not just analytical issues).
- It is important to follow the rules of coding and managing Files before you attempt to combine Projects. Most importantly, do not edit Files in Project copies or they will not merge.
- If you are working in copies of Projects use the same version of the software (including Service Packs).
- Although Projects can be saved and opened across the Windows and Mac versions, do not use this strategy with teams.
- Pilot all processes (coding, merging Projects, writing Memos, developing Maps, etc.) before you develop elaborate structures/instructions for the team.

Videos and online resources (https://study.sagepub.com/jackson3e)

Website

Help files

- *File*: Help.
- *Menu bar*: **Help > NVivo Help.**

Search for any of the following:

- Coding comparison query
- Collaborate in a server project
- Create, view, or change user profiles
- Merge projects or import items from another NVivo project
- Save and copy projects
- Strategies for teamwork
- Teamwork

Practice questions

1   What ethical issues might you need to attend to during your research that are related to teams?

2   Which of the following strategies do you think you will use for teams and why?

- A single, standalone Project that is accessed sequentially by team members.
- Multiple copies of standalone Projects that are accessed simultaneously by team members and then merged together.
- NVivo for Teams, a version that allows you to work simultaneously on the same Project.

3   How do you plan on handling the coding process in your team, including the division of labour?

4   Which of the tools for communicating as a team do you anticipate using and how will you use them (colours, Memos, Links, Annotations, Maps)?

MOVING ON - FURTHER RESOURCES

No single book can ever cover the entire range of possibilities with regard to analysis of data, whether with or without a computer. Our hope is simply that the ideas we presented will stimulate you to think about ways of exploring your data (and NVivo), of paying respect to your participants through your handling of their data, and of advancing knowledge that is both relevant and useful. Our further hope is that our guidance helped you understand the principles on which the NVivo software has been built, so you can continue to explore some of its capabilities further on your own. When you face a challenging task for which there are no straightforward instructions, think about what you want to achieve, how the tools in the software work, and be prepared to experiment (but make sure you save first!). Approach it with the attitude 'There must be a way I can make this program do what I want it to do!' – and indeed, you will often find that there is (although, of course, you must not expect one program to do it all).

If you are looking for further resources, Kristi would be happy to help you. She thrives on the interesting projects presented to her by researchers around the world and often works with teams and individuals through screen-sharing platforms. Some of these researchers have considerable experience with NVivo and require advanced troubleshooting. Others are beginning their journey and want to make sure they start experimenting with tools in the most productive way possible. No single approach is perfect for everyone, so she always focuses on the unique blend of your learning style, your preferred approaches to scholarly inquiry, your research questions, your data, and your audience. You can learn more through the following web pages:

- www.queri.com – Kristi's website with training schedules, contact details, and internationally available NVivo consulting services.
- www.researchsupport.com.au – Pat's website has links to articles and resources for qualitative and mixed methods analysis, some involving use of NVivo or computer software more broadly.
- Additional web pages and email contact information for other trainers and consultants is provided in the Acknowledgements.

In addition, the following sites offer information and resources, and carry links to further sites and resources:

- (add URL here) – Here you will find resources specifically to accompany this book, including notes and sample projects, and updates to instructions necessitated by new releases.
- Access news, tips, and videos through the Community section on the NVivo welcome screen.
- www.qsrinternational.com – The developer's site carries updates to the software, teaching resources, newsletters with articles about how other researchers are using the software, answers to frequently asked questions (FAQs), a Customer Success Center, and a link to the QSR Forum.

REFERENCES

Agar, M. (1991). The right brain strikes back. In N. G. Fielding & R. M. Lee (Eds.), *Using computers in qualitative research* (pp. 181–194). London: Sage.

Anzaldúa, G. (2015). *Light in the darkLuz en lo oscuro: rewriting identity, spirituality, reality.* Durham, NC: Duke University Press/The Gloria E. Anzaldúa Literary Trust.

Bahkali, S., Almaiman, A., Bahkali, A., Almaiman, S., Househ, M., & Al-Surimi, K. (2015). The role of social media in promoting women's health education in Saudi Arabia. *Studies in Health Technology and Informatics, 213*, 259–262.

Barnett-Page, E., & Thomas, J. (2009). Methods for the synthesis of qualitative research: a critical review. *NCRM Working Paper Series, 01/09*, 1–25. Retrieved 6 February 2012 from http://eprints.ncrm.ac.uk/690/

Bazeley, P. (2010). Computer-assisted integration of mixed methods data sources and analyses. In A. Tashakkori & C. Teddlie (Eds.), *Sage handbook of mixed methods research in social & behavioral research* (2nd edn, pp. 431–467). Thousand Oaks, CA: Sage.

Bazeley, P. (2013). *Qualitative data analysis: practical strategies*. London: Sage.

Bazeley, P. (2018). *Integrating analyses in mixed methods research*. London: Sage.

Bernard, H. R., & Ryan, G. W. (2010). *Analyzing qualitative data: systematic approaches.* Thousand Oaks, CA: Sage.

Bloomberg, L. D., & Volpe, M. (2008). *Completing your qualitative dissertation: a roadmap from beginning to end*. Thousand Oaks, CA: Sage.

Bowker, G. C., & Star, S. L. (2000). *Sorting things out: classification and its consequences.* Cambridge, MA: MIT Press.

Box, G. E. P., Hunter, W. G., & Hunter, J. S. (2005). *Statistics for experimenters* (2nd edn). Hoboken, NJ: John Wiley & Sons.

Boyatzis, R. E. (1998). *Transforming qualitative information: thematic analysis and code development*. Thousand Oaks, CA: Sage.

Bryman, A. (2006). Integrating quantitative and qualitative research: how is it done? *Qualitative Research, 6*(1), 97–113.

Bryman, A. (2007). Barriers to integrating quantitative and qualitative research. *Journal of Mixed Methods Research, 1*(1), 8–22.

Byrne, C. (2017). Anonymous social media and qualitative inquiry: methodological considerations and implications for using Yik Yak as a qualitative data source. *Qualitative Inquiry, 23*(10), 799–807. doi:10.1177/1077800417731081

Caracelli, V. J., & Greene, J. C. (1993). Data analysis strategies for mixed-method evaluation designs. *Educational Evaluation and Policy Analysis, 15*(2), 195–207.

Charmaz, K. (2006). *Constructing grounded theory*. Thousand Oaks, CA: Sage.

Coffey, A., & Atkinson, P. (1996). *Making sense of qualitative data*. Thousand Oaks, CA: Sage.

Coffey, A., Holbrook, B., & Atkinson, P. (1996). Qualitative data analysis: technologies and representations. *Sociological Research Online, 1*(1). Retrieved 1 September 2011 from http://www.socresonline.org.uk/1/1/4.html

Corbin, J., & Strauss, A. L. (2008). *Basics of qualitative research* (3rd edn). Thousand Oaks, CA: Sage.

Dixon-Woods, M., Agarwal, S., Jones, D., Young, B., & Sutton, A. (2005). Synthesising qualitative and quantitative evidence: a review of possible methods. *Journal of Health Services Research & Policy, 10*(1), 45–53.

Duchinsky, R. (2013). Abjection and self-identity: towards a revised account of purity and impurity. *The Sociological Review, 61*(4), 709–727.

Elliott, J. (2005). *Using narrative in social research: qualitative and quantitative approaches*. London: Sage.

Eyman, D. (2015). *Digital rhetoric: theory, method, practice*. Ann Arbor: University of Michigan Press.

Fairclough, N. (2014). *Language and power* (3rd edn). London: Routledge.

Flick, U. (2007). *Designing qualitative research*. London: Sage.

Flyvbjerg, B. (2004). Five misunderstandings about case-study research. In C. Seale, G. Gobo, J. F. Gubrium, & D. Silverman (Eds.), *Qualitative research practice* (pp. 420–434). London: Sage.

Fox, B., Hayashi, M., & Jasperson, R. (1996). Resources and repair. In E. Ochs, E. Schegloff, and S. Thompson (Eds.), *Interaction and grammar* (pp. 185–237). Cambridge: Cambridge University Press.

Freeman, M. (2017). *Modes of thinking for qualitative data analysis*. New York: Routledge.

Fuchs, C. (2017). *Social media: a critical introduction*. London: Sage.

Geertz, C. (1973). Thick description: towards an interpretive theory of culture. In C. Geertz (Ed.), *The interpretation of cultures: selected essays* (pp. 3–30). New York: Basic Books.

Gilbert, L. S. (2002). Going the distance: 'closeness' in qualitative data analysis software. *International Journal of Social Research Methodology, 5*(3), 215–228.

Gilbert, L., Jackson, K., & di Gregorio, S. (2013). Tools for analyzing qualitative data: the history and relevance of qualitative data analysis software. In J. M. Spector, M. D. Merrill, J. Elen, & M. J. Bishop (Eds.), *Handbook of research on educational communications and technology* (4th edn). London: Routledge.

Glaser, B. G., & Strauss, A. L. (1967/1999). *Discovery of grounded theory*. New York: Routledge.

Guest, G., & McLellan, E. (2003). Distinguishing the trees from the forest: applying cluster analysis to thematic qualitative data. *Field Methods, 15*(2), 186–201.

Guetterman, T. C., Fetters, M. D., & Creswell, J. W. (2015). Integrating quantitative and qualitative results in health science mixed methods research through joint displays. *Annals of Family Medicine, 13*(6), 554–561. doi: 10.1370/afm.1865

Hair, J. F., Black, W. C., Babin, B. J., & Anderson, R. E. (2010). *Multivariate data analysis* (7th edn). Upper Saddle River, NJ: Prentice Hall.

Hinchliffe, S. J., Crang, M. A., Reimer, S. M., & Hudson, A. C. (1997). Software for qualitative research: 2. Some thoughts on 'aiding' analysis. *Environment and Planning A*, *29*(6), 1109–1124. doi:10.1068/a291109

Howe, K., & Dougherty, K. (1993). Ethics, Institutional Review Boards, and the changing face of educational research. *Educational Researcher*, *22*(9), 16–21.

Howe, K. R., & Moses, M. S. (1999). Ethics in educational research. In A. Iran-Nejad & P. D. Pearson (Eds.), *Review of Research in Education, 24* (pp. 21–60). Washington, DC: American Educational Research Association.

Jackson, K. (2014). *Qualitative methods, transparency, and qualitative data analysis software: toward an understanding of transparency in motion*. Available from ProQuest Digital Dissertations. (AAT 3621346)

Jackson, K. (2017). Where qualitative researchers and technologies meet: lessons from interactive digital art. *Qualitative Inquiry*, *23*(10), 818–826.

Jackson, K., Paulus, T., & Woolf, N. H. (2018). *The Walking Dead* genealogy: unsubstantiated criticisms of qualitative data analysis software (QDAS) and the failure to put them to rest. *The Qualitative Report*, *23*(13), 74–91. Retrieved from http://nsuworks.nova.edu/tqr/vol23/iss13/6

Katzenback, J. R., & Smith, D. K. (1993). *The wisdom of teams*. Cambridge: Harvard Business Review Press.

Kelle, U. (1997). Theory building in qualitative research and computer programs for the management of textual data. *Sociological Research Online*, *2*(2).

Kelle, U. (2004). Computer-assisted qualitative data analysis. In C. Seale, G. Gobo, J. F. Gubrium, & D. Silverman (Eds.), *Qualitative research practice* (pp. 473–489). London: Sage.

Kemp, L. (1999). *Charting a parallel course: meeting the community service needs of persons with spinal injuries*. Unpublished PhD thesis, University of Western Sydney, Sydney.

Kemp, L., Harris, E., McMahon, C., Matthey, S., Vimpani, G., Anderson, T., Schmied, V., Aslam, H., & Zapart, S. (2011). Child and family outcomes of a long-term nurse home visitation programme: a randomised controlled trial. *Archives of Disease in Childhood*, *96*(6), 533–540.

Kvale, S. (1996). *InterViews: an introduction to qualitative interviewing*. Thousand Oaks, CA: Sage.

Lakoff, G., & Johnson, M. (2003). *Metaphors we live by*. Chicago: University of Chicago Press.

Lave, J., & Wenger, E. (1991). *Situated learning: legitimate peripheral participation*. Cambridge: Cambridge University Press.

MacQueen, K. M., McLellan-Lemal, E., Bartholow, K., & Milstein, B. (2008). Team-based codebook development: structure, process and agreement. In G. Guest & K. M. MacQueen (Eds.), *Handbook for team-based qualitative research* (pp. 119–135). Lanham: AltaMira Press.

Maxwell, J. A. (2013). *Qualitative research design* (3rd edn). Thousand Oaks, CA: Sage.

Maxwell, J. A. (2016). Expanding the history and range of mixed methods research. *Journal of Mixed Methods Research*, *10*(1), 12–27. doi: 10.1177/1558689815571132

McCay-Peet, L. & Quan-Haase, A. (2017). What is social media and what questions can social media research help us answer? In L. Sloan & A. Quan-Haase (Eds.), *SAGE handbook of social media research methods* (pp. 13–26). London: Sage.

Merchant, R. M., Elmer, S., & Lurie, N. (2011). Integrating social media into emergency-preparedness efforts. *New England Journal of Medicine*, *365*(4), 289–291.

Miles, M. B., & Huberman, A. M. (1994). *Qualitative data analysis: an expanded sourcebook*. Thousand Oaks, CA: Sage.

Miles, M. B., Huberman, A. M., & Saldaña, J. (2014). *Qualitative data analysis: a methods sourcebook*. Thousand Oaks: Sage.

Mishler, E. G. (1991). Representing discourse: the rhetoric of transcription. *Journal of Narrative and Life History*, *1*(4), 255–280.

Mitchell, C. (2011). *Doing visual research*. London: Sage.

Mohameden, M., Alkhairi, B., Issa, S., Mohameden, A., & Yuvienco, C. (2017). YouTube videos on rheumatoid arthritis: a qualitative analysis of views and content [abstract]. *Arthritis & Rheumatology*, *69*(suppl 10). Retrieved 30 July 2018 from https://acrabstracts.org/abstract/youtube-videos-on-rheumatoid-arthritis-a-qualitative-analysis-of-views-and-content/.

Morse, J. M. (1999). Qualitative methods: the state of the art. *Qualitative Health Research*, *9*(3), 393–406.

National Commission for the Protection of Human Subjects of Biomedical and Behavioral Research. (1978). *The Belmont report: ethical principles and guidelines for the protection of human subjects of research*. Bethesda, MD: The Commission.

Ochs, E. (1979). Transcription as theory. In E. Ochs & B. B. Shieffelin (Eds.), *Developmental pragmatics* (pp. 43–72). New York: Academic Press.

Patton, M. Q. (2002). *Qualitative research and evaluation methods* (3rd edn). Thousand Oaks, CA: Sage.

Patton, M. Q. (2008). *Utilization-focused evaluation*. Thousand Oaks: Sage.

Paulus, T., Jackson, K., & Davidson, J. (2017). Digital tools for qualitative research: disruptions and entanglements. *Qualitative Inquiry*, *23*(10), 751–756.

Peräkylä, A. (2004). Conversation analysis. In C. Seale, G. Gobo, J. F. Gubrium, & D. Silverman (Eds.), *Qualitative research practice* (pp. 165–179). London: Sage.

Pink, S. (2001). *Doing visual ethnography*. London: Sage.

Poirier, S., & Ayres, L. (1997). Endings, secrets, and silences: overreading in narrative inquiry. *Research in Nursing & Health*, *20*(6), 551–557.

Rich, M., & Patashnick, J. (2002). Narrative research with audiovisual data: Video Intervention/Prevention Assessment (VIA) and NVivo. *International Journal of Social Research Methodology*, *5*(3), 245–261.

Richards, L. (2009). *Handling qualitative data* (2nd edn). London: Sage.

Richards, L. (2015). *Handling qualitative data* (3rd edn). London: Sage.

Richards, L., & Morse, J. M. (2012). *Readme first for a user's guide to qualitative methods* (3rd edn). Thousand Oaks, CA: Sage.

Richards, L., & Richards, T. (1994). From filing cabinet to computer. In A. Bryman & R. G. Burgess (Eds.), *Analyzing qualitative data* (pp. 146–172). London: Routledge.

Riessman, C. K. (2008). *Narrative methods for the human sciences*. Thousand Oaks, CA: Sage.

Rinehart, E. (1998). Fictional methods in ethnography: believability, specks of glass, and Chekhov. *Qualitative Inquiry*, *4*(2), 200–224.

Sagun, K. K., & Luyt, B. (2017). Cultured and popular literary circuits on Facebook: a case study of Singaporean print culture in social media. *Information Research*, *22*(2), 1–15.

Saillard, E. F. (2011). Systematic versus interpretive analysis with two CAQDAS packages: NVivo and MAXQDA. *Forum Qualitative Sozialforschung/Forum: Qualitative Social Research*, *12*(1), Article 34. Retrieved 1 September 2011 from http://www.qualitative-research.net/index.php/fqs/article/view/1518.

Saldaña, J. (2013). *The coding manual for qualitative researchers* (2nd edn). London: Sage.

Saldaña, J. (2016). *The coding manual for qualitative researchers* (3rd edn). London: Sage.

Sanders, C. B., & Cuneo, C. J. (2010). Social reliability in qualitative team research. *Sociology*, *44*(2), 325–343.

Schwandt, T. A. (1997). *Qualitative inquiry: a dictionary of terms*. Thousand Oaks, CA: Sage.

Seale, C., Gobo, G., Gubrium, J. F., & Silverman, D. (2004). Introduction: inside qualitative research. In C. Seale, G. Gobo, J. F. Gubrium, & D. Silverman (Eds.), *Qualitative research practice* (pp. 1–11). London: Sage.

Seidel, J. (1991). Method and madness in the application of computer technology to qualitative data analysis. In N. G. Fielding & R. M. Lee (Eds.), *Using computers in qualitative research* (pp. 107–116). London: Sage.

Silver, C. A., & Lewins, A. (2014). *Using software in qualitative research: a step-by-step guide* (2nd edn). London: Sage.

Silver, C., & Patashnick, J. (2011). Finding fidelity: advancing audiovisual analysis using software. *Forum Qualitative Sozialforschung/Forum: Qualitative Social Research, 12*(1), Article 37. Retrieved 1 September 2011 from http://nbnresolving.de/urn:nbn:de: 0114-fqs1101372

Silverman, D. (2010). *Doing qualitative research* (3rd edn). London: Sage.

Strauss, A. L. (1987). *Qualitative analysis for social scientists.* Cambridge: Cambridge University Press.

Strauss, A., & Corbin, J. (1998). *Basics of qualitative research* (2nd edn). Thousand Oaks, CA: Sage.

Tesch, R. (1990). *Qualitative research: analysis types and software tools.* London: Falmer.

Tilley, S. A., & Powick, K. D. (2002). Distanced data: transcribing other people's research tapes. *Canadian Journal of Education, 27*(2&3), 291–310.

Townsend, L., & Wallace, C. (2016) *Social media research: a guide to ethics.* University of Aberdeen. Available at: www.gla.ac.uk/media/media_487729_en.pdf

Warr, D. J. (2005). 'It was fun … but we don't usually talk about these things': analyzing sociable interaction in focus groups. *Qualitative Inquiry, 11*(2), 200–225.

Wickham, M., & Woods, M. (2005). Reflecting on the strategic use of CAQDAS to manage and report on the qualitative research process. *The Qualitative Report, 10*(4), 687–702.

Williams, M. L., Burnap, P., Sloan, L., Jessop, C., & Lepps, H. (2017). Users' views of ethics in social media research: informed consent, anonymity, and harm. In K. Woodfield (Ed.), *The ethics of online research* (Advances in Research Ethics and Integrity, *Volume 2,* pp. 27–52). Bingley, UK: Emerald Publishing Limited.

Woolf, N. H., & Silver, C. (2017). *Qualitative analysis using NVivo: The Five Level QDA®️ method.* London: Routledge.

Yin, R. K. (2003). *Case study research: design and methods* (3rd edn). Thousand Oaks, CA: Sage.

INDEX

advanced find, 160, 253
aggregate, 119–122, 330
annotations, 27–28, 71, 98, 240–241,
  265–268, 322–323
assumptions, 7
attributes and values, 45, 52–53, 57,
  137–144, 150–155
  importing, 153–154
  reporting, 155
audio
  coding, 276–277
  coding stripes, 277–278
  exporting, 280–281
  importing, 270–271
  linking, 275
  playing, 271–272
  transcribing, 272–275
  use of, 259–262
auto coding, 50, 54, 112–113, 124–126,
  148–150, 177, 195, 275–276
auxiliary project, 329, 331

backing up, 33–34, 327–328
bibliographic database, 250–252

cases, 45–53, 57–58, 137–141,
  146–155, 176–178, 214–215,
  269–270, 275–276, 296–297
case types, 137–138

chart
  coding query, 209
  compound query, 211
  crosstab query, 159
  group query, 212
  hierarchy, 202–204
  matrix coding query, 208
  node, 93–94
classifications, 57, 126, 141–142, 145, 150–155
classification sheet, 152–154
closeness to data, 66, 111–112
cluster analysis, 174, 190–194
codes and coding (*also see* nodes), 64–99,
  101–132
  a priori, 73
  adding to, 76–77, 79, 85, 91, 98, 108, 110,
    116, 120, 122, 130
  and analysis, 91–92
  approaches to, 68–76
  automating, 50, 54, 112–113, 124–126,
    148–150, 177, 195, 275–276
  balancing act, 110–112
  broad, 69
  checking, 210–211
  coder agreement (%) (*also see* coding
    comparison query), 334–335
  conceptual, 75–76
  context, 84–86, 323–324
  defining, 67–68

detailed, 69–72
exploratory, 204–207
identifying codes, 71–76
in vivo, 73
media, 276–277
naming codes, 71–76
narrative and discourse, 74
recoding, 86–87
reference (coding reference), 78, 143
reliability (*also see* coding comparison
    query), 212–214, 315–316, 333–335
selecting first files, 66–67
starting, 18–19
team, 314–315
time needed, 76–77
uncoding, 82, 84, 86, 88–89
web pages, 301
coding comparison query, 212–214,
    226–227, 333–335
coding query, 96–97, 209–210, 214–215,
    223–224
coding stripes, 83–85, 98, 181–182, 212, 266,
    277–278, 331–333
Cohen's kappa, 334–335
colour, 22, 77, 80, 82–82, 88, 244, 320–321
companion website, xix
comparative analyses, 155–159, 171,
    182–184, 186–187
comparison (*also see* coding comparison
    query), 72, 142–143, 171, 214–216
comparison diagram, 94–96
complementary analyses, 170–172, 181–182
compound query, 210–211, 252–253, 224–225
concept map, 23–26, 117–118
concepts, 66–67, 124–126
copy project, 33–34, 237–238
conversion, 172–174
cross-case analysis, 214–216
crosstab query, 143, 155–160, 183–186,
    189–190, 207–209, 215, 221–223
custom fields (media), 275–276
customizing display, 89–90

datasets, 176–180, 179–180, 195,
    294–297, 299
date and time, 21
dendrogram, 190–193
detail view, 16, 115

EndNote, 250–252
Environmental Change project, 12–18, 46
ethics, 310–312
external files, 54

Facebook, 286–298
files
    exploring, 15–16

formatting, 48–53
importing, 26–27
managing, 54–58, 144–145
naming, 49
printing, 92–93
folders, 54–55
framework matrices, 182–183, 216,
    229–230

group query, 160–161, 212–214, 225–226,
    278–280

heading styles, 50–51, 124–125
hierarchical name, 154
hierarchical nodes (*see* node hierarchy)
hierarchy chart, 202–204
highlight, 85–86, 96
hyperlinks, 33, 264–265, 275, 302

illustrations, 264
import
    audio, 270–271
    classification sheet, 153–155
    Excel (*see* classification sheet *and* survey)
    NCapture, 293–295, 299–301
    pdf, 26–27, 246
    picture, 265–267
    project, 331–332
    Qualtrics, 180
    reference manager (EndNote, Mendeley,
        RefWorks, Zotero), 250–252
    social media, 293–295
    survey, 175–181, 195
    Survey Monkey, 180
    text, 22, 26–27
    video, 270–271
    web page, 301
    YouTube, 298–301

joint display, 182–183
journaling, 20–22, 33–34, 66

kappa, 334

links, 30–33
    exploring, 32
    hyperlink, 33, 264–265, 275, 302
    memo link, 29–30, 116, 301, 321
    see also link, 30–33, 240–241, 265,
        268, 275, 321–322
list view, 13
listing nodes, 89–90, 113–114
literature, 7–8, 174, 236–255

Mac instructions, xx, 11, 13–15, 17
maps, 23–26, 117–118, 216, 217, 323
    concept map, 25–26, 117

mindmap, 23–24
project map, 123–124
master project, 329, 331–332
matrix coding query, 109, 116, 186–190,
    208–209, 215, 222–223
memos, 20–22, 240–241
    file memo, 29
    in teams, 308, 321
    memo link, 116, 268
    node memo, 116
menu bar, 17
merging nodes, 88–89, 121–122
merging projects, 329–332
metaconcept, 124
methods-with software, 5–6
mindmap, 23–24
mixed methods, 167–196
multidimensional scaling (MDS), 191–192
multimedia data, 259–261
multivariate displays, 190–192

navigation view, 13–15
NCapture, 293–295, 299–301
nodes, 77–97
    aggregate, 119–122
    case nodes, 189, 331
    chart, 93
    child, 119–121
    codebook, 92–93, 114
    context, 84, 91–92
    create, 79–81
    custom display, 89–90
    delete, 88
    descriptions, 79–80, 111–112
    hierarchy, 103–110, 117–123, 242–243
    list, 92–93, 113–114
    managing, 88–97
    merging, 88–89, 121–122
    moving, 88, 105–107
    organizing, 103–106, 121–122
    parent, 119–121
    printing, 92–93, 114
    retrieval, 30, 67, 170, 181–182, 248
    reviewing and re–examining, 113–118
    sentiment, 112–113, 177–179
    structuring, 104–110, 117–119, 121–123
    theme, 112–133
    viewing, 113–115
    viral coding structure, 107–108, 110, 122
    vista coding structure, 108–110
notes, 5–8, 14, 30, 42, 240–241
NVivo – and qualitative analysis, 8–9
    install, 10–11
    project, 54

open items list, 17
output, 14, 334

passwords, 324
pattern analysis, 105, 155, 186–190, 202
pdf files, 236, 244–250
    coding, 246–250
    importing, 246
pictures, 258–270
    adjusting, 267
    coding, 268–269
    exporting, 280
    importing, 265–266
    linking, 168
    log, 267
    technical options, 263–265
    use of, 261–262
piloting, 52–53, 123, 245, 259–260, 313
play media, 271–272
practice questions, 36, 60, 99, 122, 163, 196,
    233, 254–255, 282, 304, 337
printing node content, 92–93
privacy (*also see* passwords), 291
project
    auxiliary, 329, 331
    copy, 33–34, 237–238
    create, 18–20
    design and structure, 40–60
    log, 326–327
    master, 329, 331–332
    merge, 329–332
    planning your project, 6–8
project map, 123–124

Qualitative Data Analysis Software (QDAS) –
    origin and evolution, 3–5
    don't put the cart before the horse, 5
    silver bullet, 4–5
    snake oil, 5
Qualtrics, 180
queries, 200–233
    add to project, 126–128
    coding, 96–97, 209–210, 214–215,
        223–224
    coding comparison, 212–214, 226–227,
        333–335
    compound, 210–211, 252–253, 224–225
    creating, 218
    crosstab, 143, 155–160, 183–186, 189–190,
        207–209, 215, 221–223
    group, 160–161, 212–214, 225–226,
        278–280
    matrix coding, 109, 116, 186–190, 208–209,
        215, 222–223
    saving, 228–229
    text search, 126, 129–130, 205–207,
        220–221
    word frequency, 126–128, 130, 204–205,
        218–219
quick access 13

reference material (*also see* EndNote,
Mendeley, RefWorks, Zotero), 250–252
RefWorks, 250–252
region coding, 249–250, 268–269
relationships, 207
reliability, 212, 315–316, 335
reports, 114, 155, 160, 230–232
Researchers project, 12, 15
results (*see* query results)
ribbon, 13
rigour, 260

sample projects
Environmental Change, 11–18
Researchers, 12, 15
saving, 33–34, 228–229
scoping, 160–161
search, 129–130, 205–207, 214, 217–221
searching text, 129–130
see also link, 30–33, 240–241, 265, 268, 275,
321–322
sentiment, 77, 107, 112–113, 177–179
sets, 56, 124, 144–145, 160–161, 278–279
share, 93, 114, 186, 228
social media, 288–291
attributes, 169
auto coding, 296–297
importing, 293–295, 298–299
social media dataset, 297–296
stemmed search, 129
stop words, 128–129
survey data, 176–181
form view, 180
table view, 180
Survey Monkey, 180

tagging data, 44–45
teams, 308–377
coding, 314–316
communication, 320–322
management, 317–320, 323–328
maps, 323
memos, 308, 321
preparation, 329–330

project management, 318–320
reliability and validity, 315–316
training, 317–318
text search query, 126, 129–130, 205–207,
220–221
theory-building, 201–204
tips, challenges and warnings, 35, 59,
97–98, 131, 162, 194–195, 232–233, 254,
281–282, 303–304, 336
transcription, 42–43, 259, 272–275
transformative analysis, 172–174, 184–186
Twitter, 286–298

uncoding, 82, 86–88
users, 324–328, 332–335

variables, 138, 172, 176
video
coding, 276–277
exporting, 280–281
importing, 270–271
linking, 275
playing, 271–272
transcribing, 272–275
use of, 259–260
violence prevention project, 54–58
viral coding structure, 107–108, 110, 122
vista coding structure, 108–110
visualizing (*also see* charts, cluster analysis,
coding stripes, comparison diagram, highlight, maps), 216–217

web pages, 301–302
coding, 302–303
importing, 299–301
within-case analysis, 214–215
Windows instructions, xx, 11, 13–16
word frequency query, 126–128, 130,
204–205, 218–219
word tree, 206

YouTube, 298–299

Zotero, 250–252